Armed America

The Remarkable Story of How and Why Guns Became
as American as Apple Pie

CLAYTON E. CRAMER

NELSON CURRENT

A Subsidiary of Thomas Nelson, Inc.

Published in Nashville, Tennessee, by Nelson Current, a division of a wholly owned subsidiary (Nelson Communications, Inc.) of Thomas Nelson, Inc.

ISBN–10: 1–59555–069–0
ISBN–13: 978–1–59555–069–9

Printed in the United States of America

ALSO BY CLAYTON E. CRAMER

Concealed Weapon Laws of the Early Republic: Dueling, Southern Violence, and Moral Reform

Black Demographic Data, 1790–1860: A Sourcebook

Firing Back: A Clear, Simple Guide to Defending Your Constitutional Right to Bear Arms

For the Defense of Themselves and the State: The Original Intent and Judicial Interpretation of the Right to Keep and Bear Arms

By The Dim and Flaring Lamps: The Civil War Diary of Samuel McIlvaine

Table of Contents

To Ron & Norma Kennemer:

You were a continuing source of encouragement when this project seemed like a bedraggled puppy, looking for the pound.

Acknowledgments & Technical Notes

I would like to thank those who have contributed sources, suggestions, and constructive criticism: Norman Heath, Daniel Lo, Chuck Anesi, Philip F. Lee, Joseph Schechter, J. L. Bell, James F. Lindgren, Joyce Lee Malcolm, Byron C. Smith, Gary Brumfield, Richard Frazier, David Golden, Billie J. Grey, Ron and Norma Kennemer, and John Maraldo. Certainly the greatest contributor in volume was Peter Buxtun, and his extensive library on early American guns. Many others, names now forgotten, also provided useful suggestions for sources to check. I am grateful to the libraries at Sonoma State University; University of California, Berkeley; Boise State University; University of Idaho; Eastern Washington University; as well as the Historical Society of Pennsylvania; the Massachusetts Historical Society; and the Hagley Museum and Library. The Idaho Historical Museum, the J. Earl Curtis Exhibition at the Old Idaho Penitentiary, and the Pennsylvania Longrifle Heritage Museum provided most of the early American firearms photographs.

In the final editing stages, Alan G. Eisen, David Golden, Daniel Lo, Eric Archer, Paul Norris, Paul Gallant, Joanne D. Eisen, Paul Schechter, Kevin J. Shannon, Michael S. Brown, Kurt Williams, Patrick Cox, Jim Wolfe, Matthew Peters, and Seth Vose III of the Massachusetts Historical Society, provided a detailed reading of the text with fresh eyes, catching many typos, clumsy sentences, and inartful transitions. David Golden also arranged for all these volunteer editors. Thanks also to my agent, Ed Knappman, for the hard work required to interest a major publisher in this book. Joel Miller and Alice Sullivan at Nelson Current made innumerable suggestions and changes to turn this from a scholarly sleep aid into something a bit more entertaining.

As always, my wife Rhonda L. Thorne Cramer, provided the final critical eye, for sentence structure, tone, and form of argument.

As I neared completion of the research on this project, the National Rifle Association Civil Rights Defense Fund provided a generous grant that allowed me to travel to a number of archives in Massachusetts, Pennsylvania, and Delaware. At no point did they provide any direction or suggestions as to the research or the direction of this book. I also thank John Saillant, moderator of the H-NET/OIEAHC Electronic Association in Early American Studies mailing list, for providing helpful suggestions.

COLONIAL CURRENCIES & PRICES

Throughout this book, I use the notation £2:14:7 to indicate £2, 14s., 7p. This simple and compact notation was used in at least some contemporary documents. Unless otherwise specified, I assume that prices were in local currency. Many colonies issued their own money, using the same units as English currency, but at a lower value than pounds sterling. When conversion ratios to pounds sterling were available (almost always from John McCusker's *Money and Exchange in Europe and America*),[1] I have provided that equivalent. While the pound sterling did not suffer the relentless inflation of modern money in the seventeenth and eighteenth centuries, the reader is cautioned against comparing a 1640 price with a 1780 price.

Where I have mentioned prices of goods or fines, I have looked for modern equivalents. Comparing goods or fines to Colonial and early Republic daily wages, clothing, and food, is on somewhat safer ground. Advances in manufacturing and technology, however, render all price comparisons difficult.

DATES

In 1752, Englishmen everywhere (as most Americans considered themselves), switched from the Julian to the Gregorian calendar. Along with the loss of eleven days, the beginning day of the year changed from 25 March to 1 January. Consequently, dates in the first three months of a year are often expressed as 1639/40. A date in February of 1639 as Americans kept the calendar then would be February of 1640 by the modern calendar. The abbreviation O.S. occasionally appears in this book to indicate Old Style, or Julian calendar.

SPELLING AND GRAMMAR

Throughout this book, I have preserved original spelling and grammar in the older quoted material without marking what would otherwise be a sickening number of "[*sic*]" notations. The alternative was to modernize spelling and grammar—at the risk of unintentionally altering the document's original meaning.

FIREARMS

I have included a glossary of common firearms terms with photographs in the Appendix.

Creating A Useable Past:
Michael Bellesiles and Revisionist History

Here's a history of guns in America in fifty words: Minutemen. Fur trappers. Davy Crockett. The shot heard 'round the world. Pioneers circling the wagon trains. Cowboys and Indians. Jesse James. Wyatt Earp. Buffalo Bill. The OK Corral. Abraham Lincoln, John F. Kennedy, and Martin Luther King, Jr., downed, one and all, by gunmen. *Rambo. Dirty Harry. Lethal Weapon.* Columbine.

It's undeniable. Guns are at the center of much of America's history, its legends, and its horrors. Guns have aided and abetted in acts of great heroism and fierce independence as well as the darkest, most shameful moments in our country. For many Americans, and for those who observe the United States from afar, guns seem to be a fundamental part of the American experience—and always have been.

But is this an accurate picture of American history? In 1996, Emory University history professor Michael A. Bellesiles published a startling paper in the *Journal of American History* that challenged this conventional wisdom. According to Professor Bellesiles, guns were *not* common—they were the exception, as were hunting and violence (not counting violence directed against blacks and Indians). He claimed that it was only marketing geniuses such as Samuel Colt and aggressive efforts by the government that made guns as American as apple pie—and then, only after the Mexican War and Civil War flooded the market with inexpensive firearms.[1]

I was initially intrigued by Bellesiles' claims in the *Journal of American*

History. I was working on my master's thesis at Sonoma State University in California—and my topic was the development of concealed weapon regula-tion in the early Republic (the period between the American Revolution and the Mexican War of 1846). I spent a bit of time trying to see how Bellesiles' claim might explain the South's early lead in weapons regulation—but the more I compared Bellesiles' vision of the early Republic with the evidence that I could find, the more apparent it was that Bellesiles had been somehow led astray. I believed that it was an honest mistake that reflected his obvious dis-approval of gun ownership. I wrote a letter to the *Journal of American History*, published in 1998, citing a number of works from the early Republic period that suggested that at least in some parts of the country, gun ownership and white-on-white violence, contrary to Bellesiles' claims, were very common.

Four years later, Alfred A. Knopf published a book version of Bellesiles' theory: *Arming America: The Origins of a National Gun Culture*. Throughout American history, opined Bellesiles, the militia was ineffective; in the Colonial period, the government tightly regulated gun ownership and use; guns were very scarce before 1840; there was essentially no civilian market for handguns before 1848; violence between whites was rare; few Americans hunted until the 1830s when members of the upper class sought to imitate their British equivalents.[2]

Political activists in favor of restrictive gun control laws were beside them-selves with delight at this novel revision of history. They proclaimed that *Arming America* was a powerful new tool for understanding the US Constitution's guarantee of a right to keep and bear arms. At last the world could know the truth: the Second Amendment did not exist to protect *indi-viduals'* rights to keep and bear arms. Absolutely not. These advocates used Bellesiles' claims as evidence that the Second Amendment protected only the right of the government to organize the citizens into a military force. The firearm was not a symbol of independence, but of government prerogative.[3] Activists hoped that this new model would influence future rulings in the courts' interpretation of the Second Amendment.

As I read through *Arming America*, I found myself increasingly mystified at where Bellesiles could have found Colonial sources that presented such aston-ishing evidence. Had I (and several generations of historians) so *completely* missed the mark? Then I reached the section of Bellesiles' book that I knew best—the early Republic—and I found him citing works that I had read—indeed, works that I had cited in my 1998 letter to the *Journal of American History*. What was especially troubling is that much of the evidence that the information in *Arming America* was wrong came from travel accounts that Bellesiles cited to prove just the opposite. I had read some of those accounts while writing my master's thesis, which is part of what piqued my curiosity about Bellesiles' claims.

As we will see in the last three chapters, of the thirteen of Bellesiles' sources for this claim that I checked, each and every one showed that the travelers did indeed notice that, "they were surrounded by guns and violence," contrary to Bellesiles' claim. In one of these accounts that Bellesiles cited, references to guns or violence (and sometimes both) appear on twelve percent of the pages. Another account Bellesiles cited devotes whole *chapters* to target shooting and hunting, and an entire chapter to frontier vigilante justice—using firearms. Several of the accounts, even while generally positive about America and Americans, acknowledge that violence (with and without guns) was depressingly common. I could have read all eighty of the sources Bellesiles cites for this claim, but when the first thirteen sources I checked were so emphatically contrary to Bellesiles' characterization of them, there seemed little point in reading the rest.

Bellesiles repeatedly misquoted and misrepresented primary sources. Bellesiles changed the text of the federal Militia Law of 1792 to exactly reverse its meaning. He argued that the law required Congress to arm militiamen, and this was evidence that guns were so scarce that the government had to supply them:

> Further, "every citizen so enrolled, *shall . . . be constantly provided* with a good musket or firelock, a sufficient bayonet and belt, two spare flints," and other accoutrements. Congress took upon itself the responsibility of providing those guns . . . . [emphasis added]

The document that Bellesiles cited for that claim, however, had a substantially different text:

That every citizen so enrolled and notified, shall within six months thereafter, *provide himself* with a good musket or firelock, a sufficient bayonet and belt, two spare flints . . . . [emphasis added]

Bellesiles' "quote" was not just missing some words—he changed them to hide that this law required individuals to arm *themselves*—it was not Congress that was to arm them. When I brought this to Bellesiles' attention in various public forums, he first insisted that I did not know to how look up federal statutes, then, after I provided photocopies of the statute, he started (and kept) changing his explanation for his "misquote" without ever admitting that it was wrong.[4]

I had read through Bellesiles' discussion of Colonial America, and I confess that while his claims were startling, I had lacked the detailed knowledge of the period to say anything more than, "This does not sound quite right." Once I found that Bellesiles was actively making false statements in a period that I knew well, I returned to the Colonial section of his book, and started checking his footnotes.

Bellesiles claimed, as part of his evidence that guns were scarce in Colonial America, that

[i]n 1630 the Massachusetts Bay Company reported in their possession: "80 bastard musketts, with snaphances, 4 Foote in the barrill without rests, 6 long Fowlinge peeces." There were thus exactly one hundred firearms for use among seven towns with a population of about one thousand.[5]

But the source he cited shows that this was not a list of arms "in their possession" in the New World in 1630. Instead, it was the Massachusetts Bay Company's shopping list—the guns that they expected to purchase for the *company*, and *not* a list of all firearms in both public and private hands. Nor could it have been a list of guns "in their possession" in 1630. This shopping list was dated 1628/29—before the colony's first large settlement in Massachusetts. The date 1630 appears nowhere on the pages cited by Bellesiles.[6]

Bellesiles claimed that the Colonial governments ordered freemen to *own* guns, but did not trust them to actually *possess* them:

Colonial legislatures therefore strictly regulated the storage of firearms, with weapons kept in some central place, to be produced only in emergencies or on muster day, or loaned to individuals living in outlying areas. They were to remain the property of the government. The Duke of York's first laws for New York required that each town have a storehouse for arms and ammunition. Such legislation was on the books of colonies from New Hampshire to South Carolina.[7]

As a later chapter will demonstrate, this is exactly the opposite of Colonial laws. When I started to examine the citations that Bellesiles used to back up that claim, I discovered that the fraud was nearly perfect. There were dozens of pages from nineteen different sources in Bellesiles' footnote. I was able to locate seventeen of those sources (and the remaining two were secondary sources, of lesser significance than the actual statutes passed by these governments). One *page* from one of his sources could be carelessly misread to match Bellesiles' claim,[8] provided one did not read any of the other pages Bellesiles cites from that same source. Every other cited page from these seventeen sources either directly contradicts Bellesiles' claims, is silent, or is utterly irrelevant. I lost interest in checking the other two sources to see if *any* of the nineteen fit Bellesiles' description. You do not need to bite into every chocolate in the box if seventeen of the first nineteen you bite into contain worms.

Hundreds of such misreadings, altered quotes, altered dates, and grossly-out-of-context quotes appeared in *Arming America*. (I found, over the next two years, that I could open *Arming America* at random, and find at least one such falsification on almost every page.) Yet when I first pointed out these serious errors, Bellesiles compared me to a Holocaust denier.

Inevitably, a historian's political leanings will have some influence on how he interprets historical facts and the conclusions that he draws from it. Ideally, the facts will influence a historian's political leanings. Realistically, which facts a historian considers important to include, and which to leave out, will often be influenced by the wishes of his political heart. What happened with Bellesiles, however, was substantially worse than this. Bellesiles' political leanings did not influence the selection of historical facts; his political purpose caused historical facts to change. Like the infinitely malleable past in George Orwell's *1984*,

Michael Bellesiles treated American history as something to be changed at will. Unlike *1984*'s Ministry of Truth, Professor Bellesiles did not have the option of making inconvenient copies of his primary sources disappear.

I wrote this book largely because I was dumbfounded at how *Arming America,* a book that was so clearly and grossly in error, could receive so much initial critical acclaim, not just from book reviewers, but from eminent historians and law professors.[9] Only a few early reviewers suggested that *Arming America*'s astonishing revision of the place of guns in American history might have been in error or overstated the case[10]—and only one of those critical reviews was by a history professor.[11]

In 2001, Columbia University awarded Bellesiles a Bancroft Prize (the most prestigious award for an American history book) for *Arming America.* Within two years, Bellesiles' meteoric success was followed by an even more spectacular fall. A devastating *William & Mary Quarterly* symposium in January of 2002 demonstrated that many of Bellesiles' claims about the number of guns in early America, about the competence of militias, and about violence in early America, were insupportable—indeed, sometimes contrary to Bellesiles' own sources.[12] *Yale Law Journal* published an article in 2002 showing that Bellesiles' probate record data was mathematically impossible, and his cited sources contradicted him in ways that seemed hard to blame on simple error or carelessness.[13] A swarm of newspaper and magazine journalists looked into Bellesiles' work and came to similar conclusions.[14]

In some cases, the fraud was so obvious that I found myself wondering if he *wanted* to get caught. Bellesiles made use of Gold Rush San Francisco probate records. As Professor James Lindgren discovered, and as reporters for the *Boston Globe* and *National Review* confirmed, such probate records do not exist, having been destroyed in the 1906 earthquake. Bellesiles also, under questioning by the *Boston Globe* reporter, acknowledged that he had repeatedly misread descriptions of guns in Vermont records as "old" or "rusty" when those words did not appear.[15]

Finally, Emory University chartered a distinguished committee of scholars to examine some of the claims of fraud. The committee report largely substantiated claims of unprofessional sloppiness, and suggested that Bellesiles had engaged in intentional deception. Bellesiles resigned his tenured position at

Emory.[16] Within a few months, Columbia University had taken the unprecedented step of revoking Bellesiles's Bancroft Prize—and asked him to return the prize money.[17] The following month, *Arming America*'s publisher announced that they would no longer publish it—and copies returned by bookstores would not be sold as remainders, but pulped instead.[18] (This scandal, however, did not prevent another respected publisher, Oxford University Press, from publishing other books by Bellesiles.)[19] Bellesiles and his defenders continued to argue, even after revocation of the Bancroft Prize, that the problems with *Arming America* were confined to a few paragraphs concerning guns in probate records. Because the investigative committee examined only that small part of Bellesiles' book, Bellesiles' defenders argued that it *could* be that the committee was right about that small portion, and yet, *Arming America* might still be a generally accurate portrayal of guns in early America.[20]

Why did *Arming America* initially receive such a sterling collection of reviews from some of America's most respected historians? I fear that it is because there is a distinct lack of diversity among historians today. While history departments pride themselves on the diversity of their faculty in the areas of sex, sexual orientation, race, and ethnicity, there is really no *political* diversity. (While I often hear this denied by history professors, when pressed, their response is reminiscent of the bartender in *The Blues Brothers* when asked what kinds of music they play there: "We play *both* kinds: country *and* western.")

It should not surprise anyone who read *Arming America* that it had a clear-cut public policy conclusion, even if it was more implied than explicit. As Stewart Udall said on the dust jacket of the book, "Thinking people who deplore Americans' addiction to gun violence have been waiting a long time for this information." The idea that *Arming America* was intended to promote—that the Second Amendment's guarantee of a right to keep and bear arms was not only an anachronism today, but was stillborn—is presently very popular in academic circles.

Not surprisingly, nearly every historian who reviewed *Arming America* felt no need to check the accuracy of Bellesiles' more controversial claims. It is a rare person indeed who checks the accuracy of books with which he agrees—and this is quite unfortunate. It does not say much for the quality of the American academic community that a book so grossly and obviously wrong received such glowing praise. Something went terribly wrong with *Arming America*. That so many prominent historians defended such an obviously flawed work suggests that there is also something terribly flawed in academia today as well.

The book you are holding right now takes a fresh look at the question of how common guns were in early America—the question raised and falsely answered—by Bellesiles' *Arming America*. It comes to radically different conclusions, and for a very simple reason: The historical evidence gives no other choice. Whatever interpretive tools historians use to understand the presence of guns in early America, when eyewitnesses consistently and clearly tell us a fact that contradicts elegant theories, the only sensible response is to believe those who lived in that time. To do otherwise is to turn history into polemic.

The evidence this book examines is very clear. Guns were a fundamental part of the American experience from the founding of the first English colonies. Americans used guns initially as tools for individual self-protection and hunting, but by the time of the American Revolution, firearms became symbols of citizenship, intimately tied to defending political rights. Gun ownership was not universal in early America—but in every period, in every region, the evidence from written accounts, from probate inventories (the documents assessing the value of an estate after a person's death), from archaeological digs, and from official records demonstrates that gun ownership in our nation's early history was the norm—not the exception.

NAVIGATING PRIMARY SOURCES

Rhode Island passes a law to track illegally transferred guns. In New Haven, Connecticut, a man files suit after being seriously injured in a gun accident. The Massachusetts legislature regulates the firing of guns, complaining about reckless gunfire. Connecticut passes a law regulating the carrying of guns. Government authorities pass public safety laws regulating how guns are kept in private homes. Today's news?

No. Rhode Island passed that law in 1650, to stop gun sales to Indians.[21] The product liability suit in New Haven? That was 1645. A relative of mine, a gunsmith, was a witness for the injured party.[22] (We will examine this lawsuit in more detail in Chapter 4.) Massachusetts passed the law regulating gunfire "within the town and harbour of Boston" at the 1713–14 session.[23] Connecticut regulated the carrying of guns in 1643—and it did not *prohibit* the carrying of guns—it *required* at least one adult man in every house to carry a gun to church or other public meetings.[24]

This book makes extensive use of eyewitness accounts, and it is appropriate to ask questions about how to interpret such sources. For example, consider what would happen if, today, a resident of New York City encountered a deer in Central Park. How different would the New Yorker's experience be from that of a resident of a rural settlement such as Cougar, Washington, who met a deer in his downtown? The New Yorker would certainly comment on the presence of a deer with great amazement, perhaps writing a letter to the newspaper, leaving it for future historians to cite as evidence. The resident of Cougar would find a deer so unremarkable that there would certainly be no written record. Yet, in which city today is one more likely to encounter a deer?

When looking at eyewitness accounts, we must ask, how typical was this person's experience? When numerous accounts from both American and foreign writers, pertaining to different regions of early America, all report seeing a particular object or activity, it would suggest that this object or activity was common. However, when examining eyewitness accounts—especially those of travelers to America—we must also consider that people often overgeneralize from a small number of examples. This is especially so if these experiences were outside of the writer's normal experience. A traveler from a nation where firearms or hunting was less common than in America, because of the novelty, might overstate how common these situations were here. Still, when travelers from abroad regularly give reports consistent with native writers and other, more objective evidence, it is difficult to dismiss these accounts.

We must distinguish accounts that describe what *should* be from what *is*. Bellesiles, attempting to prove that guns were not a common part of the culture in early America, points to an 1843 children's book that condemns guns as evidence that the public was "completely uninterested in firearms."[25]

Lesson 42 in McGuffey's 1836 *Eclectic First Reader*, another children's book of the same era, heartily condemns rum and whiskey,[26] but no one who has read Rorabaugh's *The Alcoholic Republic* would consider McGuffey's condemnation to be evidence about the scarcity of alcohol in antebellum America.[27] The authors of children's literature often discouraged behaviors that were too common among the adult population or that were inappropriate for children.

How a historian interprets a source often reflects the assumptions that he brings to it. Samuel Wilson's 1682 account of Carolina (not yet split into North and South) discussed available game: "The Woods abound with Hares, Squirrels, Racoons, Possums, Conyes and Deere, which last are so plenty that an Indian hunter hath kill'd nine fatt Deere in a day all shott by himself, and all the considerable Planters have an Indian hunter which they hire for less than twenty shillings a year, and one hunter will very well find a Family of thirty people with as much Venison and Foul, as they can well eat."[28] One *could* interpret this passage as indicating that whites did not hunt in Carolina, but only purchased wild game from Indians. An equally legitimate reading would be that this passage tells us nothing about whether poorer whites hunted wild game. Since Wilson's account encouraged immigration because of the bountiful supply of game, this discussion could also be legitimately interpreted as an indication that hunting would be common among the settlers.

When evaluating primary sources, we must also wrestle with the question of what "arms" meant a few hundred years ago. A dictionary definition of "arms" includes not just firearms, but also swords, pikes, clubs, and other weapons. In at least one primary source, "armed" means "with armor."[29] Many primary sources mention "arms" without specifying "firearms." We must not assume "arms" means "firearms" unless this is the only plausible meaning. For example, "The People of this place and countrey . . . rose up in Arms. . . . The Fort being Surrounded with above Fifteen hundred men was Surrendered."[30] Why would a fort surrounded by people armed with swords and pikes surrender? Such a narrative makes far more sense if those "arms" included some large fraction of guns. In other texts, the characteristics of the "arms" clearly identify that the writer meant firearms. When Connecticut, in

April 1775, directed purchasing "three thousand stands of arms," they also specified: "the length of the barrel three feet ten inches, the diameter of the bore from inside to inside three-quarters of an inch."[31]

Historians have long recognized that a primary source may be intentionally deceptive, as people of the past attempted to put the best possible light on their actions, or on those of others. In the last twenty years, some historians have employed deconstructionist theories to add still more layers of interpretation, arguing that primary sources are so influenced by the gender, class, race, ethnicity, and sexual orientation of the writer (and the reader) as to make it impossible to determine objective truth. One need not agree with all the excesses of deconstructionism to recognize that reading primary sources requires great care, especially when seeking to understand the motives that drove historical actions, and how contemporary writers perceived those actions. Some questions remain unanswerable, of course, especially when it comes to weighing intentions; we may not be able to arrive at an "ultimate truth." Most of the questions that *this* book asks, however, are not in that category. There is nothing subtle, nothing that requires a careful teasing out of information from ambiguous and uncertain texts to answer this question: How common were guns in early America?

Part I

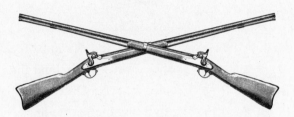

Colonial America

Colonial America often seems like a short period—at least the way that most Americans learn about it in school—but it stretches from the settlement of Jamestown in 1607 to the outbreak of the Revolution in 1775. The first settlements were primitive encampments between a vast, sometimes hostile continent, and an ocean sometimes bearing privateers, pirates, or navies of hostile European powers. By the time of the Revolution, as much as Britons might look down their nose at their American cousins, the Colonists lived better than Englishmen—and those primitive encampments were now hundreds of miles inland.

A Lonely Outpost: Militias in Colonial America

In every American colony at the start of the American Revolution, a militia—a part-time civilian army—existed to protect the colony against outside threats and ensure order within. The creation of the colonial universal militia, with its duty to be armed for the common defense, was a return to an already obsolete English tradition. From the Anglo-Saxon period (ninth century A.D.), English law had always required freemen to fight in defense of the realm. Called variously the *fyrd* or the militia, this obligatory duty atrophied as the medieval period waned.

By the sixteenth century, driven by changing warfare technology and tactics, the English government replaced the universal militia system with a more highly trained select militia. Because of Queen Elizabeth I's fear of a lower class uprising, these "trainbands" or "select militias" were drawn from the middle classes or higher whenever possible. The rest of the militia was still available for military service, but most often operated as an inactive reserve, only called up for the most extreme emergencies.[1]

The conditions of the New World revived this near-archaic universal militia system. The American colonies were, at first, a lonely outpost of Englishmen between a vast untamed continent and the Atlantic Ocean. The new and largely unknown world of America demanded both foresight and courage. The colonists lived in dread of attack by Indians and England's European enemies. Requiring every freeman to participate in the common defense of the colony was both prudent and built on a well-established English legal tradition. By 1740, all the American colonies were under British rule and, correspondingly, colonial militia laws reflected both English traditions and royal instructions to the governors.[2]

These militia laws (with a few exceptions) required every freeman (sometimes with an upper age limit) to own guns for militia duty—and in some cases, woman heads of household were similarly obligated to own guns for their militia-age sons or servants. In many colonies, adults were ordered to arm themselves for the purpose of self-defense while traveling or attending public meetings, or church. These laws varied from colony to colony and from year to year. Due to the peculiar conditions of frontier life—with its threats of Indian attack and, later, slave rebellion—the laws varied from colony to colony, and often from year to year.

Such an obligation to serve in the militia was no different from other communal obligations, such as street maintenance, fire protection, and policing.[3] One representative example is Connecticut's 1650 militia statute that required, "That all persons that are above the age of sixteene yeares, except magistrates and church officers, shall beare arms." As part of that obligation, "every male person with[in] this jurisdiction, above the said age, shall have in continuall readiness[s], a good musk[e]tt or other gunn, fitt for service, and allowed by the cl[e]rk of the band."[4] The head of the household was obligated to arm any of his sons or servants who were subject to militia duty. Similar laws existed in Massachusetts,[5] Plymouth Colony,[6] Rhode Island,[7] Providence (until absorbed by Rhode Island),[8] New Haven Colony (until absorbed by Connecticut),[9] New Hampshire,[10] New York,[11] New Jersey,[12] Delaware,[13] Virginia,[14] North Carolina,[15] and Georgia.[16] South Carolina's 1671 militia statute did not require gun ownership by militia members, but 1724, 1739, and 1743 statutes required militia members to carry guns to church, effectively imposing gun ownership.[17] Some towns also imposed their own requirements, either in addition to the colony statutes,[18] or before colony-wide statutes existed.[19]

Maryland's militia statutes are murkier than other colonies' regulations: The 1642 militia law required all "English able to bear arms" to be trained as part of the militia. This law also required every housekeeper to be armed, but also to arm "each person able to bear arms" who lived in the household as well. Maryland revised the law in 1654, so that "all persons from 16 yeares of age to Sixty shall be provided with Serviceable Armes & Sufficient Amunition of Powder and Shott ready upon all occasions and that Every master of families provid Armes & amunition as aforesaid for Every such Servant . . . ." The 1658, 1676, and 1692 laws were less universal; while all freemen *might* be called to militia duty, the number required to do so was dependent on how many the governor believed were necessary.[20] These later militia laws did not explicitly obligate every freeman to own a gun; however, 1699 and 1715 statutes required masters to provide a gun to every freed male indentured servant. The previous laws mandating gun ownership still appear to have been in effect.[21]

Pennsylvania was distinctly different from the other American colonies. The Duke of York imposed a militia law similar to that of New York in 1671, but Quaker opposition soon rendered the law ignored and unenforced.[22] A continued three-sided struggle throughout the eighteenth century between governors, Quakers, and non-Quakers, led to the formation of voluntary militias, under the encouragement of Benjamin Franklin (among others),[23] followed by passage of a voluntary militia law in 1756. This law explained that the Quakers "do not . . . condemn the use of arms in others, yet are principled against bearing arms themselves" and allowed militia companies to organize themselves with approval of the governor. Those under 21 years of age were specifically prohibited from joining, along with all "bought servant[s] or indent[ur]ed apprentice[s]" without consent of parents, guardians, or masters. The Crown vetoed this law, however, because militia duty was voluntary, and because it did not require conscientious objectors to pay for a substitute.[24]

The following year, Pennsylvania's legislature passed a more typical militia statute, requiring all men 17 to 55 to enroll in the militia, with exemptions for members of "those religious societies or congregation whose tenents and principles are against bearing arms." The law also exempted "all papists [Catholics] and reputed papists" from militia duty (presumably because they were not trustworthy while Britain was at war with Catholic France). Like the other Colonial militia statutes, all militia members "shall be sufficiently armed with one good musket, fuzee or other firelock well fixed" and were to appear at musters "with the accoutrements, arms and ammunition aforesaid in good order."[25]

Not everyone required by law to own a gun actually did so. Laws and records of fines suggest that this failure to be armed became more common in the eighteenth century. Poverty seems to be the principal reason for this failure. A 1757 Rhode Island order required that "every commissioned officer, and soldier, who has a gun fit for service, shall make use of the same; and those who have none, shall be provided for."[26] Because money was often in short supply in the American colonies, some of these laws allowed bartering crops for guns. Connecticut's 1650 militia law required any person who "cannot purchase them by such means as he hath, hee shall bring to the cl[e]rk so much corne or other merchantable goods" to pay for them. The value of the arms was appraised by the clerk "and two others of the company . . . as shall be judged of a greater value by a fifth parte." In other words, the man without a gun would be provided one by the government for only twenty percent above the market price. The government acted, in effect, as a finance company.[27]

Other colonies had different methods for arming members of the militia too poor to arm themselves. Plymouth and Virginia colonies passed laws to supply public firearms for those too poor to buy their own.[28] Virginia's 1748 militia law recognized that, "it may be necessary in time of danger, to arm part of the militia, not otherwise sufficiently provided, out of his majesty's magazine and other stores within this colony." The phrase "part of the militia" suggests that while some members of the militia were too poor to arm themselves, this was the exception, not the rule.

Why was there this decline in gun ownership by the poor? The gap between rich and poor Virginians widened in the Colonial period, but the rising economy meant that even poor Virginians in the eighteenth century were better off than they had been in the seventeenth century. The decline in gun ownership among poor Virginians in the eighteenth century may have been because the Indians were no longer a threat. Poor Virginians, when deciding what to buy, may have found other goods of greater utility to them, when they no longer feared Indian attack.[29]

Laws requiring gun ownership were not enough; just as now, they required follow-up tactics to ensure the compliance of independent-minded citizens. Many of these laws provided for inspection to verify that militiamen were armed and ready to fight. The 1643 Portsmouth, Rhode Island government ordered militia officers to go "to every inhabitant [in Portsmouth and] see whether every one of them has powder" and bullets.[30] Notice that the government felt no need to make sure that everyone had a gun in which to fire that ammunition.

Maryland even hit upon a crafty incentive strategy to secure good work among its inspection officers. Militia officers verified compliance with the duty to be armed by a monthly "Sight or view of the said armes and ammunition." Those lacking arms and ammunition were fined thirty pounds of tobacco (equivalent to about £4 sterling, or a month's wages), payable to the inspecting militia officer. The commander could arm the unarmed, and force the militiaman to pay "any price . . . not extending to above double the value of the said armes and ammunition according to the rate then usual in the Country."[31]

Records of fines exist in at least one colony. In New Haven Colony, on 4 January 1643/4, twelve men were fined two shillings each "for defect[ive] guns." Four other men were fined one shilling each, "for defect in their cocks," indicating that their guns would not cock or fire, although this was considered a less serious problem than the two shilling fine defects. Two of the twelve men who were fined two shillings for defective guns were also fined six pence "for want of shott," and two others were fined one shilling for "want of shott and pouder."[32] These fines were equivalent to part of a day's wages—enough to get a colonist's attention and compliance.

Militiamen were not the only persons obligated to own a gun. While most free white men were obligated to *possess* a firearm for militia duty, the obligation to *own* a firearm in many colonies applied to the head of the household—possibly a woman.[33] Maryland's "Act for Military Discipline" of 1638 required "that every house keeper or housekeepers within this Province shall have ready continually upon all occasions within his *her* or their house for him or themselves and for every person within his *her* or their house able to bear armes one Serviceable fixed gunne of bastard muskett boare" along with a pound of gunpowder, four pounds of pistol or musket shot, "match for matchlocks and of flints for firelocks."[34]

At least two colonies required immigrants to bring guns with them to the

New World or required gun ownership as a condition of receiving land title. Lord Baltimore's instructions to settlers immigrating to Maryland provided a detailed list of tools, clothing, and food to bring. For each man, "one musket ... 10 pound of Powder ... 40 pound of Lead, Bullets, Pistoll and Goose shot, of each sort some."[35] One of the conditions for receiving title to land in Maryland beginning in 1641 was bringing "Armes and Ammunition ... for every man betweene the ages of sixteene & fifty years w[hi]ch shalbe transported thether." The arms required were similar to those mandated for immigrants.[36] New Jersey seems to have imposed a similar requirement from the very beginning of settlement.[37]

The political structure of militias varied from colony to colony. New England militias had a strongly democratic form to them—often more democratic than legislatures and local governments. Governor John Winthrop described the election of militia officers in 1647 Roxbury, Massachusetts, with one faction supporting one Prichard, "a godly man and one of the chief in the town," while the majority preferred a George Denison. Denison, however, was not yet a citizen of the town, and could therefore not legally hold the captaincy.[38] In other colonies, governors appointed militia company commanders, and predictably, the better class of colonists usually ended up commanding in all colonies.[39]

EXCEPTIONS AND EXEMPTIONS

From the very beginning, a few people enjoyed exemption from militia obligations. Only clergymen and a handful of Colonial officials were exempted from duty by seventeenth century militia laws. Gun ownership was also optional for these men. In the eighteenth century, several colonies expanded the exemptions list. New Jersey's 1703 statute exempted ministers, physicians, school masters, "Civil Officers of the Government," members of the legislature, and slaves.[40]

Delaware's 1742 militia statute shows more complexity than most: "[E]very Freeholder and taxable Person residing in this Government" had to possess a "Firelock or Musket," appear at militia musters, and turn out in the event of war. However, "all Justices of the Peace, Physicians, Lawyers, and Millers, and Persons incapable through Infirmities of Sickness or Lameness, shall be exempted and excused from appearing to muster." (Millers were engaged in a critical occupation, especially in wartime—the making of flour. Why were lawyers exempted? One guess is that it was for the same reason that some states until recently exempted lawyers from jury duty: Lawyers write the laws, and jury duty was a distraction that lawyers did not wish to suffer.) They were exempt from musters, but still required to own a gun and turn out to fight in the event of war.

Delaware Quakers were exempt from all obligations related to militia duty: gun ownership, muster attendance, nightly watch duty, and, of course, fighting. Instead, to redress the imbalance, Delaware required Quakers to pay two shillings, six pence for every day that "others are obliged to attend the said Muster, Exercise, or Watch."[41]

When the American Revolution erupted, *every* Colonial militia law required most free adult men, as well as many female heads of the household, to own guns.

The Duty to Carry Firearms

In at least six colonies, part of the civic duty to be armed included bringing guns to church and other public meetings, or while traveling. The statute that most clearly states the intent of such laws is a 1643 Connecticut order, "To prevent or withstand such sudden assaults as may be made by Ind[i]ans upon the Sabb[a]th or lecture dayes . . . ." Within a month, Connecticut passed a new law that complained that, "[T]he late Order for on[e] in a Family to bring his Arms to the meeting house every Sabb[a]th and lecture day, hath not bine attended by divers persons . . . ." The new law thus imposed a fine for failing to do so.[42] Similar laws appeared in Maryland,[43] New Haven,[44] Virginia,[45] and Portsmouth, Rhode Island.[46]

An even more rigorous 1743 South Carolina statute required "every white male inhabitant of this Province, (except travelers and such persons as shall be above sixty years of age,) who [are] liable to bear arms in the militia of this Province" who attended "church or any other public place of divine worship" to "carry with him a gun or a pair of horse-pistols . . . with at least six charges of gun-powder and ball . . . ." Those who did not would be fined twenty shillings—a week's wages for many colonists. Other provisions required church-wardens, deacons, or elders to check each man coming into the church, to make sure that he was armed. The purpose was "for the better security of this Province against the insurrections and other wicked attempts of Negroes and other Slaves . . . ."[47] Georgia adopted a very similar statute in 1770.[48]

Massachusetts Bay Colony also imposed a requirement to come to church armed—but this law was repealed and reinstated several times as fear of Indian attacks rose and fell. Because of the danger of Indian attacks, and because much of the population was neglecting to carry their guns, a 9 March 1636/7 law ordered every person above eighteen years of age (except magistrates and elders of the churches) to "come to the publike assemblies with their muskets, or other peeces fit for servise, furnished with match, powder, & bullets, upon paine of 12*d*. for every default . . . ."[49] The Massachusetts government repealed this requirement in November 1637 (probably because of the Antinomian crisis, to be discussed in Chapter 2).[50] A 1643 order that directed the military officer in each town to "appoint what armes to bee brought to the meeting houses on the Lords dayes, & other times of meeting" suggests that this requirement was again back in force. The purpose of the 1643 law was to prevent theft of arms while the inhabitants were attending church.[51] Plymouth's 1641 law required at least one member of each household to bring weapons to church during that part of the year when Indian attack was most feared: "one of a house from the first of September to the middle of November, except their be some just & lawfull impedyment."[52]

Along with the duty to be armed at church and public meetings, several colonies required travelers to be armed. A 1623 Virginia law (reissued in similar form in 1632) required, "That no man go or send abroad without a sufficient parte will armed . . . ."[53] During a 1642 Indian scare, the militia commander of Northampton County, Virginia, announced that those traveling without "theire guns fixed and a quantitye of powder and shott with them" would be punished. Seven persons caught unarmed were sentenced to cut weeds at the parish church.[54]

Massachusetts imposed a similar requirement in 1631, ordering that no person was to travel alone between Massachusetts Bay and Plymouth, "nor without some armes, though 2 or 3 togeathr." While the law did not specify that "armes" meant firearms, it would seem likely, considering that Massachusetts' other laws required all militiamen to own a gun.[55] The measure was strengthened in 1636: "And no person shall travel above one mile from his dwelling house, except in places wheare other houses are neare together, without some armes, upon paine of 12*d.* for every default . . . ."[56]

These laws provided personal protection for the individual colonist. In a time when the Colonial population was small, this individual self-protection thus guarded the entire community, by preventing the society from being picked off, one colonist at a time.

"HANDS OFF MY GUN!"

Were these guns the property of the militiamen who held them, or were they public property? Certainly the government imposed a requirement to own guns, sold guns to militiamen, and imposed militia duty on the population. Contrary to the claim that some have made that firearms in private hands "were to remain the property of the government,"[57] the evidence is very clear that guns were usually private property, and as wartime actions, laws regulating sales of guns to the Indians, and personal negligence lawsuits prove, the Colonial governments recognized this.

References to guns and military equipment carried or lost in war suggest that guns were the private property of the militiaman. In 1639, after the Pequot War, Connecticut's government directed that a recovered "musket with 2 letters I W" "should be delivered to Jno. Woods friends until other appeare."[58] It seems unlikely that the government would turn over a gun to Woods' friends, unless that gun was the private property of Woods. In 1645, Connecticut directed Hartford's constables "to gather up the knapsacks, pouches, powder & bullets" used in a recent expedition—but made no mention of gathering up any firearms.[59] The knapsacks, pouches, and ammunition issued for a military expedition were property of the colony—but not the guns that were used to fire that ammunition. A 1650 account describing Massachusetts militia duty also demonstrates a clear distinction between publicly and privately owned arms.[60] A 1675 statute of Massachusetts Bay directed that persons exempt from militia training were to provide a specific number of "fire armes, muskets, or carbines" and ammunition. "[A]ll such persons as shall be assessed, and shall accordingly provide three fire armes, shall be freed from being sent abroad to the warrs, except in extreame & utmost necessity."[61] As much as the government needed these guns, it did not believe that it had the authority to simply confiscate them.

Maryland clearly recognized a distinction between public arms and privately owned guns. In 1676, at the height of Bacon's Rebellion in neighboring Virginia, the Maryland government requested of Maryland's Lord Proprietor, "that you will otherwise encourage the merchant to send in armes to sell that the house Keeper may purchase Sufficient for the defence of his house."[62] A Maryland statute of 1733 passed "to prevent the Embezzlement of the Public Arms," ordered marking of public arms "to denote such Arms to belong to the Public" and that "no Person or Persons whatsoever, shall presume to Sell or Purchase" public arms.[63]

In 1756, Maryland ordered militia officers to make a diligent search for arms and ammunition, demanding that everyone show what guns they had because publicly owned weapons "have been Sold or Sent from one to another and it is represented that the Locks have been taken off from many of the Said Arms and put to private Use."[64] This careful search for publicly owned arms, distinguishing them from private property, would make no sense if *all* guns were government property.

Several colonies issued orders to the militia to appear for service that provide clear evidence that militiamen owned their guns, and that the governments considered these guns to be private property. One example is Massachusetts Governor William Shirley's 1755 order: "To such of them as shall be provided with sufficient Arms at their first Muster, they shall be allowed a *Dollar* over and above their Wages, and full Recompence for such of their Arms as shall be inevitably lost or spoiled."[65]

Governor Shirley believed that some members of the militia, contrary to the law, did not have firearms appropriate to military service. He also believed some members could show up appropriately armed, and he was prepared to pay them extra because of it. Most importantly regarding the question of private versus public ownership, "full Recompence" shows that militiamen would be compensated for the loss of privately owned guns. In 1763, Massachusetts Governor Francis Bernard reimbursed Enoch Kidder

By His EXCELLENCY

WILLIAM SHIRLEY, Efq;

Captain-General and Governour in Chief in and over the Province of the Maſſachuſetts-Bay in New-England.

To ~~John Bewsh Capt'~~

SIR,

AS you have receiv'd Beating-Orders from Me to enliſt Men into His Majeſty's Service for the Expedition intended,

In the Management of that Truſt, I give you the following Directions;

1. You are to enliſt no Perſon under the Age of eighteen Years, nor above Forty-five Years.

2. You are to enliſt none but able-bodied effective Men, free from all bodily Ails, and of perfect Limbs.

3. You are to enliſt no Roman-Catholick, nor any under five Feet two Inches high without their Shoes.

4. You are to aſſure ſuch Perſons as ſhall enliſt, That they ſhall enter into Pay, ~~...~~ upon their first general Rendezvous

5. That they ſhall at the Day of their Enliſtment receive a good Blanket ~~...~~

6. That their Pay will be *Twenty-ſix Shillings and eight Pence,* per Month, lawful Money, during their Service. ~~...~~

7. That they ſhall be exempt from all Impreſſes for Three Years next after their Diſcharge.

8. To ſuch of them as ſhall be provided with ſufficient Arms at their firſt Muſter, they ſhall be allowed a *Dollar* over and above their Wages, and full Recompence for ſuch of their Arms as ſhall be inevitably loſt or ſpoiled.

9. You are to enliſt no Perſon but ſuch as you can be anſwerable for that they are fit for Service; and whom you have good Reaſon to think will not deſert the Service.

10. You are before your delivering the Blanket allowed, or any other Bounty that may be allowed by this Government to any Perſon, cauſe the ſecond and ſixth Sections of War to be read to them, and have them alſo ſworn before, and their Enliſting atteſted by, a Juſtice of the Peace.

Given under my Hand at Boſton, *the* Seventeenth *Day of* April 1755, *in the Twenty-* Eighth *Year of His Majeſty's Reign.*

T. Hutchinſon
by Govr. Shirley's order

GOV. WILLIAM SHIRLEY CALLS UP THE MILITIA

"for the Loss of his Brother Samuel's Gun in 1758" while on militia duty.[66] It is unlikely that the government would compensate militiamen for loss of government property. There are similar examples in 1759 Maryland.[67]

In contrast, during the French & Indian War (1754–63), we have one example of the royal government offering to provide arms, ammunition, and tents for North Carolina volunteers, with no apparent expectation that any militiamen would bring their own guns,[68] but this is the only example of such an offer that I have found.

Virginia also distinguished between public firearms and private firearms. In both 1672 and 1691, the Colonial government made a curious guarantee: it would pay gunsmiths for any repairs performed on privately owned guns. This willingness to pay for repairs to privately owned guns might seem evidence that the government considered all guns to belong to it, but a more careful examination of the payment mechanism shows quite the opposite. In both statutes, the government promised to pay gunsmiths for repairs—but the owner would be required to reimburse the government for that expense. The government's goal was to guarantee timely payment of gunsmiths for their labor so that the militia would be ready to fight; the gun's owner was still ultimately responsible for payment.[69]

Philip Bruce points to Virginia orders to return arms to the county courthouse after a 1677 expedition that clearly distinguished those public arms from arms sold to militiamen under the 1673 statute. Similarly, Bruce points to an order to return public arms after a 1684 emergency that distinguishes public arms from privately owned arms.[70] A 1676/7 Virginia law concerning the sale of firearms was consistent with private property rights in firearms, but contrary to an assumption that firearms were automatically government property: "It is ordered that all persons have hereby liberty to sell armes and ammunition to any of his majesties loyall subjects inhabiting this colony."[71]

A 1650 Rhode Island statute also demonstrated a clear understanding that firearms could be—and often were—privately owned. The law specifies how to determine whether privately owned guns, "his owne proper goods," had been sold to the Indians.[72] There being no serial numbers on guns at the time, tracing an illegally transferred firearm was not a trivial matter. Some gun control laws we might think are new, really are not.

Criminal prosecutions also give no hint that the government considered all firearms to remain government property. Connecticut on several occasions fined colonists for selling guns to the Indians with no suggestion that these were publicly owned arms.[73] A 1764 prosecution of two men for theft in Pennsylvania caused the court to run an ad that "as the said Rifle and Fowling Piece appear not to belong to the Public, but to be private Property," the owners were requested to apply for return of their property.[74]

Civil suits also provide no evidence that guns were assumed to be government property. What is doubtless America's first firearms product liability suit took place in 1645 New Haven. A Stephen Medcalfe went over to visit a friend named John Linley. "Francis Linley, his brother, being in the house, told him he would sell him a gun. . . . Stephen asked him if it were a good one, he answered yea, as any was in the town, whereupon they bargained, and Stephen was to give him 17s."[75] Nowhere in the course of the trial is there even a hint of any perceived impropriety in selling this musket.

In a few colonies, guns were exempted from various forms of civil processes, much as bankruptcy laws today exempt certain essential property from seizure. In April of 1673, Virginia's governor and council directed militia officers to make sure that an excess of guns in any house be redistributed to those militiamen who were short of guns.[76] But eleven years later, in 1684, Virginia passed a law that sought to encourage private ownership of guns by exempting privately owned guns from such impressments in the future. To encourage the inhabitants to be "well and compleatly furnished when commanded to musters" all "swords, musketts . . . pistolls, carbines, guns, and other armes and furniture, as the inhabitants of this country shall provide and furnish themselves with, for their necessary use and service, shall henceforth be free and exempted from being impress[sed] . . . ."[77] The law thus gave privately owned arms a special protection from government seizure, not shared by other private property.

Maryland exempted not just guns from civil "Attachments or executions" in March 1647/8, but also food, bedding, pots, "and necessary labourers tooles with such like household implements and Ammunition for subsistence . . . ."[78] Guns were thus included among the necessities of life—no different from any other private property.

In times of crisis, some Colonial governments redistributed privately owned guns, as they might do with any goods necessary to the defense of the colony. Other Colonial governments were more inclined to offer incentives to obtain such weapons, instead of simply seizing guns from individuals. All the evidence suggests that guns were often privately owned—and were not automatically the property of the government.

ASSESSING MILITIA COMPETENCE

How well-armed militia units were—and sometimes, how remarkable it was when they were not well-armed—provides evidence that gun ownership was very common in Colonial America. At the start of the French & Indian War, and just before the Revolution, we have evidence that militias were generally armed—and exceptions were noteworthy. During the 1756 emergency call-up of the Virginia militia, Colonel George Washington complained about some of his militia units:

> I think myself under the necessity of informing your Honor, of the odd behaviour of the few Militia that were marched hither from Fairfax, Culpeper, and Prince William counties. Many of them unarmed, and *all* without ammunition or provision. Those of Culpeper behaved particularly ill: Out of the hundred that were draughted, seventy-odd arrived here; of which only twenty-five were tolerably armed.

Washington considered the militia arriving inadequately armed to be "odd behaviour," and worth mentioning. This suggests that other militia units *were* adequately armed, and brought ammunition. Washington sought to have the unarmed militiamen punished, which suggests that their behavior—arriving inadequately armed, without ammunition—was exceptional, not typical.[79]

All the laws previously discussed requiring gun ownership and regular militia musters were for one purpose: to create a competent military force against Indians, other Europeans, and in some colonies, against rebellious slaves or even criminal mobs.[80] Did they make the colonists effective in that capacity? While the population seems to have been well armed (as subsequent chapters will demonstrate), their effectiveness as military units was mixed. In some colonies, at some times, militias demonstrated discipline, military competence, and skill in the use of arms. At other times, militias showed none of those traits. For every sparkling success, such as the seizure of Louisbourg on Cape Breton Island by New England militias in 1745, there were far more failures caused by internal conflict, desertion, illness, and shortages of provisions.[81]

Accounts from the Colonial period suggest that some militias did not compare well with professional soldiers. Jasper Danckaerts, a Dutchman visiting America, described an annual militia muster held in 1680 in New York City: In the course of this exercise, "two young men on horseback [rode] as hard as they could . . . dashed against each other, and fell instantly with their horses." At first taken for dead, both recovered.[82]

Half a century before, evidence reveals that the Massachusetts militia of farmers who ran off the British Army in 1775 evolved from something akin to the Three Stooges. At a 1632 training in Watertown, one militiaman fired an "unloaded" musket, injuring three men with shot, although none seriously. Later that year, the militia commander's attempt to inject some realism into a night drill demonstrated that they were not yet ready for action.

Yet by 1639, Governor Winthrop was able to describe two regiments of militia "to the number of one thousand soldiers, able men" "very skilful and ready in divers sorts of skirmishes and other military actions."[83] In 1641, Winthrop happily described two days of militia training at Boston: "About 1200 men were exercised in most sorts of land service; yet it was observed that there was no man drunk, though there was plenty of wine and strong beer in the town, not an oath sworn, no quarrel, nor any hurt done."[84]

Danckaerts was very positively impressed with a militia muster near Boston in 1680. He witnessed a total of eight infantry companies and one cavalry company, divided into two opposing forces, who "operated against each other in a sham battle, which was well performed." The "sham battle" was fought with some seriousness, with at least one officer injured by a gunshot.[85] Between the almost comical 1632 training, and these later exercises, Massachusetts militia units had participated in real combat against multiple enemies, most notably against Indians in the Pequot War, and King Philip's War. For all soldiers, whether full-time or militiamen, real combat is a transforming moment.

Virginia's militia often performed credibly. In 1667 and again in 1673, Governor Berkeley led the Virginia militia to prevent Dutch invasion. While Governor Berkeley was fearful of bringing together so many armed men—many of them landless freemen, and some of them indentured servants—he evidently feared the Dutch more. In a real crisis, not in a muster, the Virginia militia performed well.[86]

At the beginning of the eighteenth century, South Carolina's militia attack on St. Augustine in Spanish Florida showed more skill than their commander. Subsequent attacks into Florida showed competence, and when the militia defended Charles Town from attack by a French and Spanish fleet, "the victory was an impressive one." When fighting the Indians, South Carolina's militia turned in a more mixed performance, winning the Yamasee War (1715–1718) with more effort than their technological advantage over the Indian alliance should have required.[87]

The competence of militias varied substantially not only from year to year but region to region. Geographic differences meant that some colonies had a more effective militia:

New England towns were more scattered than Chesapeake farms, but each town had a capacity for armed resistance that was lacking in an individual plantation. A town could bear the burden of a military draft and still hope to maintain itself against attack, while the loss of a man or two from a single, remote household often meant choosing between abandonment and destruction. Despite shortages and complaints, a New England town could usually house and feed a company of soldiers besides its own, thus acting as an advanced military base .... [T]he clustering of manpower and the cohesive atmosphere in the town community gave New England greater military strength.[88]

Along with the question of competence, there was also the question of willingness. The effectiveness of militias was somewhat dependent on the laws under which they were organized. Governor Horatio Sharpe of Maryland repeatedly complained about the difficulties in using his militia as an effective fighting force during the French & Indian War: "[F]or want of such a Militia Law as is in force in the Northern Provinces we can scarcely oblige the people to act in the Defence of themselves & properties when immediately attacked." The people "have no . . . notion of Arms or Military Duty."[89] The problem was not only lack of military feeling or training, but also an unwillingness to follow orders: "I hope the General does not depend on the Militia of this Province to garrison Fort Cumberland[;] if he does he will most certainly be disappointed for I am satisfied it will not be in my Power to prevail on a single Company to march thither."[90]

The following year, General Webb marched the New York militia north to relieve Fort William Henry during the French & Indian War—but arrived too late. Nonetheless, he needed the militia to continue forward to prevent an invasion by the French and their Indian allies—but "all the Militia, except those of the County of Albany, had deserted in a mutinous manner."[91] Desertion seems to have been a common problem with Colonial militias; theoretically, it could be punished with great severity, but in practice, Colonial juries showed considerable mercy to their neighbors who found the hardships of military life excessive.[92]

A series of 1754 letters by Virginia's Lieutenant Governor Dinwiddie, commanding North Carolina militia, reveals another rather comical problem. The government set too high a daily pay rate for the soldiers, hence, "The Soldiers were so elated with their high Pay, that they made slow Marches, and before (reaching) the other places, the £12,000 was near all expended, and they w[oul]d not serve" any longer, without security for pay above and beyond the amount originally budgeted.[93]

As the threat of Indian attack waned in the eighteenth century, colonists in the more settled areas along the coast increasingly regarded militia duty as a burden to be avoided. The evidence appears in the increasingly strict laws designed to catch those who were not armed for militia duty, and the increasing complaints from governors about militiamen doing their best to avoid their duty.

While Colonial governors frequently complained about inadequately armed militias, only one of these complaints quantified this failing. In a 1756 letter, Governor Sharpe of Maryland complained that,

The Militia of this Colony are near 16500, One third of whom at least are entirely destitute of Arms & many of the Guns that are the property of the Rest are very bad & scarcely fit for use. For want of a proper Militia Law (which the assembly has been frequently in vain sollicited to make) the people are undisciplined as well as badly armed & cannot be compelled to serve in Defence of the Country.[94]

Even a governor complaining about the poor state of his militia believed that a majority of the militia possessed guns, even if "scarcely fit for use" for militia purposes.

Tension always exists in human societies between social obligations and personal desires. In 1713, Virginia Lieutenant Governor Spotswood attempted to prepare for possible hostilities with the Tuscarora Indians, who were then at war with North Carolina. Spotswood soon discovered that ordering out the militia was a waste of breath—it had been too long since the Indian threat had been a motivating force to keep the militia operational. Spotswood could issue all the mustering orders he wanted; he would not have an effective militia in time to defend the colony from an immediate threat. On the other hand, events such as the 1704 Indian raid on Deerfield, Massachusetts, had been recent enough that New England's militiamen were aware of the hazard, and prepared to fight.[95]

Even when external threats should have been sufficient motivation, economic interest sometimes trumped collective defense. The year after the 1622 Indian attack that had killed one fourth of the colony, Virginia's government found it difficult to persuade the militia to leave their tobacco crops and fight. The pursuit of tobacco wealth took precedence over what should have seemed to be self-preservation.[96]

Darrett Rutman's study of the transformation of Boston from 1630 to 1649 argues that economic opportunities promoted an individualism contrary to the collectivist sentiment that Governor John Winthrop and other founding

Puritans held. One of the side effects was that the title of "freeman"—a full citizen of the Commonwealth, with the privilege of not only voting but also holding office—became increasingly regarded as more burden than it was worth. Many of these offices required significant investments of time, and sometimes out of pocket expense—time and money that might be better invested in improving one's own status.[97] The Plymouth Colony Constitution of 1636, for example, required that anyone elected governor who refused to serve would be fined £20—but at least, no one would be required to serve two years in a row. Holding public office, like militia duty, was a duty to the society, and one that many sought to evade as the need for it became less clear.

By the middle of the eighteenth century, the Colonial governments found it difficult to persuade militiamen to travel great distances to fight enemies who represented threats to the British Empire and its geopolitical ambitions—but not direct threats to Boston, Philadelphia, or Charleston. Colonial governors increasingly relied upon expeditionary forces made up of volunteers, substitutes hired by wealthier members of the community, indentured servants, free blacks, white vagrants, and occasionally, militiamen drafted into service. Only under extraordinary circumstances could the more respectable citizens who were theoretically the militia persuade themselves to engage in these expeditionary forces that the laws and Whig philosophy assumed that they should.[98] By mid-eighteenth century, Virginia allowed drafting only of able-bodied men who "do not follow or exercise any lawful calling or employment." Those who had the right to vote for members of the House of Burgesses were also exempt from draft.[99] These expeditionary forces made a poor impression on British officers during the French & Indian War, who assumed, a dozen years later, that they would be confronting similarly unimpressive forces at Lexington and Concord.[100]

Besides the reluctance of militiamen to give up the security, safety, and comfort of home by performing their duties, the militia was often an expression of incipient democracy. Magistrates in America discovered what their counterparts in Britain had already found out: there was sometimes significant overlap between the mob and the militia, or at least sympathy for the concerns of the lawbreakers. In such cases, calling up the militia was a waste of time.[101] Even where the militia structures accountable to the legitimate government existed, royal governors often dared not call out the militia. As early as 1747, Governor William Shirley found that the Boston militia refused to obey orders to suppress rioters whose sympathies they shared. The Stamp Act Crisis also demonstrated that the Crown's representatives were free to issue orders, and the militia, being a popular institution, was just as free to ignore those orders.[102] Royal governors realized that it was actually more dangerous to call up the militia, who would thus be assembled and organized—and might be more hazardous to the governor himself than the governor's enemies.[103]

South Carolina's 1760s Regulator movement was a power unto itself in the backcountry—and the intersection of law breaker and citizen could lead to odd tensions. The Regulators first engaged in vigilantism to deal with widespread violence, including murder, rape, torture, kidnapping, robbery, and arson. While the lawful government in Charles Town was at first hostile to the actions of the Regulators, as the details of the outrages that they sought to correct became known, the government first pardoned and then legitimized their actions.[104] Now with legal authority for their actions, the Regulators' zeal turned to defiance of the lawful government. Officials from Charles Town discovered that their writs were unenforceable because the militia was the government's only coercive tool—and there was substantial overlap between the militia and the Regulators in the backcountry. Finally, the Regulators began to commit crimes only somewhat less serious than those they had first sought to punish.[105]

When militia duty and opposition to the government went hand in hand, as it sometimes did in the Colonial period, the results could be spectacular, as a heavily armed population demonstrated what large numbers could do to intimidate regular military forces. Nathanael Byfield's account of the overthrow of Governor Andros' authority in Boston in 1689 described how "the Town was generally in Arms, and so many of the Countrey came in, that there was twenty Companies in Boston, besides a great many that appeared at Charles Town that could not get over (some say fifteen hundred)."[106] Governor Andros' report described how "the greatest part of the people . . . appeared in arms at Boston . . . to the number of about two thousand horse and foote . . . ."[107] One description of the insurrection tells us:

I knew not any thing of what was intended, till it was begun; yet being at the north end of the town, where I saw boys run along the street with clubs in their hands, encouraging one another to fight, I began to mistrust what was intended; and, hasting towards the town-dock, I soon saw men running for their arms: but, ere I got to the Red Lion, I was told that Captain George and the master of the frigate was seized, and secured in Mr. Colman's house at the North End . . . .[108]

Seventeenth and eighteenth century Whigs argued that militias were intrinsically virtuous instruments of government power because they reflected the concerns and interests of a broad, landed gentry. While these theories had been largely accepted in Colonial America, they were more abstract than heartfelt. Americans believed in the militia system because it was flexible enough to handle attacks by naval forces, Indians, or slaves, without the expense of a standing army, either raised locally, or sent from Britain. As Parliament sought to assert its authority after the French & Indian War ended in 1763, those who would later style themselves as Patriots based their arguments against standing armies in Whig terms. The role of British regulars in the Boston Massacre, and enforcing Parliament's laws punishing Massachusetts in the 1770s, both confirmed the theory, and inflamed public sentiment against standing armies.[109] These sentiments dominated American military policy into the nineteenth century.

It is easy to pick particular examples from the period 1607–1775 to demonstrate almost any level of militia competence. Colonial militia competence reflected the varying levels of recent military experience of the men involved, how necessary the citizens regarded the existence of that militia, and the extent to which colonists saw a direct connection between their own interests and military service.

Threatening Shadows:
Guns in the Hands of the Other

While Colonial governments trusted most people with guns—indeed, required gun ownership of many—this trust was not universal. Governments sometimes disarmed individuals as punishment for criminal behavior. More often, governments distrusted particular groups. Unsurprisingly, Colonial governments rarely trusted enslaved blacks and Indians with guns—but *some* masters trusted *some* slaves with guns—enough so that legislatures passed laws to either prohibit or closely regulate this practice. (Especially in the seventeenth century, Indian prisoners of war were often enslaved. South Carolina's slave population in 1708 was one-third Indian.)[1]

The laws concerning guns and *free* blacks varied from colony to colony, and from decade to decade. Catholics, heretics, and individual criminals were occasionally subject to legal disabilities concerning gun ownership, although with far less regularity than the laws aimed at blacks. Many colonies also passed laws regulating the use of firearms with the goal of preventing accidents.

INDENTURED SERVANTS

Indentured servants were sometimes part of the militia and sometimes not—reflecting both their fettered status, and the more than occasional fear that their masters had of them. The first Africans in the American colonies were apparently treated not as slaves, but as indentured servants. But as the colonies formalized slavery along racial lines, masters feared indentured whites less, and regarded them as allies against the common enemies: slaves and Indians.[2]

Almost from the very beginning of Colonial Virginia, leaders such as John Smith, Lord De La Warr, Sir Thomas Gates, and Sir Thomas Dale sought to create a universal militia, with every man, regardless of race or status, armed and trained in military exercises. While the desire for a universal male militia is certain, the statutes actually passed are unclear as to how broad the militia was in these first few years of the colony's existence. Conflict with the Indians climaxed in the 1622 massacre, in which a coordinated attack against multiple settlements killed one-quarter of the colonists in a few hours in a nearly perfect surprise attack. (A few friendly Indians warned settlers of an imminent attack, without which the death toll would have been higher.) The survivors had no choice but to improve the colony's military preparedness, even if it meant risk on other fronts:

> [T]o defend every house and hamlet in the colony would require placing guns and other weapons permanently in the hands of hundreds or thousands of unsupervised individuals—an alarming innovation for the seventeenth century. Up to this time relatively few Virginians possessed their own weapons, and the supply of arms left over from the military regime of the earliest days was kept locked away in company magazines scattered about the colony.[3]

In desperation, Virginia's leadership armed the entire population. By 1624, the legislature imposed a duty on all able-bodied men to perform militia duty, exempting only those settlers who had arrived before 1612.[4] Later laws hint that "all able-bodied men" included blacks both free and indentured, as well as white men. Over the next few years, the law defining who was obligated to perform militia duty in Virginia and consequently arm himself, or be armed by his master, became more explicit. Governor Yeardley's instructions of 1626 required that all men above seventeen and below sixty were "liable to be summoned to war." Along with those settlers who arrived before 1612, and who perhaps were exempted because they were in positions of political power, men who had recently arrived were also exempt from militia duty. The records do not tell us why newcomers were exempt, but it seems probable that the newcomers would not yet know the countryside and were not yet armed. The requirement to be armed was not just theory. John Smith, writing from London around 1629, but presumably based on information from Virginia, wrote that most settlers owned a firearm.[5]

But such all-inclusiveness was not to last. In 1639, the first racial divide in the militia appears; black slaves were no longer obligated to serve.[6] Probably this indicates that slave masters' economic interests took precedent over militia muster—slave labor was just more tangibly advantageous than the less quantifiable value of the militia protection. It is possible that some slaves continued to serve in the militia, but we have no evidence that tells us how many slaves—if any—remained.

This racial division soon encompassed not only slaves but free blacks as well. A 1639/40 statute requiring all men (free and indentured) to arm themselves, or be armed by their master, seems to be the first that associated race instead of servitude with militia duty: "All persons except Negroes to be provided with arms and ammunition or be fined at pleasure of the Governor and Council."[7] A few months later, the statute was restated in slightly different form, but with the same result: All white men were obligated to militia duty. Free white men must arm themselves; masters must arm their indentured white servants. A 1640 order from the Colonial government directed all able-bodied freemen "to arm themselves and their white servants with 'arms both offensive and defense' within a year."[8]

Thus, free blacks were exempted from the obligation to arm themselves, and masters of both slaves and indentured blacks (as some still were) were exempted from the duty to arm their charges. While *slaves* were clearly excluded from the arms-bearing militia by 1640, the lack of laws regulating black gun ownership suggests that *free* blacks retained the right to possess firearms, both individually, and as voluntary members of the militia, into the beginning of the eighteenth century.

The 1639 and 1640 laws of Virginia demonstrate that indentured *white* servants were still trusted enough that masters were required to arm them. But a growing mistrust of these servants appears in some towns starting in the 1660s, with a number of towns excluding indentured servants from militia duty.[9] York County experienced a servant rebellion in 1661. Gloucester County uncovered a servant conspiracy in 1663 that planned "to seize their masters' arms and lead a march of servants on the governor to demand their freedom."

This mistrust also seems to spread to the poorest freemen during this period, and not just with respect to militia duty. In 1665, Lancaster judges found themselves on the run from a population angry that they had sentenced a man to the stocks. Governor Berkeley found himself having to suppress two "mutinies" related to a new tax in 1674.[10] In 1670, the assembly limited the vote to "landowners and housekeepers," on the grounds that landless freemen had "little interest in the country" and were more likely to cause "tumults at the election" than to use their votes constructively.[11] In later decades, this contraction and expansion of the franchise in Virginia often paralleled the contraction and expansion of militia duty.[12]

The localized suspicion of the poorest whites, the indentured servants, became colony-wide in the 1670s. In 1672, the colony's militia law changed; masters were now only obligated to arm indentured white men whose contracts were close to expiration. When Virginia Governor Berkeley ordered the militia to repel a Dutch invasion in 1673, planters brought their indentured servants because they feared leaving the servants in charge of their homes and families.[13]

Virginia's 1673 militia law, like the 1619 and 1632 statutes, leaves it unclear as to who was required to own a gun.[14] In light of the status of white indentured servants, after the 1672 law removed most of them from the militia,[15] this vagueness is quite understandable. Only free white men, and a few indentured white men, were now members of the militia.

Each of these changes to the Virginia militia law was relatively minor—and we often lack contemporary explanations for why these changes took place. Yet this drastic change between the 1620s, when Virginia enjoyed a universal militia, and 1672, when only part of the white male population was obligated to fight and bear arms, has explanations that can be deduced from later accounts by the House of Burgesses (the Virginia legislature). In 1699, when Governor Nicholson proposed to restore all indentured servants to militia duty, the House of Burgesses came up with two reasons to maintain the status quo. The

Burgesses' first reason for keeping nearly all indentured servants out of the militia was that calling up the militia would create a hardship on planters who would lose so many of their workers. Militia musters took place on three days of the year—hardly a significant loss of labor in peacetime. This concern about lost labor would only make sense in wartime—but it is hard to imagine that the absence of workers then would injure the planters more than the absence of a military force to protect those plantations.

The second reason seems more plausible. The Burgesses supported keeping most indentured servants out of the militia because of the fear that masters now had of their white indentured servants. Many of the indentured servants were Irish, suffering from "incorrigible rudeness and ferocity," and of suspect loyalty in a war against a European foe. Many other indentured servants were convicts transported for a fixed term of years. The Burgesses claimed that it was hard enough to control white laborers when they were unarmed, and "if they were armed and permitted to attend musters, they might be tempted to seek to obtain their freedom by slaying their masters."[16] Arming an indentured servant whose term was close to expiration might have seemed safe enough. Such a servant was close to being free and would have had little reason to free himself at gunpoint (an action that, if it failed, would cause the courts to stretch his period of servitude, if not his neck) and much reason to acquit himself in an honorable manner.

Along with a series of minor rebellions by indentured servants and poor free whites, Bacon's Rebellion in 1676 dramatically transformed the political landscape of Virginia. Bacon's Rebellion in the perception of historians has changed quite dramatically over the last two centuries. When concern for the rights of the Indians was somewhat less dominant, historians interpreted this uprising as a forerunner of the American Revolution, with Nathaniel Bacon leading the poorest whites in rebellion against a privileged elite. As sympathy for Indians has increased, Bacon and his followers have been increasingly regarded as a dangerous band of racists. The fight between Bacon's followers and Governor Berkeley thus stemmed from Berkeley's defense of Indian rights against frontiersmen who sought government assistance in exterminating Indians occupying lands that poor whites wanted.

There is considerable merit in both explanations; the elite of Virginia *were* hogging the good lands and had no interest in a costly war that might lead to Indian attacks not just on the frontier, but in the tidewater counties that were far removed from the Indian-frontiersmen conflict. At the same time, the elite could afford to take a principled position in favor of the land claims of the Indians; they were wealthy in land holdings. Expanding the available land at the expense of the Indians would draw poor whites to the frontier, reducing the supply of free labor available to the largest tidewater planters.

Throughout the thirty years after Bacon's Rebellion in 1676, who was to be armed, and who was not, was a source of considerable debate. King Charles II put Herbert Jeffreys in Berkeley's place as Virginia's governor to restore order, but Jeffreys died within two years. To deal with the continuing threat of Indian attack, William Byrd and Laurence Smith proposed that the colony establish two frontier towns, each with 250 soldiers who would be guaranteed "freedom from arrest and from lawsuits for twelve years, and freedom from taxes for fifteen years" as a recruiting incentive. The House of Burgesses and the governor's council approved this proposal, which would have created what was effectively a standing army. However, certain prominent men in Virginia perceived some real danger in allowing William Byrd— who had already shown some skill at leading discontented men during Bacon's Rebellion, to create his own frontier society, one likely to attract the poorest freemen—armed, and exempt from arrest. The Privy Council in London recognized the danger that Byrd might well end up with the power to follow in Bacon's footsteps, and vetoed the scheme.[17]

Lord Culpeper served as Virginia's governor from 1680 to 1683. King Charles II's orders to Culpeper included resolving the problem of the "big men" of the colony who had abused poor whites so severely that they had revolted. Charles' motivation does not appear to have been a concern for justice, but a pragmatic interest in Virginia's production of tobacco, which paid taxes to the royal treasury. The king's instructions included drafting a law to see that "all planters and their Christian servants were furnished with arms" for the purpose of protecting the colony from Indian attack. This would have included almost every white man in the colony—reversing the gradual removal of servants from the militia that had taken place in the period 1660–1672.[18]

Virginia required masters to supply their indentured servants with certain goods when they had completed their term of service. These "freedom dues" were certainly granted in the seventeenth century, but masters sometimes offered servants an early end to their term of service in place of these goods. These goods included necessary tools for a freeman just getting started, and this exchange put servants in the difficult position of taking early liberty—or being able to make a proper start as self-reliant freemen. Consequently, in the aftermath of Bacon's Rebellion, the Virginia legislature prohibited masters from offering servants such a choice.[19] It was better for the stability of the colony that freemen be adequately equipped to make an independent living, rather than have a population of poor and unhappy freemen. From 1705 onward, Virginia law required that the freedom dues for men include "one well fixed musket or fuzee, of the value of twenty shillings, at least." A master who refused to issue the specified goods could find himself ordered to do so by the county court.[20]

Nothing indicates that Virginia ever required indentured servants to serve in the militia during the eighteenth century (except when drafted into expeditionary forces), or required their masters to arm them (except as part of freedom dues). Delaware's 1742 militia statute very clearly prohibited indentured servants from serving in the militia, or bearing arms,[21] as did Pennsylvania's 1756 statute, except with permission of one's master.[22] None of these laws explicitly prohibited indentured servants from possessing arms, and we have at least one example of an indentured servant in 1656 Maryland who owned a firearm, and disobeyed his master's order: "[H]e Should not goe out to use his Gunn on the Sabboth."[23] Surely few servants could have afforded to buy a gun of their own, which may explain the absence of laws prohibiting indentured servants from owning guns.

BLACKS AND GUN LAWS

Virginia passed its first comprehensive slave code in 1705, the same year that the law required masters to arm their freed indentured servants with guns.[24] This increasing desire of the legislature to see every freeman armed may reflect an increasing fear of slave rebellion—and the need to have every white man prepared to fight immediately. Maryland, also a large slave colony at this time, passed a similar law within a few years of Virginia, requiring masters to arm indentured servants at the end of their terms.[25] In the case of Maryland, the first of these laws arming indentured servants appeared a few years after the colony made the decision to rely on black slaves for field labor instead of white indentured servants.[26] North Carolina, while it held slaves as well, held them in very small numbers—yet also passed such a law requiring guns as part of freedom dues by 1715.[27]

The laws concerning guns and *free* blacks varied from colony to colony, and from decade to decade—much more so than did the laws concerning white ownership, and these prohibitive laws generally became more restrictive over time. This racially-based discrimination has been common throughout American history, deriving its origins from fear of slave rebellion and a belief that free blacks might assist their slave brethren.[28] At least part of this increasing regulation of black gun ownership was also because blacks in the American colonies may at first have been treated more like indentured servants than slaves. While the evidence is "too fragmentary to prove" that Virginian blacks were treated identically to white indentured servants in the 1620s and 1630s, by the 1640s we have clear evidence of the development of black slavery.[29] As the status of black workers hardened into race-based slavery, several colonies first disarmed slaves in the seventeenth century, then free blacks in the eighteenth century.

Virginia's laws provide an especially salient record of this changing attitude towards guns and blacks. Virginia's 1639/40 law requiring every man "except Negroes" to be armed—apparently at his own expense or that of his master—did not distinguish between free blacks and slaves. However, this law only excluded blacks from mandatory militia membership, and repealed the obligation of masters to arm black servants and slaves; it did not prohibit either free blacks or slaves from owning or carrying arms.[30] The increasingly stringent laws regulating slave possession of guns—along with the indication of a perceived need for these laws—suggest that at least a few masters had armed at least some slaves. In 1680, fear of slave insurrection caused Virginia to require slaves to carry a pass from their master when traveling away from home.[31] The same year, Virginia also prohibited "any negroe or other slave to carry or arme himselfe with any club, staffe, gunn, sword or any other weapon of defence or offence. . . ."[32] This statute *might* be read as an indication that *all* blacks were prohibited from carrying guns, but "negroe or other slave" seems to mean slaves, both black and Indian.

By 1723, Virginia had become increasingly fearful of its growing black population, spurred by a series of slave conspiracies and uprisings in the period 1709–1722. Virginia's slave population grew rapidly in the late seventeenth century mostly due to importation of Africans instead of births among existing slaves.[33] Those who had been born free in Africa were less willing to accept the status of slave than those who had been born slaves and had never known any other way of life. Consequently, Virginia adopted a variety of laws intended to keep both slaves and free blacks in a subservient position. These laws imposed servitude requirements on free children of racially mixed parentage, prohibited voting by non-whites, and barred blacks from testifying in court concerning whites.[34]

During this same legislative session, Virginia passed a law regulating gun ownership by free blacks and Indians: "That every free negro, mulatto, or indian, being a house-keeper, or listed in the militia, may be permitted to keep one gun, powder, and shot." Those blacks and Indians who were "not house-keepers, nor listed in the militia" were required to dispose of their weapons by the end of October 1723. Blacks and Indians living on frontier plantations were required to obtain a license from a justice of the peace "to keep and use guns, powder, and shot."[35]

The problems of slave unrest continued through the 1720s and 1730s; consequently, the Colonial government attempted to strengthen county militias to defend against this threat,[36] establishing Virginia's first slave patrols in 1727.[37] Slave patrols would travel the countryside looking for slaves away from their plantations without permission of their owner. In some colonies slave patrols also performed preventative searches of slave quarters for weapons and other contraband.

Even the small number of blacks and Indians who were householders or members of the militia were apparently no longer trusted with guns in public by 1738. They were still required to muster but were not allowed to bear arms during the exercises.[38] Unsurprisingly, the 1727 slave patrol law was expanded in 1738, giving militia commanders authority to order "all men to go to church armed with weapons."[39] The 1738 statute did not explicitly prohibit free blacks from owning guns, but because the 1723 statute only allowed gun ownership by free blacks and Indians as part of militia duty, the 1738 law meant that free blacks no longer had any legal right to own guns.

Maryland echoed Virginia's 1680 law with a 1715 statute that ordered, "That no Negro or other slave, within this Province, shall be permitted to carry any Gun or any other offensive Weapon, from off their Master's Land, without Licence from their said Master."[40] Like Virginia's, the wording of the statute is ambiguous as to whether it applied to all blacks, or only to slaves—and unlike Virginia's 1723 statute, no later clarification exists. Maryland also went through a complex and still imperfectly understood process of changing the status of blacks from indentured servants into hereditary slaves whereby the children of slaves automatically became slaves as well.[41] (As with Virginia, historians are still arguing about the exact process in Maryland.)

South Carolina appears to have followed a similar sequence to Virginia and Maryland in its laws regulating race and guns. Like its neighbors to the north, the distinctions between white indentured servants and black slaves seem to have been less dramatic in the first few years of South Carolina's existence. Some slaves, both Indian and African, were freed by their masters and formed a small free black and mulatto class in the colony at the close of the seventeenth century. South Carolina armed slaves in 1672 to defend the governor's plantation from Spanish and Indian attack, in 1708 to resist French invasion, and during the Yamasee War a decade later.[42]

In both 1704 and 1708, South Carolina passed laws that included in the militia "every Male Person from 16 to 60 Years of Age, to bear Arms," and provided that a slave who killed an enemy during invasion earned his freedom.[43] But a 1720 slave rebellion ended the use of armed slaves in the militia along with this provision extending freedom.[44]

In spite of increasingly restrictive laws, at least some South Carolina slaves remained armed right up to the American Revolution. Slaves clearly had some access to firearms for the purpose of hunting in the first few decades of South Carolina's history. A 1703 statute paid bounties for destroying wolves, panthers, bears, and wild cats—and explicitly recognized that either a white person or a slave might be the hunter. After a 1712 slave conspiracy came to light, South Carolina prohibited a slave from possessing guns outside his master's property without his master's permission. Masters were ordered to keep guns in "the most private and least frequented room in the house" and regularly search slave quarters for guns and other weapons. Yet masters were still obligated to arm slaves for militia duty (at least through 1720),[45] and there were many other exemptions that left slaves armed at their master's discretion: Some slaves were allowed guns in order to hunt, keep varmints under control, slaughter cattle, or tote guns for their masters.

As was often the case with the slave codes, the gap between the law and its enforcement seems to have been rather wide. Slaves were still hunting, with guns, as late as 1775—and, "Lead shot and gunflints have been found at almost all the [South Carolina] Lowcountry (and many Chesapeake) slave sites."[46] Perhaps an indication of how commonly guns were found in slave hands, one of the inducements to persuade whites to accept slave patrol duty was that they were allowed to keep any guns confiscated from slaves.[47]

As in Virginia, the change from a frontier society to a more settled colony producing staples for export caused increasing racial distinctions.[48] The exact mechanism by which settlement lowered the social and legal status of blacks remains a subject of debate among historians, but at least in part, the fear of Indian attack on the frontier was greater than the fear of slave revolt. Some of the staples produced for export also required a large labor force prepared to work in a hot and humid climate, with malaria-bearing mosquitoes—conditions for which Africans were better suited by genetics. (Carriers of sickle-cell anemia are less prone to malaria and its debilitating symptoms.) Americans repeated this pattern as the frontier moved westward, and probably for the same reasons. Armed blacks, even armed slaves, were considered less dangerous than attacking Indians, and on the frontier the laws often allowed for slaves to be armed with their master's permission.[49]

The increasing racial distinctions written into the laws of South Carolina were not limited to the issue of gun ownership, but appear with respect to other fundamental rights of citizenship. At least some blacks (presumably free blacks) voted in the 1701 South Carolina elections—and they lost the franchise in 1721. A 1722 law required freed slaves to leave the colony within a year, or be re-enslaved. Similar to Virginia and Maryland, South Carolina's first law prohibiting both interracial marriage and sex, in 1717, came as both free blacks and slaves were losing their right to vote and be armed.

Unlike Virginia, where a shortage of white labor may have caused these distinctions, South Carolina's change seems based on the rapid growth of its black population as the seventeenth century waned. Lacking a large crop that required slave labor to harvest, South Carolina had few slaves until the 1690s, when rice and tar became major exports. South Carolina's first legislation devoted only to slavery did not appear until 1690, but was disallowed by the colony's owners.[50] The first comprehensive slave code did not appear until 1696,[51] suggesting that slaves had become a significant legislative concern at this time. By 1708, blacks were a majority, and this black majority grew larger from the combination of natural increase and slave importation.[52]

In 1721—the same year that free blacks lost the vote—South Carolina merged its militia and slave patrols. In addition to checking to see if traveling slaves possessed passes, the slave patrol was supposed to search black homes for "firearms or other weapons" as well as stolen goods—with no apparent distinction between slaves and free blacks. From the beginning, these patrols were armed, and blacks suffered "a high mortality rate," since the patrols were authorized to kill those resisting arrest.[53]

By the 1730s, as the percentage of African-born slaves reached its high water mark, a series of slave conspiracies added to the existing fears of the shrinking white minority.[54] The government of Spanish Florida exacerbated matters by encouraging slave revolt and runaways as part of the global conflict between Britain and Spain. Spanish authorities spread the word that runaway slaves from the British colonies could be free, just a bit farther south.[55] Yet in spite of what should have been fear on the part of South Carolina masters, slaves continued to have access to guns. A 1734 account described how a runaway slave was taken captive by "a white Man and one of His Excellency's Negroes . . . each with a Musket loaded with Swan-shot."[56]

On Sunday, 9 September 1739, a group of about twenty slaves forced entry into a store about twenty miles from Charles Town, South Carolina, seizing guns and powder for sale, and decapitating the store keepers. As they moved through the countryside, they killed most (but not all) whites with which they came in contact, recruiting (and in some cases, kidnapping) slaves along the way. Over the next month, militia units first defeated the main body of sixty to one hundred slaves, and then went after smaller bands of rebels.[57] The South Carolina legislature passed "bring your guns to church" laws in 1724 and 1739—and Peter Wood argues that imminent enforcement of the 1739 law provoked the rebels to launch their attack when they did—on a Sunday before the new, more stringent law required all white men to be armed at church.[58]

The Stono Rebellion of 1739 was as successful as it was partly because the slaves gained access to guns and ammunition so quickly. The following year, a somewhat larger rebellion involving 150 to 200 slaves failed because they were betrayed by another slave before they were able to reach Charles Town, where they hoped to secure guns by breaking into a store—suggesting that the business on the Stono River raided for guns and powder was not unique.[59] As with many of the other colonies, slave rebellion provoked legislators both to pass laws forcing the white population to be armed—and increasingly stringent laws to disarm not only slaves, but in some colonies, free blacks.

Even without the provocation at Stono, there were reasons for the white population to be worried. The slave population of South Carolina outnumbered the whites at least two to one by 1730, and even more dramatically in the low country.[60] The low country whites became increasingly concerned about both slave rebellion and by the possibility of an alliance between runaway slaves and Indians on the frontier. Runaway slaves at least occasionally formed "maroon" communities (where runaway slaves developed their own society) in the wilderness in the mid-eighteenth century—and in at least one such community, formed their own militia organization apparently patterned on the system of their former masters.[61]

Laws prohibiting slaves from possessing guns did not always create the desired effect. Some masters showed such a notable trust in at least some of their slaves that grand juries in South Carolina complained that masters were bringing guns to church, as the law required, then handing them to slaves to hold during services.[62] Complaints are also on record of slaves carrying guns home from militia musters, and firing them in the streets "to the great Terror of many Ladies."[63]

In North Carolina, unlike other Southern colonies, the definition of militia member under both the 1715 and 1746 militia statutes did not explicitly exclude free blacks.[64] While other laws limited blacks to serving only as musicians, these laws were frequently ignored, with both slaves and free blacks armed for militia duty until at least 1812. There also seems to have been no statutory prohibition of free blacks possessing weapons—and the colonial laws allowed a master to request permission for his slaves to carry guns, which was apparently granted quite freely to masters of high status.[65] After the Revolution, free black men served in the militia in North Carolina with no record of any racial tension or discrimination.[66]

Slavery developed much more slowly in North Carolina than in its sister colonies of Virginia and South Carolina. North Carolina's first comprehensive slave code was not passed until 1715, and it was much later in developing slave patrols than other Southern colonies.[67] Fear of slave rebellion, however, played an important role in encouraging North Carolina to maintain the militia system. A 1741 letter from Henry McCullough to the Lords Commissioners for Trade and Plantations described the Assembly's concerns after the 1739 Stono Rebellion in South Carolina. The Assembly's proposal was to require every slaveowner to "provide one able white man for the Militia" to counterbalance some yet-to-be-determined number of slaves.[68] A somewhat similar idea lay behind 1720s laws requiring planters "to supply armed whites in proportion to their holdings in land and slaves."[69] Similarly, there were proposals in 1730 South Carolina for establishing frontier townships where white immigrants would act to counterbalance the dramatic slave majority in the lowlands— where blacks outnumbered whites two to one.[70] Slaves were a kind of public hazard; if a master wished to buy more slaves, he was obligated to provide white members of the militia.

While these laws disarming blacks were most common in the Middle and Southern colonies, some New England laws show a similar concern. Massachusetts, apparently in the midst of a military crisis, on 27 May 1652 required all "Scotsmen, Negers, & Indians inhabiting with or servants to the English" between 16 and 60 to train with the militia. (Much as with the southern colonies, there is an interesting parallel between militia duty and voting. A 1655 report complained that "scotch servants, Irish negers and persons under one and twenty years," were voting.) In May 1656, perhaps after the military crisis had passed, "no Negroes or Indians . . . shalbe armed or permitted to trayne."[71] Unlike the 1680 Virginia and 1715 Maryland statutes, which are ambiguous as to whether they applied only to slaves or to all blacks, the Massachusetts law clearly applied to all blacks. It is unclear, however, if this was intended as a ban on gun ownership by blacks, or only a prohibition on blacks being armed and trained as part of the militia.

All colonies, before the Revolution, had slaves. Not surprisingly, while there are variations in how different colonies regulated slave possession of firearms, Georgia, New Jersey, Delaware, and Pennsylvania also passed laws attempting to disarm slaves.[72]

While the institutionalization of race-based slavery played a part in excluding all blacks from the armed militia, most colonies seem not to have prohibited free blacks from possessing or carrying firearms in a *private* capacity. Was this because free blacks were few in number? Did white Colonial society use extralegal means to discourage free blacks from owning guns? Or did the governments feel no need to restrict gun ownership by free blacks? This is certainly a topic worthy of deeper investigation.

Untrustworthy Whites

While blacks and indentured white servants were often not enough trusted with guns to serve as armed members of the militia, free whites were *generally* trusted with firearms. There were some exceptions: Particular religious minorities were not trusted; individual whites were distrusted because of past behavior. One early example of an untrusted religious minority was Anne Hutchinson's Antinomians. *Johnson's Wonder-Working Providence* describes how the Massachusetts Bay Colony dealt with this heretical schism in 1637: "[S]ome persons being so hot headed for maintaining of these sinfull opinions, that they feared breach of peace, even among the Members of the superiour Court . . . those in place of government caused certain persons to be disarmed in the severall Townes . . . ."[73] Many people were armed (as the laws required), and only as punishment for a specific crime was a small fraction of the population disarmed. The number disarmed—77 out of a population then in the thousands, most of whom were required to own guns—is far less than the percentage legally prohibited from gun ownership in America today.

In England, the Disarming Papists Act (1689) prohibited Catholics from possessing "any arms, Weapons, Gunpowder, or Ammunition (other than such necessary Weapons as shall be allowed to him by Order of the Justices of the Peace, at their general Quarter sessions, for the Defence of his House or Person)."[74] The law prohibited Catholics from possessing arms, and yet allowed them, under some restrictions, to have at least defensive arms. Professor Joyce Lee Malcolm argues that, "This exception is especially significant, as it demonstrates that even when there were fears of religious war, Catholic Englishmen were permitted the means to defend themselves and their households; they were merely forbidden to stockpile arms."[75]

At least in times of crisis, this law seems to have been the justification for disarming Catholics. In Britain, for example, the death of Protestant Queen Anne in 1714 caused orders that, "The Lords Leiutents of the severall Countrys were directed to draw out the Militia to take from Papists & other suspected Persons their Arms & Horses & to be watchfull of the Publick Tranquillity."[76] The Protestant government of England feared that Catholics might attempt to place a Catholic monarch on the throne—and the 1715 rebellion in Scotland, in favor of the Old Pretender (James III), a Catholic, shows that this fear was well-founded.

While the Disarming Papists Act was occasionally used to disarm Catholics in Britain, Catholics do not ever appear to have been legally disarmed in America. The only *attempt* at disarmament seems to be in 1756 Maryland, where the legislature declined to pass a bill that would have ordered seizure of "all Arms Gunpowder and Ammunition of what kind soever any Papist or reputed Papist within this Province hath or shall have in his House or Houses . . . ."[77] That the governor considered this provision necessary suggests that the Disarming Papists Act of 1689 did not grant authority to disarm Catholics in America.

Georgia passed a superficially similar statute, and yet more careful reading shows that it was not a ban on Catholic gun ownership. At the start of the French & Indian War, British forces demanded that the French population of Nova Scotia swear an oath of allegiance to the crown. The government forcibly removed those who refused this oath to other British colonies. Some of these Acadians (the ancestors of the Cajuns) were bound as indentured servants in

Georgia. A 1756 law regulating their terms of indenture prohibited Acadians "to have or use any fire Arms or other Offensive Weapons otherwise than in his Masters Plantation or immediately under his Inspection."[78] No general prohibition on Catholic ownership of firearms seems to have existed in Georgia; the Acadians were disarmed because they had refused to be loyal subjects of the British government, and this disloyalty remained after they settled in Georgia.

There is one curious form of religious discrimination in 1665 Dutch New Amsterdam with respect to militia duty, and based not on questions of loyalty. Jews were exempted from militia duty, and obligated to pay a special tax instead; because, "first the disgust and unwillingness of these trainbands to be fellow soldiers with the aforesaid nation and to be on guard with them in the same guard house and on the other side, that the said nation was not admitted or counted among the citizens" in Amsterdam "nor (to our knowledge) in any city in Netherland."[79] There is no evidence, however, that this prohibition from militia duty prohibited Jews from owning guns.

Along with classes or groups that Colonial laws sometimes disarmed because they were considered untrustworthy, individual freemen (regardless of race) might have their possession or use of a gun restricted. A 1645 Norfolk, Virginia, court prohibited George Kemp from hunting in the woods "with a dog or gun" as punishment for killing hogs in violation of the law, and did similarly to Denis Dally "nearly twenty-five years later . . . ." In the aftermath of Bacon's Rebellion, a petition from Westmoreland County, Virginia, requested that the rebels who had been pardoned be "forbidden to carry guns or swords"—a punishment for their disloyalty to the Colonial government.[80] Such limitations on individuals were clearly punishments for individual criminal acts.[81] While our ideas today about who should and should not be armed have radically changed, the concept that gun ownership is tied to one's participation as an adult, law-abiding member of the society remains the same.

Uneasy Alliances: Guns and Indians

One indication of how ubiquitous guns were in early America is how rapidly Indians assimilated firearms into their culture, in spite of both royal and colonial efforts to keep guns a white monopoly. Especially where colonists had recently fought Indians, or expected to do so again, simple self-interest should have been enough reason to obey injuctions to withhold guns from Indians—and yet this was not enough to stop the flow of guns.

Very little legislative history exists on the subject for those colonies that came into existence late in the seventeenth century.[1] The earlier colonies, however, reveal a complicated history of their efforts to keep guns out of the hands of the Indians. The sometimes high severity of the punishments suggests that not all the colonists shared the government's concern in keeping Indians unarmed. At the same time, these laws seesawed between severe punishments and complete laissez-faire, as relations with the Indians—and other colonies—changed. A March 1657/8 Virginia statute provided that "what person or persons soever shall barter or sell with any Indian or Indians for peice, powder or shott, and being lawfully convicted, shall forfeite his whole estate." Any Virginian who found an Indian with gun, powder, or shot, was legally entitled to confiscate it. By the following year, however,

[I]t is manifest that the neighbouringe plantations both of English and [foreigners] do plentifully furnish the Indians with guns, powder & shott, and do thereby drawe from us the trade of beaver to our greate losse and their profit, and besides the Indians being furnished with as much of both guns and ammunition as they are able to purchase, *It is enacted*, That every man may freely trade for gunns, powder and shott: It derogateing nothing from our safety and adding much to our advantage . . . . [emphasis in original]

In October 1665, Virginia again prohibited the sale of guns and ammunition to the Indians. The statute admitted that Dutch sales of guns to the Indians had made the March 1657/8 law unenforceable, saying that "those envious neighours are now by his majesties justice and providence removed from us." The ban was again in force—but not obeyed. In March 1675/6, Virginia enacted a new statute, complaining "the traders with Indians by their [avarice] have soe armed the Indians with powder, shott and guns, that they have beene thereby imboldened." The new statute made it a capital offense to sell guns or ammunition to the Indians, and also declared that any colonist found "within any Indiane towne or three miles without the English plantations" with more than one gun and "tenn charges of powder and shott for his necessary use" would be considered guilty of selling to the Indians, and punished accordingly.[2]

Contemporary accounts of Bacon's Rebellion in 1676 refer to gun battles with the Indians in which multiple guns in a single Indian home were unsurprising.[3] Bacon himself complained that Governor Berkeley had restored firearms to the Indians, and supplied them with ammunition in violation of the law.[4] (At least some of the tribes supplied by Governor Berkeley were regarded by him as allies, or at least friendly; his goal was to assist them to fight against less friendly tribes farther back from the frontier.) After the rebellion, Charles City complained that Berkeley's friends had supplied ammunition to the Indians: "[W]ith ammunicon they were better furnished by the traders then wee his majesties subjects . . . ."[5] In spite of (or perhaps because of) Virginia's vacillating policy about gun sales, the Virginia frontiersmen had much to fear from well-armed Indians.

New England colonies also wrestled with the pros and cons of placing guns in the hands of Indians. When the Pilgrims arrived in 1620, the local Indians had no guns. By 1623, Indians unfriendly to the Pilgrims had been "furnished (in exchange of skins) by some unworthy people of our nation with pieces, shot, [and] powder." Those "unworthy people" were Thomas Morton and associates at Merrymount, among others. By 1627, the Indians of Massachusetts Bay were believed to have at least sixty guns, largely supplied by Morton, in violation of the royal proclamation against supplying the natives with firearms, powder, or shot.[6] While Merrymount's licentiousness offended their Pilgrim and Puritan neighbors with drunkenness, Indian concubines, and Sabbath-breaking, when Miles Standish of Plymouth Colony led an expedition to arrest Morton and close down his scandalous establishment, the Pilgrims' primary motivation was suppressing Morton's arming of the Indians. Morton's force was adequately armed but too drunk to defend themselves from the similarly armed, but sober Pilgrims.[7]

Massachusetts Bay Colony initially sought to limit the supply of guns to the Indians. In 1632, within three years of the colony's settlement, Massachusetts courts sentenced a Watertown settler to whipping and branding in the cheek for "selling a piece and pistol, with powder and shot" to an Indian.[8] (While harsh by modern standards, whipping and branding were common punishments in English law at the time, in an era before the modern prison system.) In 1642, Massachusetts Bay complained that "some of the English in the easterne parts" who were under no government, were supplying gunpowder and ammunition to the Indians, and sought to punish the sellers.[9]

Later in 1642, as Massachusetts became concerned about an emerging coalition of hostile Indian tribes, the government "thought fit, for our safety, and to strike some terror into the Indians, to disarm such as were within our jurisdiction." After having disarmed some of these Indians, Massachusetts, finding "no ground of suspicion" of them taking part in the conspiracy, restored their weapons.

By 1647, the United Colonies (into which most of New England's English settlements were now confederated) gave "strict orders to restrain all trade of powder and guns to the Indians." Governor John Winthrop acknowledged that this accomplished less than it seemed because "the greatest part of the beaver trade was drawn to the French and Dutch, by whom the Indians were constantly furnished with these things."[10] In 1668, the Massachusetts General Court licensed the sale of "pouder, shott, lead, guns, i.e., hand guns" to Indians "not in hostility with us or any of the English in New England."[11]

Connecticut repeatedly prohibited sale of guns or ammunition to the Indians—and found the experience of gun control as frustrating as some modern governments. The first entry in *Public Records of the Colony of Connecticut* of 1636 complains that "Henry Stiles or some of the ser[vants] had traded a peece with the Indians for Corne." Because merchants in the Dutch and French colonies were selling guns to the Indians, Connecticut next prohibited the sale of guns outside the colony. Finally, foreigners were prohibited from doing business with Indians in Connecticut as retaliation for continued Dutch and French sales of guns to the Indians.[12] John Winthrop reported that the Dutch governor of New Netherlands in 1648 tried to prevent gun sales to the Indians, but he also had no luck preventing his people from gun trading.[13]

Having failed to disarm the Indians, Connecticut pursued a more realistic policy of disarming Indians within the English settlements. In 1660, Connecticut ordered that "if any Indians shal[l] bring in Guns into any of the Townes" that the English were to seize them. The Indians could redeem them for 10s. per gun, with half paid to the Treasury, and the other half paid to the Englishman who seized the gun. The following year, Connecticut repealed this rule for Tunxis Indians that lived near the towns, who "have free liberty to carry their guns, thro[ugh] the English Townes, provided they are not above 10 men in company."[14]

In the Carolinas, the government armed its Indian allies. One of Thomas Newe's letters written in 1682 mentioned one of the hostile Indian tribes of Carolina that had recently committed atrocities against the settlers: "There is a small party of English out after them, and the most potent Kingdome of the Indians armed by us and continually in pursuit of them."[15] Newe's letter does not say, "armed by us with guns," but it is hard to imagine that the English were supplying the Indians with bow and arrow. By 1746, South Carolina Governor James Glen had agreed to arm the Choctaws to assist them in rebelling against the French.[16]

By the latter decades of the seventeenth century, the failure of laws intended to disarm the Indians led to a more realistic goal: controlling the supply of guns and ammunition to reward friendly tribes, and punish hostile acts. Now huge numbers of firearms were shipped to North America for sale to the Indians. In the period 1674–1781 (with many gaps in the records), 79 London manufacturers shipped 46,000 firearms intended for Indian sale to the Hudson's Bay Company alone. We know that other firms sold guns to the Indians as part of the fur trade, although we do not have any counts.[17] Winthrop described a 1644 shipment of 4,000 pounds of gunpowder and 700 guns intended for the use of Dutch settlers at Fort Orange (now Albany, New York) as trade goods for the Indians.[18] Presumably there were other shipments.

GUNS IN THE GROUND

Archaeological evidence suggests that guns were common among some Indian tribes during the Colonial period. One study examined 198 gun artifacts, focusing on "fifty-three more or less complete flintlocks of the period of c. 1620–1690, all recovered within twenty miles of the City of Rochester." Other gun artifacts found in these digs included five pistol butts, eleven trigger guards, thirty-six hammers, eleven barrels, and many other odds and ends. This enormous miscellany of parts implies a much larger number of guns in Indian hands that were *not* found "more or less complete."

An Indian burial site unearthed in 1934 near Rochester contained 426 flintlock parts "deposited at the back of the head and presumably was at one time the contents of a sack." Many of the parts were in sufficiently good condition that they "were assembled into completely functioning locks with which muskets were fired." The design of the locks, and the number of them, suggests that the grave was an Indian gunsmith, operating "between 1650 and 1670," although the lack of gunsmith's tools in the grave casts doubt on this hypothesis.[19]

A dig at a Susquehannock village in Lancaster County, Pennsylvania, occupied between 1600 and 1620 reveals bullets and swan shot. Digs at Seneca villages in New York occupied about 1630 have gun parts in them. Digs in circa 1650 Seneca villages have enough gun parts to demonstrate that flintlocks had replaced earlier firearms designs, such as the matchlock. Yet white settlers commonly robbed Seneca graves of any useful materials, including anything made of iron. That guns remain so common among the grave goods that survived grave robbers suggests that guns were fairly common among the Seneca—and at a time when there were no nearby European settlements.[20]

One reminder of the difference between what an archaeologist finds—and what the people of the period actually used—is a dramatic reduction in guns found in Seneca graves after 1675. The beaver market changed in that year, and Indians found themselves far less able to buy guns because of this. The Seneca no longer lavishly used trade guns as grave offerings. Guns probably became much more scarce in graves than they were in daily use.

In spite of the early attempts at preventing the Indians from obtaining guns, Indians swiftly became dependent on firearms for survival. As early as 1641, the Iroquois claimed that they needed guns to hunt. While the Iroquois perhaps exaggerated their hunting need (warfare likely being the more pressing reason), it does suggest that the Iroquois were using guns sufficiently often for hunting that this would be considered a plausible excuse. Examination of Seneca and Susquehannock archaeological sites shows that arrowheads were rare after 1640, suggesting that guns had replaced the bow and arrow as the dominant weapon.[21]

Visitors to the New World quickly noticed how dependent Indians in contact with Europeans had become on guns. Danckaerts described hiring an Indian guide on the upper Delaware River in 1679 who put off the trip so that he could have a gunsmith fix his gun: "[The Indian guide] had a fowling-piece with him which he desired first to take and have repaired at Burlington, and would then come back." Danckaerts complained about the immorality of the whites, selling alcohol to the Indians, and thus corrupting them: "[F]or they all solicit the Indians as much as they can, and after begging their money from them, compel them to leave their blankets, leggings, and coverings of their bodies in pawn, yes, *their guns and hatchets, the very instruments by which they obtain their subsistence.*"[22]

Another account that suggests that Indians became highly dependent on guns and gunpowder described events in 1689 New England. Defending Governor Andros' actions to pacify the Indians, it described how Andros "took from them . . . their powder, some pistols and Musquet barrels . . .

whereby they were reduced to very great poverty and forc[ed] to the use of their bows and arrows again, soe that in a little time they must have rendered themselves to his Mercy."[23]

By the eighteenth century, the English capture of non-English colonies and the increasingly effective enforcement of law within the English colonies meant that the Colonial governments had an effective monopoly on guns and ammunition. Providing guns and gunpowder became a mechanism by which Colonial governments could reward Indian good behavior—and in some colonies, the records of this are quite extensive. *Pennsylvania Archives* lists guns, gunpowder, lead, and flints given to various Indian tribes as tokens of friendship during the Colonial period—and the quantities involved suggest that the Indians had many guns.[24]

Not only guns and gunpowder, but also gunsmiths, were a necessity for Indian tribes. In 1751, Benjamin Franklin suggested:

Every one must approve the proposal of encouraging a Number of sober discreet Smiths to reside among the Indians. They would doubtless be of great Service. The whole Subsistence of Indians depends on keeping their guns in order; and if they are obliged to make a Journey of two or three hundred miles to an English Settlement to get a Lock mended; it may, besides the Trouble, occasion the Loss of their Hunting Season.[25]

If the Indians depended on guns and gunsmiths for subsistence, the Indians must have owned a lot of guns. A number of white gunsmiths catered to the Indians: Philip Ryley, who worked among the Indians at Cayuga, New York, 1747–48;[26] Thomas Burney, who was a blacksmith and gunsmith to the Ohio tribes in the years 1750–52; Thomas Copelen, killed near Ft. Pitt in 1763; and Noah Coply, who worked among the Indians in 1749 Lancaster Co., Pennsylvania.[27] Doubtless there were many others who left no records of their work.

A 1933 archaeological dig provides further evidence of gun culture among Indians. A road excavation near Malta Bend, Missouri, uncovered a wooden chest containing 108 gun parts and eighteen gunsmithing tools. The chest's contents suggest that this was the property of a gunsmith. The location and age of the gun parts imply it was associated with a nearby Osage village abandoned before 1780.[28]

T.M. Hamilton's survey of Indian trade guns in the Colonial period includes examples of guns of English origin recovered from many parts of North America, demonstrating how widespread this trade was across parts of North America where few whites traveled. Hamilton was able to typify the guns based on multiple copies found across large geographic areas. Hamilton identified one particular type, "Type K," of the 1730–1775 period, based on one found in Michigan, and two examples from separate Osage villages in Missouri. Subsequently, incomplete Type K guns were identified from "six Indian village sites and two forts, distributed over six states: Michigan, Missouri, Oklahoma, Texas, Alabama, and Georgia."[29]

Charles Heath, an archaeologist with the Center for the Environmental Management of Military Lands at Colorado State University, has done extensive research and archaelogical fieldwork focused on Native-American and Euro-American sites dating to the Colonial period and later. He dismisses any denial of pervasive gun ownership: "Anyone who concludes that firearms ownership or firearms access was not generally ubiquitous in eastern North America during the Colonial era, or in later time periods for that matter, is essentially ignorant of the archaeological record." He continues,

> In my experience, it is readily evident that ammunition and firearms related accoutrements (e.g., gun parts, gunflints, percussion caps, etc.), as well as faunal remains from hunted game, are quite common in artifact assemblages recovered from the historic period archaeological sites (ca. 1584–1860) where I have worked. I actually find it somewhat unusual when at least some quantities of such materials are not recovered from either Colonial or post-Colonial period habitation sites, be they Euro-American, Native-American, or even enslaved African-American sites. Although firearms related artifacts may be more common on "frontier" or rural sites (I have not actually conducted comparative statistical analyses), I have even recovered weapons related accoutrements (e.g., ammunition and gunflints) from early 19th century, middle-class urban sites. . . .

I have conducted excavations on several post-Contact period Native-American sites (Tuscarora and Carolina Algonkian habitation sites, ca. 1650–1760) in eastern North Carolina where firearms, gun parts, ammunition and other related accoutrements are commonly recovered. It defies logic to suggest that European settlers, who actively participated in the "global economy" of the Colonial period—as actively, if not more so than their Indian neighbors—could not afford to purchase the same European produced weapons that were traded to the Indians in return for deerskins or other animal pelts.

While there were no major weapons production facilities in Colonial North America, any local blacksmith with basic skills could repair European produced weapons or forge and fit replacement parts. Archaeologists often find "spare" trade gun parts on 17th and 18th century Indian habitation sites in the Southeast and Middle-Atlantic regions of North America. The presence of such parts certainly suggests that Native-Americans quickly developed the basic weapons maintenance and repair skills necessary to keep their firearms functional for hunting, raiding, or defense. European produced firearms, particularly export guns shipped to North America for the Indian trade, were readily available and comparatively inexpensive.

[Thus] firearms seem to have been commonly possessed and frequently used for various purposes by ethnically diverse peoples during both the Colonial and Antebellum periods in eastern North America. While there are certainly exceptions to my generalizations . . . any claim which suggests firearms were not commonly owned or used in Colonial America is problematic.

Perhaps some future interdisciplinary study of the problem from a combined archaeological and historical perspective might shed additional light on this controversial issue.[30]

In the 1820s and 1830s, John Jacob Astor's American Fur Company contracted with Pennsylvania gun makers for rifles to trade for furs with the Indians. Starting in 1826 and continuing until at least 1831, the Henry family of Nazareth, Pennsylvania, became the only contractor for American Fur, and manufactured about 2,300 rifles for this trade, as well as shotguns. The US government also contracted for trade guns, many of them rifles, to satisfy treaty obligations associated with the westward removal of Indian tribes. At least eighteen manufacturers contracted with the US government to make thousands of Indian trade rifles in the period 1800–09. Henry Deringer contracted to make 8,500 rifles in 1837 and 1840; 2,500 of these rifles were explicitly "Indian rifles," and some of the remaining 6,000 may have been as well.[31]

How long did firearms last in Indian hands? One might assume, because of the difficulties of repair, that Indian guns would be short-lived. (The United States government, as part of treaty obligations, did sometimes provide gunsmiths to the Indians.)[32] Yet the evidence suggests otherwise. Excavation of gun parts and bullets from Osage villages of the eighteenth century shows that guns were common items, with more than one hundred gun barrels excavated at one site—and when these gun barrels outlived their usefulness, they were broken up for use as tools. Yet the barrels are the caliber of *seventeenth* century French trade guns—implying that guns survived for decades in Indian hands.[33] Similary, H.E. Leman of Lancaster, Pennsylvania, contracted to make 500 Indian rifles for the US government during the 1830s. When the Sioux and Cheyenne surrendered most of their firearms in 1877, four decades later, 94 were Leman rifles.[34]

The eyewitnesses and the archaeological evidence powerfully argue that guns were widely owned by American Indians, even those not in direct contact with Europeans—and these guns moved from European to Indian hands with astonishing speed. A number of tribes owned guns, and enough tribes had them in quantity to become dependent on them for hunting. It is hard to imagine, contrary to Bellesiles' claim that "the Eastern Woodland Indians possessed more firearms per capita than any other society in the world,"[35] that guns were more common among the Indians, than among the American colonists who supplied the guns.

Guns in Official Records and Personal Narrative

Counting guns in Colonial America is a complex though not hopeless problem. Today we have public opinion surveys, manufacturing records, and in some states, governmentally mandated gun registration records. By contrast, the historian evaluating Colonial gun ownership must rely on incomplete and easily misunderstood data sources such as court records, probate inventories, eyewitness accounts and even letters and journals which may be quite removed from the actual event. Some of these official records and personal recollections may be incomplete or even incorrect in places. But nonetheless, taken altogether, they overwhelmingly speak of prevalent gun use in early America.

NOT JUST A MALE ACCESSORY: GUNS IN PROBATE RECORDS

Probate inventories in Colonial America assessed the value of a dead person's estate, resolved debts, and clarified what portion of the property belonged to the widow and children.[1] Probate inventories are probably the single most complete and objective method of counting guns in early America, simply because they are among the few surviving common lists of personal property. The objective nature of this evidence was Bellesiles' most persuasive argument that guns were actually pretty scarce in early America—until it turned out that his use of this data was novel, not in the sense of "new" but in the sense of "fiction."

Yet the attempt to infer information about gun prevalence from probate records can be problematic. Probate records are widely scattered and incomplete, with very complete sets published in some states, while in other states these records remain in archives or county courthouses.

Even once the historian has found the probate records (instead of just imagining them as suits his fancy), legitimate questions arise about how well probate records represent what average Americans owned. Were probated estates more likely to represent the wealthy, literate, or urban?[2] Historians who have studied colonial probate inventories believe that while they are incomplete, "the early records appear to have [consistently] covered most of the spectrum of deceased freemen."[3]

Still, the pointed difference between what probate inventories record, and what archaeological digs unearth, reminds us that inventories, while perhaps consistent across the classes, are still an incomplete record. Judith A. McGaw's study of eighteenth century agricultural tool ownership in the middle colonies points out that sewing implements and poultry were uncommon in probate inventories, and yet we know from archaeological excavations that needles were common, and "domestic fowl contributed substantially to the diet." We should therefore consider probate inventories a *minimum* count of what was present.[4] Another example of the problems of probate inventories is the collection covering the period 1639 to 1663, found in the first volume of *The Public Records of the Colony of Connecticut*. The thirty-four probate inventories often lump together many household goods under the category of "tools." Nonetheless, these estate inventories provide a minimum count of guns that these colonists owned when they died.

Guns were not just a male accessory. Thomas Scott's estate inventory shows that Mrs. Scott received a fowling piece, a matchlock musket, a sword, and a pair of bandalers (used for carrying ammunition). The three daughters received a snaphance flintlock and "1 cok mach musket," apparently a matchlock.[5]

Two estates list ammunition—worth as much as £5 in one case, and £4 in the other (more than a month's wages for a skilled laborer)—but no guns. Both estates were quite valuable, and it is tempting to assume that because guns were of fairly low value, that they were not listed. Another possibility is that the ammunition was left over from a time when these men owned a gun, and the gun had been sold or given away before their deaths, but the ammunition remained. For purposes of our analysis, we assume that those estate inventories that list ammunition but mention no arms did not have a gun.

Accurate inventory counts can be a challenge because of idiosyncratic handwriting, spelling, and inconsistencies in how the inventories were taken. Four Connecticut inventories show how a quick read might miss the presence of guns. John Porter's estate inventory lumps together disparate items: "five silver spoons; and in pewter and brass, and iron, and armes, and ammunition, hempe and flax and other implements about the roome and in the sellar."[6] Were these "armes" guns? The inclusion of "ammunition" suggests yes, and so we assume at least one gun was included among "armes." The same assumption can be made for Abraham Elsen's estate inventory that includes "his arms and munition" valued at £1:15:0, John Elsen's "arms and ammunition" valued at £2, and Henry Smith's "armes and ammunition" valued at £4. We have assumed that these represent one gun, although it is possible, with these valuations, that these could have been both a musket and a pair of pistols, or a musket and a fowling piece.

Of the thirty-four estates, twenty-three—or 71 percent—explicitly list guns, or list "armes and ammunition," for a total of 41 guns. (Excluded are William Whiting's "two great guns," cannons on board his ship.) Even excluding the four estates that list "armes and ammunition," 59 percent of the thirty-four estates had guns. The largest number of guns in an estate inventory is six, for James Olmestead: "3 musketts, one fowleing peece, 2 pistolls." The average number of guns in these Connecticut estate inventories that list guns or "armes and ammunition" was 1.78. with a maximum value of £1:3:0. The average for all estates is 1.21 guns.

An examination of 135 Plymouth Colony probate inventories (representing 138 deceased persons) for the period 1628–1687 reveals similar results: 90 (66.7 percent) included at least one firearm.[7] There was an average of 1.48 guns per inventory for all estates, or 2.22 guns per inventory among those estates that listed at least one gun. The largest number of guns was 38, belonging to Thomas Willett, a very wealthy man of some importance.[8] The value of the firearms averaged £1:0:8, and like the Connecticut probate inventories, because firearms were assessed together with other goods, this represents a *maximum* value. Like Connecticut, guns are more commonly associated with male probate inventories than female, but two out of eight female probate inventories at Plymouth Colony listed firearms—two firearms in each of these two estates.[9]

Other historians who have studied gun ownership in other colonies have found similar or even higher rates of gun ownership. McGaw found that about sixty percent of middle colony frontier county probate inventories showed guns, and a somewhat lower figure—fifty percent—in longer-settled regions.[10] Probate inventories of York County, Virginia, for the period 1660–1676 show that "more than 80 percent of the estate inventories included guns, muskets, pistols, or other 'pieces.'" Of the 20 percent that showed no guns, one quarter had powder horns or pistol holsters, items suggesting gun ownership.[11] Gloria Main's analysis of Maryland probate inventories of young fathers (defined as men with minor children) in the late seventeenth and early eighteenth centuries found that "arms," which would include at least some non-firearms, were present in seventy-eight percent of the estates. Even in the poorest estates, those with a personal property worth £15 or less, fifty percent listed arms.[12] This is unsurprising: Men with minor children would have been disproportionately militia members. In New England, just before the Revolution, probate inventories show gun ownership as common. Of 186 estates from Colonial Providence, Rhode Island, 153 were of male adults, and 149 had usable itemized personal property inventories. Of those 149 estates, 63 percent had guns.[13] Guns were only slightly less common than axes and knives and more common than many other common household goods:

> Guns were as commonly listed in Providence estates (63%) as all lighting items combined (60%): candles, tallow, candlesticks, oil, lamps, and lanterns. Gun ownership is as common as book ownership (62%) and much more common than the ownership of Bibles (32%).[14]

How common were guns in New York? A search for "gun," "pistol," and "fowling piece" in a data base of New York City wills and estate inventories from 1665 through 1790 found hundreds of matches.[15] The context demonstrates that guns were personally owned, and that some people owned multiple guns. One such example was Solomon Peters, a prosperous free black New York farmer at the close of the seventeenth century. His 1694 will bequeathed his guns, swords, and pistols to his sons.[16] One recent survey of probate inventory studies shows that across many regions and decades of Colonial America, a majority of homes had guns.[17]

One obvious problem with all probate inventories is that they represent a disproportionately aged population, and thus those who were less likely to be subject to militia duty. The high average age of this population suggests that they would be less likely to use guns for hunting due to physical infirmity and declining eyesight. Even with this limitation—which would tend to understate gun ownership—this sampling of probate inventories suggests that gun ownership was the norm—not the exception. Because the laws required gun ownership of most men, this is not a surprise.

CHEAP SHOTS

In 1702, the royal government supplied weapons to the Virginia government and included an invoice of the costs (presumably expressed in pounds sterling, not Virginia currency). There were 1,000 muskets, priced at 20s. (or £1) each, and 400 carbines (a shorter musket), priced at £1:6:0 each, and "[p]istols, with Holsters, 400 pair at 30s. [£1:10:0] a pair."[18] A set of purchase records for Georgia from 1737 lists thirty "Guns," priced at 23 s. each, and four "Fowling pieces & Cases," totalling £4:18:8. The average value of these thirty-four guns—all, apparently, new merchandise—was £0:13:1—or about the price of 39 pounds of smoked beef.[19]

Why such low prices? There was no Wal-Mart around to roll back prices. Either guns were common, but they were in larger supply than demand, or guns were rare, but cheap because there was little demand for them. Sampling the thousands of surviving eighteenth century issues of the *Boston Gazette* gives some clues as to which was more likely. At least one ad among the surviving 1720 issues offered goods salvaged from a wreck off the South Carolina coast, including, "Six blunderbusses . . . Ten muskets . . . Two pistols." Later in 1720, an ad appears offering gunpowder for sale. By 1730, the quantity of such ads increases. Ads offering shot and gunpowder appear in four out of fifty-one issues published 12 January 1730 through 5 April 1731. Firearms, some described as "fit for Guinea" (suitable for sale in West Africa), and others described only as "Musketts" appear in three ads.[20] Some ads were a bit more familiar. For example, one ad read, "if any Person . . . has left any Gun in the Hands of Mr. Richard Gregory late of Boston Gunsmith" they should come retrieve it.[21]

Issues of the *Boston Gazette*, dated 17 November 1741 through 13 September 1742, are awash in gun ads. The 17 November 1741 ad from John Gerrish offered a variety of consumer goods, including cloth, flour, stockings, furniture, and "Fire Arms" and "Pistols" for sale. Variations of this ad, with slightly different collections of goods, sometimes specifying "neat Fire Arms" but not pistols, and sometimes "Guns, Pistols, &c." appear in a total of sixteen ads over the next ten months.[22] (Many issues in this series were damaged or missing, making a complete count for this period impossible.) In six issues, there are two different vendors offering guns for sale, one of whom advertises himself as a gunsmith.[23]

Either there was a market for guns in Colonial America, or a lot of merchants wasted their money advertising them. Ads for guns, like ads for other commodities in these newspapers, very seldom list prices, but the frequency of these ads suggests that guns were not unusual items to offer for sale. An online search of the *Pennsylvania Gazette* from 1728 through 1800 found far more ads for guns, gunpowder, flints, and gun parts than there was time to catalog—and far more than you will read before falling asleep.[24]

Gunpowder import records also suggest widespread gun ownership and use. Surviving British Board of Trade records from just before the Revolution show quantities of gunpowder imported into the American colonies, totalling 1,030,694 pounds for the years 1769, 1770, and 1771.[25] Of course, this shows only gunpowder imported with the knowledge of the Crown; Americans smuggled goods quite regularly during those years, and there was some domestic production of gunpowder as well.[26] Colonial Americans used gunpowder not only for civilian small arms, but also for cannon, blasting, and (in extremely small quantities), for tattooing. It seems likely that at least some of this million pounds of gunpowder ended up being sold to the British military or Colonial governments, or the Indians. Nonetheless, the quantity is enormous. Even if only one-quarter of that million pounds of gunpowder was used in civilian small arms, that is enough for eleven to seventeen million shots over those three years.[27]

REVEALING REPORTS

Probate inventories offer compelling evidence of the ubiquity of guns in Colonial America, but they do not tell us much about how or how often Americans used these guns. Here lies the strength of the eyewitness accounts of life in Colonial America, along with other indirect evidence. While far less quantitative than probate lists, these accounts reveal the central role of guns in everyday colonial life and the cultural attitudes, rituals, and anecdotes surrounding them.

Plymouth Colony was well armed from the beginning. When a party of twenty men went ashore at Cape Cod on 11 November 1620, each one carried a firearm.[28] We know that at least two more guns remained aboard the *Mayflower*, because *Mourt's Relation* (one of the contemporary accounts) reports that while John Billington was ashore, one of his sons obtained gunpowder and shot from "a piece or two, and made squibs, and there being a fowling-piece charged in his father's cabin, shot her [the gun] off in the cabin; there being a little barrel of powder half full, scattered in and about the cabin . . . and yet, by God's mercy, no harm done."[29] Forty-one adult men signed the Mayflower Compact,[30] and twenty were ashore with guns, with at least two guns remaining on the ship. We therefore know that there were guns for *at least* half of the men at Plymouth.

Mourt's Relation described an incident on Christmas night, 1620. The colonists, hard at work, "heard a noise of some Indians, which caused us all to go to our muskets."[31] Edward Winslow, another of the colonists, described the rumored arrival of a French ship in November 1621; the governor called "home such as were abroad at work; where-upon every man, yea, boy, that could handle a gun, were ready."[32] While one could read these passages in several different ways, the most obvious interpretation is that all or nearly all of the male colonists had guns.

Visitors to Plymouth described widespread ownership of guns. Emmanuel Altham, visiting in 1623, reported the arrival of the Indian chief Massasoit at Governor Bradford's wedding. Massasoit arrived with "four other kings and about six score men with their bows and arrows—where, when they came to our town, we saluted them with the shooting off of many muskets and training our men." Issack de Rasieres, a Dutchman visiting Plymouth about 1627 described a militia muster: "They assemble by beat of drum, each with his musket or firelock, in front of the captain's door." Plymouth had about fifty families; there were at least fifty muskets or firelocks present.[33] De Rasieres also described "the Sabbath-day procession up the hill to worship, every man armed and marching three abreast." When war with the Narragansetts seemed likely in 1645, Plymouth contributed forty soldiers to a New England force that met at Seekonk: "They were well armed all, with snaphance pieces."[34]

When Plymouth Colony's first governor, John Carver, died in April 1621, "He was buried in the best manner they could, with some volleys of shot by all that bore arms." Firing a salute at a funeral was not unusual in the American colonies. The tradition seems to have Old World origins. Shakespeare, at the end of *Hamlet*, has Prince Fortinbras order Hamlet's corpse to be carried off to "soldiers' music and the rites of war," saying, "Go, bid the soldiers shoot."

French pirates robbed a Plymouth Colony settlement at Penobscot in 1633. The manner in which Bradford described how the pirates gained the upper hand suggests that guns were common, and had not only a utilitarian significance, but a social function as well: "[S]eeing but three or four simple men that were servants, and by this Scotchman understanding that the master and the rest of the company were gone from home, they fell of commending their guns and muskets that lay upon racks by the wall side, and took them down to look upon them, asking if they were charged."[35] This tactic of admiring another's gun might be used as easily today on an unsuspecting gun owner. By comparison, had the pirates asked to look at a hammer or an axe, even the credulous servants would have grown suspicious.

Others used guns in more functional ways. The sober and upright

Plymouth colonists were antagonized by the settlers at Merrymount because of their riotous, unsober living. This hedonistic trading post established by Thomas Morton in the mid-1620s was not far (enough) from Plymouth Colony. At Merrymount, lawyer Thomas Morton and his men engaged in drunkenness, traded guns to the Indians for furs, and took Indian concubines. Morton's description of the Maypole at Merrymount tells us that, "And upon Mayday they brought the Maypole to the place appointed, with drumes, gunnes, pistols, and other fitting instruments, for that purpose."[36]

Guns were apparently widely distributed among the population of Massachusetts Bay Colony, and available for purchase. A 5 April 1631 directive ordered every man that "findes a musket" to have ready one pound of gunpowder, "20 bulletts, & 2 fathome of match . . . ." Militia captains were ordered to train their companies every Saturday.[37] The Colonial government evidently believed that its citizens would purchase guns, presumably from England, or from other colonists. That same year, Governor Winthrop recorded an attack and murder of settlers at Pascataquack (now Portsmouth, New Hampshire), and reported as unsurprising that the Indians "burn the house over them, and carried away their guns and what else they liked."[38]

Just as Plymouth did, Massachusetts Bay colonists recognized important comings and goings by firing guns. The 1631 arrival of Governor John Winthrop's family was a joyful public occasion of honor: "[T]he captains, with their companies in arms, entertained them with a guard, and divers vollies of shot." Lord Ley and Sir Henry Vane, departing for England in 1637, enjoyed a similar salute, as did the departure of a French dignitary in 1644.

Guns were so central to daily life that, in 1635, Massachusetts Bay incorporated ammunition into their currency system. Brass farthings (a coin worth one-fourth of a penny) were prohibited by the colony, and replaced with musket bullets to "to pass for farthings."[39] Musket bullets were readily available—and they would certainly have been valuable in a frontier society.

SUITS AND ARMS

Lawsuits offer unique insight into both the legal and personal details of gun ownership, showing that guns were never treated as unusual, and guns were not expensive. One Connecticut lawsuit filed in 1639 was "Jno. Moody contra Blachford, for a fowling peece he bought and should have payd for it 40s." In 1640, William Hill was fined £4 "for buying a stolen peece of Mr. Plums man." In 1644, Robert Bedle was fined for stealing gunpowder from a Mr. Blakman.[40] There is nothing in these reports that suggests that guns were rare or unusual items—certainly not if a fowling piece was worth only 40s (£2 sterling). A civil suit in 1668–69 Plymouth by an Indian against Francis West for the theft of a hog and a gun treated the gun as an ordinary item. The court ordered West to pay for the stolen hog and return the gun to the Indian.[41]

A New Haven Colony civil suit in 1645—perhaps the first firearms product liability suit in the American colonies—suggests that guns were both inexpensive and common. A Stephen Medcalfe purchased a gun from a Francis Linley, as a spur of the moment decision: "Stephen Medcalfe complained that he going into the howse of John Linley, Francis Linley, his brother, being in the howse told him he would sell him a gunne. . . . Stephen asked him if it were a good one, he answered yea, as any was in the towne, whereupon they bargained, and Stephen was to give him 17s. As Stephen was going out of [doors] he questioned the sufficiency of the locke, Francis told him indeed John Nash told him she was not worth 3d." (John Nash was the son of the colony's armorer, Thomas Nash, and appears also to have been a gunsmith.) John Nash had earlier warned Linley that the gun was defective and dangerous. When Medcalfe fired "said gunne, the [breech] flew out & struck into his eye and wounded him deepe and dangerously into the head."[42] Nothing in the suit suggests that there was anything unusual about this transaction—except for the unfortunate ending.

A 1656 New Haven Colony statute ordered towns to provide "suitable sad[d]les, bridles, pistols" and other military equipment for the defense of the colony, including halberds, drums, pikes, and half a pound of gunpowder per soldier. The gunpowder requirement for each soldier, and a requirement that the militia practice "by shooteing at a marke three times in a yeare . . . " shows that guns were present. Because the equipment that each town was supposed to provide did not include long guns, it suggests that individual militiamen had their own guns. (Pistols, on the other hand, were provided by the town.)[43]

Both archaeological evidence and eyewitness accounts of Colonial

Virginia suggest that guns were common. Recent excavations at Jamestown have uncovered many surviving guns and associated paraphernalia. In 1994, "Excavations recovered parts from at least three matchlocks but only one fragment of its contemporary, the flint-striking snaphaunce. Fragments of three musket rests were also in the pit fill. . . . "[44] Excavations in 1995 and 1996 reported: "The matchlock is often found on early Virginia sites, and it is the only type of ignition system represented in the pit." Through June of 1997, the dig had recovered parts of at least eight different matchlocks, one snaphaunce pistol, and one other snaphaunce, six musket rests, two bullet moulds, a musket scourer, 2,807 pieces of lead shot, 223 bullets (defined as lead shot over 10mm diameter, but excluding artillery projectiles), at least thirty bandoliers, nine gunflints, and a bullet bag.[45] Of some obvious significance are the remains of a settler buried 1607–10, who died of a gunshot wound.[46] At this early date, in the first three years of the colony's existence, it seems implausible that an Indian shot him.

Of greater significance is the nearby burial of a white woman. The dirt on top of her coffin, apparently the subsoil excavated for her burial, contained lead balls and shot.[47] The presence of lead balls and shot in a graveyard is consistent with the 1655/6 Virginia statute that prohibited promiscuous shooting—except at marriages and funerals.[48] Of course, for volleys of gunfire to have put shot into the graveyard (rather than have it land some distance away) would require firing vertically—or indicate that a lot of shot and bullets were fired somewhere outside the graveyard. Either way, a lot of shooting was going on from the very beginning of the colony.

Along with the archaeological evidence, we have direct statements about the prevalence of guns in Virginia. William Blathwayt, auditor general of the colonies, in 1691 observed that "there is no Custom more generally to be observed among the Young Virginians than that they all Learn to keep and use a gun with a Marvelous dexterity as soon as they have strength enough to lift it to their heads."[49] Robert Beverley's description of the Virginia militia in 1705 also shows that guns were a fundamental part of Virginia culture:

Every Freeman, (by which Denomination they call all, but indented, or bought Servants) from Sixteen, to Sixty years of Age, is listed in the Militia; which by a Law, is to be Mustered in a General Muster for each County, once a year; and in single Troops and Companies, three or four times more . . . . The People there are very Skilful in the use of Fire-Arms, being all their Lives accustom'd to shoot in the Woods. This, together with a little exercizeing would soon make the Militia little inferior to Regular Troops.[50]

Other evidence that suggests that the laws requiring gun ownership were generally obeyed comes from the runaway servants ads in eighteenth century Virginia newspapers. The way in which firearms are mentioned in these ads suggest that they were not particularly unusual items, and that guns were easy to steal. Seven ads for runaway indentured servants in one newspaper in 1737 and 1738 mention that the missing man had either stolen a gun (presumably from his master), or had a gun with him.[51] A 1743 ad in the *Pennsylvania Gazette* advertised for the return of two runaway indentured servants from Virginia. "They took with them two Guns, one long the other short . . . ." An online search of the *Pennsylvania Gazette* for the period 1728–1800 found similar results. Guns appeared frequently in runaway slave or servant ads. Ads that mention the fugitives had taken either long guns or pistols, or both, were too numerous to sample more than a few.[52] A 1775 ad indicates that some runaway servants carried away a number of guns: "They had, and took with them, a country square-barrelled smooth bore gun rifle-stocked, one pistol, and other fire-arms." There are also occasional references to simple thievery, such as a 1746 ad that complained of a deserter from the "Northampton Muster in North-Carolina" who stole, among other articles, a "Pocket Pistol."[53]

Runaway slaves also had no problem finding guns, including pistols. As early as 1737, two slaves who ran off were reported as having "robb'd a House, and took a Pair of Pistols . . . ."[54] Many other ads list runaway slaves and indentured servants who carried away long guns and pistols.[55] Similarly, an ad in 1768 Cumberland County, Virginia, reported the capture of a runaway slave with a horse and a rifle.[56] One group of thirty South Carolina slaves ran away in 1743 for St. Augustine, in Spanish Florida; fifteen were reported to have guns with them.[57] One unusual combination involved two runaway slaves and two runaway Irishmen: "They stole from the said Masters a new yellow stocked trading Gun."[58]

Guns were also a reward for the return of runaway slaves. In 1722, Governor William Keith of Pennsylvania offered Indians capturing runaway slaves "one Good Gun and two Blankets for each Negro . . . ."[59] Similarly, South Carolina made treaties with the Creek and Cherokee Indians in 1721 and 1730 for the return of runaway slaves. The Creeks would receive "four blankets or two guns" for returning a runaway; the Cherokees agreed to do so for "a musket and match coat per slave, alive or dead."[60] The Creek treaty indicates that a gun was worth two blankets—hardly a sign of either scarcity of guns, or of a high price.

William Black's 1744 description of a practical joke played on some Maryland fisherman also suggests that guns were common:

> Towards the going down of the sun we saw a boat and canoe fishing inshore. We hailed them with, "Have you got any fish?" They returned with, "Have you got any rum?" We answered, "Yes, will you come on board and taste it?"
>
> Then they untied and made directly for us, but were very much surprised with the manner of reception they met with. We had the [blunderbuss] ready loaded and aimed on the side while they were to board us. Mr. Littlepage, who was to act the part of the lieutenant of a man of war, was furnished with four loaded pistols and the like number of swords. . . .
>
> Several more of our company were armed each with a drawn sword and cocked pistol. Several pistols, three fowling pieces loaded, and some drawn swords were lying in view on a table on the main deck.[61]

Yale's 1745 regulations for students include the following:

> If any Scholar Shall keep a Gun or Pistol, or Fire one in the College-Yard or College, or Shall Go a Gunning, Fishing or Sailing, or Shall Go more than Two Miles from College upon any Occasion whatsoever: or Shall be present at any Court, Election, Town-Meeting, Wedding, or Meeting of young People for Diversion or any Such-like Meeting which may Occasion Mispence of precious Time without Liberty first obtain'd from the President or his Tutor, in any of the cases abovesaid he Shall be fined not exceeding Two Shillings.[62]

We know other college students were hunting during this time. Nathaniel Ames, a Harvard student, "went a gunning after Robins" one April day in 1758. It was worth noting in his diary, but so was the arrival of a relative from home with linen, attending a funeral, and going fishing.[63]

Colonial writers used comparisons involving guns, suggesting that they were common enough that the writer expected others to have some understanding of firearms. Governor William Bradford's account of Plymouth Colony expected readers to know the distance a pistol bullet would travel: "[T]hey were much grieved and went to him and told him he would do no good if he did not lay his ship better to pass for she [the ship] might lie within pistol shot of the house."[64]

A 1750 letter from Benjamin Franklin described "an Experiment in Electricity that I desire never to repeat." Franklin attempted to electrocute a turkey with his static electricity capacitors. Distracted by his audience, he shocked himself into unconsciousness. "The Company present . . . Say that the flash was very great and the crack as loud as a Pistol . . . ." Where the shock entered his finger, "I afterwards found it raised a round swelling where the fire enter'd as big as half a Pistol Bullet . . . ." Franklin expected the recipient of the letter to know how loud a pistol would be, and the size of a pistol bullet. A letter that Franklin wrote two months later to an Englishman describing the same incident used somewhat different analogies: "nor did I hear the Crack tho' the By-standers say it was a loud one; nor did I particularly feel the Stroke on my Hand, tho' I afterwards found it had rais'd a Swelling there the bigness of half a Swan Shot or pistol Bullet."[65] To an Englishman, Franklin did not use an analogy involving the sound of a pistol, and even his use of a "pistol Bullet" as an indicator of size first said, "half a Swan Shot." Franklin may have believed that while Americans would know how loud a pistol was, and how big a pistol bullet was, an Englishman might not.

In the period 1768–1771, the Regulators of the backcountry of North Carolina sought to "regulate" the county governments, whose officials they believed were oppressing them with unreasonable fees for such acts as recording deeds. Governor Tryon's struggle against the Regulators in the decade before the Revolution provides a number of clues to the level of gun ownership

in that colony, and in a way that might not have otherwise ended up in any official records, if not for the rebellion.

We can see occasional hints that gunpowder was scarce in North Carolina
in 1769, with Governor Tryon complaining, "in case of war, I could not purchase here twenty barrels of powder . . . ." A more careful reading suggests
that Governor Tryon's problem was that the legislature was reluctant to buy
ammunition for the governor's troops—not a shortage of powder. Governor
Tryon made several requests to the legislature, asking them to pay for ammunition "for the protection of the Country," and found himself carefully
rebuffed at first. When the legislature finally acceded to Tryon's request, the
language used suggests that the gunpowder and musket balls were purchased
locally: "[T]he Governor be impowered to draw upon either of the public
Treasurers for money to purchase the same."[66]

A thorough reading of *Colonial Records of North Carolina* for 1769–1771
shows that guns appear frequently. One example is the depositions concerning murders committed by felons being pursued by the Sheriff of Dobbs
County.[67] Another example is Governor Tryon's order of 7 February 1771
that prohibited "for a reasonable time from vending or disposing of any fire
arms and ammunition lest the same should come into the hands of the said
people called Regulators or the Mob. . . ." This order applied to "all Merchants,
Traders and others . . . till further notice."

The Regulators were already at least partly armed with guns. Colonel
Spencer's letter to Governor Tryon of 28 April 1768 describes how the
Regulators "came up to the Court House to the number of about forty
armed with Clubs and some Fire Arms . . . ." The Regulators were careful to
keep guns out of town when engaged in violent disruptions of the court system, and some contemporary accounts express some uncertainty as to
whether their men out of town had guns or not. Regulators having guns outside of town was expressed as a strong possibility, and not a startling one.

As the crisis grew, other evidence suggests that the population was widely
armed with guns. An Anglican minister named Cupples described the difficulties in mustering the militia in Bute County for an expedition against the
Regulators: "The Col. of this county was by his instructions only to raise

Fifty men exclusive of officers, yet he told me, when he called a general muster that though there were betwixt eight or nine hundred men under arms, there was not any would list . . . and proclaimed themselves for the Regulators . . . ."[68] It is possible that not all of these "arms" were guns, but it is a strained reading, especially as we will see in discussions of the gun battle between the Regulators and Governor Tryon's militia.

In this crisis, militiamen were certainly armed with their own guns. The only mention of unarmed militiamen is the levying of fines on 8 May 1771, against some militiamen that showed up "without Arms . . . ." Governor Tryon complained that "this service was undertaken without money in the Treasury to support it, no armory to furnish arms, nor magazines from whence we could be supplied with ammunition . . . ." Tryon seems to have exaggerated the lack of financial support, and the absence of ammunition, because orders to various militia colonels indicate that they were to purchase provisions, gunpowder, and lead for their soldiers, "and to defray the expence thereof I will give you a Draft on the Treasury." Soldiers were expected to bring at least some of the ammunition: "Ammunition to be provided by the men agreeable to Law and what is further wanting will be supplied from the Magazine in Newbern." The only logical reading of such documents is that guns were commonly owned, and ammunition was available for purchase in North Carolina. Other evidence that there was a wide variety of guns in private hands can be found in the order from General Waddell, commanding Tryon's forces, that twenty-four rounds of ammunition be supplied to each soldier, "Bullets, Lead or Swan Shot at the discretion of the Captain of each company."[69] Giving soldiers their choice of lead suggests that the militia possessed guns in a variety of calibers.

Once Governor Tryon mobilized his forces, contemporary accounts demonstrate that the Regulators were well armed with guns. About 4,000 men were part of the Regulator force that battled against Governor Tryon. Governor Tryon described how the offer of amnesty, provided "the rebels . . . surrender up their arms, take the oath of allegiance and oath of obligation to pay all taxes," had led 3,300 to surrender themselves. While these 3,300 had only surrendered 500 arms (presumably firearms, from the accounts of the battle), Tryon clearly knew that far more had failed to do so: "[M]any of those that surrendered asserted that they were not in the battle, while others pretended to be in the battle without arms." At least twenty-five guns were taken from the rebels immediately after the battle.[70]

Morgan Edwards toured North Carolina the year following the battle. He described the results of the battle as 4,000 Regulators fighting 2,000 of Governor Tryon's men, but that many shots hit no one: "lodging in the trees an incredible number of balls which the hunters have since picked out and killed more deer and [turkeys] than they killed of their antagonists." Since the weapons of the time were slow to reload single shot muskets and rifles, *many* Regulators must have been firing guns. Another contemporary account, from the Boston *Gazette* of July 1771, similarly shows that the Regulators were well armed. It described how, "the Almighty Ruler of Heaven and Earth could guide the Balls from the Rifles of the Regulators to fly over the Heads of our Troops in the Day of Battle, as they did by ten Thousands; which otherwise, as they were at least five Times the Number of our Troops, must have cut them off by Hundreds, and left the Field a dismal Scene of Blood and Carnage."[71] The *Gazette*'s account claims that so many shots going astray was miraculous. The Regulators might have been poor shots, but in the American context, this was regarded as amazing, not the norm. It seems likely that *most* of the 4,000 Regulators were armed with guns.

Official records and contemporary accounts show that guns were widely owned and inexpensive. To argue otherwise requires absurd assumptions about atypical probate inventories, atypical events recorded by observers as though they were common, and merchants repeatedly advertising goods for which there was little or no demand.

Intent to Kill:
Man Against Man and Man Against Nature

Hunting was a common pastime of the first colonists, and it appears in every account as unremarkable. Chief Massasoit in the early 1620s may have been the first and last person to request English food as his dying request: Edward Winslow described how Massasoit, close to death, asked Winslow to take his gun, and "kill him some fowl, and make him some English pottage [a meat and vegetable soup], such as he had eaten at Plymouth." Winslow did so, and Massasoit recovered.[1]

The conditions of pioneers landing in a wilderness were different from a more settled colony, but later descriptions suggest that hunting was still common. Emmanuel Altham's 1623 account of Plymouth Colony described this new land as rich in both fish and fowl: "Here are eagles of many sorts, pigeons, innumerable turkeys, geese, swan, duck, teel, partridge divers sorts, and many other fowl, [so] that one man at six shoots hath killed 400." At least some of the Pilgrims hunted deer as well; Altham listed seven or eight venison provided by the inhabitants of Plymouth for Governor Bradford's wedding, in addition to three or four brought by the Indians.[2] *Mourt's Relation* also discussed the abundance of fish and fowl at Plymouth. Colonists were encouraged to bring guns with them: "Bring every man a musket or fowling-piece; let your piece be long in the barrel, and fear not the weight of it, for most of our shooting is from stands."[3] Issack de Rasieres' circa 1628 account of Plymouth Colony described hunting birds: "Sometimes we take them by surprise and fire amongst them with hail-shot, immediately that we have made them rise, so that sixty, seventy, and eighty fall all at once."[4]

Hunting was common in other New England colonies. Francis Higginson described 1630 Massachusetts:

> Fowls of the air are plentiful here, and of all sorts as we have in England as far as I can learn, and a great many of strange fowls which we know not. Whilst I was writing these things, one of our men brought home an eagle which he had killed in the wood. They say they are good meat. Also here are many kinds of excellent hawks, both sea hawks and land hawks. And myself walking in the woods with another in company, sprung a partridge so big that through the heaviness of his body could fly but a little way. They that have killed them say they are as big as our hens. Here are likewise abundance of turkeys often killed in the woods, far greater than our English turkeys, and exceeding fat, sweet and fleshy, for here they have abundance of feeding all the year long. . . . In the winter time I have seen flocks of pigeons, and have eaten of them. . . . [T]his country doth abound with wild geese, wild ducks, and other sea fowl, that a great part of winter the planters have eaten nothing but roastmeat of divers fowls which they have killed.[5]

Massachusetts Governor Winthrop described getting lost in the woods one night in 1631. He "walked out after supper, and took a piece in his hand supposing he might see a wolf, (for they came daily about the house, and killed swine and calves, etc.)." There was nothing remarkable about carrying a gun in the hopes of killing a predator. The only time that Winthrop regarded hunting as remarkable was when game was a blessing from God.[6]

George Alsop, an English colonist who spent four years in Maryland as an indentured servant around 1666, reported not only that Indians hunted game for sale to the settlers, but also that large numbers of animals were "killed by the Christian Inhabitant, that doth it more for recreation, than for the benefit they reap by it." Alsop also inventories, with some dismay, his master's vast store of game: "[My master] had at one time in his house fourscore Venisons." What was a delicacy in England, Alsop explains, had become dull: "[P]lain bread was rather courted and desired than it." Alsop also described guns used to protect sheep from wolves and to hunt waterfowl, with no indication that either was unusual. He also observed that there was relatively little work to be done in winter for servants, "unless their Ingenuity will prompt them to hunt the Deer, or Bear, or recreate themselves in Fowling, to slaughter the Swans, Geese, and Turkeys.... For every Servant has a Gun, Powder and Shot allowed him, to sport him withal on all Holidayes and leasureable times, if he be capable of using it, or be willing to learn."[7]

Some historians suggest that Alsop's time as an indentured servant was with a "most humane and generous master" and that perhaps his experience was unusual.[8] Others believe the account is disingenuous: that the Lord Proprietor of Maryland may have given financial encouragement to Alsop to tell his tale as propaganda in order to lure colonists to Maryland. Aubrey C. Land writes, "While technically correct in most statements, Alsop is misleading." But Land says nothing that disputes Alsop's account of servants hunting. Elsewhere, Land describes how for seventeenth century Marylanders, "Hunting, sometimes for sport but mainly for [consumption], occupied many hours."[9] Alsop's account certainly seems as though it was intended to lure more indentured servants into Maryland. Nonetheless, it is consistent with the Maryland militia laws of 1638, 1642 and 1658, which required every householder to have a gun for every man in the house, including servants.[10] It is also consistent with other Maryland, Carolina, and Virginia accounts which indicate that settlers and servants hunting with guns was commonplace.[11]

A 1632 Virginia statute licensed hunting wild pigs, but "any man be permitted to kill deare or other wild beasts or fowle in the common woods, forests, or rivers.... That thereby the inhabitants may be trained in the use of theire armes, the Indians kept from our plantations, and the wolves and other vermine destroyed."[12] A March 1661/2 statute prohibited "hunting and shooting" on land without the owner's permission "whereby many injuryes doe dayly happen to the owners of the said land." A 1699 statute, "prohibiting the unseasonable killing of Deer" complained about how about the deer population being much "destroyed and diminished" by killing "Does bigg with young."[13] (It was not only whites that engaged in wasteful hunting practices; Indians in South Carolina in 1748, hunting with guns "and leaving the carcasses to rot, supplied approximately 160,000 skins" for export from Charles Town.[14])

The motivations for some of Virginia's hunting regulations were a bit more complex than simply preventing injuries and protecting wildlife. The enormous population of cattle and hogs roaming free meant that "it was not difficult for a man with a gun to keep alive indefinitely without owning or renting land." Such a man had little interest in working for others—and Virginia's planters needed labor to work their fields.[15] Hunting regulation thus kept the poorest whites working for planters, instead of living independently.

Robert Horne's 1666 description of Carolina (before it was split into North and South), was explicit that every freeman who arrived before 25 March 1667 would receive a large allotment of land, "Provided always, That every Man be armed with a good Musquet full bore, 10 [pounds] Powder, and 20 [pounds] of Bullet, and six Months Provision for all, to serve them whilst they raise Provision in that Countrey." While not explicit that settlers required muskets and ammunition to feed themselves, the preceding pages of Horne's account described the variety and abundance of game available in the Carolina woods.[16] Other accounts of early Carolina were explicit that hunting was both for food and for sport. Thomas Ashe wrote, "Birds for Food, and pleasure of Game, are the Swan, Goose, Duck, Mallard, Pigeon, Teal, Curlew, Plover, Partridge, the Flesh of which is equally as good, tho' smaller than ours in England."[17] Ashe also told merchants planning to bring commodities to include "all kinds of Ammunition, Guns, Fowling-pieces, Powder, Match, Bullet . . . ." Ashe was not explicit that these items were for sale to the white population, but the other commodities that Ashe lists seem to be for the settlers, not for the Indians.[18] John Archdale's 1707 description of Carolina told how whites purchased both skins and deer meat from the Indians, but also how the land contained, "vast Quantities or Numbers of wild Ducks, Geese, Teal" and that because there was no need to cut and store winter fodder, one "can employ their Hands in raising other Commodities as aforesaid." Archdale's unclear sentence *seems* to say that in winter, when there were few farm chores, the profusion of wild game meant that the hired hands could be out hunting food—essentially what Alsop said Maryland servants did in winter, four decades earlier.[19]

Travelers' accounts of late seventeenth century America frequently referred to guns in private hands, usually used for hunting. Jasper Danckaerts, visiting America from the Netherlands in 1679–80, described a marsh near Flatbush, New York, where the inhabitants "go mostly to shoot snipe and wild geese." Danckaerts also described how Shooter's Island in New York (then Schutter's Island) received its name: "This island is so called, because the Dutch, when they first settled on the North River, were in the practice of coming here to shoot wild geese, and other wild fowl, which resorted there in great numbers." On Long Island, "We dined with Jaques; and his little son came and presented us a humming-bird he had shot." On Staten Island, Danckaerts reported, "Game of all kinds is plenty, and twenty-five and thirty deer are sometimes seen in a herd. A boy who came into a house where we were, told us he had shot ten the last winter himself, and more than forty in his life, and in the same manner other game."

Somewhere between New York City and Maryland, Danckaerts told of a miller with whom he had stayed: "The miller had shot an animal they call a muskrat, the skin of which we saw hanging up to dry." At a plantation on Chesapeake Bay, Danckaerts stayed the night. In the morning, he and his traveling companion were given directions by "the son, who went out to shoot at daylight." Danckaerts expressed amazement at the number of ducks together in front of the house. The son was not alone: "There was a boy about twelve years old who took aim at them from the shore, not being able to get within good shooting distance of them, but nevertheless shot loosely before they flew away, and hit only three or four, complained of his shot, as they are accustomed to shoot from six to twelve and even eighteen or more at one shot." Duck hunting was not peculiar to this one plantation, apparently, because Danckaerts described a few days later the noise from flocks of waterfowl: "[I]t is not peculiar to this place alone, but it occurred on all the creeks and rivers we crossed, though they were most numerous in the morning and evening when they are most easily shot."[20]

Hunting remained a common pastime in eighteenth century Colonial America. Robert Beverley's 1705 description of Virginia described hunting with guns as a widespread sport: "I am but a small Sports-man, yet with a Fowling-Piece, have kill'd above Twenty of them at a Shot. In like manner are the Mill-Ponds, and great Runs in the Woods stor'd with these Wild-Fowl, at certain seasons of the Year." After describing how the "Inner Lands . . . have the Advantage of Wild Turkeys, of an incridible Bigness, Pheasants, Partidges, Pigeons, and an Infinity of small Birds," Beverley lists "Bears, Panthers, Wild-Cats, Elks, Buffaloes, and Wild Hogs, which yield Pleasure, as well as Profit to the Sports-man." Beverley's description of "the Recreations, and Pastimes used in Virginia" includes "Hunting, Fishing, and Fowling." While hunting included pursuit with dogs on horseback, Beverley is explicit that Virginians killed wolves with guns, using bait tied to the trigger, "so that when [the wolf] offers to seize the Bate, he pulls the Trigger, and the Gun discharges upon him."[21] Gloria Main has analyzed Virginian William Byrd's meals in the period 1709–11 (based on Byrd's diaries). Domestic animals such as cattle, pigs, sheep, and chickens provided the majority of this wealthy Virginia planter's diet—but the table included at least occasionally venison, goose, blue-winged teal, turkey, pigeon, duck, squirrel, and partridge.[22]

Two laws regulating hunting appear in New Jersey and North Carolina colonies in the first half of the eighteenth century; both statutes suggest that hunting was common. A 1722 New Jersey "Act to prevent the Killing of Deer out of Season" prohibited deer hunting from January through June. That same law included a provision prohibiting "Persons carrying of Guns, and presuming to Hunt on other Peoples Land" explaining that it was required because "divers Abuses have been committed, and great Damages and Inconveniencies arisen."[23] A 1738 North Carolina "Act, to Prevent killing Deer, at Unseasonable Times" made it unlawful "to kill or destroy any Deer . . . by Gun, or other Ways and Means whatsoever" from 15 February to 15 July.[24]

David Humphreys' *circa* 1740 account of a Connecticut wolf hunt indicated that when a particular wolf's predations became serious enough,

> Mr. Putnam entered into a combination with five of his neighbors to hunt alternately until they could destroy her. . . . By ten o'clock the next morning the bloodhounds had driven her into a den, about three miles distant from the house of Mr. Putnam.

The people soon collected with dogs, guns, straw, fire, and sulphur, to attack the common enemy.[25]

A 1760 account by Andrew Burnaby described why white pines in New York, New England, and New Jersey were protected for the use of the Royal Navy:

This restriction is absolutely necessary, whether considered as securing a pro-vision for the navy, or as a check upon that very destructive practice, taken from the Indians, of fire-hunting. It used to be the custom for large compa-nies to go into the woods in the winter, and to set fire to the brush and under-wood in a circle of several miles. This circle gradually contracting itself, the deer, and other wild animals inclosed, naturally retired from the flames, till at length they got herded together in a very small compass.

Then, blinded and suffocated by the smoke, and scorched by the fire, which every moment came nearer to them, they forced their way, under the greatest trepidation and dismay, through the flames. As soon as they got into the open daylight again, they were shot by the hunters, who stood without and were in readiness to fire upon them.[26]

Fire-hunting was not confined to those colonies; Colonial Virginia and Maryland either prohibited fire-hunting with reference to guns,[27] or licensed hunting on the frontier in an attempt to control fire-hunting.[28] There is nothing in Burnaby's description that indicated that fire-hunting was wide-spread—but in forests as large as those in Colonial America, the imposition of such restrictions, and the repeated need to control it suggests that there must have been many people engaged in such practices, both to justify the prohibition, and for it to become widely known.

Scharf's *History of Western Maryland* described how frontier Marylanders lived at the time of the French & Indian War, and quoted one of the settlers of the time about the early education of boys in imitating the various ani-mals of the forest:

This faculty was not merely a pastime, but a very necessary part of education, on account of its utility in certain circumstances. The imitations of the gobbling and other sounds of wild turkeys often brought those keen-eyed and ever-watchful tenants of the forest within reach of the rifle. The bleating of the fawn brought its [mother] to her death in the same way . . . .

A well-grown boy at the age of twelve or thirteen years was furnished with a small rifle and shot-pouch . . . . Hunting squirrels, turkeys, and raccoons soon made him expert in the use of his gun . . . . Shooting at a mark was a common diversion among the men when their stock of ammunition would allow it.[29]

At about the same time, describing growing up in Philadelphia *circa* 1765, Alexander Graydon gave this picture of his boyhood pleasures:

For those of running, leaping, swimming and skating, no one had more appetite. . . . To these succeeded a passion for fowling and boating. . . . If furnished, on Saturday afternoon or other holyday, with cash enough for the purchase of powder and shot, or the hire of a batteau or skiff, as the propensity of the day might incline, I had nothing more to wish for.

In my water excursions, the sedgy shores of the Delaware, as well as the reedy cover of Petty's, League and Mud Islands, were pervaded and explored in pursuit of ducks, reed-bird and rail.[30]

Just before the Revolution, hunting became popular enough that it created some friction in the southern colonies. The Cherokees complained to the North Carolina Colonial government in 1769 of "numerous bodys of hunters from North Carolina having this year infested their hunting Grounds and destroyed their game."[31] Similarly, one of the complaints of the South Carolina Regulators in the mid-1760s was that the poorest and most disreputable whites of the backcountry who relied upon hunting needed to be brought under some form of regulation. Hunters were killing deer for the skins alone, leaving animal carcasses unburied in the forest. The rotting meat was attracting wolves, to the hazard of livestock. The men were hunting "at night by torch-light," leading to accidental shootings of both people and cattle.[32] (As is the case today, when it gets dark enough, or the hunter is drunk enough, cattle and deer have an astonishingly similar appearance.)

Virginia, in 1772, passed a statute regulating deer hunting that complained of "many idle people making a practice, in severe frozen weather, and deep snows, to destroy deer, in great numbers, with dogs, so that the whole breed is likely to be destroyed, in the inhabited parts of the colony." The government's concern with this was that "numbers of disorderly persons . . . almost destroyed the breed, by which the inhabitants will . . . be deprived of that wholesome and agreeable food . . . ." Therefore, deer hunting was completely prohibited until 1 August 1776.[33]

As the evidence shows, hunting was not only central to survival of the colonists, but a national pastime as well. In a country where there were few legal restrictions prohibiting hunting, game was abundant, and there was not much else to do for entertainment, how could it be otherwise?

SAFETY REGULATIONS

Colonial gun safety regulations were similar to, though less restrictive, than current laws. The existence of (and therefore the need for) such laws strongly suggests that guns were widely distributed, widely used—and widely misused. A March 1655/6 Virginia statute, for example, prohibited shooting "any guns at drinkeing (marriages and funerals onely excepted)" because gunshots were the common alarm of Indian attack, "of which no certainty can be had in respect of the frequent shooting of gunns in drinking."[34] Similarly, a 1642 Maryland statute also ordered, "No man to discharge 3 guns within the space of ¼ hour . . . except to give or answer alarm."[35] In 1631 Massachusetts, the shooting of guns as an alarm was apparently common, leading to orders "that no man should discharge a piece after sunset, except by occasion of alarm."[36] Delaware's 1742 militia law also prohibited firing guns at night to prevent false alarm.[37]

Occasionally, a regulation was created for the economic benefit of an individual. In 1638 Massachusetts, when an Emanuell Downing had "brought over, at his great charges, all things fitting for takeing wild foule by way of [decoy]," the General Court felt it necessary to order "that it shall not bee lawfull for any person to shoote in any gun within halfe a mile of the pond where such [decoy] shalbee placed."[38] The goal was to prevent hunters from scaring off the fowl that Downing hoped to catch.

Negligent misuse of firearms in Colonial America also received its share of attention in the law.[39] A 1713–14 Massachusetts statute complained, "Whereas by the indiscreet firing of guns laden with shot and ball within the town and harbour of Boston, the lives and limbs of many persons have been lost, and others have been in great danger, as well as other damage has been sustained" and thus, the legislature prohibited firing of any "gun or pistol" in Boston ("the islands thereto belonging excepted").[40] Perhaps for a similar reason—or just to allow the inhabitants to get some sleep—Georgia in 1759 made it unlawful to fire "any great gun or [small] arm in the town or harbour of Savannah after Sun Set without leave or permission from the Governor."[41]

Pennsylvania—being home to one of the few large Colonial cities—passed gunpowder storage laws by the beginning of the eighteenth century. A 1701 measure made it unlawful to store "more than six pounds of gunpowder . . . in houses, shops, or warehouses, unless it be forty perches distant from any dwelling" in the towns of "Bristol . . . Philadelphia, Germantown, Darby, Chester, New Castle, and Lewes." As with other fire prevention measures, such as a 1721 prohibition on setting off fireworks and rockets without license from the governor, a 1725 statute established a privately owned powder magazine and required storage of more than twelve pounds of gunpowder within Philadelphia to be at the powder magazine. Perhaps because this measure was effectively a monopoly granted to a private party, by 1760 the legislature allowed the powder magazine storage requirement to lapse.[42]

MAN AGAINST MAN

Michael Bellesiles argues that violence among whites, especially gun violence, was rare in early America, and violence for political ends, especially involving guns, was almost unheard of until just before the American Revolution:

> White Americans had long demonstrated a capacity for violence against Indians and blacks, but, at least in the Colonial period, indicated a remarkable hesitance to kill one another. . . . Political and social conflicts among whites almost never involved violence—until 1768 [with the formation of the North

Carolina Regulators]. In that year English colonists exchanged deadly gunfire with other colonists for the first time.

Furthermore, he explains that the England from which the settlers came was almost immune to violence: "Most personal violence in early modern England occurred not on lonely highways but at public festivals, often between competing teams of Morris dancers and such other representatives of communal pride."[43] Not true. Some parts of England were quite peaceful, but other parts were extraordinarily violent.[44] Bellesiles implies that the absence of guns in private hands played a part in this almost violence-free society. The evidence—including evidence that Bellesiles cites—shows that this is wrong on every count.

In Colonial America, white-on-white gun violence, even of a political nature, was not particularly rare. Murder rates are devilishly difficult to calculate for the Colonial period, and even into the early Republic, because court records are so incomplete. By sampling court records, historian Randolph Roth's review of murder in early America concludes that at various times in the Colonial period, murder rates in New England were as much "as 11 to 14 times the rate today"—and Virginia and Maryland were much worse.[45] As the following accounts demonstrate, gun violence, and violence in general, were depressingly common.

In 1630, ten years after his arrival at Plymouth, John Billington, who had been in continual trouble at Plymouth, was convicted of murdering John Newcomen with a blunderbuss, after some quarrel now lost to history.[46] In a community that averaged only a few hundred souls, even one murder in ten years is quite dramatic.[47] A dispute over beaver trapping rights on the Kennebec River in 1634 led to the shooting death of Moses Talbot by a Captain Hocking, and in turn the shooting death of Hocking by Talbot's partner.[48] At Massachusetts Bay, John Winthrop recorded at least twelve murders (two with long guns, two with pistols) either in his colony, or adjoining English plantations (excluding incidents involving Indians), and two killings in self-defense (one with a long gun).[49]

Augustine Herrman, a Dutch diplomat en route from New Netherlands to Maryland in 1659, observed frequent gun use: "Nothing occurred on the way except hearing a shot fired to the north of us, which the Indians doubted not was by an Englishman. Whereupon we fired three shots, to see if we should be answered, but heard nothing." Two days later, having stopped at a Swedish settlement, Herrman was in a dispute as to the ownership of a boat: "Abraham with one Marcus, a Finn, came to our side in a canoe, and would not let us pass . . . and this Marcus drew a pocket-pistol and threatened to fire if we would not stop. They had, besides, two snaphances [an early form of flintlock musket]. On leaving the river, we heard heavy volley firing on Colonel Utie's island . . . which we presumed must have proceeded from fifty or sixty men. . . . This lasted until night."[50]

Bacon's Rebellion in 1676 Virginia is an especially clear example of white on white political violence involving guns. Nathaniel Bacon led largely frontier Virginians in a war first against the Indians, then against Governor William Berkeley who sought to protect the rights of the Indians. A contemporary description of Bacon's first expedition against the Indians was that they were "about 300 men together in armes . . . ." When Bacon later marched into the capital to demand a commission from the governor, he led a force of "1000 men well arm'd and resolute. . . . " Other accounts refer to guns in the hands of both Bacon's men, and the governor's force.[51] Governor Berkeley later described Bacon's arrival as "six hundred of the meanest of the People, Came into the court and Assembly with their Guns ready to fire."[52] Near the end of the rebellion, Berkeley's forces captured "four hundred English and Negroes in arms" and confiscated about 500 muskets and fowling pieces. Another 100 men refused to turn over their arms.[53] Governor Berkeley's complaint captures how difficult it was to control an armed population: "How miserable that man is that Governs a People when six parts of Seaven at least are Poore Endebted Discontented and Armed and to take away their Armes now the Indians are at our throates were to rayse an Universal Mutiny."[54]

Other colonies also suffered from political violence, often involving guns. A description of a 1677 insurrection in North Carolina depicts a Captain Gilliam with thirty to forty men who "with armes of the [said] Gilliam . . . with force and arms *vid.* Swords, guns, and pistols" forced entry into a victim's home. The author also described threats he had received from others of "hanging, pistolling, or poisoning."[55]

Guns played a large role in the Battle of Severn in 1655 Maryland, and contrary to Bellesiles' claims, white colonists killed each other over political concerns.[56] This battle was an extension of the English Civil War, with 200 to 250 men "mustered in Arms" on the Royalist side, and at least 120 on the Puritan side. Both sides were Marylanders, although a merchant vessel from England, with cannon, also participated. Dozens were killed or wounded.

Contrary to Bellesiles' claim that the small arms used by the Royalists were all publicly owned, the Royalists had plundered many homes for guns and ammunition, "taking all the Guns, Powder, Shot, and Provision, they could anywhere finde." A Puritan account described how the Royalists had stripped the Country bare of men, "as also of Arms and Ammunition; the poor women urging this to them, What should they do if the Indians come upon them, being thus strip'd of men and Arms to defend them." Guns were regarded by at least that author, who lived in Maryland, as a normal and necessary part of one's home. A Royalist account does not dispute that they took "Arms from those of Patuxent."[57] Every reference to a gun seized by the Royalists is either silent as to its origin, or is explicit that the gun was seized from an individual's home.[58]

The merchant Jacob Leisler, hearing of the Glorious Revolution (1689) in England that had replaced James II with William & Mary, led a rebellion against the royal government of New York. One account described how Leisler's men fired into the city, "whereby several of his Majesties Subjects were killed and wounded as they passed in the street . . . ."[59] Other accounts in that same source, seeking to justify Leisler's actions, reduced the number killed by gunfire from Leisler's men, but do not dispute that it happened.[60] Another account that portrayed Leisler very darkly, described how men under Leisler's command went to him "and threatened to shoot him if he did not head them." (Leisler was believed to have persuaded his men to pretend to threaten him, so that he would have an excuse for leading the rebellion.) Another section described how Leisler "sends severall Armed men, with no other warrant their Swords and Guns" to arrest a prominent merchant.[61] The willingness of colonists to kill each other in the pursuit of political goals was not rare.

Tenant uprisings against landlords in upstate New York appear repeatedly in the mid-eighteenth century. One such disturbance in 1766 aimed at obtaining more secure land tenure from the owner of Livingston Manor. The tenants, armed only with sticks, were dispersed by forty men bearing guns. Apparently recognizing that sticks were not enough of a weapon, "Seventeen hundred of the Levellers with fire arms are collected at Poughkeepsie."[62] There were at least 1,740 guns in the hands of one group of insurgents and their opponents in one region of one colony.

The accounts of political violence, riot, and murder in Charleston between Dissenters and Anglicans in 1701/2 are still somewhat shocking today. Daniel Defoe quoted a petition to the England-based proprietors of Carolina: "[S]ome of the said Rioters, whilst the Riot was at the Church, went one Night to the House of John Smith, a Butcher in Charles Town; and there being a Woman big with Child in the said House, they with Force open'd the door, threw her down, and otherwise mis-used her, that she brought forth a dead Child, with the Back and Skull broken."[63]

Disputes over the borderline between Pennsylvania and Maryland turned into deadly gunfire in 1736. "[A]n armed Force of about three hundred Men was sent up by our Governor in a Hostile Manner . . . ." Cressap, leading the Maryland forces, brought "a large Quantity of Arms and Ammunition." By the time the dispute was over, at least one person had been killed by gunfire, apparently by one of Cressap's men.[64] The documents expressed horror at the lives that were lost, but no surprise at the presence of guns.

The South Carolina Regulator movement of the 1760s started because the backcountry had become lawless in a way that is still horrifying today: men murdered, their wives and ten year old daughters raped, people tortured with hot irons and eyes gouged out to force disclosure of money, arson of homes, and kidnapping and debauching of young girls. At least part of this problem was because the lowland government failed to provide the judicial institutions for maintaining order. As on later American frontiers, where official structures failed to protect the innocent, vigilantes organized. Even before this lawlessness developed, the South Carolina backcountry relied on the militia to maintain order—and where every person was responsible for defending self, family, and home, shooting matches were a part of Saturday social meetings. Repeatedly, criminal violence and the attempts by the Regulators to restore order made use of guns.[65]

While Roth's work on murder rates shows that Colonial America was not an Eden before the Fall,[66] we do see examples of self-restraint because of cultural factors that limited violence in heavily armed Colonial America. In 1695, a French diplomat described the love of fighting in England. After observing that even among adults, minor disputes would turn into fights, with large crowds gathered to egg on the participants: "They use neither sword nor stick against a man that is unarmed; and if any unfortunate stranger (for an Englishman would never take it into his head) should draw his sword upon one that had none, he'd have a hundred people upon him in a moment."[67] A description of the riots in 1746 New Jersey quoted the rebels, "And that they were resolved [should] they be opposed by Fire Arms, to take up Fire Arms to defend theirselves."[68] It would appear that the rebels had guns and were prepared to use them only if guns were used against them; like the Englishmen that Misson de Valbourg described, there was a notion of proportionate response in the type of arms to be used.

Along with cultural restraints on the use of guns, there was a popular perception that the use of a gun might show a murderous intent in court. Just before the Revolution, Tory Peter Oliver claimed that Bostonians were arming themselves with clubs because, "Guns they imagined were Weapons of Death in the Eye of the Law, which the meanest of them was an Adept in; but Bludgeons were only Implements to beat out Brains with."[69] This might also explain the North Carolina Regulators limiting themselves to clubs in Colonel Spencer's account, as well as the tenants of Livingston Manor exchanging clubs for guns after being confronted by men with guns, as discussed in Chapter 5.

As the use of militia threats in 1774 (discussed in Chapter 8) showed, Colonial leaders were well aware, in Pauline Maier's words, that "unrestrained popular violence was counter-productive. They organized resistance in part to contain disorder. Building associations to discipline opposition, they gradually made popular self-rule, founded upon carefully designed 'social compacts,' a reality."[70] Historians who have examined mob behavior suggest that this admirable self-restraint was typical of the Age of Reason, in contrast to the previous century's excesses.

PISTOLS IN COLONIAL AMERICA

How common were pistols before the Revolution? The evidence from probate inventories, advertising, and from surviving pistols demonstrates that Americans made handguns before the Revolution, that there was a civilian market for them in at least some cities, and that pistol ownership was unremarkable. An analysis of all Plymouth Colony probate inventories found that of 339 listed firearms, forty-four, or thirteen percent, were pistols, and 54.5 percent of lead projectiles recovered from Plymouth Colony digs were pistol ammunition.[71]

While Americans made pistols early in the eighteenth century, most colonists preferred to buy pistols imported from Britain, perhaps because of price or prestige, and only a few pre-Revolutionary War American-made pistols have survived. Pistols manufactured in America before and during the Revolutionary War, however, show some interesting innovations, such as sights and rifled barrels at a time when both were uncommon in British pistols.[72] Surviving pistols made for William Smith of Farmington, Connecticut, by Medad Hills in 1771, were equipped with American-made barrels, and apparently English locks.[73]

Advertising and news reports show that merchants offered pistols for sale in Colonial America. Such ads appear in the *Boston Gazette* as early as 1720. Sampling ads from the 1741–1742 period reveals at least two different merchants offering pistols for sale, one of whom, Samuel Miller, identified himself as a gunsmith.[74] A gang of robbers, having terrorized New York City, moved on to Philadelphia in 1749. A newspaper account of their crimes reported that "two Men, unknown, were lately at Mr. Rush's, a Gun smith, enquiring for six Pair of Pocket Pistols, to make up twelve Pair, having as they said, got the six Pair at some other Place."[75] In 1772 and 1773, Heinrich Diebenberger advertised in Pennsylvania newspapers that he sold pistols,[76] as did Henry Deabarear, who sold "pistols for holsters and the pocket . . . ." Philadelphia merchants advertised pistols for sale repeatedly from 1744 onward.[77]

Pistols appear in journals and newspaper articles throughout the Colonial

period—and while the crimes committed with them are sometimes shocking, the *presence* of pistols is never remarkable. Governor John Winthrop
made several references to pistols in New England in the nineteen years that
his journal covers. One was a 1641 theological dispute at Pascataquack (now
Dover, New Hampshire) that led the factions to arm themselves and march,
at least one member identified as armed with a pistol. There were murders
with pistols at Stamford, Connecticut, and at Penobscott in 1644, and an
attempted murder with a pistol at Cape Sable in 1646.[78] Winthrop never
expressed any surprise or disgust over the presence of pistols—and he was
not a man inclined to withhold his moral revulsion.

Eighteenth century accounts also mention pistols. Eliza Lucas Pinckney
described the suicide of Anne LeBrasseur with a pistol as "melancholy and
shocking," but newspaper accounts suggest that what was shocking was
not the weapon, but that she was "a Disciple of Mr. Whitefield's" (the noted
evangelist).[79] In 1749, the *Pennsylvania Gazette* reported that "Sunday night
last, about eight a Clock, Richard Green, coming to Town from
Kensington, was stopt on the Road, and his Money demanded, by two Men
with Pistols . . . ."[80] There are other examples available in the *Pennsylvania
Gazette* of the criminal misuse of and accidental deaths from pistols; they
are never surprising.[81] Pistols appear among the South Carolina Regulators
and the criminals to whom they administered frontier justice.[82] Nor was
there any surprise when pistols appear in the hands of the law-abiding,
such as a description of Rev. Whitfield preaching in Massachusetts: "[H]e
was attended by many Friends with Muskets and Pistols on Account of the
Indians . . . ."[83]

Enough pistols were present in private hands in Pennsylvania in 1774
for the legislature to include handguns in a law regulating New Year's Day
festivities. This statute made it illegal that "any person or persons shall, on
any thirty-first day of December, or first or second day of January, in
every year, wantonly, and without reasonable occasion, discharge and fire
off any handgun, pistol, or other firearms, or shall cast, throw or fire any
squibs, rockets or other fireworks, within the inhabited parts of this
province . . . ."[84]

**PAUL REVERE'S VERY COMPACT POCKET PISTOL,
COURTESY OF THE MASSACHUSETTS HISTORICAL SOCIETY**

ACCIDENTAL VIOLENCE

Gun accidents were commonplace in early Massachusetts. At a 1632 militia muster in Watertown, a supposedly unloaded musket discharged, hitting three men, although no permanent injuries resulted. Other accidents seem to be hunting-related: "Three men coming in a shallop from Braintree, the wind taking them short at Castle Island, one of them stepping forward to hand the sail, caused a fowling piece with a French lock, which lay in the boat, to go off." The goose shot went through the thigh of one man and struck another man in the chest. The third man was able—barely—to steer the ship home.

The third type of accident is chillingly modern—and a reminder that irresponsibility is not new. The parents went to church, leaving three children at home. The eldest went outside; the middle child removed his father's fowling piece from the mantle, cocked the hammer, "and blowed in the mouth of the piece, as he had seen his father also do, and with that stirring the piece, being charged, it went off, and shot the child into the mouth and through his head." In another accident, an eight-year-old boy killed his ten-year-old sister with their father's gun.[85]

John Winthrop recorded an astonishing number of gunpowder accidents in the first ten years of the Massachusetts Bay Colony. There may have been other gunpowder accidents as well; it seems likely that similar accidents outside of Boston might have escaped Winthrop's notice. Yet the number and nature of the gunpowder accidents that *Winthrop's Journal* records suggests that while gunpowder was widely distributed, the colonists were not sufficiently careful with it. Many of these accidents involve colonists using fire to dry wet gunpowder—a common problem in a wet climate.

One gunpowder gaffe sounds worthy of Wile E. Coyote, setting his traps for the Roadrunner. On 19 March 1632,

> Mr. Maverick, one of the ministers of Dorchester, in drying a little powder, (which took fire by the heat of the fire pan,) fired a small barrel of two or three pounds, yet did no other harm but singed his clothes. It was in the new meeting-house [church], which was thatched, and the thatch only blacked a little.

But other accidents were not so funny: disasters that could easily have caused far more deaths. In late 1636, again at Dorchester, a Mr. Glover attempted to dry sixty pounds of gunpowder in the end of the hearth, with predictable results:

> A maid, which was in the room, having her arms and neck naked, was scorched, and died soon after. A little child, in the arms of another, was scorched upon the face, but not killed. Two men were scorched, but not much. [Many firearms], which lay charged in several places, took fire and went off, but did no harm. . . . The house was thatched, yet took not fire; yet when the smoke was gone, many things were found burnt. Another great providence was that three little children, being at the fire[place] a little before, they went out to play . . . and so were preserved.

Another incident in 1632 involved a small boat, a barrel of gunpowder, and an impatient smoker. Another sailor asked him to wait until they reached shore before lighting his pipe. The man with the pipe responded, "that if the devil should carry him away quick, he would take one pipe." The resulting explosion tore the boat to pieces. The smoker's body was found a few days later, "his hands and feet torn off."

One other gunpowder accident in April of 1645 shows how unconcerned the people were in storing large quantities in their homes. The home of John Johnson, the colony's "surveyor general of the ammunition," and keeper of the colony's public firearms, caught fire. His neighbors came to help salvage his property, as well as seventeen barrels of gunpowder: "[M]any were in the house, no man thinking of the powder, till one of the company put them in mind of it, whereupon they all withdrew, and soon after the powder took fire, and blew up all about it, and shook the houses in Boston and Cambridge, so as men thought it had been an earthquake."[86]

English law, until the 1600s, did not generally recognize a right to keep and bear arms. The laws of England attempted to restrict gun ownership among the lower classes, as part of the effort to preserve the privileges of the nobility. During the reign of Elizabeth I, when most of these colonists would have grown up, the English government replaced the universal militia system with a more highly trained select militia.[87] Consequently, in the New World, where the English colonists resurrected the universal militia, more than a few had not learned the lessons of gunpowder safety at their father's knee.

As with so many other categories of evidence, eyewitness accounts show that white-on-white violence, with and without guns, was common in the Colonial period. Guns, including pistols, were widely owned, and often used. To the extent that gun violence did *not* happen, it was not an absence of guns that restrained the colonists, but the cultural values against escalating violence.

Part II

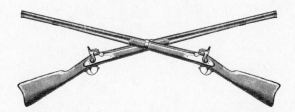

The Shot Heard 'Round the World

The Revolutionary War (1775–1783) occupies only eight years, but occupies a disproportionate part of this book. The reason is simple: Governments fighting wars keep detailed records. As a result, we have extraordinarily detailed information on gun ownership, prices, and manufacturing for these years. Without question, gun manufacturing increased, and demand for guns (both from governments and individuals) increased as well. How much it increased is hard to know with any certainty. Both before and after the Revolution, when firearms ownership and manufacturing were primarily a matter of private property, the records are far less complete.

It would hardly seem necessary to prove that guns were common in Revolutionary America—where "the embattled farmers stood, / And fired the shot heard round the world."[1] Yet, one historian's claim that Americans were desperately short of guns at the start of the Revolution, had little or no competence with guns, and were almost completely incapable of making guns during the Revolution[2] briefly became generally accepted among historians who should have known better.

Guns in Revolutionary New England

In the years between the 1770 Boston Massacre and the Battle of Lexington, 19 April 1775, a variety of private organizations in New England resisted the authority of the British crown. Many of the challenges to royal authority before Lexington relied on the effectiveness of intimidation by sheer numbers, although in some cases, British officers had the good sense to back down, rather than risk gunfire from American militants. When the British government took away the authority of the Massachusetts colonists to control their own government, they set the stage for the inevitable conflict between a government whose many members were independent, strong-willed, and heavily armed, and the servants of the Crown, who were separated by three thousand miles from reinforcements and supplies.

Guns were widely owned in New England. In the days after Lexington and Concord, General Gage was understandably nervous about being attacked from the rear by armed rebels. Many Bostonians were also deeply interested in leaving town, both because of the increasing poverty caused by the Boston Port Act of 1774 (which closed the port to all commercial traffic), and the likelihood that the rebel army would attack Boston. General Gage consequently ordered the people of Boston to turn in their arms. As an incentive, General Gage offered passes to leave Boston to all who turned in their weapons because no weapons or ammunition were allowed to leave town. The arms to be turned in were to be "marked with the names of the respective owners . . . that the arms aforesaid, at a suitable time, would be returned to the owners."

On 27 April, "the people delivered to the selectman 1778 fire-arms, 634 pistols, 973 bayonets, and 38 blunderbusses."[1] The term "fire-arm" seems not to have included "pistols" and "blunderbusses"—both of which would also be considered "firearms" in the modern sense. This may at least partly explain why some historians have misinterpreted the number of guns in Colonial America.[2] (In the interests of clarity, this work always uses the term "firearm," except when quoted, in the modern, inclusive sense of the word.)

At first glance, this count of firearms does not sound so impressive: 2,450, in a town that had, before the Boston Port Act, a population of 17,000 people or less. If averaged over the entire population, this would mean that 14.4 percent of the population owned a gun. But this overlooks several important qualifiers. First, many Bostonians had left town in the weeks before Lexington, as it became increasingly apparent that war was coming. Ammunition, military stores, muskets, and even publicly owned cannon "were carried secretly out of Boston."[3] The quantities involved seemed to have been quite large; Lieutenant Frederick Mackenzie's diary describes one amusing example:

A Country man was Stopped at the Lines, going out of town with 19,000 ball Cartridges, which were taken from him. When liberated, he had the insolence to go to Head quarters to demand the redelivery of them. When asked who they were for, he said they were for his own use; and on being refused them, he said he could not help it, but they were the last parcel of a large quantity which he had carried out at different times. Great numbers of Arms have been carried out of town during the Winter; and if more strict search had been made at the Lines, many of them, and much Ammunition might have been seized.[4]

It seems unlikely that rebel forces would have left large numbers of guns in Boston where British forces could easily seize them. The guns surrendered to General Gage must therefore be regarded as only a *part* of the guns that had been in Boston before the crisis began. Furthermore, General Gage's proclamation of 19 June 1775 complained that contrary to the claims of the selectmen of Boston that "all the inhabitants had delivered up their fire-arms," he had suspected, and now had proof, "that many had been perfidious in this respect, and had secreted great numbers."[5]

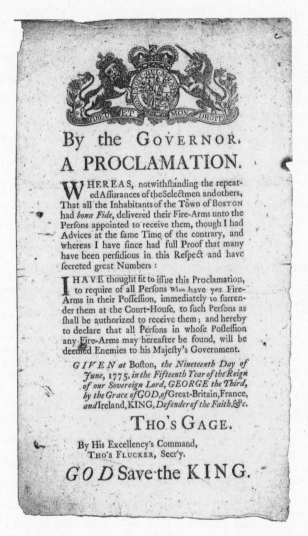

By the GOVERNOR,
A PROCLAMATION.

WHEREAS, notwithstanding the repeated Assurances of the Selectmen and others, That all the Inhabitants of the Town of BOSTON had *bona Fide*, delivered their Fire-Arms unto the Persons appointed to receive them, though I had Advices at the same Time of the contrary, and whereas I have since had full Proof that many have been perfidious in this Respect and have secreted great Numbers :

I HAVE thought fit to issue this Proclamation, to require of all Persons who have yet Fire-Arms in their Possession, immediately to surrender them at the Court-House, to such Persons as shall be authorized to receive them ; and hereby to declare that all Persons in whose Possession any Fire-Arms may hereafter be found, will be deemed Enemies to his Majesty's Government.

GIVEN at Boston, *the Nineteenth Day of June,* 1775, *in the Fifteenth Year of the Reign of our Sovereign Lord,* GEORGE *the Third, by the Grace of* GOD, *of* Great-Britain, France, *and* Ireland, KING, *Defender of the Faith,* &c.

THO'S GAGE.

By His Excellency's Command,
THO'S FLUCKER, Secr'y.

GOD Save the KING.

GOVERNOR GAGE DEMANDS CITIZENS TURN IN THEIR GUNS

If Gage's claim was accurate—and not just his excuse to keep civilians in Boston—the 2,450 firearms surrendered on 27 April were just a fraction of the weapons that had been in Boston before the Battle of Lexington, eight days earlier. And if Gage was telling the truth that Bostonians had not turned in all their guns, he was not upset because just a *few* guns were still in hiding. Colonists had been smuggling guns out of Boston for many months. We can say with certainty that there were *at least* 2,450 privately owned firearms in Boston on 27 April 1775. Probably many more had been present a year earlier, now smuggled out of town or hidden.

There is also a demographic difference between 1775 Boston and any modern American city that makes a 14.4 percent gun ownership rate misleading. Families were larger, and the average lifespan was substantially shorter than today. At least some of the residents were slaves. The number of free adult males (those most likely to possess a gun for either hunting or militia duty) was a relatively smaller percentage of the population than today. Using Madison's formula in "Federalist 46" for estimating the number of those "able to bear arms" suggests that no more than 4,250 Bostonians would have qualified as members of the militia. The surrender of 2,450 guns suddenly seems quite impressive. The people of Boston, who would have been overwhelmingly suspicious of General Gage's intentions, surrendered to him enough guns to arm 57 percent of the town's militia.

MASSACHUSETTS

One of Bellesiles' more startling claims concerning guns in Revolutionary Massachusetts is that, "Massachusetts conducted a very thorough census of arms, finding that there were 21,549 guns in the province of some 250,000 people."[6] This astonishingly low number of guns comes from an inventory of "Warlike Stores in Massachusetts, 1774" contained in the *Journals of Each Provincial Congress of Massachusetts*. But that inventory, dated 14 April 1775, does not tell us what categories of firearms it included. The orders to the committee charged with gathering the information were explicit that they should count town stockpiles: "receive the returns of the several officers of militia, of their numbers and equipage, and the returns from the several towns of their town stock of ammunition." It did not clearly order a count of *all* the guns in the province. While one could read "of their numbers and equipage" as requiring a count of militiamen's privately owned arms, this is only implied.[7]

Other evidence in that same source suggests that guns were not in short supply. On 25 October 1774, a committee "appointed to take into consideration and determine what number of ordnance, [and what] quantity of powder and ordnance stores will be necessary for the province stock" came up with a fairly extensive and expensive wish list, including twenty cannon, four mortars, "10 tons bomb-shells," one thousand barrels of powder, 75,000 flints—and only "5,000 arms and bayonets" at £2 each (equivalent to £1:14:2 sterling).[8] If guns were actually quite scarce just before the Revolution, it is a bit strange that the elected government of Massachusetts, painfully aware of their need for artillery, gunpowder, and flints, concluded that 5,000 "arms and bayonets" would be sufficient for a province with almost 350,000 people, with only 21,549 guns stored in the town stocks. This suggests that the militia of the province were still armed with their own firearms, as the law required.

The Provincial Congress thought it was plausible to buy 5,000 guns, and at the very reasonable price of £2 each, in local currency.[9] At least some town governments shared the Provincial Congress' understanding. The town of Lunenburg "assembled in legal town-meeting, and voted 100£ L[awful] M[oney] [about £75 sterling] for the Purpose of purchasing Fire-Arms with Bayonets, and other Implements of War . . . ." The Lunenberg town meeting must have thought that guns were available for purchase.[10] A petition from Maine frontier settlers requested ammunition "and a few small arms," with the clear implication that while they had almost enough guns, they did not have enough ammunition for them.[11] Other evidence that suggests that guns were widely owned comes from a coy little mention in the *Essex Gazette* that, "POWDER bears a very good price in this town; the people from all parts of the country, the fall past, having bought up almost all there was, to defend themselves against *wolves*, and *other beasts of* PREY."[12] The "beasts," of course, were the royal government.

The Provincial Congress assumed that the whole population was armed, or could be armed. A 27 October 1774 order directed inhabitants of Massachusetts to be "properly and effectually armed and equipped" and that "if any of the inhabitants are not provided with arms and ammunition according to law" the town was to arm them. These resolutions were repeated at later times in similar form, sometimes limited to militiamen and Minutemen, other times addressed to all the "inhabitants of this colony."

A Provincial Congress committee appointed to examine the problem of soldiers who lacked firearms reported on 9 May 1775 that only "a few of the inhabitants of this colony" were "destitute of fire arms" and other "accoutrements." The committee ordered the towns to find out which of their townspeople were lacking in arms in order to "supply them out of the town stock, and *in case of a deficiency there, to apply to such inhabitants of their respective towns and districts as, in their opinions, can best spare their arms or accoutrements*, and to borrow or purchase the same for the use of said inhabitants so enlisted."[13] This suggests that there were quite a number of guns in private hands, and the Provincial Congress believed that it would be possible to "borrow or purchase" guns readily enough to arm the "few" that were not armed. It seems hard to imagine that they printed up a standard form such as this otherwise:[14]

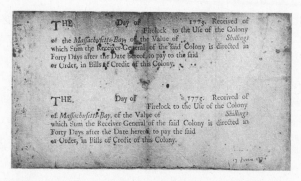

MASSACHUSETTS FIRELOCK PURCHASE RECEIPT

While an incomplete collection of records from 1776, one bound book recording equipment distributed to and received from militiamen listed cartridge boxes, bayonet belts, and gun slings—but no guns.[15]

Contemporary accounts also show that the population was well armed. At Cambridge, just a few months before the Revolution started, Tories found themselves menaced by patriot mobs. Tory Thomas Oliver described the crowd that surrounded him: "[I]n a short time my house was surrounded by three or four thousand people, and one quarter in arms."[16]

Tory Anne Hulton's letter from Massachusetts on the eve of Revolution described, "The People in the Country (who are all furnished with Arms & have what they call Minute Companys in every Town ready to march on any alarm)."[17]

A Tory account of mob violence just before the Revolution reported that, "At Worcester, a mob of about five thousand collected, prevented the court of Common Pleas from sitting, (about one thousand of them had fire-arms)." Why was only one-fifth of the mob armed? Because the "mob" had previously, "Voted, not to bring our Fire-Arms into Town the 6 Day of Sept." They believed that there would be no military force brought to bear against them, and firearms would be unnecessary for the intimidation of royal officials. Some militias left their guns out of town; others did not bring them. At least one thousand militiamen either did not get the message, or brought their guns anyway.[18]

While the militia laws required every man to own a gun, there was little uniformity of weapons, other than the requirement that it be a flintlock, leading to an interesting characteristic of American militia weapons:

> The average colonist could not afford to own a selection of guns, and so he normally chose one which would serve him well in hunting and also pass inspection on muster days. Thus the distinction between military and sporting arms is almost lost. Some examples of each, of course, are quite obvious, but a great many fall in between and are known to collectors generally as "semi-military." These arms are usually sturdy pieces. Their caliber varies normally between .70 and .75. They do not have sling swivels, and since a man was allowed his choice between a sword and a bayonet, they usually do not have bayonet studs.[19]

One account of the Battle of Bunker Hill refers to "the few who had bayonets" as distinguished from the mass of the militia.[20] If most militiamen were armed with privately owned "semi-military" muskets that lacked bayonet lugs, then this lack of bayonets at Bunker Hill is not a surprise.

In the months before the Battle of Lexington, the Provincial Congress discussed procuring and protecting bayonets, but not procuring muskets upon which to mount those bayonets. One resolve particularly emphasizes that the Provincial Congress should "possess themselves of all the same bayonets and implements of war" to be distributed "for the use of the province, to such persons . . . as they shall think proper."[21] The energies of the Provincial Congress seem more focused on acquiring an accessory only useful for muskets, than on acquiring muskets themselves.

As the Revolutionary War continued, the Massachusetts Provincial Congress again discussed the need to arm those soldiers "who are destitute of arms," but these discussions give no indication that this was a major concern. The Provincial Congress on 17 June 1775 (almost two months after Redcoats fired on Minutemen at Lexington) recommended to non-militia members "living on the sea coasts, or within twenty miles of them, that they carry their arms and ammunition with them to meeting on the [S]abbath, and other days when they meet for public worship."[22] If militiamen were short of guns and ammunition, it is a bit peculiar that non-militia members still had enough arms and ammunition that they were encouraged to bring them to all public meetings, rather than arming the militia.

If guns were rare in Revolutionary Massachusetts, their price should have been high. There was no way to immediately import more guns from Europe, and arms and powder had been prohibited for importation for a year.[23] But gun prices were markedly low. The Provincial Congress of Massachusetts bought weapons from many private owners in the colony in the first few months of the war, sometimes purchasing as many as 100 weapons in a single transaction. Interestingly enough, they appear not to have seized these weapons, but repeatedly appealed to the patriotism of private gun owners.[24] (The Provincial Congress was painfully aware that they were not, by the standards of the day, a legal government.)

The *Journals* records at least 946 guns, "fire-arms," and "small arms" purchased from private parties for which there is both a count and total price.[25] (The *Journals* also list other transactions totaling 547 small arms or guns without a recorded price.)[26] The average appraised value of these 946 guns and small arms comes to £1:18:7 in local money (£1:13:0 sterling). Some of these weapons contained in transactions labeled "small arms" were probably pikes, bayonets, or swords—although we know that at least one group of thirty-seven "guns" is next described with the less specific "small arms." The transactions explicitly labeled "fire-arms" or "guns" (of which there were 339) show an average price of £1:19:1 (£1:13:5 sterling)—not a trivial amount of money for the time—but less than a sergeant's monthly wages in the Massachusetts army—and less than one-third the price of a suit.[27]

Militiamen were not the only ones who were armed. The baggage train of the British soldiers marching towards Concord on 19 April 1775, had twelve men guarding it. On the road, "about a dozen of the elderly men of Menotomy, exempts [from militia duty] mostly, assembled near the center of the village and awaited the arrival of the baggage train . . . ." They shot and killed two British soldiers, wounded several others, took the rest prisoner, captured the baggage train, and obliterated all marks of the struggle from the road. There is nothing that identifies how many of these non-militiamen had guns, but the implication is that many of them did, if not all.[28] It seems unlikely that twelve British soldiers could be killed, wounded, or captured if only one or two of their attackers had guns.

Other non-militiamen shot British soldiers that day. "Jason Russell, aged fifty-eight years" unsuccessfully defended his home from British soldiers on the Concord road with a gun. "Samuel Whittemore, aged eighty years," upon seeing British soldiers marching towards Concord, prepared by oiling "his musket and pistols and sharpening his sword." When the soldiers returned,

> Whittemore had posted himself behind a stone wall, down Mystic Street about four hundred and fifty feet . . . . The distance seemed an easy range for him, and he opened fire, killing the soldier he aimed at. They must have discovered his hiding place from the smoke-puff, and hastened to close in on him. With one pistol he killed the second Briton, and with his other fatally wounded a third one. In the meantime, the ever vigilant flank guard were attracted to the contest, and a ball from one of their muskets struck his head and rendered him unconscious. They rushed to the spot, and clubbed him with their muskets and pierced him with their bayonets until they felt sure he was dead . . . . Whittemore lived eighteen more years, dying in 1793 at the age of ninety-eight.[29]

Another incident involving a non-militiaman shooting at the British troops happened as the retreat reached Somerville: "James Miller, about sixty-six years old, stood there awaiting the British. With him was a companion, and both fired with deadly effect, again and again, as the British marched by in the road below."[30]

In Charlestown, the opening shot of a gun battle involving British troops retreating from Concord was described by Mercy Tufts Boylston as started when "A careless, excited [N]egro discharged his musket . . . ." The British troops returned fire, killing Mrs. Boylston's cousin.[31] If guns were scarce, why was a black man, by law not a member of the militia, carrying a musket?

Samuel Thompson, the eldest of three brothers, told his fifteen year-old son Jonathan to stay home and take care of his mother while Samuel went off to fight the British. "But the father had hardly gone before the boy borrowed an old musket and a horn of powder . . . and thus armed and equipped, he, too, set off for Concord."[32]

Multiple anecdotes do not produce a statistically significant body of data; a collection of such examples does not give us much evidence of the number of the guns in private hands. They do, however, suggest that guns were not scarce, when so many examples of non-militiamen turning out to fire at retreating British soldiers have been preserved.

There were 3,763 militiamen who turned out along the road to Concord to fight against 1,800 British soldiers on 19 April 1775—delivering a devastating defeat to a professional European army. A poorly armed and unskilled militia would not have generated the terror among the British officers that they did. Especially with the inherent inaccuracy of muskets that the Massachusetts militia owned, these farmers were either very well armed, or excellent shots—or both.

Who kept all these guns in working order, and where did they come from? In Massachusetts, the Revolutionary government had more gunsmiths available to it shortly after the start of hostilities than it was prepared to hire—and could be picky about whom it put to work.[33] While the evidence is scattered, we know that there was some manufacturing of guns in Massachusetts immediately before the Revolution,[34] and some of these makers received payment for making guns for the Revolutionary government.[35]

CONNECTICUT

Like Massachusetts, Connecticut provided that one-fourth of the militia was to be organized for service on very short notice (hence the term "Minutemen"). As an encouragement to compliance,

[A] premium of fifty-two shillings per man shall be advanced and paid to each non-commissioned officer and inhabitant upon their inlistment, they supplying themselves with a blanket, knapsack, cloathing, &c . . . .

That each inhabitant so inlisted shall be furnished with good fire-arms, and that the fire-arms belonging to this Colony, wherever they are, shall be collected and put into the hands of such inlisted inhabitants as have not arms of their own; and that each inlisted inhabitant that shall provide arms for himself, well fixed with a good bayonet and cartouch box, shall be paid a premium of ten shillings.[36]

From this and similar provisions adopted two years later,[37] it appears that "such inlisted inhabitants as have not arms of their own" were the exception, not the rule. A militiaman who showed up with "blanket, knapsack, cloathing, &c" would receive fifty-two shillings (thirty-nine shillings sterling), while the militiaman who showed up with a gun would be paid only ten shillings (7.5 shillings sterling). This suggests that militiamen with guns were more common than militiamen with "blanket, knapsack, cloathing" and other camping gear.

If a militiaman lost his "arms and implements," the colony would reimburse him, deducting the ten shillings premium paid for showing up with his own arms. If this premium failed to produce enough militiamen with their own guns, "sufficient arms shall be impress'd, completely to arm and equip said inhabitants; the said impress to be limited only to the arms belonging to house-holders and other persons not on the militia roll . . . ." The owners would be paid four shillings for the use of impressed guns, and "the just value of the such gun" if lost.[38] Similar examples of the government offering a premium for those soldiers who were "providing themselves with good and sufficient arms" appear in the records as late as May of 1777.[39]

Even as late as March of 1776, almost a year into the war, Connecticut's government was not terribly concerned about a shortage of guns. The governor and Council of Safety directed that "the Guns, Barrels, and Gun-Locks, lately imported into New-Haven by Colonel Sears, be purchased (if suitable, and to be reasonably had) for the use of the Colony."[40] If guns were in short supply, it seems unlikely that the Connecticut government would haggle over the price.

In June of 1776, obeying orders from the Continental Congress, the Assembly ordered guns taken from "enemies to this country" to arm Connecticut's militia and soldiers. The details of the guns so impressed, with their appraised value, were to be carefully recorded for later reimbursement. The selectmen of the various towns were directed "to purchase or hire arms to furnish such soldiers of any of the battalions . . . as cannot furnish themselves." The selectmen were to allow "to the owner of each gun so hired the sum of six shillings,"[41] not a particularly large amount of money.

The government was not bashful about discussing shortages of needed goods, but guns do not appear to be among the items in short supply. In November of 1776, the Connecticut government gave orders for the collecting of blankets for the militiamen. The government was not discussing gun shortages, but it was buying guns—or at least, one would draw that conclusion from the detailed instructions that the General Assembly gave that same month for proof testing guns "to be made and procured within and for the use of this State."[42] ("Proof testing" is the firing of a gun with a larger than normal charge to make sure that it is strong enough to tolerate prolonged firing with a normal charge of gunpowder.)

In December of 1776, Connecticut revised its militia law, but still required that those militiamen who were not part of the Minuteman units "to equip themselves with such arms and accoutrements as by law is directed for those of the train-band in the militia." Towns were obligated to supply public arms to any militiaman who was "unable to equip and arm himself."[43] If militiamen lacked guns—but towns could purchase guns for them—then guns were not scarce; some militiamen were just too poor to buy guns themselves.

Official records of gunsmiths repairing guns in Connecticut seem to be scarce, perhaps for the same reason as in Massachusetts—that the government hired gunsmiths as employees. We do have occasional references to gunsmiths engaged in the repair of firearms for the Revolutionary governments (sometimes on an industrial scale), with no indication that gunsmiths were in short supply. In some cases, the records are unclear as to whether a gunsmith simply repaired guns, or made them.[44] We do have clear evidence that the Connecticut government was paying substantial bounties to gun makers, and that gun makers responded to these bounties by making guns for public service.[45] However, not all gunsmiths were of equal skill, and Connecticut formed a commission to investigate and prosecute those who had engaged in "fraud and breach of trust" in their manufacturing.[46]

RHODE ISLAND

In the last months of 1774, Rhode Island prepared itself for the coming war, and purchased ammunition "so that each soldier, equipped with arms, according to law, may be supplied with such quantities thereof, as by law is directed." The government discussed issuing the colony's public arms to the various towns, but at the same time, "each enlisted soldier, who shall not be provided with a sufficient gun, or fuzee . . . shall be fined two shillings . . . for each deficiency." Soldiers were also obligated to have "a good bayonet fixed on his gun" or pay a fine of four pence.[47] Rhode Island's militiamen were still obligated to own a gun.

In January 1775, while gunpowder was in short supply, gun ownership and use was sufficiently common that the government felt it necessary to give directions for the proper use of gunpowder: "That there be no firing of cannon, upon any public occasion, or of small-guns, especially by the Militia, or incorporated Companies, on days of exercising, excepting only for perfecting themselves as marksman, under the immediate direction of the commanding officer for the day." While the government felt comfortable giving orders to the militia about wasting gunpowder, it felt less sure of its authority to direct the private use of firearms: "And that it be, and hereby is, recommended to all the inhabitants of this colony, that they expend no gunpowder for mere sport and diversion, or in pursuit of game."[48] Such tentative wording suggests that the nascent government recognized the frequency of such activities and hence the sacrifice it was requiring of its civilians.

Once the war was under way, the government made fewer distinctions between public and private property. In June of 1775, the Rhode Island General Assembly ordered a committee to count the powder, arms and ammunition in each town in the colony, both in public and private stocks.[49] Providence took this step even earlier, ordering a committee to count its citizens' firearms and military equipment. The town also directed the committee to supply "all able-bodied men" who were unable to arm themselves, and to organize them into military units.[50]

A February 1775 letter to Governor Nicholas Cooke requested, "[W]e Shall Want to [equip] the men Now Enlisted 140 Guns and Expect to have them from providence[;] pray send as many New Guns as you Can . . . ."[51] While the soldiers needed guns, this letter seems more an indication that guns were not in the right place, rather than that guns were scarce. In May 1775, the Rhode Island Assembly offered forty shillings for each militiaman who could "find himself a Small-Arm, Bayonet, and other Accoutrements" but only twenty-four shillings for those who could not. Offering only sixteen shillings more (at most, a few days wages) for those who arrived armed for warfare does not suggest a dramatic shortage of firearms. The same day, the Assembly ordered 1,500 "Small-Arms and Bayonets . . . be immediately procured on the Colony's account."[52] If the militia was adequately armed, it seems rather strange that the Assembly would order purchase of 1,500 muskets—and yet the small bonuses offered to militiamen who were already armed do not suggest a shortage in general. Obviously there were guns available for purchase. The ordering of 1,500 muskets would suggest that there was some shortage of guns—but the small bonus to militia men who had armed themselves indicates that the shortage was not severe.

The following year, the General Assembly was again looking to purchase firearms, "two thousand stand of good fire-arms, with bayonets, iron ramrods and [cartridge] boxes . . . ."[53] It is unclear if the government was purchasing new guns or used, but the General Assembly apparently did not regard a purchase of this size as especially difficult—and at this point, there had been no importation of guns from Britain for two years, and large shipments of guns from Europe had not yet started. We do not have documentary evidence showing that gunsmiths delivered these "two thousand stand" of firearms, nor showing what price Rhode Island paid for them, but we do have some accounts that suggest that guns purchased by Rhode Island or its towns were not extraordinarily expensive, and therefore, could not have been very scarce: "Samuel Wall, for four guns with bayonets, and three cartridge-boxes, purchased by order of the town council of Coventry £17:14:0"[54]—or less than £3:15:8 sterling per gun and bayonet. This is a bit more expensive than prices paid in other New England colonies, but apparently these were new guns.

While weapons purchased by the state government would be issued to towns to arm those militiamen who had not armed themselves, the General Assembly clearly believed that militiamen who were not armed had only themselves to blame. The law allowed towns to declare that some persons were "incapable of providing themselves [with firearms.]" All others were "by law obliged to equip themselves with a good fire-arm." Those who failed to do so were subject to a £5 fine[55]—equivalent to several month's wages. A May 1778 statute almost doubled the fine.[56]

The evidence suggests that guns were not scarce in Rhode Island, although individual militiamen might be too poor to buy one. The Rhode Island government's plans to purchase muskets early in the Revolution suggest either a large supply of used muskets was already present, or that there was substantial manufacturing capacity in or near the state.

NEW HAMPSHIRE

The government of New Hampshire also seems to have believed that there were many firearms in private hands. On 18 May 1775, the Provincial Congress directed John Hale to procure "Fire-Arms and Gunpowder" on the promise of eventual payment by the government. Hale's job was difficult because he would have to obtain both on credit, instead of for cash. The next day, the legislature ordered towns to provide guns to those of their militiamen serving under Colonel Stark who were "destitute of Fire-Arms," with the colony to purchase guns in the event the towns were unable to do so. Not every militiaman had a gun, but the instructions suggest that these were the exception, not the rule.

A month later, the New Hampshire Committee of Safety ordered towns to "supply their men with Fire-Arms," presumably those outside of Boston, where New Hampshire forces stood shoulder to shoulder with Massachusetts men. There is also an order on 21 June shipping 3,200 flints, 628 pounds of bullets, and ten barrels of gunpowder—suggesting that New Hampshire's militia had more than a few guns with them. There are other orders for smaller shipments of ammunition as well.[57]

On 4 July 1775, the Provincial Congress ordered that "five hundred good Fire-Arms be provided" and directed that a committee investigate "how cheap they can procure them."[58] New Hampshire has long had a reputation for frugality, but it is difficult to imagine that the Provincial Congress perceived itself in imminent danger from a shortage of guns, if it was still looking to buy them on the cheap. Nor would it appear that the Provincial Congress believed that guns were impossible to purchase. In January of 1776, the New Hampshire House of Representatives voted that "Deacon Nahum Baldwin receive out of the Treasury thirty-five Pounds, to purchase Fire-Arms for this Colony." The following day, a committee was directed "to view and buy twenty Fire-Arms, procured for the use of this Colony by Mr. Moses Parsons." Amos Eastman was also paid £32:16 "for Guns," although there is no detail as to the quantity, or enough information to determine if this was a purchase or only a repair.[59]

There are some apparently contradictory statements about the difficulty of buying guns in New Hampshire. In March of 1776, a letter from Colonel Morey to the New Hampshire Committee of Safety complains about "Great difficulty on account of the want of guns" but also "of which I have been obliged to buy many . . . ." Perhaps there was a scarcity of muskets, or a scarcity of muskets available for the government to issue. Colonel Morey first wrote that he could buy "about hundred very good guns, which will cost nigh a thousand dollars" but in a postscript changed units and reported that they would cost about £300.[60] Six months later, Deacon Baldwin was again voted £60 "to pay for Guns for the Colony . . . ."[61]

Along with purchasing existing firearms, New Hampshire legislature records demonstrate that the government believed that there was substantial gun manufacturing capacity in the colony. The legislature provided for payment of three pounds each for every new musket made to New Hampshire's specifications. The statute provided for one man in every county to be responsible for proof testing—an indication that the government believed that gun manufacturers were present throughout the state. [62]

The evidence is clear that guns were not scarce in Massachusetts, and if they were scarce in New Hampshire, Connecticut, or Rhode Island, you would not know it from the manner in which the legislature attempted to procure arms. We have evidence of gun manufacturing (although not on the same scale as the Middle Colonies) in Massachusetts and Connecticut, and circumstantial evidence of gun manufacturing in New Hampshire and Rhode Island.[63]

It is certainly possible to quote particular documents that complain about shortages of guns—but as the documents in this chapter demonstrate, guns were available, and judging by the price, not particularly scarce. In wartime, guns or other military supplies are often in shorter supply than the immediate military requirements, but such a shortage says nothing about the availability of guns in peacetime. At the start of many wars, even nations that have devoted great energy to preparing for war discover that their needs far exceed their stockpiles. We should not be surprised to find complaints about a shortage of guns as the colonists, having been largely dependent on Britain for manufactured goods, were now acting as rebels, starting to fight, and obliged to be self-sufficient.

Guns in the Revolutionary Middle Colonies

PENNSYLVANIA

The people and the government of Pennsylvania believed that guns were readily available and easy to come by. The Committee of Observation for Lancaster County on 1 May 1775, shortly after the start of the war, recommended "to the inhabitants of the county of Lancaster, immediately to associate and provide themselves with arms and ammunition . . . ."[1] Similarly, the Liberty Company of Londonderry, Lancaster County, organized itself on 17 May 1775, with ninety privates on its muster roll. Among its articles, "That each Person of the Company shall (if not already done) as soon as possible, provide, himself with a good Gun or Musket."[2] Chester County adopted a similar resolution with no indication that this was difficult.[3] The Association of Inhabitants of Donegal, Lancaster County, complained about those not prepared to join the patriot Association due to "scruple of conscience," demands on time and income, or insufficient belief in the fighting cause. Members asked the county committee to compel those who would not join to pay "for the finding of arms and other accessories to those who are willing to do it, who are not of ability to provide themselves with such." (Local committees of safety had already disarmed Non-Associators.) Even as late as July 1776, the authors of the request assumed that this was a plausible demand:

[The Association of Inhabitants of Donegal, Lancaster County request] that it be allowed that all the landholders and farmers in the County of Lancaster be obliged to find at least one good gun each, and that every other person, who is judged by the Committee to be of ability, likewise find a good gun, whether they be joined in Association or not. This will put the county in a state of defence.

Obviously, enough firearms remained in private hands or such a request would have seemed ludicrous and frivolous in war time.[4]

Orders in 1775 and 1776 for the enlisting of soldiers required that they were "to find their own arms."[5] In March 1776, the Pennsylvania Assembly instructed those "recruiting Riflemen" that, "You are to take the utmost care . . . that you inlist no man who is not provided with a good rifle-gun, perfectly fit for service, and very expert in the use of it."[6] A shortage of guns in the *government's* hands did not mean that guns were rare.

Colonel William Irvine of the 6th Pennsylvania Battalion informed John Hancock in March 1776 concerning his soldiers' guns, "Many of the arms are old, and want bayonets and other repairs. . . . I have been obliged to purchase many rifles, but they, I presume, may be changed for muskets, should the service require it."[7] Irvine purchased these rifles privately; they were not supplied by the government—and they were available for purchase, almost a year into the war, and before large shipments of guns arrived from Europe. In September 1776, the Pennsylvania Committee of Safety directed that Westmoreland County "be empowered to purchase four hundred stand of Arms for the defence of said County." We can be sure that they meant firearms, not swords or pikes, because they also ordered delivery of half a ton of rifle powder and one ton of lead "to said County for the use of the Militia."[8]

The Pennsylvania Committee of Safety, like the New England governments, purchased existing firearms, and contracted for new manufacture. While some of these purchases are quite detailed, others are unspecific as to the number of firearms purchased, or the total price paid. The most that we can say is that Pennsylvania purchased at least 711 firearms (of which 174 were made to order), with many hundreds of pounds spent for firearms in other transactions,[9] some of it reimbursement to Non-Associators for seized weapons.[10] Many hundreds of pounds in transactions are unspecific if "arms" meant guns.[11] The average price for the arms for which we have specific information of price, quantity, and that these were firearms (not swords), is £3:5:5 (£2:0:7 sterling)—not particularly expensive.

Not every militiaman owned a gun, but this was due to poverty, not gun scarcity. Three months into the war, two militia officers named Tench Francis and Bache "made application to this Board for 30 or 40 Rifle Barrel Guns, for a Number of Men in their Company who have not Rifles, neither can they afford to purchase them." The officers apparently believed that guns were available from the Committee of Safety—and they were. The Committee of Safety directed Robert Morris to provide "Eighty good Rifles" for Francis and Bache's men, twice as many as they had requested.[12]

We can see something of the diversity of guns in Pennsylvania by a June 1776 order to distribute ammunition to Chester County militias. The Committee of Safety directed the Commissary to deliver both "Cartridges for Provincial Muskets" and "Cartridges, assorted, for the other different bores of Fire-locks," and to "each of the said Colonels the same proportion of loose Powder and Lead equal to the quantity of Cartridges."[13]

regimental commander	for provincial muskets	assorted
James Moore	2,300	2,070
Thomas Hockley	2,300	2,300
Hugh Lloyd	1,840	1,610
William Montgomery	2,760	2,415
Richard Thomas	1,840	1,610
total	11,040	10,005
% of total	52.5%	47.5%

This must have been very complex from a supply standpoint, but it demonstrates the enormous range of calibers of weapons Pennsylvania's militias used—exactly the situation you would expect if almost half the guns were in a caliber other than the British military standard.

Unlike Massachusetts, Pennsylvania contracted out gunsmithing services, and official records establish that Pennsylvania was awash in craftsmen both repairing and making guns.[14] Directives from the Pennsylvania Committee of Safety to the various counties show that gun manufacturing was widely distributed throughout the state. Surviving account books demonstrate that gun manufacturing preceeded the outbreak of hostilities and continued throughout the war.[15]

NEW YORK

Once New York had armed its troops and sent them off to fight, it did experience *localized* shortages of arms. One example is Orange County, which sent a letter to the Provincial Congress on 9 February 1776, indicating that it could raise more soldiers, "but think it well out of their power to arm any considerable part of the men they raise, on account of the quantity they furnished last year—none of which have been returned. . . ."

The *general* situation of New York, however, especially at the beginning of the war, shows that guns were not scarce. In May 1775, the New York Provincial Congress recommended "to the Inhabitants of this Colony in general, immediately to furnish themselves with necessary Arms & Ammunition."[16] On 22 August 1775, it ordered, "That every man between the ages of 16 and 50 . . . furnish himself with a good Musket or firelock" with a fine "of five shillings for the want of a musket or firelock." Calvarymen were obligated to provide themselves with "a case of pistols . . . and a carabine." Every man 16 to 50 was to "furnish himself" with either a long gun or "a case of pistols."

A few months into the war, New York revised its militia law to reflect the circumstances of mobilization, when the civilian supply of many goods became inadequate. These revisions seem not to be driven by a shortage of guns, but of other military goods. The December 1775 revision specified "that no man shall be fined for want of powder and ball, who shall produce a receipt from his Captain of his having deposited in his hand Six Shillings and Nine pence for the purchase of these articles." Ammunition was scarcer than the firearms in which to fire it.[17] Demonstrating that bayonets were in short supply—or at least, in shorter supply than the muskets on which the bayonets were to be mounted—the New York government requested that every militiaman "provide himself with a bayonet properly fitted to his musket or firelock." However, the government made no changes to the requirement that every member of the militia provide himself with a firearm. That firearms were not in short supply can be deduced from a *new* provision of the militia law that specified "That although persons above 50 years of age are not required to be enrolled in the Militia, yet is most earnestly recommended to them, that they be respectively provided with arms, accoutrements & ammunition, as though they were required to be enrolled."

Instructions for the raising of the four New York regiments also shows that both the Continental Congress and the New York Provincial Congress believed that soldiers could buy guns, or bring their own from home. Instructions from the Continental Congress specified that New York should pay a "bounty of 6 2/3 dollars to every ablebodied effective man, properly cloathed for the service and having a good firelock with a bayonet and other accoutrements, and 4 dollars to every soldier not having the like arms and accoutrements." (America was beginning the transformation from pounds to dollars.) The New York Provincial Congress apparently believed that it better understood the local conditions; they modified the Continental Congress' instructions specifying that each private would be allowed "instead of a bounty, a felt hat, a pair of yarn stockings and a pair of shoes, they to find their own arms."[18] Instead of paying "6 2/3 dollars" to those who brought their own gun, bayonet, and cartridge case, the Provincial Congress considered that it was a fair trade to provide three articles of clothing instead.

Some men were too poor to buy themselves "Arms, Am[m]unition, and Accoutrements." Suffolk County reported in February 1776, that there were "poor men in this County, who are good Soldiers and friends to the Cause . . . but have no guns—we should be glad to know if a number can be procured at the public Expense for such persons as are unable to purchase them." The provincial government at one point ordered counties to purchase this equipment for the poor out of fines imposed on those who failed to report for militia duty. At another point, a letter sent to the counties directed that "It is expected that each man furnishes himself with a good Gun and Bayonet . . . but those who are not able to furnish these arms and accoutrements, will be supplied at the public expense." The cost would be deducted out of each soldier's monthly pay "'till the whole are paid for, then they are to remain the property of the men."[19]

A March 1776 order to the commander of the 2nd Battalion shows that at least some privates could not "be supplied with Arms immediately," and should therefore be put to work on fortifications. The use of the word "immediately" suggests that this was not a general problem of New York, but specific to a particular battalion's location. An April 1776 report shows that Colonel Ritzema requested that the government supply "Arms for some of the Men" of his regiment "who are destitute."[20] Ritzema's request suggests that guns were available; only those who were "destitute" could not purchase a gun of their own. This does not appear to have been a widespread problem.[21]

The New York Provincial Congress believed that it could buy firearms from private citizens. In June 1775, the Provincial Congress ordered its commissary to order up cloth for uniforms, "1000 Stand of Arms," 20,000 flints, 8,000 pounds of lead, cartridge paper, tents, and other army gear. A little more than three months later, a letter to New York's delegates at the Continental Congress reported that New York had successfully armed four regiments, although not all with military arms: "The first and second Regiments and some part of the other Regiments are armed with the best of muskets and bayonets and the others with firelocks of the widest bore, which could be found, repaired where it was necessary . . . ." Civilian firearms supplemented the military muskets in the third and fourth regiments: "A great part of our arms have been procured by purchase; some have been hired—and from necessity, to compleat some Companies, a few arms have in some places been impressed."[22] (It seems that there was some shame about impressing arms.)

Guns were also coming from somewhere outside of New York in August 1776. Thaddeus Noble, for example, delivered twenty-six muskets to the government. They were damaged, apparently in overland transit, but were still considered useable. After some discussion, the government chose to pay Noble £2:0:11 each (£1:3:10 sterling) for the guns, contracted for in April of that year.[23] The government felt that it could even bargain about the price of functioning, but damaged goods.

Occasionally during the war, the government of New York ran short of guns. On 22 February 1776, the Provincial Congress refused a request to supply arms, blankets, and clothing to General Schuyler's forces because New York had "by no means a sufficiency for the equipment of those Troops, we are about to raise."[24] This letter (as well as several others) suggests that New York's efforts to arm its own four regiments had exhausted not only the local supply of arms, but also of blankets and clothing. (New York was not the only state suffering a blanket shortage.)[25] Most likely this was a temporary or localized shortage. As evidence for this, we have a complaint two months later from a precinct committee to the Committee of Safety that "we have a number of good muskets, or firelocks . . . which Captain Denton would not give us his receipt for, because his soldiers did not please to take them."[26]

The New York militia's success in disarming those loyal to the Crown to arm themselves is another indicator of gun availability. (The counties in and around New York City were a hotbed of Loyalist sentiment.)[27] Major William Williams, ordered to disarm Tories in Jamaica and Hempstead, was not short of work to do. His report of the reaction of the Tories has something of the flavor of the modern "from my cold, dead fingers." "The people conceal all their arms that are of any value . . . and say that they would sooner lose their lives, than give up their arms, and that they would blow any man's brains out that should attempt to take them from them." Williams also reported that Tories were seizing County-owned guns from Patriots. He added, "[H]ad we the Battalion, we believe we should be able to collect a very considerable number of good arms . . . but without it shall not."[28]

In April 1776, Tories in Queens County requested exemption from militia duty, claiming they had been disarmed.[29] In May 1776, the Provincial Congress ordered Dutchess and Ulster Counties to complete the arming of a Continental Army regiment with arms "collected by disarming disaffected persons in their respective Counties & districts . . . ." Westchester and Suffolk Counties received similar orders concerning arms confiscated from "disaffected persons." For Westchester, the order is explicit that these were firearms: "Gun Musket or Firelock." If these counties disarmed "disaffected persons" (those still loyal to the Crown), it must not have been entirely effective, or arms were seeping in from somewhere else. Less than two months later, there was again concern about "sundry disaffected and dangerous persons in the Counties of Dutchess and Westchester, who do now greatly disturb the peace of the said Counties and will probably take up arms, whenever the Enemy shall make a Descent upon this Colony." We have counts of those armed and unarmed: A 4 September 1776 report by the Revolutionaries describes how West Chester, Orange, Dutchess, and Ulster Counties contained 3,100 "Armed and well affected Militia," 2,300 "disarmed and disaffected," and 2,300 slaves.[30] Yet in spite of disarming those still loyal to Britain, there were *still* more firearms out there in private hands—enough of them that a number of officers were directed

> to proceed from House to House . . . and purchase at the cheapest Rate they can be obtained . . . all such good musketts and firelocks fit for the use of Soldiers, as can be spared by the Inhabitants of the Townships—That those Gentlemen respectively be requested not only to purchase arms as cheap as they can, but in no case to exceed the price of four pounds [equivalent to £2:6:7 sterling] for any one Gun Muskett or Firelock . . . . And it is hereby recommended to the Inhabitants of the said Townships to sell such muskets or firelocks as they can spare retaining arms for their own use.[31]

June 1776 orders concerning the dispatch of detachments to Canada directed that each unit "be completely provided with Arms, Accoutrements & Ammunition." Each unit's "deficiencies in these particulars if any such there be" were to be made up from the other men in each battalion "either by purchase to be deducted out of the pay of the several person detached . . . or by Loan as the respective Owners shall chuse . . . ." Enough militiamen owned multiple firearms to arm those who still lacked guns.

As late as 10 August 1776 there were still guns in private hands. Orders for mobilizing militia regiments directed the regimental commanders "to furnish all as have no arms by taking them from those who are not drafted and such other persons in the districts as have arms . . . ." The commanders were to assess the value of the arms taken from private parties for reimbursement in the event that the arms could not later be restored to them.[32]

In addition to guns already present in New York, the state government also believed that there were gun makers present—although not as many as were required by the circumstances of the Revolution. A series of discussions with Robert Boyd and Henry Watkeys starting 13 June 1775, concerned the making of one thousand muskets for the soldiers of New York. (Since New York was planning to raise and equip three thousand soldiers, this suggests that the Provincial Congress believed that its militia already had, or could purchase, at least two thousand muskets.)[33] Watkeys failed to deliver the required gunlocks and probably never intended to make them. Watkeys deserted to the British and after the war, resumed his career in Canada.[34] Watkeys' failure may reflect his political sympathies as much as technical inadequacies.

Other contracts to make guns for New York were clearly successful, with a number of manufacturers either fulfilling contracts for more than 100 muskets, or receiving gunpowder from the state for proof testing new muskets. Other evidence also implies that gunsmiths were making guns in New York, but there were not enough to meet wartime demands.[35] The state government advertised both for existing and new gun makers,[36] and offered subsidies to those who erected gunpowder mills, made gunlocks, or gun barrels—but only for new factories, and only for those who had not already contracted to make guns for the state.[37]

MARYLAND

In November 1775, Stephen West, gunsmith, writer of prolix letters to the Maryland Council of Safety, and apparently an unrecognized expert on just about everything, asked for the job of Commissary General. While West complained that ammunition had been greatly available the previous December, "it has most shamefully been wasted in Xmas Guns, fired away at birds and squirrels so that now I fear there is very little in the County and that little growing less every day." (Instead of caroling, many Americans in the nineteenth century fired guns on Christmas.) West complained about the poor organization of the militia (which he, of course, would correct), but his proposal makes an interesting claim: "[A]ll the old Arms shou[l]d be collected and repaired without delay and new ones as fast as Possible provided, there are a great many good Arms in the Province if all were Collected and repaired &c put into proper hands & places."[38]

Maryland's government believed that rifles were available for purchase. A February 1776 order directed that "the Company of Light Infantry, in the regular forces of this Province, be armed with Rifles." John Hanson, Jr.,

Charles Beatty, and James Johnson were "requested to provide and furnish the said Company good substantial and serviceable Rifles." A letter from the Maryland Council of Safety to a Captain Beall informed him in a postscript, "When we get our Rifles which we expect daily we will change, and give you rifles for some of the worst of your musketts." A letter a few days earlier directed that muskets made by John Yost should be shipped to Captain Beall. (John Yost made both rifles and muskets for Maryland.)[39]

We have gun purchase records that give some indication of their market value. The Maryland government purchased at least fifty-seven muskets, blunderbusses, rifles, and other firearms in 1776.[40] Baltimore County seized eighteen guns from Tories between 8 March and 3 April 1776 and reimbursed the owners for them at what the government thought was their market value.[41] Other transactions involve sizeable sums, although they do not specify how many firearms were purchased.[42] The value of these guns for which we can identify numbers and prices—totaling seventy-nine firearms—averaged £3:7:7 (£2:0:6 sterling)—a fairly low price: Again, the logical conclusion is that guns were common.[43]

The Maryland government bought large quantities of gun supplies, such as 24 September 1776 contracts with Joseph Selby and George Gordon for a total of 3,000 "Cartouch Boxes, Bayonet Belts and Gunslings, to be delivered in one month from this date."[44] These orders would only make sense if the government were either buying 3,000 muskets, or believed that it would have 3,000 militiamen with muskets available to it, in the next thirty days. Other orders to the Commissary are interesting for what was *not* included. The Commissary was directed to "deliver to Colonel Griffith 588 Knapsacks and Haversacks, 110 Camp-Kettles, 105 Tents, 678 Priming-Wires with Brushes, 658 Canteens, 50 pounds Gunpowder and Lead in proportion, 100 Gun-Flints, and as many Cartouch-Boxes, with Slings, Bayonet-Belts, and Gun-Slings, not exceeding 588 of each, as may be necessary for his Corps." All the military goods required to arm a regiment of 588 soldiers are listed—except for the guns. There are similar examples that suggest that many combat accessories for guns were in short supply—but not the guns that would require them.[45] Even a year and a half into the war, militia captains or soldiers were purchasing at least some guns on their own, or bringing them from home. Either there were still arms in private hands, or there were manufacturers making them for private purchase.

Like Pennsylvania, Maryland relied upon contracts with gunsmiths for repairs and new gun manufacturing. Also like Pennsylvania, the records demonstrate that gunsmiths were plentiful.[46] Gunlocks (which had been largely imported from Britain before the Revolution) were the limiting factor on gun manufacturing, but not an insurmountable obstacle, with many individual gunsmiths making guns for the state government, typically for £4 to £5 each.[47]

Flint lock mechanism

WHY AMERICANS USUALLY IMPORTED THE LOCK—LOTS OF LABOR.

There *are* reports that complain about the difficulty in obtaining guns—although even these reports acknowledge that Americans were making guns, and that guns were available for purchase, even as late as August 1776. Guns could be purchased for "£4 5s. in Virginia [£3:10:10 sterling], for muskets, that currency."[48] The problem was not that guns were scarce, but that it was difficult to borrow "firelocks from such of the Militia as will lend," because of concern that the government, if it lost the Revolution, would be unable to pay for lost or captured guns.[49]

Later in the same report, the Council of Safety informed the Eastern Shore committees:

> We will send you, by the first opportunity, some cash to buy guns and blankets with, which we request you will lay out accordingly. We have not exceeded £4 5s. for a musket [£2:10:11 sterling], with a steel ramrod and bayonet, but upon this occasion would have you go as high as £4 10s. [£2:13:11 sterling]. Guns which you may purchase without either, ought not to cost so much that the necessary repairs and providing ramrods and bayonets will carry them above £4 5s., unless they are very good, in which case we will also allow £4 10s.[50]

The Council of Safety sent similar instructions, with identical amounts to pay for guns, to the Committees of Safety for the Western Shore.[51] Such unwillingness to pay too much for guns does not suggest a severe shortage.

NEW JERSEY

At various times during the Revolution, and in particular regiments, New Jersey suffered from shortages of guns. It is difficult to examine the official records, however, and see much evidence that these shortages were widespread, or evinced much concern from the government. A 3 June 1775 document from the Provincial Congress directed that militias should reform themselves and instructed "Each person inlisted, to be equipped as soon as possible, with arms, ammunition, &c."[52] In October of 1775, the Provincial Congress revised the militia law, and ordered that "all persons . . . capable of bearing arms, between the ages of sixteen and fifty years" enroll in the militia "and shall, with all convenient speed, furnish himself with a good Musket or Firelock . . . ." Failure to have a gun would be punished with a two-shilling fine. Conscientious objectors were allowed to pay four shillings a month for exemption from militia duty.[53]

Surviving reports show that other common items were in as short supply as guns. A "Return of Arms, Accoutrements, Camp and Barrack Furniture" for one regiment shows that it still needed 269 firelocks—but also 234 bayonets, 685 tomahawks, 72 axes, 578 knapsacks, 218 hats, and 266 blankets.[54] One could cite this as evidence that guns were not common in New Jersey at the start of the American Revolution—but this same evidence would suggest that knapsacks, hats, and blankets were also scarce. It is more plausible that the shortage was because the government lacked the funds to buy needed goods, and sellers were reluctant to extend credit.

While few firearms purchase records appear, even in published sources where one might expect to find them, the prices of guns that New Jersey purchased do not suggest great scarcity.[55] One list of accounts approved for payment on 21 August 1776 purchased "seventy-nine stand of Arms" for a battalion, and reimbursed one person for a "a Gun lost in the service of this State . . . ."[56] The New Jersey gunsmith (and apparently gun maker) Benjamin Yard received payments for at least three shipments of muskets in 1776 and 1777, totaling thirty-five muskets.[57] The average value of these 125 guns was £4:6:4 or £2:10:11 sterling—a price so low it suggests that guns were common.

If New Jersey made guns before the Revolution, the quantity appears to have been quite small. New Jersey was repeatedly overrun by British forces and unsurprisingly, there is little evidence of gun manufacturing in the state—and what exists is contradictory. The New Jersey Committee of Safety established the New Jersey State Gunlock Factory at Trenton late in 1775; whether it successfully made gunlocks before Lord Cornwallis occupied Trenton in December 1776 is unclear. A March 1776 letter from the Newark Committee of Safety suggests that they were successful. The letter refers to two prisoners of war who were working for a Mr. Alling in the making of guns and gunlocks. There was some interest in moving these POWs away from Mr. Alling's gun manufacturing operation, and the Newark Committee was attempting to keep them: "Alling, in consequence of the leave obtained from Congress, had contracted to supply upwards of two hundred gun-locks for the use of the United Colonies, *which contract was in part executed*, but he would be very unable to fulfill his contracts, if Thompson should be taken from him."[58]

Delaware

Delaware's somewhat scanty records also give no indication of a gun scarcity. There are directions to deliver public arms, and a payment of £600 to a Colonel Paterson for purchasing blankets and bayonets—but no discussion of purchasing muskets upon which to mount those bayonets. A September 1776 order for raising militia companies instructs officers: "YOU are to take especial Care that those you [enlist] have Arms fit for Service, with Bayonets, Cartouch Boxes, Haversacks, Knapsacks and Blankets . . . ." Delaware government had few guns to distribute to militiamen; but the Delaware government also believed that it would have no problem enlisting militiamen with their own guns, more than a year into the war.

Delaware, like New Jersey, would seem to have little or no gun industry before the Revolution—but the state government made an effort to correct this situation. On 21 September 1776, the Convention negotiated with Duncan Beard "for erecting a Gun-Lock Manufactory in this State" for the purpose of making guns. Beard, better known as a clocksmith and silversmith, supplied two samples, and they were of sufficient quality for the government to contract with him to make gunlocks for £1:2:6 each.[59] Frederick Shraeder, of Wilmington, also made gunlocks for Delaware.[60]

The middle colonies varied substantially in their level of Colonial gun manufacturing. In New Jersey, the evidence is scanty, but there is at least a credible case that while the right *kind* of guns were often in short supply, guns of all types were not particularly scarce—at least, compared to blankets and hats. Especially for Maryland, Pennsylvania, and New York, the evidence is quite clear: Guns were sometimes in short supply in particular locations or at particular times, but not *generally* in short supply. There were enough guns in private hands to purchase them, rent them, impress them, and even expect soldiers who owned more than one to loan them to their comrades. Government complaints about a shortage of guns appear to be a shortage of guns in *government* hands, but not necessarily a shortage of guns in *private* hands. Gun manufacturers made guns in nearly all of the Middle Colonies— and in industrial quantities in Maryland and Pennsylvania.

8

Guns in the Revolutionary South

In 1774 and early 1775 it was obvious throughout the American colonies that the conflict between New England and the Crown was headed towards war. While the Crown enjoyed considerable support throughout the American colonies, this support was especially strong in the southern colonies—and oddly enough, in places such as North Carolina, this support often came from those who had rebelled against the colonial government just a few years before. The North Carolina Regulators who regarded the tidewater colonial government with contempt, sided with London. Highland Scots who had fought against George II in 1745, and then immigrated to America, formed regiments to fight on behalf of George III. Often as not, what made a person a Tory in some of the southern colonies was reaction to who was on the Revolutionary side.

The official records of South Carolina and Georgia are disappointingly scanty. South Carolina was occupied by British troops very early in the war, with a consequent loss of many records. Georgia's records from this period are somewhat scarce, at least partly because so much was destroyed a century later during General Sherman's March to the Sea. Many of the records we have for Colonial Georgia were painstakingly reconstructed from British archives after the Civil War, and it is unsurprising that these are less complete than the records of other colonies.

VIRGINIA

It was obvious to anyone who read the colonial newspapers in 1774 and 1775 that rebellion against the Crown was likely. Virginia Revolutionaries planned for the coming fight. Virginia's resolutions of 23 and 25 March 1775 called for the restoration of the Colonial militia, "That a well regulated Militia, composed of Gentlemen and Yeomen, is the natural strength, and only security of a free Government." The detailed organization of infantry and cavalry units ordered "that every man be provided with a good Rifle, if to be had, or otherwise with a common Firelock, Bayonet, and Cartouch-box . . . and four pounds of Ball, at least, fitted to the bore of his Gun." While other provisions of the 25 March resolution ordered counties to provide ammunition for the militiamen, this resolution said nothing about providing firearms.[1] In Augusta County, the local committee echoed this resolution—again, directing the county to provide ammunition but saying nothing about providing firearms.[2]

The frontiers of Virginia produced riflemen who were the terror of British soldiers besieged in Boston.[3] When Virginia received a request for 500 riflemen at the beginning of the war, there were so many available that the colonel who organized the regiment used a shooting competition to make his selection—and there was no shortage of crack shots from which to pick.[4] A letter from New Jersey's Loyalist Governor William Franklin on 4 July 1775 seems to mention this regiment: "I am just informed that 300 Rifle-Men are to march this Day from Philadelphia to join the New England Army at Cambridge; and that they are soon to be followed by 500 more."[5] On 10 August a New York newspaper reported that "[t]he remainder of the rifle men consisting of 100 passed though Newark last Friday."[6]

A July 1775 Virginia militia statute provided that regular soldiers would be armed at public expense "with one good musket and bayonet." This might indicate that militiamen were not sufficiently armed, but the same statute also directed that "until such muskets can be provided, that they bring with each of them the best gun, of any other sort, that can be procured; and that such as are to act as rifle-men bring with them each one good rifle, to be approved by their captain," with similar provisions for Minutemen (who constituted a select militia of the best trained and conditioned men). Each militiaman not part of the Minuteman units, "shall furnish himself with a good rifle, if to be had, or otherwise with a tomahawk, common firelock, bayonet, pouch, or cartouch box, three charges of powder and ball . . . and shall constantly keep by him one pound of powder and four pounds of ball."[7]

Why, if the law required militiamen to arm themselves, and as the law assumed, most men were actually already in possession of a gun, did Virginia provide public arms? As Don Higginbotham observes, while the population was well armed,

> [F]lintlocks wore out, needed new parts, and the bores of older guns varied so profusely that each man often needed a separate mold to shape bullets for his own weapon. Some soldiers left their muskets at home for the benefit of their families. Indeed, a man who contributed his own firearm made a notable sacrifice if it was damaged or destroyed; its worth was most likely equal to two weeks' pay for a laborer.[8]

While the law made exceptions for those unable to purchase powder because it was unavailable, this excuse was *not* available for lack of a gun. Virginia's government knew that not everyone could get a rifle—but assumed that everyone had, or at least could get, a "firelock." A person might be too poor to buy a gun—but Virginia's government assumed that guns were available for purchase by the committee of the county for those "so poor as not to be able to purchase the arms aforesaid . . . ."[9] The Virginia Committee of Safety on 19 June 1776 directed delivery of shot to "Captain Washington of the fourth Battalion"[10]—which is what we would expect if large numbers of militiamen were armed with fowling pieces, not muskets. Perhaps the most astonishing indicator of how widespread guns were is what happened when residents of the Eastern Shore searched the slave quarters (who might take seriously all this Revolutionary talk of human rights and liberty): "They collected about 'eighty Guns, some Bayonets, swords, etc.' from their slaves."[11]

If guns were in short supply in the first two and a half years of the war, the *Calendar of Virginia State Papers* is curiously silent. There *are* letters such as

George Mason's of 14 July 1775 that talk about reorganizing Virginia's militia. Mason lists many tasks before his committee, including "to provide arms, ammunition &c, and to point out ways & means of raising money." A month later, Mason refers to "Arms, Tents, &c to be provided for the Minute men at the public charge." But as we have previously seen, government provision of arms did not necessarily mean that guns were rare. A number of war materials were in short supply. Mason, for example, expressed his desire for laws "encouraging the making [of] Salt-petre, Sulphur, [both ingredients of gunpowder] Powder & Lead" but said nothing that suggests guns were in similarly short supply.[12] Richard Henry Lee's letter of 24 November 1777 shows a great concern about clothes for the army.[13]

The *Journals of the Committee of Safety of Virginia* demonstrates that guns were not in short supply. There are contracts that refer to purchase of "the arms offered to this Board by Mr. _____ West . . . ." This contract refers both to existing arms purchased, "and if any should be manufactured under this contract they are to correspond with the model heretofore established by this Board." There is an order to a John Bannister to "deliver, out of the Rifles which he contracted to furnish for the public use . . . twenty three" for the use of a particular company.[14] In addition to contracts, the first month of the *Journals of the Committee of Safety* contains so many individual purchases of guns that there was no purpose in continuing to gather the data beyond that point.

In June 1776, the Committee of Safety purchased 174 firearms at an average price of £4:2:2 Virginia money, or the equivalent of £3:8:6 sterling—and this is more than a year into the war, when demand should have driven up prices.[15] There are also at least sixteen payments in less than a month totaling more than £1,275 sterling for "arms purchased" that are unspecific as to whether these were firearms, or unspecific as to count or purchase price.[16] Perhaps the best evidence that guns were not in short supply is an order from the Committee of Safety on 27 June 1776 to Snickers and Thruston, "requiring them to *desist* from making any further purchases of Rifles or Guns" [emphasis added]. There are many other examples of guns and related supplies appearing in the records that show that guns were not *generally* scarce.[17]

Lancaster County was authorized to call into service "the whole of the two Minute Companies . . . provided they can be armed."[18] In light of the enormous amount of activity with purchase and issuance of guns, however, it suggests that, like the situation in other colonies, this was a localized shortage of guns, not a colony-wide problem. If guns were in short supply in Virginia at the beginning of the Revolution, one would be hard pressed to see evidence of it from these documents—while other items, such as clothes, gunpowder, and lead were clearly matters of concern.

While gunsmiths in Virginia were not as common as in Pennsylvania or Maryland, they were present, offering to make rifles for "Four Pounds and Ten Shillings Viriginia Currency each" or muskets with bayonets for £4 each.[19] As we saw in the previous chapter, the Maryland Committee of Safety as late as August of 1776 believed that they could purchase for "£4 5s. in Virginia [£3:10:10 sterling], for muskets, that currency."[20] Stephen & Noble's Martinsburg, Virginia factory was "capable of making as many as eighteen muskets in a single week."[21]

The Rappahannock Forge in Virginia made guns during the Revolution; some of their production survives today. Nathan Swayze, an arms collector specializing in Rappahannock Forge's production, has found at least eighteen surviving guns produced during the Revolution: ten pistols, four muskets, and four "wall guns" (a type of very large musket used for defending fixed positions).[22] It seems likely that many more guns made by Rappahannock Forge were melted down, lost, or otherwise destroyed when they ceased to be useful.

NORTH CAROLINA

The North Carolina Provincial Congress on 10 September 1775 issued a variety of orders, including a recommendation "to such of the inhabitants of this Province as may not be provided with Bayonets to their Guns, to procure the same as soon as possible, and be otherwise provided to turn out at a minute's warning." If guns were scarce in North Carolina, it is exceedingly strange that the government told its people to procure bayonets, but said nothing about procuring guns on which to mount them. The Provincial Congress' expectation that the inhabitants could "turn out at a minute's warning" for warfare certainly indicates easy access to guns. It is more plausible that the population owned hunting guns, but not bayonets—an accessory only useful in warfare.

Gun powder was scarce because it was almost entirely imported from Britain. (Under the mercantilist economic system then in effect, all goods imported to America, no matter what their origin, were supposed to be shipped through British ports and merchants.) On 19 June 1775, a circular letter sent by North Carolina's delegates at the Continental Congress pleaded with the leaders of various towns and counties to encourage all to treat gun powder as a precious, even sacred resource, a means to "live and die free."

> It is the Right of every English Subject to be prepared with Weapons for his defence. . . .
>
> Carefully preserve the small quantity of gunpowder which you have amongst you; it will be the last Resource when every other means of Safety fail you—Great Britain has cut you off from further supplies. . . . [R]eserve what Ammunition you have as a sacred Deposit. He in part betrays his Country who sports it away, perhaps in every Charge he fires he gives with it the means of preserving the life of a fellow being.[23]

Guns receive no such exalted, sacramental treatment, presumably because they were not in short supply.

The provincial and local governments assumed widespread gun ownership. On 7 September 1775, the North Carolina Provincial Congress issued orders for the enrolling of Minutemen, requiring captains

> give a preference to those who have guns of their own; but if it be found necessary to take such as have none,
>
> That then the Captains certify the same to the Committees of the Countys to which they belong who shall thereupon borrow such guns as are fit for Service, giving receipts, describing such Guns, and the value thereof; to the owners, that they may hereafter get them again or the value of them . . .
>
> That an allowance be made after the rate of ten Shillings per Annum for a good smooth bore or Musket, and twenty shillings for a Rifle, to the owners for the use of their Guns, in the Case above mentioned.[24]

The Provincial Congress expected most of the Minutemen to have guns; only "if it be found necessary" would the militia officers enroll men without guns—and those could be easily borrowed from other gun owners in the county.

On 13 November 1775, the Wilmington Safety Committee directed:

> Messrs. Forster, Mallett, Wilkinson and Jewkes, go round the town and examine the arms that may be in each Family; after reserving one gun for each white man that may be in the House, the remainder shall be valued by the above Gentlemen, and a receipt given for them, mentioning their value. Those who have new Guns to dispose of shall be allowed three for one (in order to obtain an immediate supply of arms on this immergent occasion) a receipt shall also be given for such Guns on account of the public, and for the use of the first Regiment under the command of Col. James Moore.[25]

The Committee assumed that not only were there more than a few homes with more than one gun per white man, but that there were a number of *new* guns available for purchase.

On 4 May 1776, the North Carolina Provincial Congress issued orders defining the militia, which "shall consist of all the effective men from 16 to 60 years of age." Each militia member "shall be furnished with a good gun, bayonet, cartouch box, shot bag and powder horn, a cutlass or tomahawk." But who was to furnish the gun? "[W]here any person shall appear to the field officers not possessed of sufficient property to afford such arms and accoutrements, the same shall be procured at the public expence." These guns for the poor men were to be issued when the militia was called into service, and recovered when the militia was no longer in service.[26] There were North Carolinians too poor to own a gun—but the combination of the statute requiring militia men to arm themselves, and language to deal with any "person . . . not possessed of sufficient property" suggests that these were the exception, not the rule.

What were the actual numbers of armed militia? We have the records of Colonel Thomas Brown's militia battalion and Colonel Dauge's militia regiment dated 31 July 1776. Brown's battalion included 659 "rank and file" of whom only 447 were "Present fit for Duty." (The remainder were either sick and wounded, on furlough, absent, deserted, or in the curious category, "On Command.") These 447 available soldiers had 519 "Guns Fixed" and 10 "Guns not Fixed." Every man fit for duty had a gun—though ammunition was clearly in very short supply. Colonel Dauge's regiment had 491 "Present fit for Duty" and 551 "Guns Fixed" and "35 "Guns out of Fix."[27] Both regiments had more guns than soldiers.

A careful reading of *Colonial Records of North Carolina* for 1775 and 1776 suggests that guns were sometimes in short supply in *some* counties at the start of the Revolution, while abundant in other counties. While both the state and county governments were buying and disbursing large quantities of lead and gunpowder for use of the militia—who, presumably, had guns in which to fire all this ammunition—there are only occasional discussions of a shortage of guns.[28]

The quantities of lead and gunpowder purchased were substantial. The Wilmington Safety Committee, for example, paid a number of people for gunpowder and flints at the very start of the war in 1775. In a single county, merchants had large quantities of powder and flints available to sell, almost a year after Britain had prohibited the export of ammunition to America. William Mactier sold 200 pounds of gunpowder; Burgwin, Humphrey & Co. sold 350 pounds; 133 ½ pounds were purchased from Yelverton Fowkes. Charles Jewkes received payment 12 August for 300 flints. All this took place in one county, in just a few months.

New Hanover County purchased 400 pounds of gunpowder from two parties (merchants, perhaps) on or before 19 June 1775—and in a county with only a few thousand people. Tryon County disbursed 500 pounds of gunpowder, 600 pounds of lead, and 600 gunflints to Daniel McKissick on 14 August 1775—after a year of British embargo. On 6 February 1776, the Rowan County Safety Committee ordered confiscation of gunpowder from a James Cook for public use. The quantity was apparently large enough that if he did not turn it over voluntarily, two militia captains were ordered to raise whatever number of militia were required to take it from Cook.[29] The Safety Committee never stated the quantity of powder, but it is hard to imagine that they were sending a detachment of militia to get a pound or two of gunpowder.

Even as late as 8 May 1776, more than a year after the start of hostilities at Lexington, when gunpowder from abroad would not yet have been arriving in quantity, Rowan County's Safety Committee requested 500 pounds of gunpowder, as well as flints, from neighboring counties, expecting that such would be available for purchase.[30] Did they get it? The records are silent (or perhaps insufficiently scrutinized), but it seems unlikely that the Safety Committee would waste the time making the request if gunpowder was not available. On 9 July 1776, the North Carolina Provincial Congress gave orders for moving a total of six tons of gunpowder. On 23 July 1776, the Halifax Council of Safety gave directions for what to do with two tons of gunpowder recently arrived by wagon from Virginia. Even when officials asserted that "Powder is scarce with us," they still shipped 500 pounds of gunpowder on request. There are other large shipments of gunpowder as well, totaling more than ten tons.[31]

A 25 June 1776 letter from William Purviance describes his trip into town for ammunition and provisions for his soldiers. More than a year into the war, and almost two years after the shut off of exports of powder from Britain, ammunition was easier to obtain than pork and bread. General Griffith Rutherford, begging the Provincial Congress for gunpowder on 12 July 1776, asked for at least "1000 lbs. more Powder, besides what you first Voted, for People in the [frontiers] will move off if not [supplied] with that article." (Apparently, the gunpowder shipped 21 July 1776.)[32]

While the war made gunpowder scarce, there was quite a bit of it around before the war—a situation consistent with widespread gun ownership and hunting. North Carolina's delegates to the Continental Congress knew well the state they represented. When they asked their people to preserve the "small quantity of gunpowder" in North Carolina, the quantity was "small" only relative to the amount needed for a prolonged war.

The Revolutionary records also treat the government's purchasing of guns as unremarkable. After the Continental Congress ordered the colonies to disarm Loyalists, the North Carolina Provincial Congress appointed officials to "to receive, procure and purchase fire arms for the use of the troops." This included confiscation of arms from the disaffected, specifying that they were to be returned to the owners at a later date. A committee of seventy men—

two in each of thirty-five counties—was appointed to "purchase all Fire-Arms which are good and sufficient and fit for immediate use; and also such as may be repaired, and put in such order as to be made useful." These seventy men were to purchase not only arms confiscated from Tories, but also other arms that were available. Quakers, Moravians, and Dunkards, "who conscientiously scruple bearing arms," were encouraged to sell their guns to the firearms purchasing commissioners. This was explicitly a voluntary transaction providing that "no compulsion be exercised to induce them to this duty." Once all regiments were armed, *surplus* arms were to be delivered to the Commissary of Stores.[33] On 21 October 1775, the Provincial Council directed Richard Caswell to "purchase from David Baron of Newbern all the new serviceable Guns, and all the Gunpowder he may have for sale at the lowest price they can be had for."[34] Six months into the war, North Carolina's government still believed there were "new serviceable Guns" for sale.

On 17 January 1776—nine months into the war—the Wilmington Safety Committee responded to a request for "50 stand of Arms" from Colonel Moore by sending a committee out "to call respectively on the inhabitants of this town tomorrow and borrow from them such guns as they can spare."[35] On 12 June 1776, Colonel William Bryan complained of his difficulty in borrowing guns from independent-minded townspeople: "I have Indeavoured to borrow or hire Guns though in vain; I then ordered the [captain] to send out his S[e]argants to [im]press Guns, but the people Hides their guns and would not show them and says They do not know how soon they may have Occasion to turn [out] with them themselves." Bryan added to his grievances his concern that Congress (probably the Provincial Congress) had purchased all the spare arms in the county, apparently for North Carolina's contribution to the Continental Army, "so close that it is Impossible to furnish the militia with arms." While guns were now scarce *for purchase* (because the population would not sell them) in Colonel Bryan's part of North Carolina, this does not indicate a scarcity of guns before the Revolution. And obviously the army would not have wasted time and soldiers by sending them in search of something they did not expect to find.

Of course, orders might have been issued to buy or borrow guns that were not actually available. But we do have fragmentary records indicating that the government was successfully buying guns—and at very reasonable prices. The Wilmington Safety Committee purchased at least thirty-three muskets sometime before 22 December 1775, for less than £90 (£51:8:7 sterling). On 23 January 1776, the Pitt County Safety Committee gave a receipt "for arms Received from Mr. Robt Jameson for the use of the Continental Army" but without any information on the number of arms, or the price. Charles Jacocks was reimbursed for "arms, camp kettles and camp equipage" that he purchased sometime before 2 May 1776. Arthur Moore of Orange County was paid £56 (£32 sterling) for seven rifles—or £8 (£4:11:5 sterling) each—sometime before 9 May 1776. On 26 June 1776, Joseph Green, one of the commissioners for purchasing guns in Dobbs County received reimbursement of £149:9:4 for forty guns.[36] Green had paid a bit less than £4 (£2:2:7 sterling) each for guns—and this more than a year after the start of the war. And occasionally, officers were even able to buy more guns than they needed for their soldiers.[37]

In total, we have records for eighty firearms purchased by North Carolina governments, averaging £3:14:1 (£2:2:4 sterling). Guns do not seem spectacularly expensive, considering a war was in progress.[38]

We do have curious letters, however, such as one from Colonel Robert Howe to the Provincial Council, in December 1775, complaining about "the Disarmed Situation of North Carolina" and that when he sent out an order "to Procure Arms for my own Regiment, the officers could find hardly any Inhabitants armed, and such as had Arms, not one in twenty fit for service . . . ."[39] The North Carolina Council of Safety's letter of 24 June 1776 to the Continental Congress complained about a "great want of Fire Arms, Ammunition and other Warlike Stores . . . ."

What are we to make of such letters? Were arms scarce in some parts of North Carolina? If there were many examples of such complaints, or no evidence that the government was successfully buying guns at very reasonable prices, we might conclude that guns were actually scarce. The bulk of the evidence, however, suggests that Howe's concern about the difficulty in procuring arms was more a matter of civilians unwilling to supply guns to the Revolutionaries—which would not be able to pay for those guns if they lost the war. As the 24 June letter also observed, "We have involved this Colony in such a load of Debt as the Inhabitants cannot possibly bear unless they receive immediate assistance."[40]

Guns were common among the Loyalists as well. On 14 August 1775, the New Bern Safety Committee ordered militia captains to disarm those suspected of Loyalist sympathies of "their Fire-arms . . . Swords, Cutlasses . . . and all Gun powder, Lead and other Military Stores," and to deliver those arms to militiamen "not having Arms . . . as may be willing to serve in the American Cause."[41] The Provincial Congress directed Colonel Long to "collect all the arms which may have been taken from the Regulators [to be discussed in the next paragraph] and Tories, and hold them ready to be delivered to new recruits, as the officers may apply for them." As late as 8 May 1776, there were still guns in private hands, with the Rowan County Safety Committee dealing with complaints from the inhabitants of Muddy Creek that the militia had taken their guns from them during an expedition. The same committee also ordered the disarming of a suspected Loyalist.[42]

The backcountry counties of North Carolina had been the scene of lethal confrontations in the years 1768 to 1771. First the Regulators fought corrupt county officials, and then the Colonial militia, which were led by the governor. After the last of these battles, the governor confiscated many hundreds of guns. Astonishingly enough, many of the Regulators sided with the British government at the start of the Revolution—regarding a king thousands of miles away as less of a threat than the tidewater Revolutionaries. Governor Martin, writing from a Royal Navy warship off Cape Fear on 12 January 1776, informed the Earl of Dartmouth that between two and three thousand of the former Regulators were ready to join the Loyalist cause, "although not half of them are provided with arms . . . ."[43] The Regulators were generally poor, and at least five hundred had voluntarily turned in their arms in 1771. Yet, somewhat less than half of them were armed *before* the British government could supply them with weapons.

The British government probably supplied some guns to these Loyalists. Martin's letter of 21 March to Lord George Germain claimed that two to three thousand Regulators were now "well armed," which would only be consistent with his letter of 12 January if the British government had supplied guns to the more than half that were unarmed.[44] (Of course, Martin might have been lying. Martin's continued self-justification and toadying to Lord Germain makes him a less than trustworthy source, and someone that I would *not* invite over for dinner.)

In early March, there is a description of the arms captured from these Regulators. The report is ambiguous as to whether the captured arms were supplied by the British government or were the personal property of the Regulators. The Revolutionaries had "taken 350 guns and shot-bags; about 150 swords and dirks; 1,500 excellent rifles . . . ." *Some* of the captured materials were almost certainly supplied by the British to the Regulators. The rifles, however, and the description of "shot-bags" (more appropriate to fowling pieces than military muskets) suggest that the Regulators were armed with the traditional hunting weapons of the American frontier.[45]

Private citizens definitely used their privately owned guns. In the vicinity of Charlotte, North Carolina, British occupation forces were under regular attack by armed civilians:

> So inveterate was their rancour, that the messengers, with expresses for the commander in chief, were frequently murdered; and the inhabitants, instead of remaining quietly at home to receive payment for the produce of their plantations, made it a practice to way-lay the British foraging parties, fire their rifles from concealed places, and then fly into the woods.[46]

In 1780, North Carolina's militia gathered into a single large force. These militia units consisted of "the wild and fierce inhabitants of Kentucky, and other settlements westward of the [Allegheny] Mountains"; followers of a Colonel Williams; and other militia from the upcountry parts of North Carolina. A British officer described them: "These men were all well mounted on horseback and armed with rifles . . . . When the different divisions of mountaineers reached Gilbert-town, they amounted to upwards of three thousand men."[47] While *muskets* were imported from Europe in large quantities starting in 1777, where did 3,000 militiamen get their rifles?

At least part of why the frontiersmen had guns was for protection from the Indians—who also had many guns, and were generally allied with the British against the Revolutionaries. The North Carolina Council of Safety reported on 30 July 1776, while planning military strategy with Virginia, "The Cherokees as we are told, can muster about 2,000 Gun Men in the whole . . . ." How well armed were the Cherokees? They had something under 2,500 warriors at that point—so about 80 percent of their warriors had guns. Reports of one battle between North Carolina troops and Indians near the start of the Revolution described how after a Cherokee and Creek war party retreated after great losses, "[W]e took a great number of Guns . . . ."

At the start of the Revolution, Colonel William Christian of the Virginia troops who fought against the Cherokees observed that the Indians depended on "ammunition to get meat" and that burning their villages and cornfields would starve them into submission.[48] Guns were not in short supply among the Cherokees; the Cherokees had abandoned their traditional methods of hunting.

One startling aspect of reading through *Colonial Records of North Carolina* is how little discussion there was of acquiring, distributing, making, or purchasing of guns—and how much time was spent discussing the importance of making, importing, and distributing *salt* or equipment for making salt. The scarcity of salt did not become apparent until partway through volume 10, but even a partial listing of the pages on which salt appeared as an important subject of discussion is fairly astonishing,[49] with similar problems in Connecticut, Pennsylvania, Maryland, Delaware, Virginia, New York, Kentucky, and South Carolina.[50] One example:

> That Colonel Ebenezer Folesome immediately call on the several Merchants and Factors in Cumberland County, whom he suspects of having Salt in their Hands and make enquiry for any that may be concealed, and take an Inventory and stop the sale of the same; and return an Account thereof to this Board: Provided, That this Resolve shall not extend to such Salt as have been purchased for the use of private Families and that he call on the Commissioners to render an Account of all the Salt delivered out and to whom, and make return thereof to the Council.

North Carolina had been dependent on salt imported from abroad, and it was now in short supply. There were similar problems obtaining clothes for the troops throughout the war.[51] The Revolution disrupted existing economic relationships, causing temporary shortages of common items of the pre-Revolutionary period.

North Carolina's records show almost no transactions for repair of guns—and yet there are statements that suggest gunsmiths were common throughout the state.[52] When the North Carolina Provincial Congress established a commission to purchase guns—with two commissioners in each of thirty-five counties—they also provided that firearms not fit for military use were to be repaired, and, "That if Armourers cannot be found in each County, sufficient for repairing such Arms, that they sent into such publick Armoury as shall be established hereafter by this Congress."[53] The Provincial Congress directed Colonel Nicholas Long to "employ at the Public Expense some Person or Persons to mend and put in fix sundry Guns now in his Possession, and in the Town of Halifax."[54] The assumption was that in many, perhaps most North Carolina counties, there were "sufficient" gunsmiths capable of repairing guns. (New York's Committee of Safety made similar provisions.)[55]

The North Carolina records show only a few instances of the government paying gunsmiths for repairs, and even then, these transactions often included the purchase of guns. The state government reimbursed the Wilmington committee £83:15:10 for purchasing "thirty-one Guns, stocking four Guns, repairing three Guns, and twelve Gun Locks" and a later transaction of £7:1:0 "for two Muskets, repairing one gun and two gun locks . . . ." Other records indicate that there were gunsmiths present, but the small number of such transactions suggests that either there were very few gunsmiths present in North Carolina, and the Provincial Council was deluded about this, or, consistent with the evidence from other states, that the records of publicly paid gunsmithing are very incomplete.[56]

North Carolina's Provincial Congress believed that there was an existing gun manufacturing industry in their state. They named eighteen men in six different districts "to direct the establishing of public manufactories in their respective districts, of good and sufficient muskets and bayonets" following the specifications of the Continental Congress. These men were to "collect from the different parts of their respective districts all gunsmiths, and other mechanicks, who have been accustomed to make, or assist in making muskets, or who may in their opinion be useful in carrying on such manufactory . . . ." Musket and bayonet together were not to exceed £5.[57]

The North Carolina Provincial Congress' records tell surprisingly little about these public gun factories, but these factories were making guns, often under quite adverse conditions. Privately owned and operated gun factories (some of which predated the Revolution) also manufactured firearms for the North Carolina government.[58]

SOUTH CAROLINA

South Carolina's records are relatively sparse. The evidence, while hardly conclusive, does not suggest that guns were particularly scarce, and does provide some limited evidence of a pre-Revolutionary gun making industry.

On 17 June 1775, the Provincial Congress "RESOLVED, That it be recommended to such of the inhabitants of this colony, as are not provided with bayonets to their guns, to procure the same without delay, and to be otherwise prepared to turn out at a minute's warning."[59] Much like Massachusetts, New York, and North Carolina, South Carolina's government assumed that bayonets were in short supply, at least relative to the supply of guns upon which to mount those bayonets.

At the start of the war, guns were apparently widely distributed, at least on the frontier. Henry Laurens' letter to the Provincial Council of Wilmington, North Carolina, dated 2 January 1776, thanked North Carolina for its help in dealing with "insurgents on our western frontier . . . [M]any of their leaders are in jail; others have fled the country; hundreds of the common class have surrendered their arms . . . ."[60]

Patriot General Robert Howe wrote to the legislature on 6 October 1776 of the need for more wagons, clothes, blankets, and the establishment of "minute battalions": more highly trained militia, comparable to the Minutemen of Massachusetts. But he said nothing about a need for more muskets, rifles, or other firearms. When, on 19 October, the House of Representatives took action on General Howe's request, they requested along with the wagons and the minute battalions, some more muskets, but their language is hardly that of crisis: "The Committee cannot conclude their Report without desiring that it may be recommended to the President [of South Carolina] to use every means in his power to procure us a quantity of ammunition and a number of good muskets with bayonets and iron ramrods, large cannon, some light field pieces, and a few mortars and howitzers with shells."[61] This is the *only* discussion of a small arms shortage contained in the surviving records of the South Carolina legislature, which cover 1776 and 1779–80. A letter from General Howe to South Carolina's President Rutledge two days later about the state of defense of South Carolina discussed his desire that the state organize Minutemen, the more highly trained militia. Howe did say that Minutemen "are generally better armed and will probably be better disciplined than militia . . . ."[62]

Not only Patriots were armed in South Carolina; so were Loyalists. British officer Charles Stedman described how, after British troops took control of South Carolina in 1778, "A great majority of the inhabitants came in, and having taken the oath of allegiance, submitted themselves again to the authority of the mother-country. Rifle companies of dragoons were formed out of those who came in to renew their allegiance . . . ."[63] Rifles were almost certainly locally supplied, although the British Army did use small numbers of European rifles in America.

South Carolina's government clearly believed that they had a gun making industry—and it seems likely that it was one that preceeded the Revolution. On 24 February 1776, South Carolina's Provincial Congress directed a sub-committee "to contract for the making, or purchasing already made, any number, not exceeding one thousand stand, of good Rifles, with good bridle-locks . . . not exceeding the price of thirty Pounds each . . . Also for the making, or purchasing already made, one thousand stand of good smooth-bored Muskets, carrying an ounce ball . . . at a price not exceeding twenty Pounds each . . . ."[64] (South Carolina currency inflated rapidly during the Revolution.) The relatively sparse records of the South Carolina government provide no information about gun manufacturing that actually took place there.

GEORGIA

Georgia's militia law of 1778 authorized the governor to "call together all Male Persons" with a few exceptions "from age of Fifteen to Sixty Years . . ."

apparently including free blacks and slaves. A later section of the statute, however, distinguished those "liable to appear and bear Arms" from the rest of the militia, implying that free blacks would work in an unarmed capacity, much like the 1738 Virginia militia statute, discussed in chapter 2.

While the law authorized the governor to "Arm and Array them," which suggests that the government was to provide weapons, a later section obligated "every person liable to appear and bear Arms at any Muster . . . shall constantly keep and bring with him, to such training, exercising or Muster, one good Gun, Bayonet, hanger, sword or hatchet" along with ammunition and cleaning tools. These items were "to be produced at Musters and at all other times retained in every Persons House . . . ." Officers were allowed to visit a militiaman's home "and to demand a sight of their Arms" with a £5 fine for failure to have these items at home, and a £10 fine for failure to be completely armed at a muster.[65]

In North Carolina and Virginia the evidence from official records shows that guns were common, although sometimes scarce in particular regions at particular times. The quantities of ammunition available for purchase from merchants in North Carolina at the start of the Revolution strongly suggest what the official documents tell us: Guns were common and widely used. In Georgia, Virginia, and North Carolina, militia statutes suggest that guns were, if not universally owned by free white men, at least commonly owned. In South Carolina there is little evidence, but what there is suggests that guns were common.

North Carolina, and to a lesser extent, Virginia, show evidence of widespread gunmaking during the Revolution, although not on the industrial scale of Maryland and Pennsylvania. Still, enough evidence exists to suggest that Revolutionary gun manufacturing was an expansion of a pre-Revolutionary tradition. In South Carolina, the evidence suggests that there was some gun manufacturing capability at the start of the Revolution.

Guns in the Continental Army & Revolutionary Militias

GUNS IN THE CONTINENTAL ARMY

Guns used by the Continental Army came in a bewildering array of calibers and types, reflecting the diversity of privately owned hunting weapons. Baron von Steuben (a German army officer whose noble title later turned out to be rather . . . creatively acquired), attempting to drill Continentals at Valley Forge in 1778, complained about the lack of uniformity of the firearms the soldiers carried: "[M]uskets, carbines, fowling pieces, and rifles were found in the same company."[1] The Continental Congress, a few months into the war ordered, "That all the Militia take proper care to acquire military skill, and be well prepared for defence by being each man provided with one pound of good gun powder, and four pounds of ball, *fitted to his gun*."[2] Each militiaman needed to supply ammunition specific to his gun, because large numbers were bringing their own guns, in non-standard calibers.

General George Washington complained that his forces had been at various times well armed, but that public arms had drifted away with the soldiers. "The scandalous Loss, waste, and private appropriation of Public Arms, during the last Campaign is beyond all conception." He asked the state governments to ask for an accounting of the public arms that had been issued to various regiments, but also made another request that shows that Washington, almost two years into the war, believed that there were still many privately owned firearms in America: "I beg you will not only do this, but purchase all, fit for the field, that can be procured from private persons, of which there must be a vast Number in the Government."[3]

How well armed—and how competent with their firearms—was the Continental Army? There are letters that suggest a shortage of guns, such as George Washington's 1777 letter to John D. Thompson: "I wish it was in my power to furnish every man with a firelock that is willing to use one, but that is so far from being the Case that I have scarcely sufficient for the Continental Troops." Later in that same letter, however, Washington indicated that there were many guns in private hands that, while not well-suited to military use, were certainly functional: "It is to be wished, that every Man could bring a good Musket and Bayonet into the field, but in times like the present, we must make the best shift we can, and I wou'd therefore advise you to exhort every Man to bring the best he has. A good fowling Piece will do execution in the hands of a Marksman."[4]

A 1778 letter from Washington complained, "I am as much at a loss as you can possibly be how to procure Arms for the Cavalry. . . . " But the rest of the sentence tells the rest of the story: "[T]here are 107 Carbines in Camp but no Swords or Pistols of any consequence. General Knox informs me, that the 1100 Carbines which came in to the Eastward and were said to be fit for Horsemen were only a lighter kind of Musket."[5] Other letters suggest that guns other than muskets were available on the private market. A letter from Washington to Elisha Sheldon directed him to raise a cavalry regiment, suggesting what type of horses he should purchase, and how he should pay for them. In the same way, Washington instructed Sheldon: "Saddles, Bridles, Carbines, Broadswords, Pistols and every other Accoutrement necessary (agreeable to a pattern herewith given you,) you will procure as cheap as possible." Nothing in the letter indicated that any of these items would be unusually difficult to obtain, nor is there any suggestion that Sheldon would have more difficulty purchasing firearms than saddles. Similarly, a 1780 letter from Washington to the War Board concerning two regiments of dragoons to be outfitted indicated that pistols were available: "There are pistols in the

Magazine, but the Horsemens swords must be made, as there are none proper for the purpose on hand, that I know of."[6]

One document records the number of firelocks and bayonets present in each regiment of "the Army in and near New-York, June 24, 1776." Of 9,088 (or perhaps 9,072—the columns do not agree) men, seventy-six percent are described as having "firelocks good," another fifteen percent have "firelocks bad," and nine percent are "wanting." It is unclear if firelocks described as "bad" are completely useless, unreliable, or perhaps of such a low caliber as to be better suited to bird hunting than combat. By comparison, fifty-seven percent have "bayonets good," one percent have "bayonets bad," and forty-two percent lacked bayonets.[7] Much like the militias of Massachusetts and North Carolina, Washington's army was better supplied with guns than bayonets. Guns were at times and in certain places, scarce; guns of the correct *type* were often scarce; and the Continental Army often had difficulty purchasing guns, but these are not necessarily evidence that guns were rare.

More typical is Washington's February 1776 complaint to the Continental Congress that the "Militia, contrary to an express requisition, are come, and coming in without ammunition; to supply them alone, with 24 Rounds, which is less by 3/5[ths] than the Regulars are served with, will take between fifty and 60 Barrels of Powder . . . ."[8] That Washington needed to supply the militia with ammunition suggests that many militiamen brought guns with them.

The Continental Congress reimbursed individuals for the loss of personally owned weapons: "[T]o Philip Melton, late a private in Captain Rippey's company of the 6th Pen[n]sylvania regiment, for a rifle-gun of his taken by the enemy, 13 60/90 dollars."[9] A 1780 letter from Washington also shows that some significant number of soldiers brought their own guns with them into service:

> There does not appear to me any reason, upon which the soldiers are intitled to, or can claim the Continental fire arms at the expiration of their times of service. The act of Assembly is very plain. *As an incouragement for men to bring their own arms into the army, it offers a certain bounty, and to such who do not, a lesser sum.* The difference which is given to the former, appears to have been designed as a compensation for the use of the arms; nor can any

construction whatsoever authorise the latter to carry off arms &c. the property of the Continent.[10]

The Continental Congress also reimbursed military officers for guns purchased for their units, of which there are a number of examples: "[T]o James Young, for 51 rifle and smooth-bore guns, 22 of which was delivered to Robert Towers and Samuel Appleton, 7 lost, and 22 delivered at Fort Washington, the sum of 571 25/90 dollars . . . ." Rifles brought into Continental Army service were privately owned and the Army, which needed those rifles very badly, sometimes bought them from soldiers who were unwilling to re-enlist: "Resolved, That General Washington be directed to order the riffles of such men belonging to the riffle regiments as will not re-inlist, to be purchased, and that the General order the payment out of the military chest."[11]

The Continental Congress disarmed Tories in March and June of 1776. A 14 March resolution directed compensating "disaffected persons" for arms taken for public use—demonstrating that even the guns of Tories were recognized as private property:

> Resolved, That it be recommended to the several assemblies, conventions, and councils or committees of safety of the United Colonies, immediately to cause all persons to be disarmed within their respective colonies, who are notoriously disaffected to the cause of America, or who have not associated, and shall refuse to associate, to defend, by arms, these United Colonies . . . ; and to apply the arms taken from such persons . . . in the first place to the arming the continental troops raised in said colony; in the next, to the arming such troops as are raised by the colony for its own defence, and the residue to be applied to the arming the associators; that the arms when taken be appraised by indifferent persons, and *such as are applied to the arming the continental troops, be paid for by Congress, and the residue by the respective assemblies, conventions, or councils, or committees of safety.*[12]

The Pennsylvania Assembly on 29 March 1776 debated a resolution implementing the Continental Congress' request. One of their concerns was that "many Fire-Arms may be taken which may not be fit for use" by either the Continental Army or Pennsylvania's troops. There were enough of such guns that the Pennsylvania government passed specific legislation describing what to do with them. The "disaffected persons" were to be paid only for the military arms; the others were to be stored "for the owners, to be delivered to them when the Congress shall direct." Later revisions of the resolution specified that the firearms to be involuntarily purchased from the disaffected were those "fit for the use of the Troops, or could be conveniently made so . . . ." While the "disaffected" were to be disarmed against their will, "well-affected Non-Associators" (those who were neutral) "possessed of good Arms" were encouraged—but not required—to sell their weapons to the government.[13]

The state laws disarming the "disaffected" tell us that gun ownership was a signifier of citizenship. Virginia required loyalty oaths of all citizens, with those refusing facing "the loss of weapons and the franchise, sacrificing as well all right to public office, jury duty, sue for debt, and purchase property."[14] Pennsylvania's 1777 Test Act similarly required all free white males to swear a loyalty oath, with those refusing prohibited from "serving on juries, suing for any debts, electing or being elected, buying, selling or transferring any lands, tenements or hereditaments, and shall be disarmed." The rationale was, "allegiance and protection are reciprocal, and those who will not bear the former are not nor ought not to be entitled to the benefits of the latter. . . . "[15] These lists included all the rights and responsibilities of citizenship, similar to how current US law prohibits firearms purchase by those who have renounced US citizenship.[16]

In June of 1776, the Continental Congress adopted Pennsylvania's policy for non-military weapons: arms unfit for the military were not compensated, because these weapons were not permanently confiscated, but were to be returned at a later time:

> Whereas in the execution of the resolve of Congress of the 14th of March, respecting the disarming disaffected persons, many fire arms may be taken, which may not be fit for use to arm any of the troops mentioned therein: Therefore, Resolved, That all the fire arms so taken, being appraised according to said resolve, none of them shall be paid for, but those that are fit for

the use of such troops, or that may conveniently be so made, and *the remainder shall be safely kept by the said assemblies, conventions, councils or committees of safety, for the owners, to be delivered to them when the Congress shall direct.*[17]

Much has been made of an order that Washington gave in 1777 ordering his officers to start carrying half-pikes. This was *not* because of a shortage of arms, but the different needs that officers had for arms compared to the men:

As the proper arming of the officers would add considerable strength to the army, and the officers themselves derive great confidence from being armed in time of action, the General orders every one of them to provide himself with a half-pike or spear, as soon as possible; firearms when made use of with drawing their attention too much from the men; and to be without either, has a very aukward and unofficerlike appearance.[18]

Firearms were available for officers; Washington's concern was that loading and firing a gun—neither a quick nor simple process in the flintlock era—distracted officers from leading their men. The use of pikes and other contact weapons was not confined to the Revolutionaries. At the start of the Revolution, British officers still carried swords or half-pikes, "and sergeants bore halberds . . . . The woody character of the country in America induced many of the officers to discard these awkward medieval weapons and to replace them with firelocks."[19]

Pennsylvania faced a somewhat similar problem, although in this case there is a suggestion of a gun shortage—at least a shortage of guns in the hands of the government. The use of the pike was suggested as a solution to the problem that "the Spirit of our People supplies more Men than we can furnish with Fire Arms, a deficiency which all the Industry of our ingenious Gunsmiths cannot suddenly supply. . . . " But a little later in the same paragraph, we see evidence that it was not *all* firearms that were in short supply but specifically muskets, because "Each Pikeman to have a cutting Sword, and where it can be procured, a Pistol."[20]

Officers on the frontier complained at times about shortages of firearms, such as a July 1779 letter from Colonel Archibald Lochry of Westmoreland County, Pennsylvania: "What few we still have are so out of repair that they are almost useless and it is out of my power to get them repaired [in] this quarter."[21] Yet oddly enough, there was at least one gunsmith working in Westmoreland County at the time, David Dickey, and no surviving evidence that Dickey was ever employed to resolve Lochry's problem.[22]

Instructions from the Continental Congress and letters from Washington suggest that such shortages were localized. In 1778, the Continental Congress discussed "the reward offered in March last to such drafts as should bring firelocks &c with them into the field" because the government owned too few "arms and accoutrements." They therefore increased the reward offered to the two new regiments "to be raised in Virginia and Pennsylvania, to induce them to come armed and accoutred . . . ." If the soldier brought "a good serviceable rifle, with a powder horn, bullet pouch, and mould, eight dollars; for a good serviceable musket, with a bayonet and a powder horn, and bullet pouch, or a good cartouch box, six dollars; for a like musket and accoutrements, without a bayonet, five dollars; for a knapsack, two dollars; for a haversack, one dollar; for a blanket, eight dollars."[23] Rifles and blankets were equally valuable on the frontier.

We have letters from Washington, late in the war, that suggest that while the Continental Army had no rifles, the civilian population was not similarly deficient. Washington wrote to Joseph Reed in June of 1781, requesting Reed's help in raising a unit of 300 riflemen in Pennsylvania. Washington expected these men to bring their own rifles:

> One of the terms should be that they are to find their own Rifles, as we have none in Store. I shall be glad to hear as soon as possible what probability there will be of succeeding in this undertaking. The greater part of the Men, must be with the Army by the 1st. of Augt. or their services will be useless afterwards.[24]

In a bit more than a month, Washington had a realistic hope that Reed would raise 300 men with their own rifles, and have them march off to join the Continental Army—and this was more than six years into the war.

Another set of combatants seemed to think that guns were common in early America—and certainly so on the frontier. At the encouragement of the British, Indians representing the Mohawks, Ottowas, Nantucas, Shawnees and Delawares traveled south to meet with the Cherokees in 1776. According to Henry Stuart, the British government's representative to the Cherokees, the Indian ambassadors described what they saw as they headed south: "[W]hen they attempted to pass through that Country from Pittsburgh to their Nation . . . they found the Country thickly inhabited and the people all in arms . . . ." The Indian ambassadors listed several forts that contained a total of 6,500 men, apparently armed, and other forts that they did not enumerate that they also believed were filled with armed men. It is possible that the Indians were falsely claiming that the Revolutionaries were well-armed as part of negotiating a better situation with respect to their coming into the war on the British side, but Isaac Thomas, a Loyalist present at the same conference, also claimed "that there were about six thousand men in Arms on the Frontiers of Virginia and North Carolina which were intended to have gone to oppose the King's Troops but they had determined to stay and oppose the Indians . . . ."[25]

During the Revolution, there were more than a few complaints about a shortage of muskets—but not necessarily a shortage of *guns*. Fowling pieces lacked the range and striking power of the musket. Rifles were popular for hunting; muskets were not. The strength of the rifle was its accuracy, which suited it to both hunting and sniper work, but rifles were slow to load, and muskets were a better choice for the massed fire that was the norm for large units. The Secretary of the Board of War, requesting that a rifle company from Maryland be armed with muskets instead, complained that there was "a superabundance of riflemen in the Army." They wanted fewer rifles, and more muskets, "as they are more easily kept in order, can be fired oftener and have the advantage of Bayonetts." A hundred men firing muskets could not be overrun as easily as a hundred men firing and then slowly reloading rifles.[26]

Even more interesting, from the standpoint of gun scarcity, is that the Secretary of the Board of War put more emphasis on *clothing* this rifle company before they came to Philadelphia than arming them: "They might be armed and accoutred, but might lie here a very considerable time before cloathes and blankets could be furnished."[27] Complaints about the inability to purchase clothes, blankets, and food appear in other colonies as well—demonstrating that scarcity for official purposes did not necessarily mean scarcity in civilian life.[28]

Rifles seem to have been common hunting weapons in some parts of America—more common than muskets, in spite of being more expensive. The disadvantage of the rifle for massed fire, however, meant that Americans were heavily armed, and yet not well-armed *for military duty*. Consider what would happen today if the government, using its authority under current federal law, called up the unorganized militia[29]—and asked Americans to muster with their own arms. Americans would show up with many small handguns, not very useful for anything but highly specialized missions. They would show up with lots of .22 rimfire rifles—only useful for training. Shotguns would be useful for guard duty and jungle warfare or certain types of urban combat, but not useful for the US Army's primary mission. Many hunters would show up with hunting rifles, in a bewildering array of calibers. Some of these hunting rifles might be useful for specialized military functions, such as sniping, but their slow reloading and the problem of ammunition resupply would make them difficult to integrate into a modern military. Two centuries from now, historians might read complaints of "not enough rifles" or "not enough military arms" and based on those complaints alone, conclude that there were few guns in America today—and be just as wrong as those who claim that there were few guns in America before the Revolution.

REVOLUTIONARY WAR MILITIA PERFORMANCE

While there were a few exceptions, Colonial militias performed disappointingly during the French & Indian War (1756–63)—partly because the American colonists did not perceive the need for this war with quite the same fervor as the British government. With the settlement of 1763, the French ceded Upper and Lower Canada to Britain, removing the French as a threat to the American colonies. The war had sufficiently reduced the number of Indians allied with the French that, except on the frontiers, Colonial militias lost much of their reason to exist. As conflict grew between the colonists and the British government, however, the militias found a new purpose. Instead of fighting Indians, foreign armies, and pirates, the new goal was to protect the liberties of the colonists.

How effective were militias in the American Revolution? How well did they follow orders? How courageous were they under fire? How competent were they with guns? The last of these questions has a rather obvious applicability to the question of how common gun ownership was in America at the start of the Revolution. It is also the question most readily subject to a quantifiable answer.

Contrary to the traditional view of American militiamen as crack shots, Bellesiles claims that contemporary accounts of American firearms prowess were simply mindless boasting, symptoms of a *rage militaire* that swept across America, deluding many Americans into believing that their countrymen were heavily armed marksmen. According to this point of view, the Americans at Lexington and Concord were not particularly skilled marksmen:

> Expert marksmanship requires training, good equipment, and a regular supply
> of ammunition for practice. These farmers rarely practiced, generally had no
> ammunition, and owned old muskets, not rifles, if they owned a gun at all.[30]

By contrast, the traditional view of historians, from the very beginning, emphasized the widespread competence of Colonial militias with guns. David Ramsay's 1789 *History of the American Revolution* observed, "For the defence of the colonies, the inhabitants had been, from their early years, enrolled in companies, and taught the use of arms," and that, "Europeans, from their being generally unacquainted with fire arms are less easily taught the use of them than Americans, who are from their youth familiar with these instruments of war . . . ."[31] Frothingham's *History of the Siege of Boston,* as another example, assumed a high quality of marksmanship among ordinary Americans:

> [A] martial spirit had been excited in the frequent trainings of the minute-
> men, while the habitual use of the fowling-piece made these raw militia supe-
> rior to veteran troops in aiming the musket.

Frothingham's account of the Battle of Bunker Hill emphasized the tremendous effectiveness of the militia in cutting down the advancing British soldiers:

Many were marksmen, intent on cutting down the British officers; and when one was in sight, they exclaimed, "There! See that officer!" "Let us have a shot at him!" – when two or three would fire at the same moment. They used the fence as a rest for their pieces, and the bullets were true to their message.

According to Frothingham, British journals explained the enormous loss of life at the Battle of Bunker Hill as evidence of both uncommon valor by British troops, and remarkable shooting by the Americans:

Attempts were made to account for the facts that so many of the British, and so few of the Americans, fell. One officer writes of the former, that the American rifles "were peculiarly adapted to take off the officers of a whole line as it marches to an attack." Another writes, "That every rifleman was attended by two men, one of each side of him, to load pieces for him, so that he had nothing to do but fire as fast as a piece was put into his hand; and this is the real cause of so many of our brave officers falling."[32]

Some of the claims about American marksmanship made just before the Revolution, it is true, show an astonishing bravado—or a carefully calculated propaganda campaign. The Continental Congress certainly believed (or claimed to believe) that the average American was intimately familiar with guns, and competent with them. In their 8 July 1775 address, "The Twelve United Colonies, by their Delegates in Congress, to the Inhabitants of Great Britain," declared "Should Victory declare in your Favour, yet Men trained to Arms from their Infancy, and animated by the Love of Liberty, will afford neither a cheap or easy Conquest."[33] This statement could well have been intended to discourage Britain from continuing the war.

Richard Henry Lee's February 1775 letter to his brother Arthur Lee is full of confidence about the ability of Virginia riflemen, quoting from a letter recently published in a Virginia newspaper. It claimed that the "County of Fincastle can furnish 1000 Rifle Men" that would make the "most formidable light Infantry in the World." Further, it claimed that every man could hit an object the size of an orange at 200 yards: "Every shot is fatal." Arthur Lee was an agent of the colonies in London, and dined with John Wilkes, London's sympathetic Lord Mayor.[34] It is possible that Richard Henry Lee intended for his brother to show the letter around, and provoke reluctance on the part of the British government to go to war against the colonies. Richard Henry Lee's letter would require *every* frontier rifleman to make shots of two and a half minutes of arc. This would not be difficult with a modern rifle, but it seems unlikely—especially in an era before telescopic sights—that this would be within the capabilities of *every* frontier rifleman. Lee's letter likely reported an exaggerated claim of the capability of the frontier riflemen—but an exaggeration sufficiently within the realm of possibility that it would unnerve British officials.

A letter that James Madison wrote on 19 June 1775 to William Bradford in Philadelphia presents a considerably more plausible claim about the skill of Virginians (including himself) with the rifle:

> The strength of this Colony will lie chiefly in the rifle-men of the Upland Counties, of whom we shall have great numbers. You would be astonished at the perfection this art is brought to. The most inexpert hands rec[k]on it an indifferent shot to miss the bigness of a man's face at the distance of 100 Yards. I am far from being among the best & should not often miss it on a fair trial at that distance. If we come into an engagement, I make no doubt but the officers of the enemy will fall at the distance before they get [within] 150 or 200 Yards. Indeed I believe we have men that would very often hit such a mark 250 Yds. Our greatest apprehensions proceed from the scarcity of powder but a little will go a great way with such as use rifles.[35]

Unlike Richard Henry Lee's letter, Madison's letter is far less expansive in its claims, and written to a fellow American who was in no position to influence British opinion. Madison's description required the average riflemen to shoot within five minutes of arc, and the very best able to hit targets within two minutes of arc—not implausible for that time. The 3 November 1775 *Virginia Gazette* reported that, "a rifle-man killed a man at the distance of 400 yards."[36] This is plausible, but probably news in the sense of "unusual."

Most of the shooting in the initial engagements would have been with muskets, because New Englanders did not make much use of rifles this early, but the frontier riflemen arrived by July of 1775. Frederick County, Maryland raised two companies of riflemen to join the army forming outside of Boston. An eyewitness account of Captain Michael Cresap's rifle company of "upwards of 130 men" described a demonstration

> to show the gentlemen of the town their dexterity at shooting. A clapboard, with a mark the size of a dollar, was put up; they began to fire off-hand, and the bystanders were surprised, so few shots being made that were not close to or in the paper.
>
> When they had shot for a time in this way, some lay on their backs, some of their breast or side, others ran twenty or thirty steps, and, firing, appeared to be equally certain of the mark. With this performance the company was more than satisfied, when a young man took up the board in his hand, not by the end, but by the side, and holding it up, his brother walked to the distance, and very coolly shot into the white; laying down his rifle, he took up the board, and, holding it as was held before, the second brother shot as the former had done.
>
> By this exercise I was more astonished than pleased. But will you believe me, when I tell you, that one of the men took the board, and placing it between his legs, stood with his back to the tree, while another drove the center?[37]

Other accounts of Cresap's company also report on their marksmanship:

> [W]e mention a fact which can be fully attested by several of the reputable persons who were eye-witnesses of it. Two brothers in the company took a piece of board five inches broad and seven inches long, with a bit of white paper, about the size of a dollar, nailed in the centre; and while one of them supported this board perpendicularly between his knees, the other, at the distance of upwards of sixty yards, and without any kind of rest, shot eight bullets through it successively, and spared a brother's thigh!
>
> Another of the company held a barrel stave perpendicularly in his hands with one edge close to his side, while one of his comrades, at the same distance,

and in the manner before mentioned, shot several bullets through it, without any apprehension of danger on either side.

The spectators appearing to be amazed at these feats, were told that there were upwards of fifty persons in the same company who could do the same thing; that there was not one who could not plug nineteen bullets out of twenty, as they termed it, within an inch of the head of a tenpenny nail. In short, to prove the confidence they possessed in their dexterity at these kind of arms, some of them proposed to stand with apples on their heads, while others at the same distance, undertook to shoot them off; but the people who saw the other experiments declined to be witnesses of this.[38]

These skills were not limited to inanimate targets, or wild game. When they reached the lines outside of Boston, they sniped British soldiers, contrary to Washington's orders, outraging the British, who called "their twisted guns the worst widow- and orphan-makers in the world." Similar actions at Quebec City—but this time operating under orders—provoked similar reactions.[39] Thatcher's military journal of August 1775, apparently referred to this same group of frontier riflemen:

They are remarkably stout and hardy men, . . . dressed in white frocks or rifle shirts, and round hats. These men are remarkable for the accuracy of their aim, striking a mark with great certainty at two hundred yards' distance. At a review, a company of them, while on a quick advance, fired their balls into objects of seven inches diameter at the distance of two hundred and fifty yards. They are now stationed on our lines, and their shot have frequently proved fatal to British officers and soldiers, . . . even at more than double the distance of common musket-shot.[40]

John Harrower recounted a no less astonishing account of how a rifle company commander in Virginia sought to identify the best marksmen out of an overflow crowd of volunteers. The colonel's solution was a shooting contest:

Col. Washington . . . made a demand of 500 Riflemen from the frontiers. But those that insisted on going far exceeded the number wanted when in order to

avoid giving offence, the commanding officer chose his company by the following method, viz. He took a board of a foot square and with chalk drew the
shape of a moderate nose in the center and nailed it up to a tree at 150 yards
distance and those who came nighest the mark with a single ball was to go. But
by the first 40 or 50 that fired the nose was all blown out of the board, and by
the time his company was [filled] up, the board shared the same fate.[41]

While not explicit that these riflemen brought their own guns, it seems
unlikely that they could demonstrate this level of skill with rifles with which
they were not intimately familiar. Yet it appears that the Continental Congress
reimbursed Frederick County $268.40 "for Rifles, &c., furnished Captain
Cresap's Company . . . ."[42] This price of slightly more than $2 per rifle and
"&c." seems more likely to be a rental fee for the use of privately owned rifles
and military "accoutrements" than a purchase price. If this *was* a purchase
price, however, it would suggest that rifles were *very* inexpensive.

British Army Major George Hanger, who held in contempt the accuracy
of the common soldier's musket, had a different opinion about America's
riflemen. He described being on horseback with Lieutenant Colonel
Banastre Tarleton, preparing an attack on the Americans. A rifleman 400
yards away fired at Hanger and Tarleton, who were less than two feet apart.
The shot killed the horse of the orderly standing between and just behind
Hanger and Tarleton.

Hanger became a prisoner of war at the Battle of Saratoga. The riflemen
told Hanger that, "an expert rifleman . . . can hit the head of a man at 200
yards. I am certain that provided an American rifleman was to get a perfect
aim at 300 yards at me standing still, he most undoubtedly would hit me,
unless it was a very windy day . . . ."[43]

The dominant military weapon of the eighteenth century, for both the
British Army, and for the American militias, was the musket. Muskets were
not rifled, so there was no rotation of the bullet as it left the barrel, and thus
no gyroscopic stabilization to improve the gun's accuracy. The fit between
bullet and barrel was relatively loose, so that muskets could be reloaded
rapidly—not a recipe for precision shooting. The reason was simple: The
dominant military doctrine of the eighteenth century emphasized massed

musket fire, not precision shooting. Mass firing was not because accuracy was impossible, but because the goal was for a group of infantrymen to fire many bullets at once—the machine gun approach in an era with only single shot technology.[44] While most British soldiers were trained to fire rapidly, not accurately, those assigned to duty as flankers, pickets, and rangers practiced marksmanship. Flankers would move alongside a column in thick terrain to provide protection for the main body of troops. Pickets performed a somewhat similar function when a body of troops was stationary. Rangers operated independently of the main body. All were somewhat specialized functions.

Unlike the British Army, which emphasized aimed fire for only specialized soldiers, the Continental Army "stressed Colonial experience in the value of aimed musket fire." Where the British Army initially deployed soldiers in America in three ranks, based on the importance of bayonet charges, Continental units were organized around the idea of marksmanship. It was a significant military innovation when the Continental Army replaced the manual of arms command "Present!" with "Take Sight!"[45]

George Washington's 1777 letter to John A. Washington described contacts between the Continental and British armies: "Our Scouts, and the Enemy's Foraging Parties, have frequent skirmishes; in which they always sustain the greatest loss in killed and Wounded, owing to our Superior skill in Fire arms. . . . " Washington believed in the marksmanship of American riflemen; his letter to Joseph Reed, requesting help in raising a unit of 300 riflemen in Pennsylvania, describes their mission as

> to fire into the embrazures and to drive the enemy from their parapets when our approaches are carried very near their Works . . . . General Lincoln informs me that the enemy made use of this mode at the Siege of Charlestown, and that his Batteries were in a manner silenced, untill he opposed the same kind of troops and made it as dangerous for the enemy to shew their Men as it had been before for him to expose his.[46]

British officers shared Washington's view of the firearms skills of the Americans. British Army officer Charles Stedman, who served under General

Howe, described why even able officers and brave men were unable to fight back effectively against the Minutemen:

> The people of the colonies are accustomed to the use of fire-arms from their earliest youth, and are, in general, good marksmen. Such men, placed in a house, behind a wall, or amongst trees, are capable of doing as much execution as regular soldiers: And to these advantages, which they possessed during the greatest part of the nineteenth of April, we may attribute the inconsiderable losses sustained by them, compared with that of our detachments.[47]

British Lieutenant Frederick Mackenzie, who was part of the expedition to Lexington and Concord, similarly seems to have been impressed with the skills of the militia:

> During this time the Rebels endeavored to gain our flanks, and crept into the covered ground on either side, and as close as they could in front, firing now and then in perfect security . . . . [N]umbers of armed men on foot and on horseback, were continually coming from all parts guided by the fire, and before the Column had advanced a mile on the road, were were fired at from all quarters . . . . As the Rebels encreased, and altho they did not shew themselves openly in a body in any part, except on the road in our rear, our men threw away their fire very inconsiderately, and without being certain of its effect . . . .
>
> During the whole of the march from Lexington the Rebels kept an incessant irregular fire from all points at the Column . . . . Our men had very few opportunities of getting good shots at the Rebels, as they hardly ever fired but under cover of a Stone wall, from behind a tree, or out of a house; and the moment they had fired they [went] down out of sight until they had loaded again, or the Column had passed.

Another officer's account, quoted at length by Mackenzie, gives a similar description, reporting that some of the rebels were on horseback. Leaving their horses at some little distance from the road, they crept down near enough to have a Shot; as soon as the Column had passed, they mounted again, and rode round until they got ahead of the Column, and found some convenient place from when they might fire again. These fellows were generally good marksmen, and many of them used long guns made for Duck-Shooting.[48]

It was certainly easier for the British to acknowledge that Americans were good shots than to admit the British side made serious tactical mistakes—but it is hard to imagine that British officers, who held the American militias in utter contempt before the war, gave them credit for better weapons or better shooting if there was not some truth to it. The evidence from eyewitness accounts seems clear enough: If every American militiaman was not a crack shot, he was certainly a good enough shot with his fowling-piece, musket, or rifle, to terrorize the finest army in Europe at the time. This level of competence did not come from a few weeks of training at the start of the Revolution, but from long experience using a gun.

Marksmanship alone is not enough to make a group of armed men into an army. An effective military unit must stand and fight when attacked. Until the twentieth century's dramatic expansion in military firepower, the greatest risk to a soldier was not if he confronted the enemy face to face, but if he turned tail and ran. The soldier that ran, instead of engaging in an orderly retreat, would be cut down by the enemy. For the individual, this willingness to stand and fight is courage; for the unit, it is discipline.[49] General Charles Lee's letter to George Washington of 1 July 1776, portrayed in a very favorable light the courage of militiamen fighting against the British in North Carolina:

The cool courage they displayed astonished and enraptured me; for I do assure you my dear General, I never experienced a better fire—twelve full hours it was continued without intermission. The noble fellows who were mortally wounded conjured their brethren never to abandon the standard of liberty. Those who lost their limbs deserted not their posts. Upon the whole, they acted like Romans in the third century.[50]

It is easy to point to examples of undisciplined militias that broke and ran when confronted by the sight of Redcoats making a bayonet charge, and conclude that the militias were a poor substitute for regular troops. Along with examples of both militia courage and cowardice, there are examples such as General Howe's landing at Kips Bay on Manhattan, where both Connecticut militias *and* Continental soldiers panicked and ran.

Militias were effective not only as reinforcements for the more disciplined Continental Army, but also in guerrilla, irregular, and low-intensity warfare against British forces. This is especially impressive considering that most of the Colonial militias had fallen into a state of disrepair by the 1770s. The coming conflict soon led New England towns to fill empty militia offices, purchase ammunition, and read freshly published books, such as Timothy Pickering's *Easy Plan of Discipline for a Militia* (1775). Militia muster days became the scene of serious drilling, instead of serious drinking. Militia members showed up with an interestingly diverse collection of arms, some dating back to Queen Anne's War (1702–1714)—but certainly deadly enough to make General Gage regret stirring up a hornet's nest at Lexington.[51]

The official British account of the events of 19 April 1775 suggest that the militia was well-armed and very effective at irregular warfare: "As soon as the troops had got out of the town of Concord, they received a heavy fire, from all sides, from walls, fences, houses, trees, barns, &c., which continued without intermission, till they met the first brigade with two field pieces . . . ."[52] British officers were convinced that at least 5,000 men were firing upon them as they retreated towards Boston.

Neither of the engagements at Lexington or Concord demonstrated spectacular competence by the American militia in face-to-face battle formations. The retreat of the British column *did* show what citizen-soldiers were good at—guerrilla warfare; firing from trees, walls, and houses while increasingly panicked Redcoats committed atrocities against non-combatants. Some British officers regarded the militia's expert use of cover as "cowardly," since it provided no chance for the Redcoats to return fire,[53] but General Gage's famous letter contrasted the behavior of American militia during the French & Indian War with their behavior at Lexington, Concord, and Bunker Hill: "These People Shew a Spirit and Conduct against us, they never shewed against the French. . . ."[54]

British officer Charles Stedman was certainly impressed with the abilities of American militias, not only at Lexington and Concord, but throughout the war. Stedman described a December 1775 battle in Norfolk, Virginia, in which American militia ambushed 120 British soldiers, killing or wounding 30 of the unit, including its captain. Similarly, Stedman described the great skill of a mixed force of Continentals and militia at Moore's Creek Bridge, North Carolina in June 1776. Again, British soldiers retreating from Ridgefield, Connecticut in April 1777 were subject to a series of attacks by small militia units. This continual low-level warfare exhausted the British soldiers, killing or wounding 200 soldiers and ten officers: "It may be reasonably doubted, whether the loss which the British sustained in this expedition, did not more than counterbalance the advantage derived from the complete attainment of their object."[55]

At Saratoga, militia played a crucial role in defeating General Burgoyne's march from Canada. Militia forces hastily recruited from Vermont and New Hampshire villages tricked, surrounded and destroyed German mercenary Lieutenant Colonel Frederick Baum's raiding party of 800 men, and then scattered and disrupted Lieutenant Colonel Heinrich von Breyman's 600 man rescue party. Throughout the lakes region, Burgoyne's forces found themselves surrounded and defeated by militiamen whose knowledge of local terrain and woodcraft far exceeded the professional soldiers. Burgoyne complained that, "Wherever the King's forces point, militia to the amount of three or four thousand assemble in twenty-four hours." Morgan's frontier riflemen and local militias soon intimidated Burgoyne's scouts, both European and Indian.

That militiamen fought well in irregular warfare, where parade ground drills were irrelevant, is not surprising. The skills of the hunter took precedence over a regiment's musket volleys, as long as the hunter kept his head down. Yet at the Battle of Bunker Hill, the militia improvised breastworks, and inflicted an enormous slaughter on a professional military. Only a shortage of ammunition caused the militia to leave the field that day—not a shortage of guns or a dearth of marksmanship. Nor was courage scarce; at least thirty Americans turned their muskets into clubs, dying of bayonet wounds rather than run. As British troops pursued the retreating militia, American snipers firing from abandoned houses harried and slowed the pursuers. The British suffered a forty-two per cent casualty rate—losses that a professional military 3,000 miles from home could ill afford. When a regular army was not available, the militia turned in a credible performance—and one that often left British forces deeply shaken.[56]

Militias, despite their many limitations, threw sand in the gears of British occupation. To the military historian John Shy, the greatest strength of the militia was as guerrilla bands. When General Charles Lee first proposed this use, Washington refused because it threatened to unleash "civil war with all its grisly attendants—ambush, reprisal, counter-reprisal." In the South, leaders such as Francis Marion did exactly that, and realized Washington's fears—and Lee's hopes.[57] Shy argues that one of the defining characteristics of the effectiveness of guerrilla warfare is persuasion of the population so that "old authority is displaced by revolutionary organization without the massive confrontations of conventional warfare or the *force majeure* of the *coup d'e-tat.*" In the first year of the conflict with Britain, this sense of community obligation meant that even before patriots had taken over existing governmental structures, volunteers were forming associations to enforce internal security, enforce boycotts against British goods, organize militias, and take steps against Loyalists. While slow to recognize the merits of this approach, the British Army eventually did likewise in the South, using Loyalists to exercise control over their own communities as a counterbalance to Patriot militias.[58]

Even without formal organization or encouragement, civilians often took the initiative. Perhaps in response to British and German abuses in 1776, New Jersey's civilians organized ambushes, leading one German officer to complain, "It is now very hard to travel in Jersey . . . ." Besides direct attacks, New Jersey militias seized over seven hundred oxen and thousands of sheep and hogs that the British Army had purchased for food.[59] British foraging parties in New Jersey found that both militiamen and irregulars were firing on them:

> While the British were loading their wagons, a single man began to fire on them from the woods. He was soon joined by more of his neighbors, who

could not patiently see their property carried away. After the foragers had been annoyed for some time by these unseen marksmen, they fancied on the appearance of General Dickenson, that they were attacked by a superior force, and began a precipitate flight.

The New Jersey militia, which had allowed British troops to pass through unmolested in 1777, soon grew tired of British depredations, and drove back the British Army: "for the Jersey militia, turned out in a very spirited manner, to oppose them .... The farmers, with arms in their hands, ran to the place of rendezvous from considerable distances."

Even engaged in the sort of battles at which militia should have been soundly routed by their more disciplined British Army opponents, the militia often performed quite effectively. Describing a battle near Burlington, New Hampshire, Ramsay wrote: "On this occasion about 800 undisciplined militia, without bayonets, or a single piece of artillery, attacked and routed 500 regular troops advantageously posted behind entrenchments—furnished with the best arms, and defended with two pieces of artillery." Similarly, 200 militia, of whom only nine were "regular soldiers," successfully drove off 200 British soldiers at Port-Royal, South Carolina in 1779. While Ramsay is clear that much of this advantage was "gained by two field pieces," even these cannon were operated by the Charleston artillery militia.[60]

At the Battle of Cowpens in South Carolina, Daniel Morgan demonstrated that properly employed, a mixed force of frontier riflemen, local militia, and Continental soldiers were capable of outstanding military performance. At the end of the day, British Lieutenant Colonel Banastre Tarleton had lost 812 men with 110 killed and 702 captured; Morgan's mixed force had twelve dead and sixty wounded. A few days later, Morgan's commander, Nathaniel Greene, made somewhat less effective use of a largely militia force to maul Cornwallis's forces at Guilford Courthouse. Don Higginbotham calls Cornwallis's victory at Guilford Courthouse "Pyrrhic," for his "army virtually ceased to exist as a fighting force." King's Mountain, a great victory late in the war, involved thousands of east Tennessee militia—without regular soldiers—who came up over the mountains, and demonstrated their proficiency at forest warfare. The British losses were 300 dead, and 700 prisoners; the militias who had come together only shortly before the battle, had only 90 casualties.

Even battles in which militia figured prominently, but that Washington lost, such as at Germantown, Pennsylvania, in 1777, demonstrated that militia, within their limitations, were a valuable addition to a regular army. The combined force of Continentals and militia gave up the field, and lost 1,000 men to British losses of 534—but Washington could replenish his militia far more easily than General Howe could obtain replacement soldiers. At the Battle of Long Island, where a combination of regulars and militia fought a losing battle, "the Americans were not so much outfought as they were outgeneraled." At the Battle of Pelham Bay, Glover's 750 Marblehead fishermen held off a 4,000-man British and German force for a whole day, causing 800 to 1,000 casualties, and saving Washington's retreating Continentals.

Along with courage and discipline under fire, another measure of the effectiveness of militias was if they showed up when called into service, and stayed in service even when there was no battle to fight. It is very easy to find stinging criticisms of these part-time soldiers on all these counts, at least partly because professional soldiers "dominated the writing of military history in the United States until recent years . . . ."[61] The professionals' disregard for amateurs is unsurprising, nor is this problem of professional contempt for amateurs limited to the occupation of soldiering. Military historians studying the American militia in the latter half of the twentieth century, however, have developed an increasing respect for the capabilities of America's Revolutionary citizen-soldiers. The American militia also earned the respect and fear of the professional soldiers against whom they fought.

George Washington was often frustrated with the reliability of the militias, as can be seen in a letter he wrote to the Continental Congress in December 1776:

> Militia may, possibly, do it for a little while; but in a little while also, the Militia
> of those States which have been frequently called upon will not turn out at all
> or with so much reluctance and sloth as to amount to the same thing. . . . Can
> any thing (the exigency of the case indeed may justify it), be more destructive

to the recruiting Service than giving 10 Dollars Bounty for Six Weeks Service of the Militia; who come in you cannot tell how, go, you cannot tell when; and act, you cannot tell where; consume your Provisions, exhaust your Stores, and leave you at last in a critical moment.[62]

Yet this same collection of militia, alongside the Continental Army, made possible Washington's nearly bloodless victory over the Hessians less than a week later. In a complex night crossing of the Delaware, Washington's 2,400 Continentals were supplemented by 3,000 Pennsylvania militiamen, as well as the Marblehead fisherman militia that ferried the troops across. This combined force of regulars and militia carried out a complex attack, killing 30 Hessians, and taking 918 prisoners—while suffering only three wounded, and no combat deaths.[63]

Along with Washington's stinging criticisms of the militia's reliability, it is also easy to find such statements as Washington's letter from Cambridge in December of 1775: "The Militia are coming fast, I am much pleased with the Alacrity which the good People of this province as well, as those of New Hampshire, have shewn upon this occasion . . . ." In June 1777, Washington again wrote: "The Militia turn out in a very spirited manner and seem determined, in conjunction with the Continental Troops, to harass and oppose the Enemy upon their march thro' the Country."[64]

Benedict Arnold's capture of Fort Ticonderoga and British warships on Lake Champlain was entirely the doing of New England militias and irregular forces such as Ethan Allen's Green Mountain Boys, showing initiative and courage. When Benedict Arnold, newly commissioned as a colonel in the Continental Army, marched north through the wilderness to besiege Quebec City (coming very close to success), he was leading entirely militia forces on one of the great military expeditions of the century. That one third of Arnold's force deserted on the orders of their immediate commander says less about the skill and discipline of the deserting militia unit, and more about their personal loyalty. The courage of the militias that stormed Quebec varied, with some retreating in a cowardly way—while others ran up to the gun ports out of which British soldiers were firing, and fired back.[65]

A regular army became necessary because the militia included an enormous age range, many of whom were not suited to the hardships of camp life. The development of a regular army was thus division of labor. Farmers and artisans returned to their fields and shops, while young men, often of the lowest rungs of the society, including indentured servants and slaves, became specialized in the demanding—and often lower paying—skills of the soldier.[66] By the end of the Revolution, the mixed performance of militias had given Washington and many of the other prominent men of the time a realistic understanding of the strengths and limitations of citizen-soldiers. They were not useless, but neither were they the equivalent of regular troops. They had one great virtue: There were many militiamen compared to the regular army that Washington commanded.

Militias provided local control when neither the American nor British armies were present, and were called out in emergencies, close to home, where their numbers made up for their lesser military skills.[67] It also seems likely that militias were more strongly motivated to protect families, friends, and homes in their own county or state, than for the still abstract notion of an American nation, or even more abstruse political ideologies. Wherever the Continental Army went, there was likely a militia that could make up in numbers and irregular fighting skills what they might lack in discipline.

The great flaw of militias was not only their localism, but also their short service. At times, this rapid evaporation of the militia can be explained as a collapse of morale, or even simple cowardice. Most often, economic necessity caused the departure of militiamen: "Within a week after the Battle of Long Island, the 8,000 Connecticut irregulars had dwindled to 2,000." This was at least partly because August and September were harvest season—and militiamen, overwhelmingly, were farmers. When the British Army overran New Jersey, unsurprisingly, militiamen ignored Washington's calls to arms, and devoted their energies to evacuating their families and possessions from the path of plundering enemy soldiers.[68]

Often enough, the Revolutionary War militias demonstrated their marksmanship and courage in fighting regular troops. Military historian John Shy—a careful and often critical chronicler of the militia's failings—echoes the view of many a British officer:

Poorly trained and badly led, often without bayonets, seldom comprised of the deadly marksmen dear to American legend, the Revolutionary militia was much more than a military joke. . . . The militia enforced law and maintained order wherever the British army did not, and its presence made the movement of smaller British formations dangerous. Washington never ceased complaining about his militia—about their undependability, their indiscipline, their cowardice under fire—but from the British viewpoint, rebel militia was one of the most troublesome and unpredictable elements in a confusing war. The militia nullified every British attempt to impose royal authority short of using massive armed force.[69]

David Ramsay's 1789 *History of the American Revolution* acknowledged that in spite of the Americans' superior knowledge of guns, the Colonials were *less* suited to military duty than Europeans since their independence of spirit made them less likely to take orders.[70] Often, it was believed, the democratic character of militias also meant a lack of consistent and stern discipline—a potential weakness. George Washington believed that militia officers who wished re-election, would be insufficiently strict in discipline.[71]

Another interpretation of popular election of officers, however, is that militiamen who had served under regular army officers during the French & Indian War had suffered brutal treatment and saw election of officers as a method of preventing abuse.[72] Steven Rosswurm argues that in the case of the Philadelphia militia, this indiscipline was because of fierce opposition by radicals to unfairness in the militia system, which allowed wealthier members of Philadelphia society to shirk their responsibilities.[73]

Even worse than the popularity-focused militia officers, as far as Washington was concerned, were the wild frontiersmen, such as Michael Cresap's Maryland riflemen. They not only broke the rules of gentlemanly warfare—to the dismay of their British targets—but refused to obey the rules of the camp, once they arrived at Washington's siege of Boston in 1775,[74] looting Loyalists along the way, and not above robbing their fellow soldiers on occasion.[75]

The democratic nature of the militia was one reason that while militias were not an adequate replacement for a standing army, Americans retained a confidence in the merits of the militia disproportionate to their skill. There were several reasons for this, both economic and political. From an economic standpoint, the militia was very attractive, consuming no wages in peacetime, but this was not the strongest argument for this system. As we will see in later chapters, many Americans, as well as foreigners visiting the United States, cherished the militia ideal. This often romantic view of the militia's virtue was not because of their actual military skill, but because they were not regarded as a threat to the liberties of the people.

For decades, Whig political theory had regarded standing armies as dangerous to political liberty. The American experience with the British Army quartered in the colonies after the French & Indian War did nothing to change their perception of the Redcoats "placed in their midst by a corrupt ministry to enforce unpopular laws and subvert Colonial liberties." The militia, by comparison, were not hirelings, but one's fellow citizens, an expression of the virtue of the yeomen of America, consistent with Whig theories of political structure in vogue among Revolutionary Americans. As Brigadier General Richard Montgomery complained about his New England militia units during the invasion of Canada, "The privates are all generals" who "carry the spirit of freedom into the field, and think for themselves."[76] Thomas Aubrey, a British officer taken prisoner of war, described his amazement at watching how three "peasants" dealt with Colonel Thomas Randolph. When Aubrey expressed amazement at their lack of deference, Randolph explained that, "every one who bore arms, esteemed himself upon a footing with his neighbour, and concluded with saying, 'No doubt, each of these men conceives himself, in every respect, my equal.'" Guns were the great equalizers of social status.[77]

British General Burgoyne, two months after the Battle of Bunker Hill, expressed the opposite form of this, arguing that, "I believe in most states of the world . . . that respect, and control, and subordination of the government . . . depend in a great measure upon the idea that trained troops are invincible against any numbers or any position of undisciplined rabble; and this idea was a little in suspense since the 19th of April."[78] The Battles of Lexington and Concord were thus the beginning of the end of the notion that the masses served the government, not the other way around.

In a society where community obligations had not yet been atomized by the rise of individualism, serving in the militia was like serving on a jury, or on night watch: a sign of one's duty, responsibility, and membership in the polity—and the right of privates to think of themselves as equals to generals. All being armed in defense of the community, all deserved an equal voice—and thus the gun was a symbol of one's duties and rights.

Part III

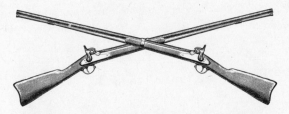

The Early Republic

From the end of the Revolution in 1783 to the Mexican War of 1846 is often described as the early Republic. In a period of sixty-three years, America transformed itself. In 1783, it was thirteen former colonies bound together by a national government so weak that more than a few Europeans (and even some Americans) wondered how long it might be before we returned to the British fold. In 1846, it was a confident, even arrogant power growing rapidly across the continent, first by purchase, and then by conquest from Mexico.

Militias in the Early Republic

While most Americans appear to have owned guns for personal use, during the early Republic militia laws also required most white men to own guns. These militia laws provide some insights into the attitudes of the Framers of our Constitution concerning gun ownership. Estimates of gun ownership in the early Republic, and evidence of gun ownership and hunting, suggest that while gun ownership was not universal, as the militia laws required, firearms were certainly very common.

The Georgia militia law of 1784 (passed the year after the Treaty of Paris formally ended the Revolutionary War) suggests that guns were widely distributed. Unlike the earlier 1778 law, which included slaves in the militia, the 1784 Georgia militia was restricted to "the Male free Inhabitants of this State" from 16 to 50 years of age. The statute still distinguished between those required to bear arms and those who were not (probably thus excluding free blacks). Like the Colonial militia statutes, the 1784 Georgia militia law required "those liable" to appear "completely armed and furnished with one rifle musket, fowling-piece or fusee fit for action" along with ammunition. Militiamen could be fined five shillings for failure to be armed at a general muster, or two shillings, six pence at an ordinary muster. The statute seemed to treat indentured servants as not free—but then obligated masters to arm their indentured servants as required for "every Male free inhabitant . . . ."[1]

Secretary of War Knox's 1790 militia proposal (not passed into law) required the federal government to arm militiamen, at least those ages 18 to 45.[2] After considerable wrangling, the next Congress passed a simpler militia law—one so simple that in some eyes, it "murdered" the militia system, and made a standing army inevitable.[3] This federal law obligated every able-bodied free white male between 18 and 45 to enroll in the militia. Among its simplifications, instead of the government arming the militia, militiamen were obligated to arm themselves:

> That every citizen so enrolled and notified, shall within six months thereafter, provide himself with a good musket or firelock, a sufficient bayonet and belt, two spare flints, and a knapsack, a pouch with a box therein to contain not less than twenty-four cartridges, suited to the bore of his musket or firelock: or with a good rifle, knapsack, shot-pouch and powder-horn, twenty balls suited to the bore of his rifle, and a quarter of a pound of powder . . . .[4]

Much like the Colonial militia laws, Congress required militiamen to provide their own guns. Congress assumed that every man either already owned a "good musket or firelock," or could obtain one.

Enforcement of the 1792 Militia Act soon led to the discovery that while many militiamen had guns, they were the wrong type. In December of 1794, Secretary of War Knox complained that the law had failed to specify a fine for failing to be properly armed. Fortunately, several states passed their own militia statutes, most providing penalties for militiamen failing to arm themselves. Still, Knox pointed out that out of 450,000 men subject to militia duty under the new law, "probably not one hundred thousand are armed as the act requires, although a greater number might be found of common and ordinary muskets without bayonets." This would indicate that less than 100,000 had military muskets, and more than 100,000 had some other type of musket. This suggests that close to half of the adult white male population possessed a musket.[5] Rifles, not then considered an appropriate militia weapon because of their slowness in reloading, and the lack of a bayonet lug, do not seem to have been considered proper militia arms by Secretary Knox. It is impossible to determine how many fowling pieces, rifles, and handguns the militia possessed in 1794, but because fowling pieces and rifles were more useful for hunting, it seems likely that these were present in similar or greater numbers than muskets.

Other evidence of an indirect nature appears in a May 1798 debate about expansion of the standing army. One proposal was to accept independent volunteer militia units into the standing army—a position that some Republicans regarded with concern, because such units would be "rich, zealous Federalists . . . under Presidential command—a praetorian guard siphoning off the best young men from the militia . . . ."[6] Federalist Representative Harrison G. Otis's argument against this fear assumed that arms were, if not universally, at least widely distributed. Being armed was not a defining difference based on either wealth or party affiliation: "Does not the militia . . . consist of citizens who arm themselves? It certainly does; therefore no proof of wealth results from this, for every soldier in the militia is as much a man of wealth as a volunteer of the corps proposed to be raised."[7]

The 1803 Militia Act, using slightly different language from the 1792 Militia Act, *could* be interpreted to mean that the government was to provide guns to militiamen, "That every citizen duly enrolled in the militia, shall be constantly provided with arms, accoutrements, and ammunition. . . . "[8] However an 1806 Congressional committee report was explicit that the individual militiaman "is put under obligations to provide himself with a good musket or rifle."[9] A Massachusetts prosecution for failure to "be constantly provided" under the 1803 Militia Act echoes this: The 1803 Militia Act was in addition to the 1792 Militia Act (not a replacement for it), and the individual militiaman was still obligated to provide *himself* with these arms and accoutrements, even in peacetime.[10]

On several occasions in the first two decades of the nineteenth century, the Secretary of War requested "militia returns," or a count of enrolled militiamen, and how well armed they were,[11] apparently to see what the actual military strength of the United States was. These militia returns turn out to be far less useful for measuring gun ownership than they might at first appear. As an example, consider the 1803 "Return of the Militia." The letter from Secretary of War Dearborn to the state and territorial governors asked them to provide information "stating the military strength of each State, the actual situation of the arms, accoutrements, and ammunition of the several corps, with the same, and every other thing which may relate to their government, and the general advantage of good order and military discipline." These militia returns tell us nothing about how many arms there were, other than those in the hands of the enrolled militia.

We can be quite sure that the guns listed in the 1803 Return of the Militia did not include any weapons owned by the federal government, and fairly confident that the guns so listed were not a comprehensive count of guns in the United States. The 1810 and 1811 Returns of the Militia are quite similar in form and method to the 1803 Return. The 1811 inventory of federal military stores is clearly *not* included in the totals contained in the 1810 or 1811 militia returns. This implies that a "Return of the Militia" included no federal arms at all.

Nor do the supporting letters or explanatory notes of the 1803, 1810, or 1811 Returns tell how many of the arms listed were privately owned, or that all privately owned guns were included in this count.[12] The firearms listed in these returns only include "pairs of pistols," muskets, and rifles. The categories suggest that this inventory included only military arms, and did not include privately owned arms that would be inappropriate for militia use, such as fowling pieces and pocket pistols.

President Jefferson's cover note to Congress on the Militia Return of 1803 apologized for its "incompleteness." Delaware, Maryland, and Tennessee filed no report, and many states that did report clearly provided incomplete data. For example, only five states reported possession of any "Tumbrils [two wheeled carts] and Wagons." Only New York and the District of Columbia reported any "Drums and Fifes"—yet every reporting state and territory except North Carolina and Indiana Territory reported "Drummers and Fifers" or "Musicians," totaling in the thousands. The counts of muskets and rifles (223,318), compared to the total of "Riflemen, Rank and File" and "Infantry, Privates" (436,735) show that at least 51 per cent of those soldiers had either a rifle or musket available to them. It is unclear which guns were included in this report, but it is interesting that the number of rifles (40,248) far exceeds the number of "Riflemen, Rank and File." Even adding in various officers of the Riflemen leaves far more rifles than riflemen shooting them.[13]

There is also an 1806 Congressional committee estimate of guns in the hands *of the militia* that has also been misread as a count of *all guns in America*, both publicly and privately owned: "a congressional committee estimated that there were 250,000 guns in America."[14] This report, however, was quite explicit that the laws of the United States required every "citizen enrolled in the militia" to "provide himself with a good musket or rifle . . . . From the best estimates which the committee has been able to form, there is upwards of 250,000 fire arms and rifles in the hands of the militia, which have, a few instances excepted, been provided by, and are the property of, the individuals who hold them."[15] Thus, there were *at least* 250,000 guns in the hands of the militia alone—and nearly all of them were privately owned. (By comparison, there were 640,000 white men of militia age in the United States at the time.[16])

The 1806 Congressional committee report also gave a count of the number of guns in the federal magazines: 132,000, of which 120,000 were "fit for use" and 12,000 "which need repairs." A count of guns in the United States would add the "upwards of 250,000" privately owned militia guns to the 132,000 guns in federal magazines, and guns in the state magazines—and the 1806 report is explicit that guns in state magazines were not counted. Guns in the hands of non-militia members would also need to be added. Depending on how one interprets the congressional committee report, it is possible that there were many firearms owned by militia members that were not considered to be military weapons, and thus not included in this estimate of "upwards of 250,000 fire arms and rifles . . . ." The most that we can conclude from the 1806 Congressional committee report is that there were *at least* 382,000 guns in the United States, and the actual number was likely much higher.

Congressional debates the next year, give reason to suspect that the population was actually well armed. Some Congressmen believed that the federal government should take it upon itself to arm the entire militia, by purchasing and providing muskets to the states. To arm the entire militia of 640,000 men would require an additional 300,000 firearms. Representative Chandler pointed to the 1806 report, and concluded that there were at least 364,000 guns in federal arsenals and in the hands of the militias, claiming, "probably at this time there was a much larger number." Chandler also argued that there was little reason to assume that the entire militia would be called out at once.

During that same debate, Representative Thomas explained that the question of whether the militia needed to be armed was not a question of whether there were enough *guns* (such as fowling-pieces, pistols, and rifles), but enough *muskets*: "It was true that there was a great deficiency of muskets in the militia of the United States, but it was also true that a great portion of them had now in their hands useful, serviceable, and efficient firelocks, and other implements of war." There were, Thomas acknowledged, some militiamen "unable to provide themselves with arms," but he contended that, "all persons who were able should provide their own arms."[17]

It is very easy to misread isolated statements by public officials of the period concerning shortages of guns for the militia and read these as a general shortage of guns.[18] When territorial governors complained about shortages, their complaints were about "battalions armed with a 'mixture of rifles, fowling pieces, broken muskets and sticks.'" However, these shortages were problems of the frontier, isolated from the manufacturing centers of the United States.[19] More careful reading suggests that what frontier militias lacked were firearms appropriate to militia duty. In some cases, the early Republic's shortages reflected not a general scarcity of guns, but a disagreement as to who should purchase militia arms: the federal government, the state governments, or the individual militiamen. Southerners seem to have been most desirous that the federal government purchase arms for the militia, on the grounds that poor men could ill afford them.[20]

An examination of both personal and official papers suggests that guns were *sometimes* in short supply on the frontiers—and then, only some types of guns. One example comes from W.C.C. Claiborne, governor of Mississippi Territory 1801–1803, and of Orleans Territory starting in 1812. Claiborne at one point observed that his efforts to organize the Mississippi militia had met "many obstacles . . . the greatest of which are the want of arms and the means of obtaining a supply." Yet, within a few months, Claiborne wrote to the Secretary of War, "The prospect of organizing the militia is flattering: the different Counties are laid off into regiments, battalions and company Districts: the officers are all appointed, and the men enrolled: a great degree of rivalry exists between the different corps: and I flatter myself that in a little time I shall have a well-armed and well disciplined militia." Later in the week, Claiborne finished his letter, "In the course of this week, I have reviewed the militia of Jefferson and Adams Counties; and can assure you that the prospect of having a well-armed militia, exceeds my most sanguine expectations."

The shortage of militia arms that Governor Claiborne complained about seems to have been a short-lived problem, and not a chronic difficulty. Governor Claiborne reported, "I received, the other day, sixty stands of muskets from Fort Adams. They have been heretofore used, and are not in good order: I propose therefore to sell them at the moderate sum of eight dollars apiece. At this reduced price I expect the militia will speedily purchase them. But I find the people here are much prejudiced against muskets, and are unwilling to depend on any other arms but rifles." Shortly thereafter, "You will discover that many of the privates are yet unarmed, but I flatter myself, this Inconvenience will soon be remedied—the Rifles (which were sent to me) are in high Estimation among the Militia, and the probability is, they will all be sold, upon the conditions, I have prescribed . . . ." Those conditions included a certificate from the militia captain that "Every Citizen applying for a Rifle" "is regularly inrolled on his Company, and in want of Arms," and that the applicant must pay $14 for it. "Upon those conditions I suppose the Rifles will speedily be disposed of to the Militia . . . . As to the Muskets, they are in no demand among the Citizen Soldiers, and I cannot persuade them of their utility . . . ." Instead, Governor Claiborne planned to store the muskets in a warehouse. If the militia was insufficiently armed, this was not because of a shortage of firearms, but a desire by the militia for rifles, not muskets. *Rifles* were scarce in Mississippi Territory that year, but not necessarily *guns*.

Claiborne sometimes expressed concern about the militia system, but not because he was skeptical of the *idea* of the militia, but rather of specific defects in the militia law of Mississippi Territory: "The exertions of the Officers to organize and discipline the Militia, have been accompanied with great success, and authorize a hope that *this best resource*, of a free people, will shortly become an efficient means of defence. Experience, however, has proven, that our militia laws are still defective." Claiborne later asked the Mississippi Territorial Legislature to correct the territory's militia laws.[21]

At the end of the Revolution, Americans were of two minds about the militias. Especially to those who had been officers in the Continental Army, militias were inferior to regular troops. Militias were less trained because they were only part-time soldiers. They were less reliable in following orders, because they were civilians, and regarded themselves as subject to civilian laws, not the harsh military codes of the eighteenth century. Militiamen were generally less physically fit, because of the range of their ages, and because in peacetime they trained for militia duty only a few days a year. Especially on the frontier, the threat of Indian attack—encouraged by British forces in Canada—seemed to argue for a standing army. Because frontier territories belonged to the federal government, not the individual states, a federal solution, not state militias, seemed an appropriate answer. Militias were limited to a defensive role in a vast wilderness where few Americans yet lived.[22]

Proponents of the militia system argued that militiamen were pragmatically superior to regular troops in three important ways. First, they were cheap. When not in actual service, they cost the government nothing.[23] They were required to arm themselves, and even though Colonial militias by the time of the Revolution were often partially armed with government weapons when called into service, it was rare for the entire militia to be called into duty at once. If there was ever an occasion where the entire militia needed to be called up, guns were already in the hands of most of the free white men who composed the militia. The government only needed to arm the very poorest men.

Secondly, militias were superior because of the vast numbers of soldiers that they could put into the field. The militia of the United States at the end of the Revolution amounted to hundreds of thousands of men. Whatever deficiencies they had in training and skill, they could certainly defeat any body of regular troops that might be thrown against them in America.

Thirdly, the militia was widely distributed throughout the United States; no matter where an invading army might land, the local militias would far outnumber the attackers—an experience that the Revolution repeatedly validated. In practice, where slavery persisted, the militia provided an adequate military force to deal with slave rebellions, as happened on occasion in the early Republic.[24]

Not everyone agreed that a professional army enjoyed superior military skills over a militia. During debate on reduction of the standing army in January of 1800, Representative Macon argued that the advantages a regular army had over militias in discipline and training were not of the greatest importance: "[T]he knowledge of the use of a gun was universal; he had never seen an American who could not shoot, and that was the principal use of a gun . . . . There could not be a doubt but if the young men were got together they would be soldiers immediately, for, understanding the use of arms, they would easily be disciplined."[25] This was a naïve view of the military profession, but one that demonstrates how Macon viewed the relationship between Americans and guns.

How seriously did the advocates of a strong militia take its supposed practical advantages over a standing army? It is hard to tell at this point. Two different philosophies of citizenship were present after the Revolution. One, sometimes called civic republicanism, stressed the individual's duty to the state. Individuals enjoyed certain freedoms, but these freedoms were dependent on the preservation of a state that protected these freedoms.[26] Whether the militia system was the best solution for the defense of the state, to civic republicans there could be no serious argument that it was part of community responsibility and duty.

The other emerging philosophy was liberalism, which stressed that individual rights took precedence over duty to the community. While not usually taken to extremes in that era, liberalism was more sympathetic to the individual's desire to look out for his own interests. In wartime, militia duty interfered with the pursuit of individual goals. Even in peacetime, however, militia musters, and keeping a firearm better suited to militia duty than hunting, were seen as obstacles to the primary goal of most Americans: getting ahead.

Richard Kohn argues that Federalists regarded the militia as worthless, and sought to destroy it by a failure to properly organize it, thus requiring the formation of a standing army. Kohn points to Federalists, such as Gouverneur Morris, who held that view. Kohn however admits that "no one will ever be certain about the framers' intent because few men in America, no matter what their private, innermost thoughts on the subject, dared advocate a permanent, exclusive reliance on a standing army for defense." Kohn argues that this reluctance makes "any definitive statement impossible" concerning Federalist opposition to reliance on the militia for defense. At the same time, Kohn points out that President Washington waited the maximum period of time to sign the law "probably to register his disgust with such a weak measure . . . ." It is just as plausible to explain the weak militia created by the 1792 Militia Act as a response to the emerging liberalism of the period.

There were certainly elected officials and militia officers in the first decades of the Republic who denigrated the value of the militia system. General St. Clair complained that in his combined force of regulars, militia, and drafts (short-term soldiers recruited from the states, but under regular army discipline), the militia was the least useful, running at the first serious fight, terrified by the sound of the Indian war whoop.[27] If, however, as Kohn argues, Federalists sought a standing army for reasons other than military necessity, such criticisms of the performance of the militia must be examined with a more critical eye.

Morally, the militia system was very gratifying. In a militia system, the free white men of the country all bore an equal responsibility for its defense. As Representative Randolph observed in a speech before Congress in 1800, standing armies were not only "useless and enormous expense," but contrary to the spirit of the Constitution: "A people who mean to continue free must be prepared to meet danger in person; not to rely upon the fallacious protection of mercenary armies."[28]

The most important virtue of the militia was its political reliability. This was sufficiently important that even proponents of a standing army acknowledged that the primary defense of a nation must be the militia. George Washington, still commanding the Continental Army in May 1783, proposed a post-war military system to the Continental Congress that consisted of 2,631 regular troops, but primary reliance on the militia:

> Altho' a *large* standing Army in time of Peace hath ever been considered dangerous to the liberties of a Country, yet a few Troops, under certain circumstances, are not only safe, but indispensably necessary. Fortunately for us our relative situation requires but few . . . .
>
> But, if our danger from those powers was more imminent, yet we are too

poor to maintain a standing Army adequate to our defence, and was our Country more populous and rich, still it could not be done without great oppression of the people.

In spite of his sometimes negative remarks during the Revolution about relying upon the militia, Washington referred to it as "this great Bulwark of our Liberties and independence . . . ." Washington's proposal also demonstrated that he saw the militia duty no differently than it had existed (at least in theory) before the Revolution:

It may be laid down as a primary position, and the basis of our system, that every Citizen who enjoys the protection of a free Government, owes not only a proportion of his property, but even of his personal services to the defence of it, and consequently that the Citizens of America (with a few legal and official exceptions) from 18 to 50 Years of Age should be borne on the Militia Rolls, provided with uniform Arms, and so far accustomed to the use of them, that the Total strength of the Country might be called forth at a Short Notice on any very interesting Emergency . . . .

Washington intended that militiamen keep the "uniform Arms" at home, it appears, because he proposed, "They ought to be regularly Mustered and trained, and to have their Arms and Accoutrements inspected at certain appointed times, not less than once or twice in the course of every [year] . . . ."[29]

Within a few weeks of Washington's report, the Continental Congress experienced the dangers of a standing army outside their meeting hall. Pennsylvania's regular army, liberally reinforced with "spirituous drink," surrounded the Continental Congress, demanding their pay. The Pennsylvania government, fearful of the upcoming elections, refused to call out the militia to drive its soldiers off—and so Congress moved to Princeton, having learned that the problem of regular soldiers making demands on the government was not theoretical, nor limited to Europe.[30]

Even strong advocates of a standing army, such as Henry Knox, Washington's Secretary of War, either believed that standing armies were a necessary evil, or knew better than to argue against the militia system. Washington submitted

Knox's proposal for "Organization of the Militia" to Congress in 1790, and its language is very clear:

> An energetic national militia is to be regarded as the *capital security* of a free republic, and not a standing army, forming a distinct class in the community.
>
> It is the introduction and diffusion of vice, and corruption of manners, into the mass of the people, that renders a standing army necessary. It is when public spirit is despised, and avarice, indolence, and effeminacy of manners predominate, and prevent the establishment of institutions which would elevate the minds of the youth in the paths of virtue and honor, that a standing army is formed and riveted for ever . . . .
>
> If it should be decided to reject a standing army for the military branch of the government of the United States, as possessing too fierce an aspect, and being hostile to the principles of liberty, it will follow that a well constituted militia ought to be established. [emphasis in original]

The report went on to argue that either the entire population must be educated and disciplined in the military arts, "by the means of rotation" or "the militia must be formed of substitutes, after the manner of the militia of Great Britain." The report held out the most astonishing hopes for the effects of all young men serving in the militia, and the results if this did not happen:

> A glorious national spirit will be introduced, with its extensive train of political consequences. The youth will imbibe a love of their country; reverence and obedience to its laws; courage and elevation of mind; openness and liberality of character; accompanied by a just spirit of honor; in addition to which their bodies will acquire a robustness, greatly conducive to their personal happiness, as well as the defence of their country . . . .
>
> But the second principle, a militia of substitutes, is pregnant, in a degree, with the mischiefs of a standing army; as it is highly probable the substitutes from time to time will be nearly the same men, and the most idle and worthless part of the community. Wealthy families, proud of distinctions which riches may confer, will prevent their sons from serving in the militia

of substitutes; the plan will degenerate into habitual contempt; a standing army will be introduced, and the liberties of the people subjected to all the contingencies of events.[31]

This hope for a universal militia that would protect the liberties of the people had examples in the early Republic. Several rebellions after the Revolution had, at least in part, provoked calling the Philadelphia Convention of 1787 that drew up the new Constitution. Shays' Rebellion in western Massachusetts is well known; less known is another rebellion in 1786 that briefly took over the New Hampshire legislative chambers.[32] The Whiskey Rebellion in western Pennsylvania in 1794, after the new Constitution was in effect, had similar popular roots. In all three cases, military force was brought to bear on the rebels. The relatively merciful punishment of the rebels suggests that the rebel concerns were sufficiently widely shared to deserve a soft answer. As with the American Revolution, these rebels used the rhetoric and mechanism of militia for the purpose of popular revolution.[33]

When ratification of the Constitution and the Bill of Rights became an all-consuming political debate in the years 1787 to 1791, many Antifederalists stressed the dangers of a standing army under the command of a President.[34] Standing armies were "engines of despotism" because they would certainly have primary loyalty to their commander. They were a "nursery of vice" because soldiers without a war to fight were well known to amuse themselves in gambling and wenching.[35] Based on the Colonial experience of British regulars—as well as the manner in which Colonial expeditionary forces had recruited the bottom of the social ladder—many Americans believed that the lowest members of the society would make up the enlisted ranks. Federalists sought to reassure those concerned about the danger of a man on a white horse leading a professional army, by pointing to the continued operation of the militia as one of those balancing forces. In "Federalist 46", James Madison pointed to the enormous numerical advantage that "a militia amounting to near half a million of citizens with arms in their hands" would have over any imaginable standing army.[36]

Within a few years of the new federal government starting operations, partisan divisions hardened into the first political parties. On the question of militias vs. standing armies, the emerging Republican Party was strongly on the side of the militia, with Federalists skeptical that militias were a substitute for a standing army—although party affiliation was not the only basis for how politicians stood. Although Federalists were *generally* supportive of a standing army, and Republicans *generally* opposed, regional differences often mattered more than party affiliation. Those Republican Congressmen who represented frontier districts often supported the new government's standing army because until 1798, that army was entirely aimed at the Indians. While a standing army was a theoretical threat to the liberties of the people, Indian conflict with frontiersmen was much more immediate and real.

At the same time, even Federalists who supported a standing army recognized that the frontier's need for it was because of white encroachments on Indian lands and the resulting hostilities. Critics of the regular army also believed that frontier militias would be better suited to fighting Indians, simply because they knew the terrain and were less burdened with baggage and artillery.[37]

As the political divisions within the new nation grew, and the prospect of war with France increased in 1797, Federalist support for a larger standing army (and not just on the frontier) increased. Federalists and Republicans had become increasingly distrustful of each other, with Republicans convinced that Federalists were more loyal to Britain than to America, and Federalists convinced that Republicans would fight on the French side if war broke out.[38] Richard Kohn argues that, "Hamilton and other Federalists who favored an army in 1797" did so because of concern about internal revolt— and not primarily slave revolt. Congressional Federalists in 1798 argued for an expanded standing army on these grounds. Federalist Representative Harrison G. Otis expressed his concern that the United States might see a change in government: "an exchange of a free for a despotic system of Government" with only a standing army as a barrier preventing this.

Republicans in 1798 saw the standing army as an instrument of political oppression. Representative Albert Gallatin observed that proponents of this enlarged standing army "speak not only of the danger of an invasion, but of the danger of a revolution—of an oversetting of the Government. . . . " Gallatin suggested that the enlarged standing army would be used in response to "fictitious conspiracies, pop-gun plots, and every other party artifice which has been practiced in England." Representative Joseph McDowell argued that the army proposed would "answer the like purposes to which a similar force had been raised in England and Ireland. And what have they been used for there but to suppress political opinion? The military force is there riding over the people, and dragging husbands and fathers from their wives and children to prison, merely because they have taken the liberty to think."[39]

When the threat of French invasion receded, Republicans demanded demobilization, while Federalists ridiculed the popular fear of a standing army. Representative Harrison G. Otis argued that if the new regiments needed to be eliminated, so must the regiments that formed the frontier force: "This alarm relative to standing armies has been at least rung a thousand times a year since the first British army was landed in this country . . . ." Otis acknowledged "the importance of the great national resource, the militia" but argued "militia in itself is calculated only for sudden emergencies. They will fight bravely while they continue in the field. They will resist an invading army, but they will not endure a series of campaigns."[40]

In spite of this clear Republican mistrust of a standing army, by 1801, the notion of keeping a standing army, while still controversial, seems to have been more broadly accepted—or perhaps Republicans were no longer afraid of a government that they now controlled. In that year, the First Inaugural Address of Thomas Jefferson, a Republican with long skepticism of standing armies, acknowledged the value of a "well-disciplined militia, our best reliance in peace and for the first moments of war till regulars may relieve them . . . ."[41] Jefferson seems to have accepted what had been the Federalist position: that militias performed a vital function in national defense, yet they were no substitute for a professional military.

The militia system never worked as envisioned by its proponents, and the universally armed militia did not materialize. By the time of the Civil War, the militia system had substantially declined in the United States. To the extent that the Southern states preserved it at all, it was because it was intertwined with the slave patrol system, for which a pressing need remained apparent.[42] The evidence suggests, however, that a majority (sometimes a bare majority) of militiamen owned at least one gun appropriate to militia duty, and gun ownership by white males was, if not universal, at least extremely common. The militia as the best defense of a free state was, almost from the beginning, a dream, but a potent dream—and gun ownership was part of that dream.

11

Ammunition in the Early Republic

Industrial gunpowder production in America did not start until the Revolution, although there seems to have been considerable domestic manufacture in the Colonial period. In Maryland, large-scale production began to satisfy the Revolutionary government's needs, although it appears that much of this production ended with the Revolution, then resumed around 1790, with gunpowder mills constructed near Baltimore. The scale of production—and the hazards of making gunpowder—is demonstrated by Maryland mill explosions in 1792, 1812, 1817, 1818, 1820, 1821, 1824, 1830, and 1833.[1] Victor Du Pont's production of gunpowder in Delaware started in 1804, and by 1806 he was advertising in New York, boasting of his product's superiority "to any Dutch or English imported . . . ."[2]

Gilbert's examination of post-Revolutionary gunpowder manufacturing mentions an incident that both illustrates how common guns were, and the hazards of unregulated manufacturing in urban areas: "An earlier explosion occurred on October 17, 1783, in the yard of a Mrs. Clement in Baltimore, where some gunpowder had been placed to dry. Three boys, two of them Negroes, went into the yard to clean their pistols. One of them carelessly fired his pistol near the powder, causing it to blow up. One boy was killed and the other two seriously injured."[3] Unsurprisingly (although perhaps because of more immediately proximate accidents) in 1797, Baltimore required gunpowder storage in public magazines.[4] It is unclear if this requirement applied

> ## Riflemen, Attention !
> # GUNPOWDER
> ### OF THE FIRST QUALITY,
> Warranted Superior to any Dutch or English imported,
> *MANUFACTURED BY*
> ### E. I. DUPONT DE NEMOURS & Co.
> *On the Brandywine in the State of Delaware.*
>
> ANY further comment to recommend the said Powder is deemed unnecessary, as its excellence is so well established by the repeated trials made of the same in several places, and especially in New-York, by order of Governor Lewis, against the best imported Gunpowder, which it was always found to surpass in point of *strength, quickness and cleanness.* To every true American it must be a satisfactory prospect to see some of the home manufactures already superior to those of the old world.
>
> Large or small quantities of the different kinds of the said Gun Powder to be had at any time, on reasonable terms, by applying to the subscriber, who will keep a constant supply of the same.
>
> Proper allowance will be made to store keepers, and a powder proof shall be found at his house for the convenience of those who may wish to have the said powder tried against any other.
>
> *Angelica Allegany county, state of*
> *New York, November 1, 1806.*   **V. DUPONT.**
>
> WILMINGTON, Printed by JANES WILSON, Market Street.

to all quantities of gunpowder or only quantities above a certain size. New Brunswick, New Jersey's 1813 ordinance regulating storage of gunpowder applied only to quantities of fifty pounds or more.[5] Boston's 1821 ordinance licensed possession of more than five pounds of gunpowder within the city. Wholesalers and retailers were regulated as to the quantities, storage methods, and public notice, but quantities under five pounds were exempt from all regulation.[6] At least one additional gunpowder licensing law from 1833 has left its mark in the form of a blank license.[7]

Another Boston storage regulation, from 1786, suggests that gun ownership was common in this period. This ordinance prohibited keeping loaded "fire-arms, or any bomb, granade, or other shell . . . in any house, outhouse, barn, stable, store, ware-house, shop, or other building . . . ." Other sections apply this to "cannon, swivels, mortars" and other military ordinances. Saul

Cornell has pointed to this law as evidence that there was no individual right to keep and bear arms at the time: "This is a law that effectively makes it illegal in the city of Boston to have a loaded firearm. To have a loaded firearm in the city of Boston in the 1780s is against the law. The founding fathers were willing to ban loaded guns in the city of Boston."[8]

A careful reading of the statute, however, reveals that its purpose was not a general ban on loaded guns in Boston, but leaving them unattended: "Whereas the depositing of loaded arms in the houses of the town of Boston, is dangerous to the lives of those who are disposed to exert themselves when a fire happens to break out in the said town . . . ."[9] The statute did not prohibit *carrying* loaded firearms within the city of Boston—only taking them into a building. Unloading a flintlock firearm (except by firing it) was a tedious task, and it is easy to see why the city felt that it was appropriate to require guns not be kept loaded and unattended. That Boston felt the need for such a law, however, suggests that gun ownership was also common, as was having loaded firearms in one's home or business. Fires were more common than today, but if only 10% of homes had a gun, and only 10 percent of those homes had a *loaded* gun, the intersection of houses on fire and houses containing loaded guns in them would have been very small. The law also clearly considered the possession of firearms, cannon, and grenades to be unremarkable, and the carrying of loaded firearms a sufficiently common practice as to need regulation—but not completely prohibited, and not prohibited while walking the streets of Boston.

Gunpowder production figures also indicate that guns were common in the early Republic. Fortescue Cuming's description of 1807 Lexington, Kentucky, lists six gunpowder mills "that make about twenty thousand pounds of powder yearly."[10] Ten years later, Henry Bradshaw Fearon's *Sketches of America* describes gunpowder mills in the same area that made £9,000 worth of goods annually. US exports of gunpowder for 1817 were worth $356,522, equivalent to perhaps thirty times that today.[11]

While the gunpowder manufacturing data in the 1810 census appears to be *more* complete than the firearms manufacturing data from that same report, it is clearly incomplete. Of the seventeen states, fourteen contained at least one commercial maker of gunpowder. Of the five territories and the District of Columbia, two reported gunpowder mills. There were at least 208 gunpowder mills in the US. Even with these incomplete results, the US manufactured at least 1,397,111 pounds of gunpowder in 1810. Connecticut and East Tennessee reported a value of gunpowder production, but not a weight.[12] If we assume that gunpowder cost about the same to produce in Connecticut and East Tennessee, as in adjoining New York and West Tennessee, this would add 161,953 pounds to the total.

Du Pont began manufacturing gunpowder in 1804, and complete production records exist from 1804 through 1815, showing quantities sold to the US government, as well as quantities sold through agents and to "others." Du Pont's 1810 production of gunpowder was 176,027 pounds, or no more than 13 percent of total reported United States gunpowder manufacturing, and only 55,000 pounds of that went to the US government (including the Indian Department).[13]

It would be tempting to use these figures to calculate private gun use, but this is a hazardous venture for a number of reasons. One problem is that sales to agents and "others" (whatever Du Pont meant by that) would almost certainly have included some sales to the state governments (and perhaps even foreign sales). State governments provided gunpowder for cannons, as well as for militia musters. Until more evidence becomes available, it is impossible to make anything but a guess as to how much of the gunpowder produced was intended for civilian, non-militia purposes.

A second problem is that Americans used gunpowder not only for small arms and cannon, but also for blasting: "Gunpowder was ubiquitous in the early republic, widely consumed and retailed, and crucial to subsequent industrial change .... Gunpowder production, then, was not unusual or esoteric. It was a central component of early American commerce, industry, and trade—an important way for individuals to pursue happiness and fortune."[14] Coarse-grained gunpowder was better suited to cannon than to small arms.[15] Unfortunately, there is nothing in the 1810 census data or Du Pont's production records that identifies for which weapons the gunpowder was manufactured, or to distinguish that intended for firearms from that used for demolition. The following graph shows Du Pont gunpowder production for 1804–1815:

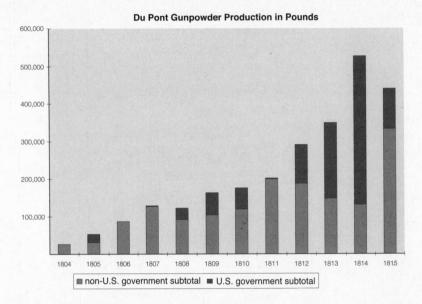

Du Pont Gunpowder Production in Pounds

■ non-U.S. government subtotal ■ U.S. government subtotal

From the available data, it seems impossible to make any authoritative statements distinguishing military from civilian consumption of gunpowder in the period 1800–1840, but during the American Revolution, 2,349,210 pounds of gunpowder were consumed (of which 2/3rds was imported), or about 335,000 pounds of gunpowder per year.[16] Per capita US production of gunpowder in 1810 was at least comparable to per capita US military consumption during the American Revolution. Du Pont gunpowder production for non-US government customers in the years 1807–1811 averaged more than 130,000 pounds a year.[17] At a minimum, the burden of proof is on those who argue against widespread gun use during this period to explain this astonishing gunpowder production (and presumably consumption) in peacetime.

Americans also imported gunpowder during at least part of the early Republic period, because there are occasional advertisements, such as ran in an 1821 Cleveland newspaper for "Best Eng[lish] Powder."[18] Gunpowder dealers and associated businesses appear in city directories, suggesting that gunpowder was a sufficiently common consumer good for retail specialization. Samuel Hastings, for example, appears in the 1800, 1803, and 1805 Boston directories as "dealer in powder."[19] Charles Munns in an 1815 Pittsburgh directory described himself as a "salt-petre refiner"[20]—saltpeter being an essential component of gunpowder. Circa 1819, E. Copeland, Jr. of

Boston advertised "Dupont's Superior Gunpowder . . . For Sale at 65 Broad-Street" with various grades for muskets and rifles.[21]

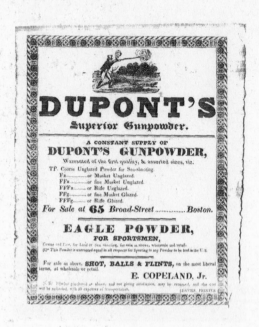

In addition to gunpowder production, we have scattered evidence that shows that Americans manufactured shot—although the reported data is very incomplete, with the 1810 manufacturing census showing data for only Pennsylvania, Virginia, and Louisiana Territory. For Virginia, the census tells us only the value of its production: $2,040. Louisiana Territory had two manufacturers, but the 1810 census gives us no weight or value of their production. The scale of production in Pennsylvania, however, shows that someone was buying a lot of lead shot: Pennsylvania had at least six manufacturers, and they made at least 575 *tons* of it in 1810.[22]

Shot manufacturing appears in other years. Perry Williamson, for example, appears in an 1814 Baltimore business directory as a shot manufacturer.[23] Bernhard, Duke of Saxe-Weimar Eisenach, visiting America in 1825 and 1826, described a tower in Philadelphia and another near St. Louis for the manufacturing of lead shot.[24] In the years 1827–30, Illinois was a major producer of lead—smelting more than 38,000,000 pounds (although much of this may have been for uses other than ammunition). Shot towers were present in

Missouri, which were associated with the extraction and refining of lead, whereby molten lead was dropped through the air to form round shot: "Many shot towers have been erected on the high bluffs along the Mississippi . . . where large quantities of shot are manufactured."[25] Because the military used bullets, not shot, this is evidence of manufacture for hunting—not for military or militia purposes.

Gunpowder production figures, without some detail as to how it was used, do not provide enough information to make anything but wild guesses about the number of guns owned by Americans, or how often those guns were fired. However, those production numbers fit well with the picture painted by many travel accounts of the early Republic in the remaining chapters: that most Americans owned guns, and hunting was a common pastime.

Pistols in the Early Republic

Part of why this book exists is that Michael Bellesiles' revisionist history argues that in the early Republic few Americans hunted, and hunting until the 1840s was done almost entirely by a small number of professional market hunters (those hunting meat or fur for sale). Most Americans, even on the frontier, according to this astonishing claim, did not hunt until the mid-1830s, when a small number of wealthy Americans chose to ape their upper class British counterparts. An even more amazing claim is that until 1848, when Samuel Colt mass marketed the revolver, violence between whites was somewhat unusual, and murder was rare. As evidence for these two related claims, Bellesiles asserts that, "an examination of eighty travel accounts written in America from 1750 to 1860 indicate that the travelers did not notice that they were surrounded by guns and violence."[1]

The remaining chapters of this book use eyewitness accounts of the early Republic to demonstrate the exact opposite of Bellesiles' claims—and include more than a dozen of Bellesiles' "eighty travel accounts." (Indeed, of the first thirteen of the travel accounts that Bellesiles cites as evidence that I checked, all thirteen contradicted him.) In the following chapters, where Bellesiles cited a travel account as evidence that "travelers did not notice that they were surrounded by guns and violence," and the source directly contradicts his claim, I have bolded the first reference in each chapter.

Bellesiles also claims that "Few pistols had been made in the United States prior to the opening of the [Colt] Hartford factory [in 1848], pistols having found little market beyond the officers in the army and navy."[2] As we saw in previous chapters, this claim about "little market" among civilians is demonstrably false for the Colonial period. The evidence is even more clear-cut for the early Republic. Much like the Colonial period, and America today, pistols appear to have been less common than long guns in the early Republic—but certainly not unusual. In modern America, handguns are disproportionately used in criminal violence (as well as in self-defense), and the situation in the early Republic does not appear dramatically different. This chapter examines the evidence from advertising, travel accounts, memoirs, newspaper accounts, and other scattered documentary evidence.

Pistols appear repeatedly in advertising of the period, in many cities, usually as a sideline of manufacturers or merchants engaged in the general firearms trade—and always treated as common or ordinary. Perkin & Coutty of Philadelphia advertised in 1781 that they made firearms "where Gentlemen may be supplied with Guns and Pistols of the neatest and best quality, on the shortest notice . . . ."[3] John Nicholson, gunsmith, offered a variety of firearms for sale in November of 1781, including "Pistols . . . upon the most reasonable terms."[4] Edward Pole advertised his "Military Laboratory"; among the items for sale were "Musket's and pistol's." That Pole's customers included civilians is suggested by the offering of "Musket cartridges in blank, for the exercise of the militia."[5]

In 1785, Anthony Desverneys, Jr., of South Carolina advertised that he "continues to make and repair all sorts of guns, Pistols and generally everything that belongs to the Gunsmith's Business."[6] Francis Brooks in 1791 Philadelphia advertised himself as a "Pistol Maker."[7] John Miles' 1798 advertisement in the *Pennsylvania Packet* made it clear that there was a civilian market for pistols: "Gun and Pistol Manufactory . . . Where Merchants, Captains of vessels, and others may be supplied with all sorts of small arms, on the lowest terms and shortest notice."[8]

Aaron Hart, in 1812 Pittsburgh, advertised his ability to furnish "Rifles, Fowling pieces, and Pistols, equal in goodness and workmanship to any

Military Laboratory,

At No. 34, Dock Street, near the Drawbridge,

PHILADELPHIA: *1789*

Where Owners and Commanders of ARMED VESSELS may be supplied, for either the use of Small Arms or Cannon, at the shortest notice, with every species of

MILITARY STORES.

VIZ.

Rammers, sponges, worms and ladles, with or without spring worms, ready covered, of all sizes, of superior quality

Copper gun ladles and double worms for every bore

Gunner's handspikes, plain or shod, and crowbars

Windlass and capstern handspikes

Best saltpetre and common match rope

Cannon priming horns, with screw bottoms

Cannon priming wires, bitts and augers

Lint-stocks, port-fire and false-fire stocks

Boarding pikes ready fitted, cutlasses and poll-axes

Musket's and pistol's

Musket and pistol balls and cartridges, with or without buck shot, either empty or filled

Musket cartridges in blank, for the exercise of the militia

Round, grape, canister, partridge, star, sliding gunter and langridge shot, either loose or quilted

Stools and bags for langridge and grape shot, of all sizes

Shot, cartridge and wad, formers & guages

Cannon cartridges, ready made to every bore

Cannon, musket cartridge and log book paper

Gun aprons, either lead or canvass

Cannon and musket cartridge boxes of every size

Tompions and port tangles

Sheep-skins for sponges, ready dressed

Musket, cannon and pistol powder & flints

Cannon provers, tryers, searchers and relievers, to discover any defect in the bore

Magazine, side, battle, poop, tin and other lanthorns, with directions how to fix the magazine lanthorn to prevent accidents

Hand cuffs and leg shackles

Port fire, slow fire, quick match, flambeaux, stink pots, fire balls, carcases, and composition for signals for convoys made up, of every description, & every species of fire work prepared at the shortest notice

Fuzes, tubes and powder chests, with full instructions for fitting them for close quarters to prevent being boarded

Sky rockets and colors of every description for signals; also fire arrows

Military drums and fifes, either plain or ornamented with United States or other arms

Hand grenadoes, filled and fused

Conductors for howitzers and carronades that are chambered

Copper and other powder measures

Musket, pistol, and cannon cartridge formes for every bore

Budge barrels, ready fitted

Flannel cartridges, fixed with either round, grape or canister shot

Marlin, sewing and whipping twine

Masters of vessels may have their cartridges filled

Gunners' spiking mallets and spiking irons

Wad, hooks and arm chests, &c. &c.

The above articles are prepared by a person who followed the business, and had full experience during the whole of the American revolution.

Any commander of an armed vessel, by leaving of his indent or order a few days previous to his sailing, may be completely furnished, with the above and many other articles without further trouble to himself.

Cannon, swivels, howitzers and carronades bought and sold on commission.

Powder proved for any person desirous of knowing its strength or quality.

Ships Colours, and Signals, of every species made at the shortest notice.

Ready money will be given for lead and military stores of every kind.

Cannon proved at a few days notice, for any person not acquainted with the business, by one who is fully experienced in that line, and had great practice both for private merchants and the public during the late American war.

Printed by R. AITKEN, No. 22, Market Street.

Edward Pole

made in the state."[9] Isaac King advertised in the 8 January 1818 *Somerset* [Pennsylvania] *Whig* that he was opening a business, and, "He has and expects to have on hand, for sale, GUNS of all descriptions, Pistols . . . ."[10] A letter of 9 November 1807 from Benjamin Prescott, Superintendent of the Springfield Armory to Secretary of War Henry Dearborn provides some indirect evidence that pistol manufacturing was not confined to just one region of the United States. In that letter, Prescott responds to Dearborn's request for pistols: "I believe Pistols and horsemens Swords can be made here as advantageously as in any other part of the country and I think I may venture to say better . . . ."[11] Along with advertising for sales, pistols are occasionally mentioned as items stolen from private parties.[12]

While Americans had *usually* imported pistols in the Colonial period, American-made pistols appear in much larger numbers after the Revolution, including a surviving pair made by J. Resor, who was among a small number of gunsmiths known to have made a large quantity of pistols in the period around the War of 1812. (Most gunsmiths who made pistols seem to have made only small quantities, perhaps because the demand was smaller than for muskets and fowling-pieces.) Other surviving pistols of American manufacture include one apparently made by Nicholas Hawk of Stroudsburg, Pennsylvania, and another made by John Armstrong of Bedford County, Pennsylvania. The lock on the Armstrong pistol appears to be Armstrong's work, based on his signature on it. A pistol from after the War of 1812 has also survived, believed to be the work of one of the Angstadt family of gunsmiths of Pennsylvania, using an imported lock.[13]

These pistols were apparently for military officers, but there are other surviving pistols of the early Republic that appear to have been made for civilians, including dueling pistols. Lindsay shows a number of these survivors from the first few decades of the nineteenth century, unmistakably American-made, by makers such as Silas Allen, Asa Waters, and Simeon North. While some have English-made gunlocks, the Asa Waters pistol is signed by Waters on the lockplate, suggesting that Waters made the gunlock, along with the rest of the pistol.[14]

James Haslett, who made muskets for Virginia government contracts, also made pistols and sold imported pistols in Baltimore at least as early

as 1806. He advertised in the 12 November 1806 *Federal Gazette & Baltimore Daily Advertiser* that he offered dueling pistols for sale, some made by him, and others that were imported from London. His pistols were of very high quality, and his customers included the governors of both Maryland and Virginia.

Gun dealers such as Halbach & Sons sold imported pistols, a number of which have survived from the period 1824–1833 with gunlocks stamped "McKim and Brother Baltimore." As was common at the time, some gunlocks imported from Britain were stamped with the American importer's name. These gunlocks were made into pistols for the civilian market after arrival in America.[15] Francis D. Poyas advertised his services as a gunsmith in 1825 Charleston, South Carolina—but Poyas did more than repair guns. The Charleston Museum has a pair of percussion lock pistols stamped with Poyas' name on the frame. It seems likely that they were his manufacture, and they were not government contract pistols.[16]

A list of debts owed to the estate of James Ross, a Steubenville, Ohio, gunsmith who died in 1816, showed that along with outstanding debts for repairs of guns, and apparently for purchases of long guns, he was also owed $45 by John Miller for a "pair of pistols."[17] S.E. Dyke's *Thoughts on the American Flintlock Pistol* shows ninety-one surviving flintlock pistols that are unquestionably of American manufacture in the period before 1840—and these are not government contract pistols of known patterns.[18]

J. Bolton and J. McNaught advertised in 1816 Richmond that they were recently arrived from England, and that their services included "All kinds of GUNS and PISTOLS made, altered and repaired in a perfect manner . . . ." The inventory of James McNaught's estate in 1826 showed a "pair of dueling pistols . . . 6 pair small dirk pistols . . . 2 pair best round stock pistols with flints . . . 2 pair percussion pistols, plain secret triggers . . . 3 pair rifle barrel pistols . . . 5 pair secret trigger pistols . . . ."[19] It seems a good assumption that these were unsold inventory, and the description of the pistols suggests that they were for civilian use.

Jacob S. Baker's "Rifle Manufactory" advertised in Whitely's *Philadelphia Directory of 1820* that "All orders for Rifles, Pistols, Fowling Pieces and Muskets, will be punctually attended to . . . ."[20] A Cleveland, Ohio, gunsmith in 1823 advertised that "Rifles, Fowling pieces, and Pistols will be furnished on short notice." While the ad is ambiguous as to whether this gunsmith made all of these items, or simply sold and repaired them, it is clear that he sold pistols, and considered that there was enough demand to justify advertising them for sale.[21] Similarly, Francis Areis advertised in 1831 that his firm were "Manufacturers and Repairer of all kinds of Fire Arms; Pistols, Guns, Swords, Gunlocks."[22] This can be read as either manufacturing or repair of pistols; either way, it appears that there was either enough demand for pistols, or enough pistols in need of repair, that Areis considered this ad worth running.

The Henry family of gunsmiths made pistols—in large quantities. Some were for military contracts, but many others are clearly pocket pistols, intended for the civilian market.

Business directories contain ads that show merchants believed that there was sufficient market for pistols to be worth advertising. In Louisville, Kentucky, Fletcher & Reeves advertised in an 1837 business directory, "Dealers in Watches, Jewellery, Silver Ware, Military Goods, Pistols,

ABRAHAM HENRY
LANCASTER, PA
CIRCA 1790 - 1811
62 CALIBER FLINTLOCK PISTOL
THIS BEAUTIFULLY MADE PISTOL WAS
PRODUCED IN LANCASTER, PA. BY WILLIAM
HENRY II's YOUNGER BROTHER ABRAHAM
HENRY APPRENTICED UNDER HIS OLDER
BROTHER IN NAZARETH UNTIL 1785. HE
THEN RETURNED TO LANCASTER WHERE
HE SET UP A SMALL GUN SHOP. THIS
PISTOL FEATURES A BRASS BARREL AND A
ORIGINAL BRASS FLINTLOCK WITH A
STEEL FRIZZEN. IT IS SIGNED AND
ENGRAVED "A. HENRY" INSIDE A SCROLL
BENEATH THE PAN. IT ALSO FEATURES A
DELICATE BRASS SKELETAL SIDE PLATE.
ABRAHAM HENRY PISTOLS ARE VERY RARE
AS HE WORKED ONLY 21 YEARS DURING
WHICH TIME HE PRODUCED MOSTLY
RIFLES AND MUSKETS IN HIS SMALL SHOP.

JAMES HENRY & SON
BOULTON, PA
CIRCA 1840-60
DERINGER TYPE PERCUSSION
POCKET PISTOL.
THIS IS A 40 CALIBER PISTOL HAVING A
PHILADELPHIA DERINGER STYLE BACK-
ACTION PERCUSSION LOCK. THE BARREL
APPEARS TO BE A CAST-STEEL OCTAGON
TO ROUND BARREL LEFT OVER FROM
THE HENRY'S 1836 1839 UNDER-HAMMER
PISTOL PRODUCTION. IT IS BEAUTIFULLY
STOCKED IN WALNUT. THIS PISTOL
IS MARKED " HENRY " ON THE
TOP BARREL FLAT.
THIS IS THE ONLY KNOWN HENRY
PRODUCED DERINGER STYLE PISTOL.
38

23

PISTOLS IN THE EARLY REPUBLIC

Surveyor's Compasses, Piano Fortes, Music, &c." In St. Louis that same year, Meade & Adriance described themselves as "Importers and wholesale dealers in . . . Guns, Pistols, Cutlery, Military and Fancy Goods, generally. . . ."[24]

Henry A. Cargill, a Nashville merchant, advertised for almost two months on the front page of the Nashville *Daily Republican Banner* "Guns, Pistols, Bowie Knives. A large and splendid assortment of the above articles . . . ."[25] A few months later, A.W. Spies advertised in every issue of the *New York Morning Herald* for several weeks: "Hardware, Cutlery, Guns and Pistols . . . . 500 Guns, 300 Rifles, 2,000 pair Pistols/Gun and sporting implements of every kind/Gun materials for Gunsmiths . . . ."

In the same paper, on many of the same days, S. M. Pike was advertising, "Particular Notice to Sportsmen—A choice assortment of fine double and single barrel guns, rifles and pistols . . . ."[26] A B. Ferguson of Huntsville, Alabama, advertised in May of 1837 that he was a "Gun and Locksmith," offering repairs and adding, "I also have on hand some Guns and Pistols for sale, and also a variety of gun and pistol locks . . . ."[27]

Travel accounts from the early Republic also show that pistols were common. **Isaac Weld's account of travels between 1795 and 1797 discussed how** in the backcountry, "The people all travel on horseback, with pistols and swords . . . ."[28] Pim Fordham, while staying at Princeton, Indiana, in 1817–18, reported that, "Yesterday 8 men on foot armed with pistols and rifles came into the town from Harmony. They had been in pursuit of an absconded debtor from Vincennes." It was no problem to persuade eight men armed with pistols and rifles to pursue a mere debtor, and Fordham found nothing surprising about them being so armed. Fordham described an associate judge as carrying "a pair of pistols at his saddle bow; and altogether [he] looks more like a Dragoon Officer in plain clothes, than a Judge." The pistols themselves were not remarkable; what was remarkable, at least to a transplanted Englishman, was that a *judge* was carrying them.

Fordham also described a party in the Illinois Territory that had excluded some "vulgar" party-crashers. Some of Fordham's party "armed themselves with Dirks (poignards [daggers] worn under the clothes)" to resist another such attempt, but later, "In going away some of the gentlemen were insulted by the rabble, but the rumour that they were armed with dirks and pistols prevented serious mischief." While the antecedent of "they were armed" is unclear, that it prevented serious mischief by "the rabble" suggests that members of Fordham's party were the ones armed; pistols were weapons commonly enough carried to be a realistic deterrent to "the rabble." According to Fordham (and many other travelers), the flatboat men who worked the Mississippi River were a wild and dangerous population. Fordham warned, "But I would advise all travellers going alone down the river, to get one man at least that they can depend upon, and to wear a dagger or *a brace of pistols*; for there are no desperadoes more savage in their anger than these men."[29]

Two days before Christmas, 1828, Mayor Joseph Gales of Washington DC issued a proclamation that suggests that guns, and specifically pistols, were common:

MAYOR GALES' PROCLAMATION

WHEREAS it has been too much the habit of idle and inconsiderate persons, on Christmas and New Year's Day and Eve to indulge in firing off guns, pistols, squibs, and crackers, and burning of gun-powder in divers other ways, to the great annoyance of the peaceable inhabitants of this city, and to the manifest danger of their persons and property—all which practices, where they are not contrary to the express ordinances of the corporation, amount to "disorderly conduct," and as such are punishable by law:

Now, therefore, with a view to prevent such disorderly practices, I, Joseph Gales, jr. Mayor of Washington, do enjoin upon all Police Constables, Ward Commissioners, and others, whose duty it is to preserve peace and good order, to be diligent in the execution of their several duties, and to apprehend and bring to justice all persons so offending against the laws.[30]

Newspaper ads throughout this period offered handguns for sale and the repair of handguns. Travel accounts and newspaper reports demonstrate that handguns were commonly carried in at least some parts of the United States, and the presence of handguns was *never* a surprise. The evidence suggests that, like today, pistols were less common than long guns—but they were not, in any sense, scarce or unusual.

Guns and Sport in the Early Republic

The accounts that this chapter examines are chronologically organized. In every region in the period 1789 through 1846, memoirs and traveler accounts either treat gun ownership as common, or explicitly tell us that it was common. Some imply, while others clearly state, that hunting was common throughout the United States, and nearly universal on the frontier. No account that I found even implied that hunting was unusual or rare. There is no evidence that hunting was in any sense an upper class phenomenon; many of the accounts are explicit that it was common or nearly universal among the lowest classes.

Excluded are accounts that describe clearly atypical occupations and travels, such as George Frederick Ruxton's *Life in the Far West*, describing fur trapping in 1847 Utah, New Mexico, and Colorado, and John Palliser's *Solitary Rambles and Adventures of a Hunter in the Prairies*. Ruxton's book is awash in guns and violence; Palliser's 1847 hunting trip is similarly awash in guns and hunting. Both books take place within the United States, but where few Americans—other than the Indians—yet lived.[1]

Isaac Weld's account of his travels in North America between 1795 and 1797 described how rifles worked for his British audience, who would have been unfamiliar with rifled weapons. Weld told how

> An experienced marksman, with one of these guns, will hit an object not
> larger than a crown piece, to a certainty, at the distance of one hundred yards.

Two men belonging to the Virginia rifle regiment, a large division of which was quartered in this town during the war, had such a dependence on each other's dexterity, that the one would hold a piece of board, not more than nine inches square, between his knees, whilst the other shot at it with a ball at the distance of one hundred paces. This they used to do alternately, for the amusement of the town's people, as often as they were called upon. . . . Were I . . . to tell you all the stories that I have heard of the performance of riflemen, you would think the people were most abominably addicted to lying.

Weld discussed the manufacture and use of rifles for hunting, and compared Canadian hunters to their American counterparts: "The people here, as in the back parts of the United States, devote a very great part of their time to hunting, and they are well skilled in the pursuit of game of every description. They shoot almost universally with the rifle gun, and are as dexterous at the use of it as any men can be."[2] The difference between Americans and Canadians, according to Weld, was that Americans used American-made rifles, and preferred smaller calibers.

Francis Baily's *Journal of a Tour in Unsettled Parts of North America in 1796 & 1797* is awash in accounts of guns and hunting, including not only his own guns and hunting, but those of Americans whom he met. Baily described an "excellent tavern" on Chesapeake Bay, "which is frequented by parties in the shooting season, for the sake of the wild fowl with which the Susquehannah so plentifully abounds . . . ." Long Island's villages, according to Baily, "are much frequented by different parties from New York [City], which go over to hunt, shoot, and fish . . . ."

Washington DC was still largely woods when Baily visited it. To emphasize how far the new capital had to go before it would be a large city, Baily reported, "Game is plenty in these parts, and, what perhaps may appear to you remarkable, I saw some boys who were out a shooting, actually kill several brace of partridges in what will be one of the most public streets of the city." It was not boys out shooting that was remarkable to Baily; what was significant is that they were shooting in what would be one of the main boulevards of America's capital.

Baily described Fredericktown, Maryland, as a "large and flourishing place" at which, "There is a large manufactory of rifle-guns carried on here; but so great is the demand for them, that we could not meet with one in the whole place; they sell in general from 15 to 25 dollars each, according to their style of being mounted." Over the mountains, Baily came to Hagerstown, which "like Frederick's-town, is a place of great trade, and also a manufactory for rifle-guns, of which we bought two at twenty dollars each."

Baily's trip down the Ohio River described how each day his party moored their boats, "so that there were fourteen or fifteen of us in company: and we every day sent out some of them into the woods with their guns to hunt for deer, turkeys, bears, or any other animals fit for food." Baily described a plantation in the wilderness from whom they asked for food, that "they were, in fact, in the same destitute situation in which we were— obliged to depend upon their guns for subsistence . . . ." After a serious boat accident, his party became more desperate for food. "Accordingly, we took it by turns to go out every morning with our gun and shoot whatever we could find; and many a time would we lay ourselves down at night without a prospect of anything wherewith to break our fast the next morning, save what our guns might procure us the next day . . . ."

Baily's description of frontier Kentucky emphasized hunting as a source of food. "The inhabitants live a great deal upon deer and turkeys, which they shoot wild in the woods . . . ." Baily went hunting there with a Dr. Bean: "We were mounted on horses, and had each a gun . . . ." Baily described how black bears were hunted in Kentucky by cutting down trees into which the bears had climbed, "and three or four of the party with loaded rifles" would shoot the bear as he climbed out of the fallen tree. Baily also made casual references to guns, such as an old man "accompanied by his dog and his gun," and how, as his party floated down the Mississippi, the first boat in the expedition fired a gun as a signal to the others.[3] Baily was certainly surrounded by guns, and by hunting.

Fortescue Cuming's *Sketches of a Tour to the Western Country* described his journey through Pennsylvania, Ohio, and Kentucky from 1807 to 1809. Throughout his journey, Cuming mentioned, with no surprise, widespread use of guns for sport, subsistence hunting, and self-defense. Cuming also distinguished between market hunters, and those hunting to feed themselves; subsistence hunting was common. In Kentucky, Cuming, like Baily, described how abundant the wildlife of the area remained, even after settlement, by reporting "that little or no bread was used, but that even the children were fed on game; the facility of gaining which prevented the progress of agriculture . . . ."[4]

Even though Cuming was a hunter, he expressed his admiration for the superior marksmanship of Western Pennsylvanians and Virginians:

Apropos of the rifle.—The inhabitants of this country in common with the Virginians, and all the back woods people, Indians as well as whites, are wonderfully expert in the use of it: thinking it a bad shot if they miss the very head of a squirrel, or a wild turkey, on the top of the highest forest tree with a single ball; though they generally load with a few grains of swan shot, with which they are equally sure of hitting the head of the bird or animal they fire at.[5]

When Aaron Burr was tried for his criminal conspiracy to detach the Southwest into its own country, one of the pieces of evidence used against him was a meeting of a Mr. Blannerhassett with a number of other conspirators—all of them armed. Burr's defense attorney argued that gun ownership was the norm in the early Republic:

Arms are not necessarily military weapons. Rifles, shot guns and fowling pieces are used commonly by the people of this country in hunting and for domestic purposes; they are generally in the habit of pursuing game. In the upper country every man has a gun; a majority of the people have guns everywhere, for peaceful purposes. Rifles and shot guns are no more evidence of military weapons than pistols or dirks used for personal defence, or common fowling pieces kept for the amusement of taking game. It is lawful for every man in this country to keep such weapons.[6]

Rev. William C. Smith's frontier account, *Indiana Miscellany*, described settlers who were heavily armed with guns for self-defense against Indians. Smith also described the morality of the early Indiana settlements by telling how "it was a rare thing to hear . . . the report of a hunter's gun on the holy Sabbath day . . . ." Smith's statement thus implied that during the rest of the week gunfire was *not* rare. During the War of 1812, Smith told of a shortage of provisions for the settlers, who had fortified their villages,

> but usually they had plenty of meat. All the men were excellent hunters—some of them real experts. The country abounding in game, they kept the forts well supplied with venison and bear-meat. . . . When considered at all admissible to venture outside the fort to labor, the men went in company, taking their trusty rifles with them. . . . Some of [the women] could handle the rifle with great skill, and bring down the game in the absence of their husbands . . . .[7]

Baynard Rush Hall's memoir of frontier Indiana life immediately after statehood (1816) contained detailed descriptions of how hunting was a common part of life for most settlers, done partly for sport, and partly because it supplied fresh meat at very little expense:

> Let none think we western people follow rifle shooting, however, for mere sport; that would be nearly as ignoble as shot gun idleness! The rifle procures, at certain seasons, the only meat we ever taste; it defends our homes from wild animals and saves our corn fields from squirrels and our hen-roosts from foxes, owls, opossums and other "varmints". . . . The rifle is a woodman's lasso. He carries it everywhere as (a very degrading comparison for the gun, but none other occurs,) a dandy [carries] a cane. All, then, who came to our tannery or store came thus armed; and rarely did a customer go, till his rifle had been tried at a mark, living or dead . . . .[8]

After listing a variety of wild game that were hunted in the forest, Hall lists, "Add—'the neighbours' hogs,'—so wild and fierce, that when pork-time arrives, they must be hunted and shot, like other independent beasts." Hall's many hunting references with guns (usually with rifles) suggest it was ordinary.

Hall used the imagery of guns to describe the height of the trees in the forest: "till their high heads afforded a shelter to squirrels, far beyond the sprinkling of a shot-gun, and almost beyond the reach of the rifle!" In describing how life on the frontier expanded a person's talents relative to those who stayed in the East, Hall compares the double-barreled shotgun with the rifle, common in his region: "Does the chap shoot a double-barrelled gun?—so can you, if you would—but transcend him, oh! Far enough with that man's weapon, that in *your* hands deals, at your will, certain death to *one* selected victim, without *scattering* useless wounds at a venture in a little innocent feathered flock."[9]

Hall's America was steeped in a gun culture. Hall devotes an entire chapter to the joy of target shooting with rifles, opening the chapter with:

> Reader, were ever you *fired* with the love of rifle shooting? If so, the confidence now reposed in your honour will not be abused, when told my love for that noble art is unabated . . . .[10]

Hall also described target shooting matches as common, and took pride in participating in a match where the prize was a half-barrel of whiskey. As president of the local temperance society, his goal was to win the prize and pour the whiskey out on the ground. The local blacksmith was also a rifle-maker, and according to Hall, his rifles were better than those made back East.[11]

The rifle was so common an implement, and target shooting so common a sport, that when Hall went out evangelizing in a sparsely settled part of Indiana, one of his fellow preachers switched in mid-sermon to a metaphor involving rifle matches to sway the audience: "My friends and neighbours don't you all shoot the rifle in this settlement?" They were becoming restless with analogies that meant nothing to them—but they understood the preacher's analogy to a rifle match. Hall also described Pittsburgh, in a whimsical style with literary allusions, as a place where guns are made: "[S]ome here make tubes of iron, with alternate and spiral 'lands and furrows,' better by far to shoot than Milton's grand and unpatent blunderbusses . . . ."[12]

Hall described a non-lethal hunting accident—and gave no indication that this was a shocking event. Hall referred to pistols on several occasions with no indication that they were either rare or regarded with any particular concern.[13] Yet Hall's references to pistols were far exceeded by his mentions of rifles and shotguns.[14] Hall's discussions of hunting, use and misuse of guns, and target shooting occur on at least seventy-seven pages of Hall's book, or twelve percent of the total volume, and are always treated as common events.

Abraham Lincoln's autobiographical sketch, prepared in 1860, described his family's movement from Kentucky to Indiana around 1816, and how, "A few days before the completion of his eighth year, in the absence of his father, a flock of wild turkeys approached the new log-cabin, and A[braham] with a rifle gun, standing inside, shot through a crack, and killed one of them." Lincoln did not continue as a hunter, but even in his family, which was not wealthy by any means, there was a rifle, and hunting was considered an appropriate action for a seven-year-old. A poem by Lincoln, "The Bear Hunt," apparently written in 1847, described, "When first my father settled here, / 'Twas then the frontier line: / The panther's scream, filled night with fear / And bears preyed on the swine. / But wo for Bruin's short lived fun, / When rose the squealing cry; / Now man and horse, with dog and gun, / For vengeance, at him fly." Another line of the poem refers to "Bang,—bang—the rifles go."[15] Hunting and guns were apparently common on Lincoln's frontier.

Pim Fordham's account of his arrival at St. Vincennes, Indiana, in 1817 described what was considered appropriate paraphernalia for traveling in the Indiana wilderness: "We were furnished with guns and tomohawks, and all things necessary to encamp in the woods . . . ." Fordham also described Indiana's "back-wood settlers, who are half hunters, half farmers."[16] He divided the frontier population of Illinois into four categories, of which the first two relied upon hunting for their survival:

> 1ˢᵗ. The hunters, a daring, hardy, race of men, who live in miserable cabins, which they fortify in times of War with the Indians, whom they hate but much resemble in dress and manners. . . . But their rifle is their principal means of support. They are the best marksmen in the world, and such is their dexterity that they will shoot an apple off the head of a companion. Some few use the bow and arrow.
>
> 2ⁿᵈ. class. First settlers;—a mixed set of hunters and farmers. . . . [17]

Fordham's letter to his brother back in Britain described his style of dress when traveling, and it suggests that this was the norm in Illinois Territory: "I wish you could see your brother mount his horse to morrow morning. I will give you a sketch. A broad-brimmed straw hat,—long trousers and moccasins,—shot pouch and powder horn slung from a belt,—rifle at his back, in a sling . . . ." Fordham observed that "should a war break out on our frontiers, I hope that there is not nor will be, a young Englishman among us, who would hesitate to turn out with his gun and blanket."[18] Fordham assumed that every "young Englishman" on the Illinois frontier owned at least one gun.

While Fordham described people who hunted at least partly to sell game to others, he also indicated that hunting for one's own table was common. His account of a Christmas Day village feast listed a variety of game being cooked, including wild turkeys. That the game were hunted, not trapped, may be inferred from the following description:

> The young men had their rifles out, and were firing *feux de joi* almost all the preceding night, all the day till late into the evening. It reminded me of Byron's description of the Moslems firing at the feast of the Ramadan in Constantinople—but we backwoodsmen never fire a gun loaded with *ball into* the town,—only from all parts of it, out towards the woods.[19]

Fordham fills his account with descriptions of settlers (including himself) engaged in hunting for sport and for food. Most significantly of all, with respect to the supposed rarity of firearms in America, Fordham wrote a letter to his brother telling him what he should bring to America, and what was not needed: "Do not bring with you any English rifles, or indeed any firearms but a pair of pistols. A good rifle gunlock would be valuable."[20] While pistols might be expensive or rare, firearms in general were readily available. It seems likely that guns in America were as cheap, or cheaper, than in Britain. This is somewhat surprising, because Britain, at the time, was a major firearms manufacturing nation.

Anne Newport Royall's description of 1818 Alabama discussed the use of guns for self-defense and hunting as completely ordinary events, incidental to the events and people that she depicts. Royall also referred to bear hunting in her native Virginia as an ordinary part of life, with no indication that it was anymore unusual than an American today driving a car.[21]

Henry Rowe Schoolcraft's 1818 journey through the Ozarks also provides evidence that firearms ownership, sport hunting, and subsistence hunting, were common. Schoolcraft's description of the frontier settlement of Sugar-Loaf Prairie shows that guns and hunting were the norm:

These people subsist partly by agriculture, and partly by hunting. . . . Hunting is the principal, the most honourable, and the most profitable employment. To excel in the chace procures fame, and a man's reputation is measured by his skill as a marksman, his agility and strength, his boldness and dexterity in killing game, and his patient endurance and contempt of the hardships of the hunter's life. . . . They . . . can subsist any where in the woods, and would form the most efficient military corps in frontier warfare which can possibly exist. Ready trained, they require no discipline, inured to danger, and perfect in the use of the rifle.[22]

At least some of Sugar-Loaf Prairie's hunting was commercial fur trapping, and so perhaps this was atypical of the region—but Schoolcraft's description of other frontier settlements shows that hunting was a common part of how settlers obtained their meat. By the time frontier Ozark children reached fourteen years of age, they "have completely learned the use of the rifle, the arts of dressing skins and making [moccasins] and leather clothes."[23] Early in his journey, much to Schoolcraft's chagrin, he failed

to engage our hostess and her daughters in small-talk, such as passes current in every social corner; but, for the first time, found I should not recommend myself in that way. They could only talk of bears, hunting, and the like. The rude pursuits, and the coarse enjoyments of the hunter state, were all they knew.[24]

At one isolated cabin that Schoolcraft and his companion visited, the lady of the house was home alone. Schoolcraft expressed amazement that the lady of the house instructed Schoolcraft and his companion not only about "errors in our dress, equipments, and mode of travelling," but also "that our [shotguns] were not well adapted to our journey; that we should have rifles . . . ." Schoolcraft and his companion were astonished "to hear a woman direct us in matters which we had before thought the peculiar and exclusive province of men."[25] Ozark women as hunters surprised a New Englander like Schoolcraft, but his comments also imply that what was surprising was the sex of his instructor, not widespread hunting and firearms.

New Yorker John Stillman Wright's acidic *Letters from the West* (1819) described the early farmers of southern Indiana as, "mostly, of indolent slovenly habits, devoting the chief part of their time to hunting, and drinking whiskey . . . ."[26] While Wright was not explicit that these farmers hunted with *firearms*, he was explicit that hunting was *not* an upper class phenomenon in southern Indiana, nor was it rare. Richard Flower's *Letters from the Illinois* described the 1820–21 Illinois Territory. At the frontier village of Albion, Sunday amusements included that "the backwoodsmen shot at *marks*, their favourite sport . . . ."[27]

A circa 1820 Du Pont gunpowder packaging illustration for Hagley Mills (as Du Pont gunpowder was marketed after 1814) also suggests that the market for gunpowder included some significant numbers of hunters. While not conclusive evidence, the hunter's attire suggests a rustic, not a member of the upper class:[28]

As we saw in chapter 11, merchants advertising gunpowder gave indications that hunters were a significant market for gunpowder: "Eagle Powder, for Sportsmen, Coarse and Fine, for Land or Sea shooting . . . ."[29]

William N. Blane's *An Excursion through the United States and Canada, during the Years 1822–3* mentioned guns and hunting on at least twenty-two pages. On the road across the Appalachians, he described his first encounter with rifles in the hands of some hunters: "As one of them, an old man, was boasting of his skill as a marksman, I offered to put up a half-dollar at a distance of fifty yards, to be his if he could hit it. Accordingly, I stepped the distance, and placed the half-dollar in the cleft of a small stick, which I thrust into the ground. The hunter, slowly raising his rifle, fired, and to my great astonishment, struck the half-dollar."

Rifles were common in the backcountry. "Go to what house I might, the people were always ready to lend me a rifle, and were in general glad to accompany me when I went out hunting." Blane described squirrel hunting with an American on an island in the Ohio River, and how the Americans were in a losing battle to exterminate them: "In parts of Ohio, the people attempted to destroy them by means of guns, dogs, and clubs. One party of hunters, in the course of a week, killed upwards of 19,000 . . . . The people are very fond of the flesh of the squirrel, roasting it, and making it into pies, soups, &c . . . ."

Blane's description of the backwoodsmen observed, "Every boy, as soon as he can lift a rifle, is constantly practicing with it, and thus becomes an astonishingly expert marksman. Squirrel shooting is one of the favorite amusements of all the boys, and even of the men themselves." Blane wrote an additional two pages about the impressive marksmanship skills of the backwoodsmen, remarking, "in these immense forests, where every tree is a fort, the backwoodsmen, the best sharp shooters in the world, constitute the most formidable military force imaginable."

Americans hunted birds as well, and Blane described the normal procedure by which Americans hunted the prairie grouse: "They are delicious eating, and are killed in great numbers by the unrivalled marksmen of this country. After driving up a flock of these birds, the hunter advances within fifteen or twenty yards, raises his long heavy rifle, and rarely misses striking the bird on the head." After admitting that he was not as good a shot, and had to resort to shooting the prairie grouse through the body (instead of the head), he writes, "the Backwoodsmen regarded my unsportsmanlike shooting with as much contempt, as one of our country squires feels, when a cockney shoots at a covey of partridges on the ground." Blane also described the astonishment when he informed Americans that British game laws prohibited hunting deer in public lands, and even limited hunting on one's own land to the wealthy: "Such flagrant injustice appeared to them impossible . . . ."[30]

Karl Bernhard, Duke of Saxe-Weimar-Eisenach visited America in 1825 and 1826. Bernhard mentioned Americans hunting on only eighteen pages, but he always treated it as an unremarkable event.[31]

Sandford C. Cox's *Recollections of the Early Settlement of the Wabash Valley* describes 1820s and 1830s Indiana, using the journals and memoirs of the early settlers, who used guns for hunting, self-defense, assisting law enforcement, and for criminal purposes. Firearms and subsistence hunting are so common in Cox's book that there is no point in giving page numbers, nor do the journal-keepers and memoir-writers show any surprise about the presence or use of guns.[32]

Philip Gosse, an English naturalist visiting Alabama in the 1830s, provided one of the more complete descriptions of the attitude of the population towards hunting and firearms:

> Self-defence, and the natural craving for excitement, compel him to be a hunter; it is the appropriate occupation of a new, grand, luxuriant country like this, and one which seems natural to man, to judge from the eagerness and zest with which every one engages in it when he has the opportunity. The long rifle is familiar to every hand; skill in the use of it is the highest accomplishment which a southern gentleman glories in; even the children acquire an astonishing expertness in handling this deadly weapon at a very early age.[33]

Gosse's account also emphasized the high level of marksmanship in America:

> But skill as a marksman is not estimated by quite the same standard as in the old country. Pre-eminence in any art must bear a certain relation to the average attainment; and where this is universally high, distinction can be won only by something very exalted. Hence, when the young men meet together to display their skill, curious tests are employed, which remind one of the

days of old English archery . . . . Some of these practices I have read of, but here I find them in frequent use. "Driving the nail" is one of these; a stout nail is hammered into a post about half way up to the head; the riflemen then stand at an immense distance, and fire at the nail; the object is to hit the nail so truly on the head with the ball as to drive it home. To hit at all on one side, so as to cause it to bend or swerve, is failure; missing it altogether is out of the question.[34]

Gosse also described widespread hunting of squirrels, wild hog, and varmints with rifles. Alabamans hunted for sport, food, and to protect crops from damage.[35]

Alexis de Tocqueville's *Journey to America,* his account of the travels that led to writing *Democracy in America,* quotes a Tennessee farmer in 1831 that

[T]he dweller in this country is generally lazy. He regards work as an evil. Provided he has food enough and a house which gives half shelter, he is happy and thinks only of smoking and hunting. . . . There is not a farmer but passes some of his time hunting and owns a good gun.[36]

Tocqueville also described a usual "peasant's cabin" in Kentucky or Tennessee: "There one finds a fairly clean bed, some chairs, a good gun, often some books and almost always a newspaper . . . ."[37] Guns and hunting were not unusual in Kentucky or Tennessee, according to Tocqueville; they were typical.

Robert Baird's *View of the Valley of the Mississippi* reads like a real estate promotional guide, emphasizing the enormous benefits from moving to these largely unsettled states—but still admits some unsavory aspects of the frontier. A few instances of violence appear in Baird's promotional work, such as St. Louis and its dueling problem, but they are usually in conjunction with a positive statement such as, "A great moral change is, however, going forward here." Baird also reported a dispute at cards aboard a steamboat: "Pistols and dirks were drawn!"[38]

While booster Baird seldom mentioned violence, he repeatedly mentioned hunting—and in a manner suggesting that the abundance of game would be an important factor when deciding where to settle. Baird wrote of

Michigan's advantages, saying that, "The wild game of this territory is simi-lar to that of Indiana, and the adjoining unsettled parts of Ohio. Deer, bears, beavers, otters, wolves, foxes &c. are numerous. Geese, ducks, and other aquatic fowls are exceedingly abundant. Wild [turkeys], pheasants, prairie hens, &c. &c. are to be found in great numbers and afford delicious food to the settlers in the autumn and winter."

Baird made similar remarks about the wild game of Illinois, Missouri, and Florida. In Missouri, Baird told of the abundance of game, describing a "semi-barbarian population" that lived off the game: "I have seen some of these men who could spend hour after hour in detailing their achievements with the 'rifle.'" Baird also describes steamboat passengers, including "the half-horse and half-alligator Kentucky boatman, swaggering, and boasting of his prowess, his rifle, his horse, and his wife."[39]

Harriet Martineau's account of mid-1830s America shows that firearms and sport hunting were common occurrences along the Mississippi, and unsurprising to her:

While I was reading on the morning of the 12th, the report of a rifle from the lower deck summoned me to look out. There were frequent rifle-shots, and they always betokened our being near shore; generally under the bank, where the eye of the sportsman was in the way of temptation from some object in the forest.[40]

"Christmas shooting" took the same place on the frontier that Christmas caroling did in the America of my youth. Gert Göbel's description of the Missouri frontier in the 1830s tells us that at Christmas, there were no reli-gious observances, and no gifts exchanged:

There was just shooting. On Christmas Eve, a number of young fellows from the neighborhood banded together, and, after they had gathered together not only their hunting rifles but also old muskets and horse pistols from the Revolutionary War and had loaded them almost to the bursting point, they went from house to house. They approached the house as quietly as possible and then fired a mighty volley, to the fright of the women and children, and, if someone did not appear then, another volley no doubt followed. But usually the man of the house opened the door immediately, fired his own gun in greeting and invited the whole company into the house. . . . After everyone had chatted for a little while, the whole band set out for the next farm, where the same racket started up anew. In this way, this mischief was carried on until morning, and since, as a rule, a number of such bands were out and about, one could often hear all night the roaring and rattling of guns from all directions.[41]

Accounts of similar practices—apparently of German origin—appear in many states, both frontier and settled, in the 1830s.[42]

Rebecca Burlend's narrative of the Missouri frontier in 1831 described bird hunting, and implied that it was not only common among British emigrants, but also among Americans. Her husband had successfully hunted a turkey—or so he thought. Rebecca had it mostly cooked for Sunday dinner, when their guest arrived and expressed surprise, "as those birds are difficult to obtain with a common fowling-piece . . . ." Mr. Burlend had bagged a vulture, not a turkey—definitely not fit for the table![43]

Frances Wright is certainly one of the most extremely pro-American British visitors of the early Republic, and her claims should be regarded with greater care than many of the other visitors. Nonetheless, her assertion, "Every man, or nearly every man, in these states knows how to handle the axe, the hammer, the plane, all the mechanic's tools in short, besides the musket, to the use of which he is not only regularly trained as a man but practised as a boy" suggests that the use of firearms in America was widespread, even granting a large dose of romantic hyperbole on Wright's part.[44]

The Anglo-Irishman Thomas Cather described emigrants headed to the frontier while crossing Michigan in 1836. Rifles were the norm, not the exception:

[E]migrants from the old states on their way to settle in the Western forests. Each emigrant generally had a wagon or two, drawn by oxen. These wagons contained their wives, children, and *rest of their baggage*. The man walked by the side of his team with his rifle over his shoulder . . . .[45]

British naval officer and novelist Frederick Marryat's account of his journey to North America described North Carolinians emigrating west in 1837:

These caravans consist of two or three covered wagons, full of women and children, furniture, and other necessaries, each drawn by a team of horses; brood mares, with foals by their sides, following; half a dozen or more cows, flanked on each side by the men, with their long rifles on their shoulders; sometimes a boy or two, or a half-grown girl on horseback.

Marryat's account of his journey frequently mentioned Americans hunting and shooting in a way that suggests that there was nothing particularly unusual about it. He described how hunting was the "principal amusement of the officers" at Fort Snelling. Captain Scott, one of those officers, had a reputation as a very great marksman, based on his ability to throw two potatoes in the air and puncture both of them with a single rifle bullet. Nor was Captain Scott's hunting a peculiarity of Fort Snelling being on the frontier. Marryat recounted Scott's hunting anecdotes as a 12-year-old in Vermont, and these accounts indicate that both hunting and gun ownership were common in Scott's youth in Vermont.[46]

British emigrant Caroline Kirkland's 1839 *A New Home—Who'll Follow?* shows that guns and sports involving guns were widespread on her frontier. Discussing the problems of church attendance, "many of the neighbours always make a point of being present, although a far greater proportion reserve the Sunday for fishing and gunning." Kirkland mentions long guns, pistols, and hunting in a manner that suggests that they were normal parts of frontier life. Hunting was unremarkable; Kirkland commented on a neighbor whose husband's love of hunting left her alone and neglected. She also reported that in the woods, "The division of labour is almost unknown" and "in absolutely savage life, each man is of necessity his own tailor, tentmaker, carpenter, cook, huntsman, and fisherman . . . ."[47]

Harriet Williams Sawyer of Maine described 1840 Indiana life. Unlike Rev. William C. Smith's somewhat earlier version of Indiana, Sabbath-breaking was a problem:

The Sabbath in the West is much desecrated; trades are transacted; labor, it is true, is generally suspended, but the Sabbath is regarded by most as a day of recreation. Hunting and intemperance are common.[48]

John James Audubon's *Delineations of American Scenery and Character* described a society awash in guns and hunting. Audubon described traveling along the Ohio River: "The margins of the shores and of the river were at this season amply supplied with game. A Wild Turkey, a Grouse, or a Blue-winged Teal, could be procured in a few moments; and we fared well, for, whenever we pleased, we landed, struck up a fire, and provided as we were with the necessary utensils, procured a good repast." Audubon's preparations for a trip in the forests of Pennsylvania, included "25 pounds of shot, some flints . . . my gun *Tear-jacket*." The result? "The juicy venison, excellent bear flesh . . . that daily formed my food, methinks I can still enjoy." Audubon described what this area must have been like before settlement: "Bears and the Common Deer must have been plentiful, as, at the moment when I write, many of both kinds are seen and killed by the resident hunters." Audubon witnessed an incident in which eight bears wandered into a clearing, driving away the woodsmen: "Down they all rushed from the mountain; the noise spread quickly; rifles were soon procured and shouldered; but when the spot was reached, no bears were to be found . . . ."[49]

Audubon's chapter on "Navigation of the Mississippi" described how boatmen would stop along the way when logs blocked their path: "The time is not altogether lost, as most of the men, being provided with rifles, betake themselves to the woods, and search for the deer, the bears, or the turkeys, that are generally abundant there." The flood stage of the Mississippi and the Ohio Rivers trapped "Bears, Cougars, Lynxes, and all other quadrapeds that can ascend the trees . . . ." The animals were "[f]atigued by the exertions which they have made in reaching the dry land, they will there stand the hunter's fire, as if to die by a ball were better than to perish amid the waste waters. On occasions like this, all these animals are shot by hundreds."[50]

Audubon described a squatter's cabin, and how squatters, "like most of those adventurous settlers in the uncultivated tracts of our frontier districts . . . [are] well versed in the chase, and acquainted with the habits of some of the larger species of quadrapeds and birds." Audubon went cougar hunting with a party of squatters. "Each hunter now moved with caution, holding his gun ready . . . ." Audubon told of a young couple's home in the back-woods, and while he emphasized how their clothes and their furniture were "homespun" and "of domestic manufacture," but a "fine rifle ornamented the chimney-piece."

Audubon described another family in the Louisiana bayous, but in this case, it was comprised of runaway slaves. Their food supply came from wild plants and deer: "One day, while in search of wild fruits, he found a bear dead before the muzzle of a gun that had been set for that purpose . . . . His slave friends at the plantation supplied him with some ammunition . . . ."[51]

In a chapter about how the burning of forests changed the nature of the trees that grew there, Audubon told of an immense forest fire in Maine, and how the settlers responded to the fire that awakened them one night: "We were sound asleep one night, in a cabin about a hundred miles from this, when about two hours before day, the snorting of the horses and lowing of the cattle which I had ranging in the woods suddenly awakened us. I took yon rifle, and went to the door to see what beast had caused the hubbub . . . ."[52]

A chapter on Kentucky sports described how Virginians moved into the Kentucky frontier: "An axe, a couple of horses, and a heavy rifle, with store of ammunition, were all that were considered necessary . . . ." Kentucky sports included target shooting with rifles, and Audubon spent four pages describing sport similar to Gosse's account of "driving the nail" that we examined in chapter 13.[53] (This was apparently not a new practice, nor spe-cific to the New World. *Mourt's Relation*, published in 1622 concerning Plymouth Colony, used this target shooting practice as a metaphor for his writing: "though through my slender judgment I should miss the mark, and not strike the nail on the head . . . ."[54])

Audubon was clearly a gun enthusiast. When a new acquaintance offered to show him the new percussion cap method of firing a gun, Audubon was keen to see it. His friend demonstrated that it could fire under water by load-ing and firing it in a basin of water—inside the house. Guns were a funda-mental part of how Audubon was able to produce his beautiful works on natural history: "I drew and noted the habits of every thing which I procured, and my collection was daily augmenting, as every individual who carried a gun always sent me such birds or quadrapeds as he thought might prove useful to me."[55]

Audubon devoted a whole chapter to "Deer Hunting" with rifles, distinguishing "Still Hunting" from "Firelight Hunting" and "Driving." "*Still Hunting* is followed as a kind of trade by most of our frontier men. To be practiced with success, it requires great activity, an expert management of the rifle, and a thorough knowledge of the forest . . . ." Another section described alligator hunting: "A rifle bullet was now and then sent through the eye of one of the largest . . . ." Audubon devoted an entire chapter to "The Moose Hunt" in 1833 Maine, and of course, the hunt was with guns. Similarly, an entire chapter is devoted to "A Racoon Hunt in Kentucky" using rifles, with a detailed and picturesque description of rifle loading.[56]

Another traveler to America was Ole Rynning, who wrote that those considering immigrating to American should bring "good rifles with percussion locks, partly for personal use, partly for sale. I have already said that in America a good rifle costs from fifteen to twenty dollars."[57] Rynning is clear that one should bring guns both to sell (indicating that there was a demand for guns in America), *and* because one would need them here.

Charles Augustus Murray's description of his hunting trip from Britain to America in the 1830s reported that both firearms ownership and sport hunting were common in rural Virginia. Murray was explicit that these hunters were ordinary farmers, and not members of the upper class:

I lodged the first night at the house of a farmer, about seven miles from the village, who joined the habits of a hunter to those of an agriculturalist, as is indeed the case with all the country people in this district; nearly every man has a rifle, and spends part of his time in the chase. My double rifle, of London manufacture, excited much surprise among them; but the concluding remark of almost every inspector was, "I guess I could beat you to a mark."[58]

The frontier, of course, would have more reason for firearms ownership than settled areas of the East, but even from the most settled parts of pre-1840 America we have ads, memoirs and travel accounts that show gun ownership and hunting was unremarkable. Jonathan Vickers advertised in a Cleveland newspaper in 1821 that he had opened a "Gun Factory" where "New Rifles and Fowling Pieces will be furnished cheap, for cash . . . ." Another ad in the same issue lists, "Best Eng. Powder, Com. Amer'n [ditto] Shot & Lead."[59]

Charles H. Haswell's *Reminiscences of New York by an Octogenarian* described New York City life from 1816 to 1860. Haswell's entry for November 1830 told of shooting a "ruffed grouse" at 144th Street and 9th Avenue in Manhattan, "and it was believed by sportsmen to be the last one to suffer a like fate on the island." Haswell also described the opening of commercial hunting clubs on Manhattan. This suggests that sport hunting on Manhattan was already common[60] at a time when Bellesiles argues that sport hunting was still unusual in America.[61]

The sources from the early Republic provide persuasive evidence that firearms and hunting were the norm and not the exception. To demonstrate that America was *not* a society awash in guns and hunting would require not just a new interpretation of the existing evidence—it would require rewriting dozens of eyewitness accounts.

Guns and Violence in the Early Republic

As newspapers, memoirs, and traveler accounts make clear, white on white violence of all sorts, including murder, both with and without guns, was depressingly common. Many of the traveler accounts in this chapter directly state that particular regions of America were prone to violence, and they place at least part of the blame on a combination of an "honor culture,"[1] and the widespread habit of carrying of guns and knives.

It is not difficult to find contemporary accounts that describe gun murders. One example is the trial of Jesse Wood in Poughkeepsie, New York, in 1806. Jesse Wood apparently had a dispute with his son Joseph concerning the collection of a debt. Both Jesse and Joseph were drunk, and shortly after Jesse exclaimed "That he would be revenged!" a shot was heard by Hezekiah Wood, Jesse's other son. Joseph Wood was found dead from a shotgun blast. Jesse Wood was tried and executed for his murder. Murder with a gun was neither shocking nor amazing to the author, just disappointing and regrettable.[2] There are many newspaper accounts of murder and attempted murder in this period; the use of guns in robberies does not ever seem to be a surprise.[3]

Pistols appear repeatedly in travel accounts of this period and newspaper stories. They are *never* identified as surprising, startling, or unusual in the American context. In a few cases, they are explicitly declared to be common. Pistols were used in ways that would not surprise Americans today: for self-defense and for criminal attack. There are many dozens of examples available from the *Pennsylvania Gazette* from the years 1784–1800; robberies, murders, attempted murders, suicides, and accidental deaths from pistols (from across the United States) were never expressed as surprising.[4]

Cuming's account of his 1807–09 journey referred to the use of firearms for law enforcement. When two Western Pennsylvanians discovered a murder (committed with a gun and a knife), they "rode on to the next house and gave an alarm, which soon mustered the inhabitants of the neighbourhood, who arming themselves, went in pursuit of the murderers. One of them resisting, when discovered, was shot, and the other apprehended . . . ." Cuming also described meeting in Kentucky "straggling parties above fifty horsemen with rifles . . . at a militia muster," apparently mostly drunk, which led to fights later in the evening.[5]

Baynard Rush Hall's memoir of frontier Indiana described the use of guns in both criminal and defensive capacities. Settlers used rifles when pursuing criminals, and criminals used rifles when trying to avoid arrest.[6] Hall also described problems with armed robbers, and explained, "We are not advocates for Lynching, but we do know that where laws cannot and do not protect backwoodsmen, they fall back on reserved rights and protect themselves. Nay, such, instead of laying aside defensive weapons . . . we know that such woodsmen will go better armed, to slay and not unrighteously on the spot every unholy apostate that *maliciously* and *wilfully* strikes down and stamps on God's image!" [emphasis in original]. In Hall's grandiloquent language, describing the conflict with legislators who sought imprisonment for robbers, and the backwoodsmen, partial to firearm solutions, "Many neighbours out there will always physic [treat] such with lead pills [bullets]—at least till Reformers have prisons prepared fit to hold their pets longer than a few hours!"[7]

Hall discussed the problem of stagecoach robberies and reported that a fellow traveler on the road to Indiana described an earlier journey: "I need hardly say I then traveled with weapons, and as we entered the mountainous country, a brace of pistols was kept loaded usually in a pocket of the carriage." Highwaymen armed with hammers, axes, and bludgeons had interrupted the traveler's earlier journey; his threat to use a pistol had driven the robbers away. Another traveler in the carriage told Hall of conflict at an inn in the South: "Of course, I barricaded the door as well as possible, and, without noise, examined my pistols—and got out my dirk . . . ." A third traveler described a journey from Charleston to Georgetown by stagecoach with slave-dealers, "Their diversion often was, to entice dogs near the stage and then to fire pistol-balls at them . . . ."[8]

The Methodist preacher Peter Cartwright described a journey through the Allegheny Mountains to Baltimore in April 1820 that shows pistols were not startling discoveries, even when found lying in the road:

> In passing on our journey going down the mountains, on Monday, we met several wagons and carriages moving west. Shortly after we had passed them, I saw lying in the road a very neat pocket-pistol. I picked it up, and found it heavily loaded and freshly primed. Supposing it to have been dropped by some of these movers, I said to brother Walker, "This looks providential;" for the road across these mountains was, at this time, infested by many robbers, and several daring murders and robberies had lately been committed.

Cartwright then recounted his use of this pistol shortly thereafter to defend himself against a robber. On his return trip, he described his carrying of a pistol to defend himself from robbery during a dispute at a toll gate. The owner of the tollgate "called for his pistols," apparently with the intention of shooting at Cartwright.

In other incidents from the 1820s, Cartwright refers to pistols in a manner that suggests that they were not at all unusual items, even if the use of them could be dramatic. Cartwright described two young men reduced to deadly enemies as a result of rivalry over a young lady: "They quarreled, and finally fought; both armed themselves, and each bound himself in a solemn oath to kill the other. Thus sworn, and armed with pistols and dirks, they attended camp meeting."[9] The pistols and the death threats disheartened, but did not surprise Cartwright.

In 1820, two young men were competing for the affections of a young lady in Lawrenceburgh, Indiana. Mr. Fuller offered Mr. Warren the chance to write a note disclaiming any interest in her, or engage in a duel. Mr. Warren declined to do either, at which point Fuller shot and killed Warren with a pistol. The report emphasized that Warren was "highly respected" and Fuller, his murderer, was "pleasing in his address, intelligence, and communicative." The report closed with, "Great God! Is this human nature? When the restraining power of offended Heaven is withdrawn, man becomes desperate, and dies by his own hand."[10] The newspaper said nothing indicating the presence of a pistol was remarkable.

William Oliver Stevens described 1820s Georgia as a place so brutal and lawless that

[N]o adult male ever went abroad unarmed. Whether it was to attend church, a social affair, or a political meeting, the Georgians carried loaded pistols, bowie knives, and sword canes. The pistols rested in the breast pockets of the coat and could be drawn quickly by both hands.[11]

Suicides with handguns appear in newspapers of the early Republic, and are portrayed as tragic events—but a pistol's presence is never surprising. A Delaware newspaper described such a death in 1825: "[B]etween the hours of eight and nine a servant girl heard the report of a pistol, she went upstairs and found Mr. Hart sitting on a chair and his cloths on fire, she asked him what was the matter, when he gave a groan and expired; she immediately went for Mr. Carter, and upon examination it was discovered that he had shot himself . . . ."[12]

William N. Blane's *An Excursion through the United States and Canada, during the Years 1822–3* is very clear about America's violence problem—especially because Blane was otherwise quite positively impressed with Americans: "A custom much to be blamed among the better class in the Western States, is that of wearing concealed weapons. So common is it to carry a dirk hid in the breast, that a Student of the Transylvanian College, Lexington, informed me that it was the practice of many of his fellow collegians. Fatal accidents are thus often occasioned; as a man when angry, is enabled, by means of the weapon he carries, to commit an act of which he may repent all the rest of his life."

Blane also discussed the problem of dueling, and why the laws against it were nearly useless: "In the United States as in England, a Jury would never find a man guilty of murder provided the affair has been honourably conducted." Blane also talked about backwoods fighting: "The object of each combatant is to take his adversary by surprise; and then, as soon as he has thrown him down, either to 'gouge' him, that is, to poke his eye out, or else to get his nose or ear into his mouth and bite it off."[13]

Blane thought highly of the American militia system, within its limitations: "[T]he militia, and particularly that of the western States, is very formidable in defending a thickly wooded country, and forms a corps of excellent light troops; but they never have been able, and they never can expect, to cope with regulars in the open field . . . ." Blane also described the militia laws and the duty to be armed. "In consequence of this admirable institution, every individual is armed, and is sufficiently a soldier, to turn out at a moment's warning, and defend his country from an enemy."[14]

Somewhat less impressed with American military preparedness was **Karl Bernhard, Duke of Saxe-Weimar-Eisenach, who visited America in 1825 and 1826.** He clearly did not think much of relying on a militia system, although Bernhard acknowledged the competence of some militia units, and that some were well armed.[15] Yet Bernhard repeatedly mentioned the presence of guns, describing various technical innovations and their disadvantages, which cities manufactured rifles, as well as the manufacturing of hunting ammunition in shot towers. In Ohio, prison inmates were at work as gunsmiths, "who make very good rifles . . . ."[16]

Concerning violence, Bernhard gives the impression that it was unsurprising to the locals. Bernhard attended a masked ball in New Orleans, and described how, "Two quarrels took place, which commenced in the ball-room with blows, and terminated in the vestibule, with pocket-pistols and kicking, without any interruption from the police." Attending a quadroon ball later, Bernhard reported that "some gentlemen had dipped too deep in the glass, and several quarrels with fists and canes took place.[17] The police [enforcement of laws] is not strict enough here to prevent gentlemen from bringing canes with them to balls."

In Kentucky, Bernhard described how a son of the governor had been arrested for robbery and murder, "and found guilty by two different juries." What made this astonishing to Bernhard was not the murder, but that the governor had attempted to replace appellate judges so as to protect his son, resulting in great political conflict. "I was assured that political struggles, often terminating in sanguinary conflicts, were the order of the day; nay, that this division had already given occasion to several assassinations."[18]

John James Audubon's *Delineations of American Scenery and Character* devoted one whole chapter to white-on-white violence, much of it involving guns.[19] Audubon stopped for the night at a frontier cabin, where the woman of the house conspired with her sons to murder him, so that they could steal his watch: "I turned, cocked my gun-locks silently, touched my faithful companion, and lay ready to start up and shoot the first who might attempt my life." Audubon claimed that such violence was unusual, "so little risk do travelers run in the United States, that no one born there ever dreams of any to be encountered on the road . . . ."

Yet Audubon devoted the entire next chapter, "The Regulators," to how frontier communities dealt with criminals by threats, then whipping, and for the most serious cases, "delinquents of the worst species have been shot, after which their heads have been stuck on poles, to deter others from following their example." Regulators would gather, "forty or fifty" on horseback, "well armed with rifles and pistols . . . ."[20] Audubon's travels and experiences were atypical, but to cite this book as an account that shows "the travelers did not notice that they were surrounded by guns and violence" defies explanation.[21]

Charles Haswell's memoir of New York City contains a February 1836 entry describing a mob that gathered to burn "Saint Patrick's Church in Mott Street." The effort failed because "the Catholics . . . not only filled the church with armed men" but put so many men on the walls, presumably armed with long guns, that he described the walls as "crenellated."[22] The attempt to burn the church was worthy of note; that the church was defended with armed men was worthy of note; that men were armed, apparently with long guns, Haswell treated as unsurprising.

Haswell described a widely reported 1830 incident in the District of Columbia. A prominent Washington newspaper editor, Duff Green, drew a concealed handgun to deter attack by a New York City newspaper editor at the US Capitol. Haswell's account of subsequent events suggests that instead of regarding this as dastardly, criminal, unrespectable, or surprising, Green's acquaintances good-naturedly ribbed him about the incident.[23] Green earned no infamy for his actions; two years later he published the 1830 census for the federal government.[24]

Charles Dickens' *American Notes for General Circulation* contains an entire chapter devoted to murders committed with both guns and knives. In addition to murder, Dickens refers to the use of guns for dueling, and incongruously, "alternately firing off pistols and singing hymns."[25]

Alexis de Tocqueville's *Journey to America* is full of reminders that some regions of America were sometimes quite violent. A young Alabama lawyer that Alexis de Tocqueville spoke with in 1831 asserted, "There is no one here but carries arms under his clothes. At the slightest quarrel, knife or pistol comes to hand. These things happen continually; it is a semi-barbarous state of society."[26]

Handguns in private hands were not in short supply in this period, and they appear in acts of violence at the highest levels of American society. The US House of Representatives tried Samuel Houston for "a breach of the privileges of the House of Representatives, by assaulting and beating Mr. Stanbery, a member of that House." The testimony included that Representative Stanbery

had a consultation with some of my friends, who agreed with me upon the answer which was sent. It was the opinion of one of my friends (Mr. Ewing, of Ohio,) that it was proper I should be armed; that, immediately upon the reception of my note, Mr. Houston would probably make an assault upon me. Mr. Ewing, accordingly, procured for me a pair of pistols, and a dirk; and, on the morning on which the answer was sent, I was prepared to meet Mr. Houston if he should assault me.[27]

Even *slaves* in some places had pistols—or at least newspapers reported that they did, and expected readers to believe it. An article from the Chickasaw, Mississippi, *Union* reprinted in the *North Alabamian* reported that, "And many of our Negroes . . . fancy that, in defence of their *honors*, they must carry loaded pistols and long knives! We do things on a magnicent scale here in Pontotoc!—Negroes going armed." The *North Alabamian* also reprinted from the Chickasaw *Union* a report of, "little boys [presumably white], just out of swaddling clothes, wielding dirk-knives and pistols with as much *sang-froid*, and manifesting as familiar an acquaintance with their use, as if they had been born with weapons in their hands."[28]

Another news account shows that both handguns and murder were, at least in the South, unsurprising:

Mr. B. D. Boyd, a highly respectable and correct young man, and an officer in the Commercial Bank, together with an another young man in the room, interfered to prevent further aggressions by either party. Stewart, however, drew a pistol, and, in mistake we presume, shot Boyd in the lower part of the abdomen. Stewart is said to be from Mississippi, and about 17 years of age.

We regret the necessity that calls for the publication of these facts, but public opinion must be made to bear upon the common practice among our young men of carrying deadly weapons in a peaceably community.[29]

The editorializing is clear: Young men carried deadly weapons far too freely, but the presence of the pistol was not particularly startling; indeed, it was all too common.

Pistols appear repeatedly in news accounts from the period 1837–38, and while the results were considered tragic, the presence of pistols was never surprising. A quarrel took place in Columbus, Georgia, between "Col. Felix Lewis and a Doctor Sullivan, the latter drew a pistol and attempted to shoot the former, when Lewis produced a Bowie knife, and stabbed Sullivan to the heart, who died in two minutes."[30] In Missouri, Alexander H. Dixon drew a sword cane on a man named Flasser. Flasser drew a pistol, and shot Dixon to death.[31] Near Natchez, Captain Crosly of the steamboat *Galenian* had a difficulty with one of his passengers, during which Crosly "drew a Bowie knife, and made a pass at the throat of the passenger," but without causing any injury. Crosly retrieved a pistol from his cabin, pointed it at the passenger, and accidentally shot him.[32]

Thomas Cather, an Ulster Scot traveler to America in the 1830s, commented on the reluctance of the criminal justice system in the South and West to interfere in violence: "Everyone goes armed with dagger, Boey [Bowie] knife, or pistols, and sometimes with all three, and in a society where the passions are so little under control it is not to be wondered . . . that murderous affrays should so often take place in the streets."[33] **British naval officer and novelist Frederick Marryatt described 1837 America as a very violent place:**

Slander and detraction are the inseperable evils of a democracy, and as neither public nor private characters are spared, and the law is impotent to protect them, men have no other recourse than to defend their reputations with their lives, or to deter the defamer by the risk which he must incur.

And where political animosities are carried to such a length as they are in this exciting climate, there is no time given for coolness and reflection. Indeed, for one American who would attempt to prevent a duel, there are ten who would urge the parties on to the conflict. . . . The majority of the editors of the newspapers in America are constantly practicing with the pistol, that they may be ready when called upon, and are most of them very good shots. . . . But the worst feature in the American system of duelling is, that they do not go out, as we do in this country, to satisfy honour, but with the determination to kill.[34]

In 1831, Arkansas Territorial Governor Pope expressed his concern about passions out of control, arguing that the willingness of juries to reduce murder to manslaughter encouraged killing: "Men should be brought to bridle their passions when life is at stake, and no excuse for shedding blood should be received but that of *absolute necessity*. The distinction between murder and manslaughter should be abolished in all cases where a dirk, pistol or other deadly weapon is used, except in cases of *self-defense*."[35]

Pistols were common in the hands of abolitionists. When Elijah P. Lovejoy (clergyman and abolitionist newspaper editor of the 1830s) and his friends defended his printing press in Alton, Illinois, with pistols, the mob of "respectable gentlemen" of Alton murdered Lovejoy. Lovejoy died with a pistol in his hand.[36] Kentucky abolitionist Cassius Clay was keenly aware of the effects of mob violence against abolitionists:

We say, that when *society fails to protect us*, we are authorized by the laws of God and nature to defend ourselves; based upon *the right*, "the pistol and Bowie knife" are to us as sacred as the gown and the pulpit; and the Omnipresent God of battles is our hope and trust for victorious vindication. "Moral power" is much; with great, good, true-souled men, it is stronger than the bayonet! But with the cowardly and debased it is an "unknown God." Experience teaches us, common sense teaches us, instinct teaches us, *religion* teaches us, that it loses none of its force by being backed with "cold steel and the flashing blade," "the pistol and the Bowie knife." [37]

Charles Augustus Murray's description of his hunting trip from Britain to America in the 1830s recounted incidents of guns and violence that occurred during his journey. Murray reported that on 3 February 1835, "a distinguished lawyer of New Orleans" entered the Louisiana House of Representatives chamber and struck the Speaker of the House with a cane. The Speaker drew a pistol and fired through the lawyer's coat, without hitting his body. The lawyer then drew a pistol and wounded the Speaker.

Murray criticized the widespread practice of carrying deadly weapons and the related problems of "rough and tumble" (as the no-limits, eye-gouging, hand-to-hand style of combat was called). Murray suggested that "constantly carrying a weapon, when their houses and families were hourly liable to be surprised by the war-whoop of the Indian" made sense, but now, "against whom is the dirk-knife now sharpened? against brothers, cousins, and neighbours! ... I trust that the progress of civilization, and increasing weight of a sounder public opinion, will soon put a stop to the custom above censured, which is not confined to Kentucky, but is more or less prevalent in the whole valley of the Mississippi, especially in Louisiana." [38]

A newspaper account of a robbery at pistol point in 1839 Delaware also gives no hint that pistols were rare or unusual items: "Warren Gibbons of this County, was on his return home from market, a short distance west of this Village his horse was stopped by three villains, two of which held him while their companions entered his dearborn, and after striking a light presented a pistol to his breast and demanded his money." [39] An 1844 incident in which William S. Moore took a shot at a member of the House of Representatives with a pistol was disappointing, but the presence of a pistol was unremarkable. [40]

Dueling oaths were a major topic of debate at the Kentucky Constitutional Convention of 1849. One delegate argued that dueling was preferable to sudden attacks in the streets. While he was only 31 years old, he lamented that of his boyhood friends, some twelve or fourteen have perished in violent affrays in the streets, and I have never known one who fell in fair and honorable duel. And why is this? It is because a thousand opportunities exist of effecting a reconciliation between parties where a challenge has passed and a duel is proposed, and the difficulty by the interference of friends may be adjusted; but in the murderous street fight the parties excited with passion, heed no one, and arming themselves, go forth in the thoroughfares and the by-ways, and there in a bloody affray, to the terror of every passer-by, settle their quarrel with the knife and the pistol.[41]

Frederick Law Olmsted's description of a not completely concealed Colt revolver on a Kentucky railroad in 1853 strongly suggests that concealed carrying of handguns was at least common, if not widespread:

In the cars in Kentucky a modest young man was walking through with the hand[le] of a Colt out of his pocket-skirt behind. It made some laugh & a gentleman with us called out, "You'll lose your Colt, Sir." The man turned and after a moment joined the laugh and pushed the handle into the pocket.

John said, "There might be danger in laughing at him." "Oh no," replied our companion, evidently supposing him serious, "he would not mind a laugh." "It's the best place to carry your pistol, after all," said he. "It's less in your way than anywhere else. And as good a place for your knife as anywhere else is down your back, so you can draw over your shoulder."

"Are pistols generally carried here?"

"Yes, very generally."

Allison said *commonly*, but he thought not generally.[42]

Kentucky, Louisiana, Indiana, Alabama, Georgia, Virginia, and Arkansas all passed laws between 1813 and 1840 that prohibited the carrying of concealed pistols (among other deadly weapons)[43]—when, according to Bellesiles, there was "little market beyond the officers in the army and navy."[44]

The sources from the early Republic provide persuasive evidence that violence, including murder with or without guns, was common enough that it was never surprising. As with the prevalence of guns and hunting, Bellesiles' claims of a society where white-on-white violence was startling and rare is directly contradicted not just by many eyewitness accounts—it is directly contradicted by the accounts that Bellesiles cited for this claim.

Epilogue

It seems almost inconceivable that anyone could seriously argue, after having read the evidence, that America was not, from the very beginning, a society in which guns played a fundamental part: for the collective military purposes of each colony; for the defense of individual families and isolated settlements; as symbols of being a citizen with the duty to defend the society; and more than occasionally, to demonstrate that nothing has changed in the human condition since Cain slew Abel.

Guns were a fundamental part of hunting, from the first settlements between ocean and forest. Americans hunted to put meat on the table, furs on the trading floor, and perhaps most often of all, for sport. Throughout all regions and all periods that we have examined, hunting was the norm, and so was gun ownership for that purpose. Even slaves, at least at times, were trusted to go hunting and to participate as armed members of the militia—in spite of the enormous risks that arming slaves might entail.

I have spent much of the last five years reading tens of thousands of pages of newspapers, law books, memoirs, travel accounts, advertisements, and secondary sources about early America. The primary sources about how common guns were in the early United States speak with one voice: Gun ownership appears to have been the norm for freemen, and not terribly unusual for free women and at least male children, throughout the Colonial, Revolutionary, and early Republic periods. To argue otherwise is only slightly more plausible than arguing that Columbus sailed from New York City and discovered Europe.

Appendix: Firearms Glossary

All firearms require a method for lighting gunpowder, which expels the projectile from the barrel of the gun. *Matchlock, wheellock, flintlock* and *percussion* describe different types of ignition systems used on all types of firearms—and were also used in that time as shorthand to describe firearms using these ignition mechanisms. Unless otherwise qualified, "matchlock" or "flintlock" in seventeenth or eighteenth documents means a musket or fowling piece using this ignition system.

MATCHLOCK

The matchlock used a slow burning material known as *slowmatch*; when you pulled the trigger, the slowmatch dropped into the pan, igniting the primer powder. The fire from the primer would burn through a small hole into the barrel, ignite the main charge, and fire the lead ball out of the barrel. (Of course, if the powder in the pan failed to set off the main charge in the barrel, there was a flash of light and smoke—but no explosion—a "flash in the pan.") In the following picture, notice the lever below the stock, which is the trigger, and the curved match holder on the right.

ARQUEBUS

An early form of the matchlock musket.

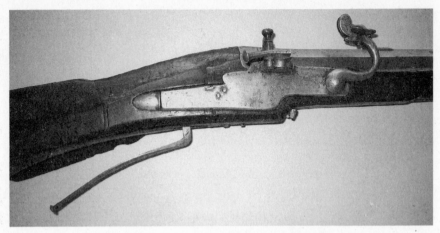

A 17ᵀᴴ CENTURY MATCHLOCK ARQUEBUS

BLUNDERBUSS

A *blunderbuss* is a short-barreled firearm designed for close range fighting, with a distinctive belled muzzle, intended to spread shot rapidly with lethal effect. Blunderbusses were tremendous, deadly weapons at close range. They were commonly carried on ships to repel pirates—but they appeared with surprising frequency among the civilian population of the United States.

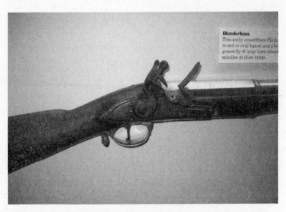

AN 18ᵀᴴ CENTURY BLUNDERBUSS

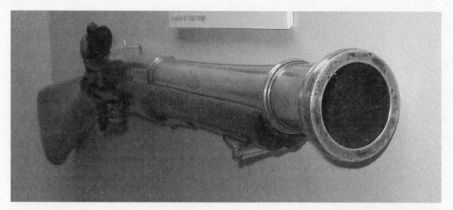

THE END OF A BLUNDERBUSS YOU DO NOT WANT TO SEE

FLINTLOCK

The flintlock strikes a piece of flint against a piece of steel. The flying sparks ignite the powder in the pan, setting fire to the main charge in the barrel. In this photograph you can see the screw mechanism that holds the flint. The hole leading into the brass barrel provides the path by which the burning gunpowder in the pan ignites the powder in the barrel. You used a *priming wire* to remove gunpowder ash from this hole.

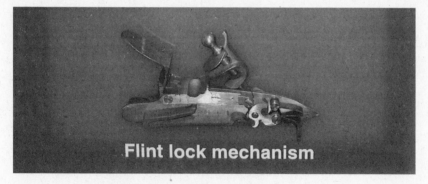

AN 18ᵀᴴ CENTURY FLINTLOCK

Flintlocks appeared in the sixteenth century and largely replaced matchlock guns in America by the mid-seventeenth century.

MUSKET

A *musket* is a *smoothbore* long gun, which means that the barrel is smooth on the inside. It may be fired with either shot or round lead balls.

"BROWN BESS": STANDARD BRITISH FLINTLOCK MUSKET OF THE LATE 18TH CENTURY

FIRELOCK

The term *firelock* was used in most of the seventeenth and eighteenth centuries to describe any wheellock or flintlock firearms. By the time of the Revolution, Americans seem to use *firelock* to refer to a smaller, civilian form of the musket.

FOWLING PIECE

A *fowling piece* is the ancestor of the modern shotgun, distinguished from a musket by being generally of smaller caliber, with lesser range, and designed primarily to fire shot, although fowling pieces could fire lead balls as well.

FUSEE, FUZEE, OR FUSIL

A *fusee, fuzee,* or *fusil* is a lighter, smaller form of the musket.

GUNLOCK

A *gunlock* refers to the lockwork mechanism of trigger and hammer (or cock) that fires the gun. Adding to the confusion, a gunlock was often simply called a *lock*, but many craftsmen who made gunlocks also worked as locksmiths, making or repairing locks for doors.

PEPPERBOX

Pepperbox pistols had multiple barrels, which enabled you to fire four or six shots without reloading. Of course, if you were unfortunate, a pepperbox might fire all shots at once, or blow up in your hand.

AN ALLEN & THURBER PEPPERBOX, EARLY 19ᵗʰ CENTURY[1]

PISTOL

A *pistol* (spelled in an astonishing number of different ways in the Colonial period) was any weapon intended to be fired one handed. Until the late eighteenth century, pistols, like almost all other firearms of the period, could fire one shot before reloading. (Adding to the complexity of reading documents of the time, a "pistole" was a coin often used in Colonial America, and merchants used "pistol" as an adjective to describe certain types of cloth.)

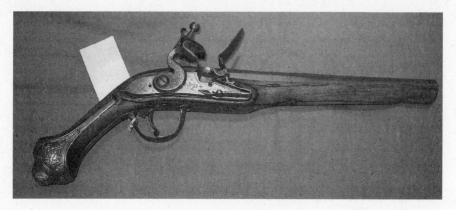

18ᵗʰ CENTURY FLINTLOCK PISTOL, IMPORTED FROM BRITAIN OR CONTINENTAL EUROPE

REVOLVER

The revolver has a single barrel and a cylinder that rotates, allowing multiple shots without reloading. While others had experimented with revolving cylinder weapons in the nineteenth century, Samuel Colt perfected it.

RIFLED BARREL

A rifled barrel (from which our word *rifle* comes) has several spiral grooves cut inside the barrel that spin a ball or bullet as it leaves the barrel. This spinning stabilizes the bullet so that a rifle is more accurate at long range than a musket.

SNAPHANCE OR SNAPHAUNCE

One particular style of flintlock mechanism is known as a snaphance, sometimes claimed to be derived from Dutch words describing a hen dropping to the ground to peck at grain.

WHEELLOCK

The wheellock works in the same way as a cigarette lighter, with a spinning piece of metal striking sparks to light the powder in the pan. The wheellock made pistols practical because of their compactness, and because you could carry such a weapon in your coat—no slowmatch setting fire to your pocket, or giving away that you were armed because of smoke. Wheellocks appear in the sixteenth century, and while already obsolete at the time the English settled the American colonies, they were still in use until the middle of the seventeenth century.

Bibliography

PRIMARY SOURCES

Acts and Laws of His Majesties Colony of Rhode-Island, and Providence-Plantations in America, (John Allen, 1179 [1719]).

Acts and Laws, Passed by the General Court or Assembly of the Province of New-Hampshire in New-England ... (1716). In Clifford K. Shipton, ed., *Early American Imprints, 1639–1800* (American Antiquarian Society, 1967), imprint 1985.

Acts and Resolves, Public and Private, of the Province of the Massachusetts Bay ... (Albert J. Wright, 1878).

Adams, Jr., Charles Francis ed. *New English Canaan of Thomas Morton* (The Prince Society, 1883; reprinted, Burt Franklin, 1967).

A Letter From a Gentleman of the City of New-York To Another ... (William Bradford, 1698). In Charles M. Andrews, ed., *Narratives of the Insurrections: 1675–1690* (Charles Scribner's Sons, 1915; reprinted, Barnes & Noble, 1959).

Allen, Jeremiah, Jeremiah Allen Account Book, 1714–1716, Massachusetts Historical Society.

Alsop, George, *A Character of the Province of Mary-land* ... (Peter Dring, 1666). In Clayton Colman Hall, ed., *Narratives of Early Maryland: 1633–1684* (Charles Scribner's Sons, 1910; reprinted, Barnes & Noble, 1959), 340–87.

"An Act in Addition to the Several Acts Already Made For The Prudent Storage of Gun-Powder Within the Town of Boston" (1786).

Andrews, Charles M. ed., *Narratives of the Insurrections, 1675–1690* (C. Scribner & Sons, 1915; reprinted, Barnes & Noble, 1959).

"A Proclamation. Mayor's Office, Washington Dec. 23, 1828," Printed Ephemera Collection; Portfolio 193, Folder 10, Library of Congress.

Arber, Edward, ed., *The Story of the Pilgrim Fathers, 1606–1623 A.D.; as told by Themselves, their Friends, and their Enemies* (1897).

Archdale, John., *A New Description of That Fertile and Pleasant Province of Carolina* ... (John Wyat, 1707). In Alexander S. Salley, Jr., ed., *Narratives of Early Carolina: 1650–1708* (Charles Scribner's Sons, 1911; reprinted, Barnes & Noble, 1959), 282–311.

A Relation of Maryland; Together with a Map of the Countrey ... (William Peasley, 1635). In Clayton Colman Hall, ed. *Narratives of Early Maryland: 1633–1684* (Charles Scribner's Sons, 1910; reprinted, Barnes & Noble, 1959), 70–112.

Ashe, Thomas, *Carolina, or a Description of the Present State of that Country* . . . (Mrs. Grover, 1682). In Alexander S. Salley, Jr., ed., *Narratives of Early Carolina: 1650–1708* (Charles Scribner's Sons, 1911; reprinted, Barnes & Noble, 1959), 138–59.

Audubon, John James, *Delineations of American Scenery and Character* (G.A. Baker & Co., 1926).

Baily, Francis, Jack D.L. Holmes, ed., *Journal of a Tour in Unsettled Parts of North America in 1796 & 1797* (Southern Illinois University Press, 1969).

Baird, Robert, *View of the Valley of the Mississippi* . . . (H.S. Tanner, 1832).

Bartlett, John Russell, ed., *Records of the Colony of Rhode Island and Providence Plantations, in New England* (A. Crawford Greene and Brother, 1856).

Bass, Sheila, comp., *Buffalo, Erie County, New York Directory, 1832* [database online] (Ancestry.com, 2001), original data: *Buffalo, New York Directory, 1832* (L.P. Crary, 1832).

[Bayard, Nicholas], *A Modest and Impartial Narrative Of several Grievances and Great Oppressions* . . . (n.p., 1690). In Charles M. Andrews, ed., *Narratives of the Insurrections: 1675–1690* (Charles Scribner's Sons, 1915; reprinted, Barnes & Noble, 1959).

Beecher, Edward, *Narrative of Riots at Alton* (1838; reprinted, E.P. Dutton & Co., 1965).

Bernhard, Karl (Duke of Saxe-Weimar-Eisenach), *Travels Through North America, During the Years 1825 and 1826* (Carey, Lea & Carey, 1828).

Bernstein, David A. ed., *Minutes of the Governor's Privy Council, 1777–1789* (New Jersey State Library, 1974).

Beverley, Robert, Louis B. Wright, ed., *The History and Present State of Virginia* (University of North Carolina Press, 1947).

Blane, William N., *An Excursion through the United States and Canada, during the Years 1822–3* (Baldwin, Cradock, and Joy, 1824; reprinted, Negro Universities Press, 1969).

Bradford, William, Samuel Eliot Morison, ed., *Of Plymouth Plantation, 1620–1647* (Alfred A. Knopf, 2001).

Boston Board of Fireworks, "An Act, Further Regulating the Storage, Safe Keeping, and Transportation of Gunpowder, in the Town of Boston, Together With the Rules and Regulations of the Firewards, Relative to the Same" (n.p., 1821).

Boston Gazette, 21 December 1719–1720, 12 January 1730–5 April 1731, 17 November 1741–13 September 1742, 16 January 1750–1755 (a few scattered issues).

Boston (Mass.) "Blank License to Keep and Sell Gunpowder in the City of Boston," (n.p., 1833), Massachusetts Historical Society.

Bradford, William, Samuel Eliot Morison, ed., *Of Plymouth Plantation, 1620–1647* (A. Knopf, 2001).

Brigham, William, ed., *The Compact with the Charter and Laws of the Colony of New Plymouth* . . . (Dutton and Wentworth, 1836).

Brookville Enquirer & Indiana Telegraph, January 1820.

Browne, William Hand ed., *Archives of Maryland* (Maryland Historical Society, 1885).

Burlend, Rebecca, *A True Picture of Emigration: Or Fourteen Years in the Interior of North America* . . . (G. Berger, 1848).

Bushman, Claudia L., Harold B. Hancock, and Elizabeth Moyne Homsey, ed., *Proceedings of the Assembly of the Lower Counties on Delaware 1770–1776, of the Constitutional Convention of 1776, and of the House of Assembly of the Delaware State 1776–1781* (University of Delaware Press, 1986).

Byfield, Nathanael, *An Account of the Late Revolution in New-England* . . . (Ric. Chitwell, 1689). In Charles M. Andrews, ed., *Narratives of the Insurrections, 1675–1690* (C. Scribner & Sons, 1915; reprinted, Barnes & Noble, 1959), 170–82.

Candler, Allen D., comp., *The Colonial Records of the State of Georgia* (Chas. P. Byrd, 1911).

Carey, John, ed., *Eyewitness to History* (Harvard University Press, 1988).

Carleton, Robert [Baynard Rush Hall], *The New Purchase, or Seven and a Half Years in the Far West* (D. Appleton & Co., 1843).

Carroll, Andrew, ed., *Letters of a Nation: A Collection of Extraordinary American Letters* (Kodansha International, 1997).

Cartwright, Peter, *Autobiography of Peter Cartwright, the Backwoods Preacher* (Jennings & Graham, 1856).

Cather, Thomas, Thomas Yoseloff, ed., *Voyage to America: The Journals of Thomas Cather* (Thomas Yoseloff, 1961; reprinted, Greenwood Press, 1973).

Claiborne, William C., Dunbar Rowland, ed., *Official Letter Books of W.C.C. Claiborne* (Mississippi Department of Archives and History, 1917).

Clark, Walter, ed., *The State Records of North Carolina* (Nash Bros., 1903).

Clay, Cassius Marcellus, *The Writings of Cassius Marcellus Clay*, Horace Greeley, ed., (Harper & Brothers, 1848; reprinted, Negro Universities Press, 1969).

Cleaveland [Ohio] *Herald*, 30 October 1821.

"Claiborne vs. Clobery et als. In the High Court of Admiralty," *Maryland Historical Magazine* 28:26–43.

Clay, Cassius Marcellus, Horace Greeley, ed., *The Writings of Cassius Marcellus Clay* (Harper & Brothers, 1848; reprinted, Negro Universities Press, 1969).

Code of 1650, Being a Compilation of the Earliest Laws and Orders of the General Court of Connecticut (Silas Andrus, 1822).

Coleman, Kenneth, and Milton Ready, ed., *Colonial Records of the State of Georgia: Trustees' Letter Book 1732–1738* (University of Georgia Press, 1985).

Collection of all the Public Acts of Assembly, of the Province of North-Carolina: Now in Force and Use . . . (James Davis, 1751).

Colonial Laws of New York from the Year 1664 to the Revolution . . . (James B. Lyon, 1894).

Colonial Records of Pennsylvania (J. Severns, 1852).

Commonwealth v. *Stephen Annis*, 9 Mass. 31 (1812).

Cooke, Jacob E. ed., *The Federalist*. (Wesleyan University Press, 1961).

Copeland, Jr., E., "Dupont's Superior Gunpowder: A Constant Supply of Dupont's Gunpowder, Warranted of the First Quality, and Assorted Sizes . . ." (Davies, ca. 1819), Hagley Museum and Library.

Costa, Tom. ed., *Virginia Runaways: Runaway Slave Advertisements from 18th-century Virginia Newspapers*, http://www.wise.virginia.edu/history/runaways/.

Cotton, Edward, *The Boston Directory: Containing The Names Of The Inhabitants, Their Occupations, Places Of Business, And Dwelling-Houses . . .* (David Carlisle, 1805).

Cox, Sandford C., *Recollections of the Early Settlement of the Wabash Valley* (1860; reprinted, Books for Libraries Press, 1970).

Coxe, Tench, *A Statement of the Arts and Manufactures of the United States of America, for the Year 1810* (A. Cornman, 1814).

Cuming, Fortescue, *Sketches of a Tour to the Western Country Through the States of Ohio and Kentucky; A Voyage Down the Ohio and Mississippi Rivers . . .* (Cramer & Bierbaum, 1810).

Cushing, John D., ed., *The Earliest Printed Laws of North Carolina, 1669–1751* (Michael Glazier, Inc., 1977).

_____. ed., *The Earliest Acts and Laws of the Colony of Rhode Island and Providence Plantations, 1647–1719* (Michael Glazier, Inc., 1977).

Danckaerts, Jasper, Barlett Burleigh James and J. Franklin Jameson, ed., *Journal of Jasper Danckaerts: 1679–1680* (Charles Scribner's Sons, 1913; reprinted, Barnes & Noble, 1959).

Defoe, Daniel, *Party-Tyranny, or an Occasional Bill in Miniature . . .* (n.p., 1705). In Alexander S. Salley, Jr., ed., *Narratives of Early Carolina: 1650–1708* (Charles Scribner's Sons, 1911; reprinted, Barnes & Noble, 1959), 224–64.

Delaware County Republican, 15 February 1839, http://www.accessible.com.

Dexter, Franklin B., *Biographical Sketches of the Graduates of Yale College* (H. Holt & Co, 1896).

Dickens, Charles, *American Notes for General Circulation* (1842), available at http://etext.lib.virginia.edu/toc/modeng/public/DicAmer.html.

Du Pont Company, "Sales of Gunpowder and Remanufactured Gunpowder Period 1810 to 1815 Inclusive," Du Pont Company Legal Dept. files, box 32, Hagley Museum and Library.

Du Pont, Victor, "Riflemen, Attention!: Gunpowder of the First Quality—Manufactured by E.I. Dupont de Nemours & Co.—to Be Had—by Applying to the Subscriber," (James Wilson, 1806), Hagley Museum and Library.

E.I. du Pont de Nemours & Company, "Hagley Mills: IIF Gunpowder," Courtesy Hagley Museum and Library.

Elliot, Jonathan, *The Debates of the Several State Conventions on the Adoption of the Federal Constitution* (Burt Franklin, 1888).

Enumeration of the Inhabitants of the United States, 1830 (Duff Green, 1832).

Essex (Mass.) *Gazette*, January 1775.

Fearon, Henry Bradshaw, *Sketches of America: A Narrative of a Journey of Five Thousand Miles Through the Eastern and Western States* (Longman, Hurst, Rees, Orne, and Browne, 1818; reprint, Benjamin Blom, 1969).

Fernow, Berthold ed., *Documents Relating to the Colonial History of the State of New York* (Weed, Parsons & Co., 1887; reprinted, AMS Press, Inc., 1969).

Flower, Richard, *Letters from the Illinois, 1820–1821: Containing An Account of the English Settlement at Albion and Its Vicinity . . .* (J. Ridgway, 1822).

Force, Peter, ed., *American Archives: Consisting Of A Collection Of Authentick Records, State Papers, Debates, And Letters And Other Notices Of Publick Affairs . . .* (1837–53; reprinted, Johnson Reprint Co., 1972).

Ford, Worthington C. *et al.,* ed., *Journals of the Continental Congress, 1774–1789* (Government Printing Office, 1904–37).

Fordham, Elias Pim, Frederic Austin Ogg, ed., *Personal Narrative of Travels in Virginia, Maryland, Pennsylvania, Ohio, Indiana, Kentucky; and of a Residence in the Illinois Territory: 1817–1818* (Arthur H. Clark Co., 1906; reprinted, Library Resources, Inc., 1970).

Franklin, Benjamin, *The Papers of Benjamin Franklin,* Leonard W. Labaree, ed., (Yale University Press, 1961).

Gosse, Philip, *Letters from Alabama* (Morgan & Chase, 1859).

Hall, Clayton Colman, ed., *Narratives of Early Maryland: 1633–1684* (Charles Scribner's Sons, 1910; reprinted, Barnes & Noble, 1959).

Hamilton, Stanislaus Murray, ed., *Letters to Washington and Accompanying Papers* (Houghton, Mifflin & Co., 1902).

Hammond, John, *Leah and Rachel, Or, The Two Fruitfull Sisters Virginia and Mary-land . . .* (T. Mabb, 1656). In Clayton Colman Hall, ed. *Narratives of Early Maryland: 1633–1684* (Charles Scribner's Sons, 1910; reprinted, Barnes & Noble, 1959), 281–308.

Harrower, John, "Diary . . . .1773–1776." *American Historical Review* [October 1900]: 65–107.

Hart, Albert Bushnell, ed., *American History told by Contemporaries* (Macmillan Co., 1898).

Hart, Albert Bushnell and Mabel Hill, *Camps and Firesides of the Revolution* (Macmillan Co., 1937).

Haswell, Charles H., *Reminiscences of New York by an Octogenarian* (Harper & Bros., 1896).

Heath, Dwight B. ed., *Mourt's Relation: A Journal of the Pilgrims at Plymouth* (Applewood Press, 1963).

Hemphill, William Edwin, and Wylma Anne Wates, and R. Nicholas Olsberg, ed., *Journals of the General Assembly and House of Representatives 1776–1780* (University of South Carolina Press, 1970).

_____. ed., *Extracts from the Journals of the Provincial Congresses of South Carolina, 1775–1776* (South Carolina Archives Department, 1960).

Hening, William Waller, ed., *The Statutes at Large; Being a Collection of all the Laws of Virginia, from the First Session of the Legislature, in the Year 1619* (R. & W. & G. Bartow, 1823).

Henry Family Papers at Hagley Museum and Library.

Henry Family Papers at Historical Society of Pennsylvania.

Herrman, Augustine, "Journal of the Dutch Embassy to Maryland." In Clayton Colman Hall, ed., *Narratives of Early Maryland: 1633–1684* (Charles Scribner's Sons, 1910; reprinted, Barnes & Noble, 1959), 314–33.

Higginson, Francis, *New England's Plantation Or A Short And True Description Of The Commodities And Discommodities Of That Country: Written By A Reverend Divine Now There Resident* (Michael Sparke, 1630).

Hoadly, Charles J., ed., *Public Records of the State of Connecticut* (Case, Lockwood & Brainard Co., 1894).

_____. ed., *Records Of The Colony And Plantation Of New Haven, From 1638 To 1649* (Case, Tiffany, 1857).

_____. ed., *Records of the Colony or Jurisdiction of New Haven, from May 1653, to the Union* (Case, Lockwood & Co., 1858).

Honeyman, A. Van Doren, ed., *Documents Relating to the Colonial History of the State of New Jersey*, 1ˢᵗ ser. (Unionist-Gazette Association, 1923).

Horne, Robert, *A Brief Description of the Province of Carolina . . .* (n.p. 1666). In Alexander S. Salley, Jr., ed., *Narratives of Early Carolina: 1650–1708* (Charles Scribner's Sons, 1911; reprinted, Barnes & Noble, 1959), 66–73.

Huntsville, Alabama, *Free Democrat*, 23 May 1837.

James, Jr., Sydney V., *Three Visitors to Early Plymouth* (Applewood Books, 1997).

Jameson, J. Franklin, ed., *Johnson's Wonder-Working Providence: 1628–1651* (Barnes & Noble, Inc., 1959).

Jefferson, Thomas. Julian P. Boyd, ed., *The Papers of Thomas Jefferson* (Princeton University Press, 1950).

Kimball, Gertrude Selwyn, ed., *The Correspondence of the Colonial Governors of Rhode Island 1723–1775* (Houghton, Mifflin & Co., 1903).

Kirkland, Caroline Matilda, *A New Home—Who'll Follow? Or, Glimpses of Western Life* (C.S. Francis, 1839), available at http://etext.lib.virginia.edu/toc/modeng/public/Eaf240.html.

Labaree, Leonard Woods, ed., *Royal Instructions to British Colonial Governors, 1670–1776* (Noble Offset Printers, Inc., 1935; reprinted, Octagon Books, Inc., 1967).

Lakin, James, *Baltimore Directory and Register, for 1814–15 . . .* (J.C. Oreilly, 1814).

Langford, John, *A Just and Cleere Refutation of a False and Scandalous Pamphlet Entitled Babylons Fall in Maryland . . .* (John Langford, 1655). In Clayton Colman Hall, ed., *Narratives of Early Maryland: 1633–1684* (Charles Scribner's Sons, 1910; reprinted, Barnes & Noble, 1959), 254–275.

Laws and Acts of the General Assembly of Her Majesties Province of Nova Caesarea or New-Jersey (W. Bradford, 1709). In Clifford K. Shipton, ed., *Early American Imprints, 1639–1800* (American Antiquarian Society, 1967), imprint 1412.

Laws and Acts of the General Assembly Of His Majesties Province of Nova Caesarea or New-Jersey . . . (William Bradford, 1722).

Laws of North Carolina–1715, In John D. Cushing, ed., *The Earliest Printed Laws of North Carolina, 1669–1751* (Michael Glazier, Inc., 1977).

Laws of the Government of New-Castle, Kent and Sussex Upon Delaware (B. Franklin, 1741).

Learning, Aaron and Jacob Spicer, *The Grants, Concessions, and Original Constitutions of the Province of New-Jersey* (W. Bradford, 1752).

Lee, Richard Henry, James Curtis Ballagh, ed., *The Letters of Richard Henry Lee* (Macmillan Co., 1911; reprinted, Da Capo Press, 1970).

Lincoln, Abraham, Roy P. Basler, ed., *The Collected Works of Abraham Lincoln* (Rutgers University Press, 1953–55).

Lowance, Mason L. Jr. and Georgia B. Bumgardner, *Massachusetts Broadsides of the American Revolution* (University of Massachusetts Press, 1976).

Loyalty Vindicated from the Reflections of a Virulent Pamphlet . . . (n.p., 1698). In Charles M. Andrews, ed., *Narratives of the Insurrections: 1675–1690* (Charles Scribner's Sons, 1915; reprinted, Barnes & Noble, 1959).

Lyford, William G., *The Western Address Directory: Containing the Cards of Merchants, Manufacturers, and Other Business Men* . . . (Joseph Robinson, 1837).

Mackenzie, Frederick, Allen French, ed., *A British Fusilier in Revolutionary Boston* (Harvard University Press, 1926).

Madison, James, William T. Hutchinson and William M.E. Rachal, ed., *The Papers of James Madison* (University of Chicago Press, 1962).

Marryat, Frederick, ed. Jules Zanger, *Diary in America* (Longman, Orme, Brown, Green, and Longmans, 1839; reprinted, Indiana University Press, 1960).

Martineau, Harriet, *Retrospect of Western Travel* (1838, reprinted, Haskell House Publishers, 1969).

Massachusetts, Governor (1760–1770: Bernard), "Pay Warrant, 14 June 1763," Miscellaneous Bound Manuscripts, Massachusetts Historical Society.

Masschusetts Militia, Massachusetts Militia Record of Firearms Distribution [1776], Ms. S–63, Massachusetts Historical Society.

Massachusetts Provincial Congress, *The Journals of Each Provincial Congress of Massachusetts in 1774 and 1775* (Dutton and Wentworth, 1838).

McCord, David J., *Statutes at Large of South Carolina* (A.S. Johnson, 1840).

McCord, Shirley S. ed., *Travel Accounts of Indiana, 1679–1961* (Indiana Historical Bureau, 1970).

McGuffey, William H., *The Eclectic First Reader for Young Children* (Truman & Smith, 1836; reprinted, Mott Media, 1982).

McIlwaine, H.R. ed., *Journals of the House of Burgesses of Virginia, 1659/60–1693* (The Colonial Press, 1914).

_____. ed., *Journals of the Council of the State of Virginia* (Virginia State Library, 1931).

(Milledgeville, Ga.) *Georgia Journal*, January 1838.

(Milledgeville, Ga.) *Southern Recorder*, January 1838.

Minutes of the Supreme Executive Council of Pennsylvania (Theo. Fenn & Co., 1852).

Mitchell, James T. and Henry Flanders, ed., *Statutes at Large of Pennsylvania from 1682 to 1801* (William Stanley Ray, 1898).

Morton, Thomas, *A New English Canaan* (Jacob Frederick Stam, 1637). In Charles Francis Adams, Jr., ed., *New English Canaan of Thomas Morton* (The Prince Society, 1883; reprinted, Burt Franklin, 1967).

Murray, Charles Augustus, *Travels in North America* (R. Bentley, 1839; reprinted, Da Capo Press, 1974).

Myers, Albert Cook, ed., *Narratives of early Pennsylvania, West New Jersey and Delaware, 1630–1707* (Barnes & Noble, 1959).

Nashville Daily Republican Banner, October-November 1837.

New Brunswick (N.J.) Common Council, "Gun-powder: an Ordinance, to Prevent the Storage, or Otherwise Keeping, Within Half a Mile of the Line of Buildings of This City, Certain Quantities of Gunpowder," (A. Blauvelt, 1813).

New York [City] *Morning Herald*, 1–17 January 1838.

New York (Colony) Legislative Council, *Journal of the Legislative Council of the Colony of New-York: Began the 8th Day of December, 1743; and Ended the 3rd of April, 1775* (Weed, Parson & Co., 1861).

New York Mercury, 29 August 1763.

New York (State) Court of Oyer and Terminer (Dutchess County), *An Account Of The Trial Of Jesse Wood For Shooting His Son Joseph Wood* . . . (n.p., 1806).

Olmsted, Frederick Law, Charles E. Beveridge and Charles Capen McLaughlin, ed., *The Papers of Frederick Law Olmsted* (Johns Hopkins University Press, 1981).

Palliser, John, *Solitary Rambles and Adventures of a Hunter in the Prairies* (John Murray, 1853; reprinted, Charles E. Tuttle Co., 1969).

Palmer, William P., ed., *Calendar of Virginia State Papers and Other Manuscripts, 1652–1781, Preserved in the Capitol at Richmond* (Richmond, 1875).

Penn, William, *Some Account of the Province of Pennsilvania in America . . .* (Benjamin Clark, 1681). In Albert Cook Myers, ed., *Narratives of early Pennsylvania, West New Jersey and Delaware, 1630–1707* (Barnes & Noble, 1959), 202–15.

_____. *Letter From William Penn to the Committee of the Free Society of Traders* (Andrew Sowle, 1683). In Albert Cook Myers, ed., *Narratives of early Pennsylvania, West New Jersey and Delaware, 1630–1707* (Barnes & Noble, 1959), 224–44.

Pennsylvania Archives (J. Severns & Co., et al., 1852–1935).

Pennsylvania Gazette, 1728–1800, searched through http://www.accessible.com.

Pennsylvania Provincial Council, *Minutes Of The Provincial Council Of Pennsylvania, From The Organization To The Termination Of The Proprietary Government* (J. Severns, 1852).

Pennsylvania Supreme Executive Council, *Minutes Of The Supreme Executive Council Of Pennsylvania, From Its Organization To The Termination Of The Revolution* (T. Penn, 1852–53).

Pinckney, Eliza Lucas, Elise Pinckney, ed., *The Letterbook of Eliza Lucas Pinckney* (University of South Carolina Press, 1997).

Pole, Edward, *Military Laboratory, at No. 34 . . .* (R. Aitken, [1789]). In Library of Congress Printed Ephemera Collection, Portfolio 147, Folder 9a.

Pope, William F., *Early Days in Arkansas* (Frederick W. Allsopp, 1895).

Report of the Debates and Proceedings of the Convention for the Revision of the Constitution of the State of Kentucky 1849 (A.G. Hodges & Co., 1849).

Rhode Island General Assembly, *Acts and Laws of His Majesties Colony of Rhode-Island, and Providence-Plantations in America* (John Allen, 1179 [1719]).

Rhode Island General Assembly, "State of Rhode-Island and Providence Plantations. In General Assembly, May Second Session, A.D. 1778 . . ." (John Carter, 1778), Early American Imprints 43541.

Ricord, Frederick W. and William Nelson, ed., *Documents Relating to the Colonial History of the State of New Jersey* (Daily Advertiser Printing House, 1886).

Riddle, James M., *The Pittsburgh Directory, for 1815 . . .* (n.p., 1815).

Robertson, David, *Reports of the Trials of Colonel Aaron Burr . . .* (Hopkins and Earle, 1808; reprinted, Da Capo Press, 1969).

Robertson, James Rood, *Petitions of the Early Inhabitants of Kentucky to the General Assembly of Virginia 1769 to 1792* (John P. Morton & Co., 1914; reprinted, Da Capo Press, 1971).

Royall, Anne Newport, *Letters from Alabama, 1817–1822* (University of Alabama Press, 1969).

Ruxton, George Frederick. Leroy R. Hafen, ed., *Life in the Far West* (University of Oklahoma Press, 1951).

Rynning, Ole, ed. and trans. Theodore C. Blegen, *Ole Rynning's True Account of America* (Minnesota Historical Society, 1926).

Salley, Jr., Alexander S. ed., *Journal of the Grand Council of South Carolina* (Historical Commission of South Carolina, 1907).

_____. *Narratives of Early Carolina: 1650–1708* (Charles Scribner's Sons, 1911; reprinted, Barnes & Noble, 1959).

_____. ed., *Journal of the General Assembly of South Carolina: September 17, 1776–October 20, 1776* (Historical Commission of South Carolina, 1909).

Saunders, William L. ed., *The Colonial Records of North Carolina* (Josephus Daniels, 1890; reprinted, AMS Press, Inc., 1968).

Schoolcraft, Henry Rowe, intro. by Milton D. Rafferty, *Rude Pursuits and Rugged Peaks: Schoolcraft's Ozark Journal 1818–1819* (University of Arkansas Press, 1996).

Shurtleff, Nathaniel B., *Records of the Governor and Company of the Massachusetts Bay in New England* (William White, 1853).

Smith, Paul H. *et al.* eds., *Letters of Delegates to Congress, 1774–1789* (Library of Congress, 1976–2000).

Smith, William C., *Indiana Miscellany* (Poe & Hitchcock, 1867; reprinted, Library Resources, 1970).

Soule, Allen, ed., *Laws of Vermont* (Howard E. Armstrong, 1964).

Stedman, Charles, *The History of the Origin, Progress, and Termination of the American War* (J. Murray, 1794).

Strachey, William, comp., *For the Colony in Virginea Britannia: Laws Divine, Morall and Martiall, etc.*, ed., David H. Flaherty (University Press of Virginia, 1969).

Strong, Leonard, *Babylon's Fall in Maryland: a Fair Warning to Lord Baltamore* . . . (Leonard Strong, 1655). In Clayton Colman Hall, ed., *Narratives of Early Maryland: 1633–1684* (Charles Scribner's Sons, 1910; reprinted, Barnes & Noble, 1959), 235–46.

Tami, Chris, *New York City Wills* 1–11 (Ancestry, Inc., 1998–99) on http://www.ancestry.com under "New York City Wills."

Thomas, Gabriel, *An Historical and Geographical Account of the Province and Country of Pensilvania* . . . (A. Baldwin, 1698). In Albert Cook Myers, ed., *Narratives of early Pennsylvania, West New Jersey and Delaware, 1630–1707* (Barnes & Noble, 1959), 313–37.

Tocqueville, Alexis de., *Journey to America*, trans. George Lawrence, ed. J.P. Mayer (Greenwood Press, 1981).

Trumbull, J. Hammond (vol. 1–3), Charles J. Hoadly (vol. 4–15), *The Public Records of the Colony of Connecticut, Prior to the Union with New Haven Colony* (Brown & Parsons, 1850).

(Tuscumbia) *North Alabamian*, February 1837.

Tyler, Lyon Gardiner, *Narratives of Early Virginia, 1606–1625* (Charles Scribner's Sons, 1907; reprinted, Barnes & Noble, 1959).

United Kingdom Public Records Office, Customs 16.

United States Congress, *American State Papers: Military Affairs*.

_____. *Annals of Congress*.

_____. *Journal Of The Executive Proceedings Of The Senate Of The United States Of America*.

_____. *Journal of the House of Representatives of the United States*.

_____. *Journal of the Senate of the United States of America*.

The Upland [Delaware] *Union*, 27 December 1825, from http://www.accessible.com.

Virginia and Maryland, or The Lord Baltamore's printed CASE . . . (n.p., 1655). In Clayton Colman Hall, ed., *Narratives of Early Maryland: 1633–1684* (Charles Scribner's Sons, 1910; reprinted, Barnes & Noble, 1959), 187–230.

Washington, George, Donald Jackson, ed., *The Diaries of George Washington* (University Press of Virginia, 1976).

Washington, George, John C. Fitzpatrick, ed., *The Writings of George Washington from the Original Manuscript Sources, 1745–1799* (Government Printing Office, 1931–44).

Weld, Isaac, *Travels Through the States of North America, and the Provinces of Upper and Lower Canada, During the Years 1795, 1796, and 1797* (John Stockdale, 1807).

West, John, *The Boston Directory: Containing the Names of the Inhabitants* . . . (Manning & Loring, 1796).

_____. *The Boston Directory: Containing the Names of the Inhabitants* . . . (John Russell, 1800).

_____. *The Boston Directory: Containing the Names of the Inhabitants* . . . (E. Lincoln, 1803).

Wilson, Samuel, *An Account of the Province of Carolina* . . . (G. Larkin, 1682). In Alexander S. Salley, Jr., ed., *Narratives of Early Carolina: 1650–1708* (Charles Scribner's Sons, 1911; reprinted, Barnes & Noble, 1959), 164–76.

Winslow, Edward, *Good Newes from New England* (n.p., 1624; reprinted, Applewood Books, n.d.).

Winthrop, John, James Kendall Hosmer, ed., *Winthrop's Journal: "History of New England" 1630–1649* (Charles Scribner's Sons, 1908).

Wright, Frances, ed. Paul R. Baker, *Views of Society and Manners in America* (Belknap Press, 1963).

Wright, John Stillman, *Letters from the West; or a Caution to Emigrants* (1819; reprint, University Microfilms, Inc., 1966).

Zavala, Lorenzo de., Wallace Woolsey trans., *Journey to the United States of North America* (1980).

SECONDARY SOURCES

Andrews, Matthew Page, *Tercentenary History of Maryland* (S.J. Clarke Publishing Co., 1925).

Ayers, Edward L., *Vengeance and Justice: Crime and Punishment in the 19th-Century American South* (Oxford University Press, 1984).

Beecher, Edward, *Narrative of Riots at Alton* (1838; reprinted, E.P. Dutton & Co., 1965).

Bellesiles, Michael A., *Arming America: The Origins of a National Gun Culture* (Alfred A. Knopf, 2000).

_____. "Gun Laws in Early America: The Regulation of Firearms Ownership, 1607–1794." *Law & History Review*, 16:575 [1998].

_____. "The Origins of Gun Culture in the United States, 1760–1865," *Journal of American History*, 83:2 [September 1996], 425–55.

Bivins, Jr., John, *Longrifles of North Carolina*, 2nd ed. (George Shumway, 1988).

Brown, Abram English, *Beneath Old Roof Trees* (Lee & Shepard, 1896).

Brown, Kathleen M., *Good Wives, Nasty Wenches, and Anxious Patriarchs: Gender, Race, and Power in Colonial Virginia* (University of North Carolina Press, 1996).

Brown, Richard Maxwell, *The South Carolina Regulators* (Harvard University Press, 1963).

Brown, M.L., *Firearms in Colonial America: The Impact on History and Technology 1492–1792* (Smithsonian Institution Press, 1980).

Bruce, Philip Alexander, *Institutional History of Virginia in the Seventeenth Century* (G.P. Putnam's Sons, 1910; reprinted, Peter Smith, 1964).

Campbell, Charles, *History of the Colony and Ancient Dominion of Virginia* (J.B. Lippincott & Co., 1860; reprinted, The Reprint Co., 1965).

Carey, John, ed., *Eyewitness to History* (Harvard University Press, 1988).

Center to Prevent Handgun Violence, *Second Amendment Symposium: After the Emerson Decision, Setting the Record Straight on the Second Amendment*, available at http://www.gunlawsuits.org/pdf/defend/second/symposium.pdf.

Coburn, Frank Warren, *The Battle of April 19, 1775*, 2nd ed. (n.p. 1922; reprinted, Kennikat Press, 1970).

Cottrol, Robert J., and Raymond T. Diamond, "The Second Amendment: Toward an Afro-Americanist Reconsideration," *Georgetown Law Journal* 80:2 [December 1991]: 309–361.

Countryman, Edward, *A People in Revolution: The American Revolution and Political Society in New York, 1760–1790* (John Hopkins University Press, 1981).

Cramer, Clayton E., *For the Defense of Themselves and the State: The Original Intent and Judicial Interpretation of the Right to Keep and Bear Arms* (Praeger Press, 1994).

_____. *Concealed Weapon Laws of the Early Republic: Dueling, Southern Violence, and Moral Reform* (Praeger Press, 1999).

_____. "The Racist Roots of Gun Control," *Kansas Journal of Law & Public Policy* 4:2 [Winter 1995] 17–25.

Craven, Wesley Frank, *White, Red, and Black: the Seventeenth-Century Virginian* (University Press of Virginia, 1971).

Curtis, Edward E., *The Organization of the British Army in the American Revolution* (New Haven, 1926; reprinted, AMS Press, 1969).

Deetz, Patricia Scott, Christopher Fennell, and J. Eric Deetz, *The Plymouth Colony Archive Project*, "Analysis of Selected Probate Inventories," available at http://etext.lib.virginia.edu/users/deetz/Plymouth/probates.html.

Demos, John, *A Little Commonwealth: Family Life in Plymouth Colony* (Oxford University Press, 1970).

Deyrup, Felicia Johnson, *Arms Makers of the Connecticut Valley: A Regional Study of the Economic Development of the Small Arms Industry, 1798–1870* (George Banta Publishing Co., 1948).

Dickson, R.J., *Ulster Emigration to Colonial America 1718–1775* (Routledge & Kegan Paul, 1966).

Dyke, S.E., *Thoughts on the American Flintlock Pistol* (George Shumway, 1974).

Fischer, David Hackett, *Albion's Seed: Four British Folkways in America* (Oxford University Press, 1989).

Franklin, John Hope, *The Free Negro in North Carolina, 1790–1860* (University of North Carolina Press, 1995).

Fraser, George MacDonald, *The Steel Bonnets: The Story of the Anglo-Scottish Border Reivers* (HarperCollins, 1995).

Frothingham, Richard, *History of the Siege of Boston, and of the Battles of Lexington, Concord, and Bunker Hill*, 6th ed. (n.p., 1903).

Gilbert, Arlan K., "Gunpowder Production In Post-Revolutionary Maryland," *Maryland Historical Magazine*, 52:3 [September 1957]: 187–201.

Grubb, Farley, "The Statutory Regulation of Colonial Servitude: An Incomplete-Contract Approach," *Explorations in Economic History* 37 [January 2000]: 42–75.

Hadden, Salley E., *Slave Patrols: Law and Violence in Virginia and the Carolinas* (Harvard University Press, 2001).

Hamilton, T.M., *Early Indian Trade Guns: 1625–1775* (Museum of the Great Plains, 1968).

_____. ed. *Indian Trade Guns* (Pioneer Press, 1982).

Hansen, Joyce and Gary McGowan, *Breaking Ground, Breaking Silence: The Story of New York's African Burial Ground* (Henry Holt and Co., 1998).

Hartzler, Daniel D., *Arms Makers of Maryland* (George Shumway, 1977).

Hicks, James E., *Notes on United States Ordnance* (James E. Hicks, 1940).

Higginbotham, Don, *The War of American Independence: Military Attitudes, Policies, and Practice, 1763–1789* (Macmillan Co., 1971).

Hindes, Ruthanna, "Delaware Silversmiths, 1700–1850," *Delaware History* 12 [October 1967]: 4, 247–306.

Hoffman, Ronald and Peter J. Albert, ed., *Arms and Independence: The Military Character of the American Revolution* (University Press of Virginia, 1984).

Isaac, Rhys, *The Transformation of Virginia: 1740–1790* (University of North Carolina Press, 1982).

Jackson, Carlton, *A Social History of the Scotch-Irish* (Madison Books, 1993).

Jones, Alice Hanson, *American Colonial Wealth: Documents and Methods*, 2nd ed. (Arno Press, 1978).

_____. *Wealth of a Nation To Be: The American Colonies on the Eve of the Revolution* (Columbia University Press, 1980).

Kauffman, Henry J., *Early American Gunsmiths: 1650–1850* (Bramhall House, 1952).

Keegan, John, *The Face of Battle* (Penguin Books, 1978).

Kelso, William and Beverly Straube, *1996 Interim Report on the APVA Excavations at Jamestown, Virginia* (Association for the Preservation of Virginia Antiquities, 1997).

Klay, Frank, *The Samuel E. Dyke Collection of Kentucky Pistols* (The Gun Room Press, 1972).

Kohn, Richard H., *Eagle and Sword: The Beginnings of the Military Establishment in America, 1783–1802* (The Free Press, 1975).

Land, Aubrey C., *Colonial Maryland: A History* (KTO Press, 1981).

Lewis, Berkeley R., *Small Arms and Ammunition in the United States Service, 1776–1865* (Smithsonian Institution Press, 1956).

Leyburn, James G., *The Scotch-Irish: A Social History* (University of North Carolina Press, 1962).

Lindgren, James and Justine Lee Heather, "Counting Guns in Early America," *William and Mary Law Review* 43:5 [2002], 1777–1842.

Lindsay, Merrill, *The New England Gun: The First Two Hundred Years* (New Haven Colony Historical Society, 1975).

Lowance, Jr., Mason L. and Georgia B. Bumgardner, *Massachusetts Broadsides of the American Revolution* (University of Massachusetts Press, 1976).

Luccketti, Nicholas M., William M. Kelso, and Beverly A. Straube, *APVA Jamestown Rediscovery: Field Report 1994* (Association for the Preservation of Virginia Antiquities, 1994).

Maier, Pauline, *From Resistance to Revolution: Colonial Radicals and the Development of American Opposition to Britain, 1765–1776* (Alfred A. Knopf, Inc., 1972).

Malcolm, Joyce Lee, *To Keep and Bear Arms: The Origins of an Anglo-American Right* (Harvard University Press, 1994).

_____. "The Right of the People to Keep and Bear Arms: The Common Law Tradition," *Hastings Constitutional Law Quarterly* 10:285–314 [1983].

_____. *Guns and Violence: The English Experience* (Harvard University Press, 2002).

Main, Gloria L., *Tobacco Colony: Life in Early Maryland, 1650–1720* (Princeton University Press, 1982).

Mayer, Joseph B., *Flintlocks of the Iroquois: 1620–1687* (Rochester Museum of Arts and Sciences, 1943).

McCusker, John, *Money and Exchange in Europe and America, 1600–1775: A Handbook* (University of North Carolina Press, 1978).

McGaw, Judith A., ed. *Early American Technology: Making and Doing Things from the Colonial Era to 1850* (University of North Carolina, 1994).

Menard, Russell R., "The Tobacco Industry in the Chesapeake Colonies, 1617–1730: An Interpretation," *Research in Economic History*, 5:109–77.

Middlekauf, Robert, ed., *Bacon's Rebellion* (Rand McNally & Co., 1964).

Mooney, Chris, "Showdown: Liberal Legal Scholars Are Supporting The Right to Bear Arms. But Will Historians Shoot Them Down?" *Lingua Franca*, 10:1 [February 2000].

Morgan, Edmund S., *American Slavery, American Freedom: The Ordeal of Colonial Virginia* (W.W. Norton & Co., 1975).

Morgan, Philip D. *Slave Counterpoint: Black Culture in the Eighteenth-Century Chesapeake and Lowcountry* (University of North Carolina Press, 1998).

Novak, William J., "*Salus Populi*: The Roots of Regulation in America, 1787–1873," (Ph.D. diss., Brandeis University, 1992).

Peterson, Harold L., *Arms and Armor in Colonial America: 1526–1783* (Stackpole Co., 1956).

Pitcavage, Mark, "An Equitable Burden: The Decline of State Militias, 1783–1858," (Ph.D. diss., Ohio State University, 1995).

Plymouth Archaeological Rediscovery Project, "Firearms in Plymouth Colony" (2002), Tables 2 and 4, available at http://plymoutharch.tripod.com/parp/id71.html, last accessed August 10, 2004.

Ramsay, David, Lester H. Cohen, ed., *The History of the American Revolution* (Liberty Fund, 1990).

Randall, Willard Sterne, *Benedict Arnold: Patriot and Traitor* (Barnes & Noble Books, 1999).

Raphael, Ray, *A People's History of the American Revolution* (The New Press, 2001).

_____. *The First American Revolution: Before Lexington and Concord* (New Press, 2002).

Ripley, Ezra, *A History of the Fight at Concord* (Allen & Atwill, 1827).

Robbins, Walter L., "Christmas Shooting Rounds in America and Their Background," *Journal of American Folklore*, 86:339 [1973] 48–52.

Rorabaugh, W.J., *The Alcoholic Republic: An American Tradition* (Oxford University Press, 1979).

Russell, Carl P., *Firearms, Traps, & Tools of the Mountain Men* (University of New Mexico Press, 1977).

Rutman, Darrett B., *Winthrop's Boston: A Portrait of a Puritan Town, 1630–1649* (W.W. Norton & Co., Inc., 1965).

Scharf, J. Thomas, *History of Western Maryland: Being a History of Frederick, Montgomery, Carroll, Washington, Allegany, and Garrett Counties From the Earliest Period to the Present Day . . .* (L.H. Everts, 1882; reprinted, Regional Publishing Co., 1968).

Scharf, J. Thomas and Thompson Westcott, *History of Philadelphia, 1609–1884* (L.H. Everts & Co., 1884).

Schwarz, Philip J., *Twice Condemned: Slaves And The Criminal Laws Of Virginia, 1705–1865* (Louisiana State University Press, 1988).

Shapiro, James, *A Year in the Life of William Shakespeare: 1599* (HarperCollins, 2005).

Shea, William L., *The Virginia Militia in the Seventeenth Century* (Louisiana State University Press, 1983).

Shy, John, *A People Numerous and Armed: Reflections on the Military Struggle for American Independence* (Oxford University Press, 1976).

Simpson, J.A. and E.S.C. Weiner, ed., *Oxford English Dictionary*, 2nd ed. (Clarendon Press, 1989).

Smith, Abbot Emerson, *Colonists in Bondage: White Servitude and Convict Labor in America, 1607–1776* (Peter Smith, 1965).

Smith, Joseph H. ed., *Colonial Justice in Western Massachusetts (1639–1702): The Pynchon Court Record, An Original Judges' Diary of the Administration of Justice in the Springfield Courts in the Massachusetts Bay Colony* (Harvard University Press, 1961).

Smith, Mark H., "Rememering Mary, Shaping Revolt: Reconsidering the Stono Rebellion," *Journal of Southern History* 67:3 [August 2001] 513–34.

Soule, John E., Milton E. Terry, and Robert S. Wakefield, comp., *George Soule of the Mayflower and His Descendants for Four Generations*, 3rd ed. (General Society of Mayflower Descendants, 1999).

Stevens, William Oliver, *Pistols at Ten Paces: The Story of the Code of Honor in America* (Riverside Press, 1940).

Stickels, George A., "The William Smith Pistols Made by Medad Hills," *The Gun Report*, September 1979, 10–12.

Stratton, Eugene Aubrey, *Plymouth Colony: Its History & People, 1620–1691* (Ancestry Publishing, 1986).

Straube, Beverly A. and Nicholas Luccketti, *APVA Jamestown Rediscovery: 1995 Interim Report* (Association for the Preservation of Virginia Antiquities, 1996).

_____. *1997 Interim Report on the APVA Excavations at Jamestown, Virginia* (Association for the Preservation of Virginia Antiquities, 1998).

Swayze, Nathan, *The Rappahannock Forge* (American Society of Arms Collectors, 1976).

Thornton, John K., "African Dimensions of the Stono Rebellion," *American Historical Review* 96:4 [October 1991] 1101–13.

US Census Bureau, "Population Of The 100 Largest Cities And Other Urban Places In The United States: 1790 To 1990," June 1998, Table 6, available at http://www.census.gov/population/documentation/twps0027/tab06.txt.

Washburn, William, *The Governor and the Rebel: A History of Bacon's Rebellion in Virginia* (University of North Carolina Press, 1957).

Wax, Darold D, "'The Great Risque We Run': The Aftermath of Slave Rebellion at Stono, South Carolina, 1739–1745," *Journal of Negro History* 67:2 [Summer 1982] 136–47.

Weir, Robert M., *Colonial South Carolina: A History* (KTO Press, 1983).

Whisker, James B., *The Gunsmith's Trade* (Edwin Mellen Press, 1992).

_____. *The American Colonial Militia* (Edwin Mellen Press, 1997).

_____. *Arms Makers of Colonial America* (Susquehanna University Press, 1992).

Willison, George F. *Saints and Strangers* (Time-Life Books, 1981).

Windell, Marie, "News Notes and Book Reports," *Delaware History* 5 [March 1953]:3, 206–21.

Wood, Betty, *Slavery in Colonial Georgia, 1730–1775* (University of Georgia Press, 1984).

Wood, Peter H., *Black Majority: Negroes in Colonial South Carolina From 1670 Through the Stono Rebellion* (Alfred A. Knopf, 1974).

Woodward, E.M. & John F. Hageman, *History Of Burlington And Mercer Counties, New Jersey, With Biographical Sketches Of Many Of Their Pioneers And Prominent Men* (Everts & Peck, 1883).

Wright, James D., Peter H. Rossi, and Kathleen Daly, *Under the Gun: Weapons, Crime, and Violence in America* (Aldine de Gruyter, 1983).

REVIEWS AND CRITICISM OF *ARMING AMERICA*

Anderson, Fred, "Guns, Rights, and People," *Los Angeles Times*, 17 September 2000.

"The Bancroft and Bellesiles," *History News Network*, 14 December 2002, available at http://hnn.us/articles/1157.html.

Chambers II, John Whiteclay, "Lock and Load," *Washington Post*, 29 October 2000, X2.

Grossman, Ron, "Wormy Apples From the Groves of Academe," *Chicago Tribune*, 23 January 2002.

Gruber, Ira D., "Of Arms and Men: *Arming America* and Military History," *William & Mary Quarterly*, 3rd ser. 59(1):217–22.

Hillel Italie, Associated Press, "Publisher Stops History Book Publication," 7 January 2003, available at http://story.news.yahoo.com/news?tmpl=story&u=/ap/20030107/ap_on_en_ot/history_book_canceled_1.

Katz, Stanley N., Hanna H. Gray, Laurel Thatcher Ulrich, "Report of the Investigative Committee in the Matter of Professor Michael Bellesiles," 10 July 2002, available at http://www.emory.edu/central/NEWS/Releases/Final_Report.pdf.

Lane, Roger, "Review of Arming America," *Journal of American History* 88:2 [September 2001] 614–15.

Levinson, Sanford, "A Startling Reassessment of Gun Ownership and Gun Culture," History Book Club, November 2000.

Lindgren, James, "Fall from Grace: *Arming America* and the Bellesiles Scandal," *Yale Law Journal* 111:2195–2249 [June 2002].

Main, Gloria L., "Many Things Forgotten: The Use of Probate Records in *Arming America*" *William & Mary Quarterly*, 3rd ser. 59(1):205–16.

Malcolm, Joyce Lee, "Concealed Weapons," *Reason*, January 2001, 47–49.

Mehegan, David, "New Doubts About Gun Historian," *Boston Globe*, 11 September 2001.

Morgan, Edmund S., "In Love with Guns," *New York Review of Books*, 19 October 2000.

Rosenberg, Paul, "Historian Explodes Myth: Gun Culture Firing Blanks," Memphis *Commercial Appeal*, 24 September 2000.

Roth, Randolph, "Guns, Gun Culture, and Homicide: The Relationship Between Firearms, the Uses of Firearms, and Interpersonal Violence," *William & Mary Quarterly*, 3rd ser., 59(1):223–40.

Seckora, Melissa, "Disarming America," *National Review*, 1 October 2001.

Seib, Philip, "'Arming' Takes Aim at America's Gun 'Mythology,'" Milwaukee *Journal Sentinel*, 24 September 2000.

————. "Shooting Holes in Myth of Gun-toting Forebears," *Dallas Morning News*, 8 October 2000, 13C.

Skinner, David, "The Historian Who Couldn't Shoot Straight: The Truth About Michael Bellesiles' 'Arming America,'" *Weekly Standard*, 25 February 2002.

Slotkin, Richard, "The Fall Into Guns," *Atlantic Monthly*, November 2000, 114–18.

Suprynowicz, Vin, "Will Rewrite Nation's History to Suit New Tenant," Las Vegas *Review-Journal*, 17 September 2000.

"Take Another Look At Gun Rights History," *San Francisco Chronicle*, 25 September 2000, A22.

Wiener, Jon, "Emory's Bellesiles Report: A Case of Tunnel Vision," *OAH Newsletter* 31:1 [February 2003], available at http://www.oah.org/pubs/nl/2003feb/wiener.html.

Wills, Gary, "Spiking the Gun Myth," *New York Times*. 10 September 2000.

About the Author

Clayton E. Cramer (http://www.claytoncramer.com) received his M.A. in History from Sonoma State University in 1998. His fifth book, *Concealed Weapon Laws of the Early Republic: Dueling, Southern Violence, and Moral Reform* was published by Praeger Press in 1999.

Mr. Cramer works as a software engineer.

Notes

Acknowledgments and Technical Notes

1. John McCusker, *Money and Exchange in Europe and America, 1600–1775: A Handbook* (University of North Carolina Press, 1978).

Creating a Useable Past: Michael Bellesiles and Revisionist History

1. Michael A. Bellesiles, "The Origins of Gun Culture in the United States, 1760–1865," *Journal of American History*, 83:2 [September 1996], 425–55.
2. Michael A. Bellesiles, *Arming America: The Origins of a National Gun Culture* (Alfred A. Knopf, 2000), 174, 212, 220–1, 301, 73, 378, 306, 322–25.
3. "Take Another Look At Gun Rights History," *San Francisco Chronicle*, 25 September 2000, A22; Philip Seib, "'Arming' Takes Aim at America's Gun 'Mythology,'" Milwaukee *Journal Sentinel*, 24 September 2000; Philip Seib, "Shooting Holes in Myth of Gun-toting Forebears," *Dallas Morning News*, 8 October 2000, 13C; Richard Slotkin, "The Fall Into Guns," *Atlantic Monthly*, November 2000, 114–18; Paul Rosenberg, "Historian Explodes Myth: Gun Culture Firing Blanks," Memphis *Commercial Appeal*, 24 September 2000; Edmund S. Morgan, "In Love with Guns," *New York Review of Books*, 19 October 2000; Gary Wills, "Spiking the Gun Myth," *New York Times*, 10 September 2000.
4. Bellesiles, *Arming America*, 230 (first printing); *Debates and Proceedings in the Congress* 3:1392–95; *Statutes at Large*, 2nd Cong., sess. 1, Ch. 33 (1792), 1:271–74. *Statutes at Large* is identical to *US Statutes*.
5. Bellesiles, *Arming America*, 63.
6. Nathaniel B. Shurtleff, *Records of the Governor and Company of the Massachusetts Bay in New England* (William White, 1853), 1:25–26.
7. Bellesiles, *Arming America*, 73.
8. Shurtleff, *Records of the Governor and Company of the Massachusetts Bay in New England*, 1:125.
9. A few examples: Edmund S. Morgan, "In Love with Guns"; Gary Wills, "Spiking the Gun Myth"; Sanford Levinson, "A Startling Reassessment of Gun Ownership and Gun Culture," *History Book Club*, November 2000; Roger Lane, "Review of *Arming America*," *Journal of American History* 88:2 [September 2001] 614–15.
10. Vin Suprynowicz, "Will Rewrite Nation's History to Suit New Tenant," Las Vegas *Review-Journal*, 17 September 2000.
11. John Whiteclay Chambers II, "Lock and Load," *Washington Post*, 29 October 2000, X2.
12. Gloria L. Main, "Many Things Forgotten: The Use of Probate Records in *Arming America*," *William & Mary Quarterly*, 3rd ser., 59(1):205–16; Ira D. Gruber, "Of Arms and Men: *Arming America* and Military History," *William & Mary Quarterly*, 3rd ser., 59(1):217–22; Randolph Roth, "Guns, Gun Culture, and Homicide: The Relationship Between Firearms, the Uses of Firearms, and Interpersonal Violence," *William & Mary Quarterly*, 3rd ser., 59(1):223–40.

13. James Lindgren, "Fall from Grace: *Arming America* and the Bellesiles Scandal," *Yale Law Journal* 111:2195–2249 [June 2002].

14. Ron Grossman, "Wormy Apples from the Groves of Academe," *Chicago Tribune*, 23 January 2002; David Skinner, "The Historian Who Couldn't Shoot Straight: The Truth about Michael Bellesiles' 'Arming America,'" *Weekly Standard*, 25 February 2002.

15. David Mehegan, "New Doubts about Gun Historian," *Boston Globe*, 11 September 2001, A1; Melissa Seckora, "Disarming America," *National Review*, 1 October 2001.

16. Stanley N. Katz, Hanna H. Gray, Laurel Thatcher Ulrich, "Report of the Investigative Committee in the Matter of Professor Michael Bellesiles," 10 July 2002, http://www.emory.edu/central/NEWS/Releases/Final_Report.pdf.

17. "The Bancroft and Bellesiles," *History News Network*, 14 December 2002, http://hnn.us/articles/1157.html.

18. Hillel Italie, Associated Press, "Publisher Stops History Book Publication," 7 January 2003, http://story.news.yahoo.com/news?tmpl=story&u=/ap/20030107/ap_on_en_ot/history_book_canceled_1.

19. Christopher Waldrep and Michael Bellesiles, *Documenting American Violence: A Sourcebook* (Oxford University Press, 2006).

20. Jon Wiener, "Emory's Bellesiles Report: A Case of Tunnel Vision," *OAH Newsletter*, 31:1 [February 2003], http://www.oah.org/pubs/nl/2003feb/wiener.html.

21. John Russell Bartlett, ed., *Records of the Colony of Rhode Island and Providence Plantations, in New England* (A. Crawford Greene and Brother, 1856), 1:226.

22. Charles J. Hoadly, ed., *Records Of The Colony And Plantation Of New Haven, From 1638 To 1649* (Case, Tiffany, 1857), 176–77.

23. *Acts and Resolves, Public and Private, of the Province of the Massachusetts Bay . . .* (Albert J. Wright, 1878), 3:305–6.

24. J. Hammond Trumbull (vol. 1–3), Charles J. Hoadly (vol. 4–15), *The Public Records of the Colony of Connecticut, Prior to the Union with New Haven Colony* (Brown & Parsons, 1850) (hereinafter Trumbull, Hoadly, *Public Records of the Colony of Connecticut*), 1:95, 96.

25. Bellesiles, "Origins of Gun Culture in the United States, 1760–1865," 439.

26. William H. McGuffey, *The Eclectic First Reader for Young Children* (Truman & Smith, 1836; reprinted, Mott Media, 1982), 138–40.

27. W.J. Rorabaugh, *The Alcoholic Republic: An American Tradition* (Oxford University Press, 1979).

28. Samuel Wilson, *An Account of the Province of Carolina . . .* (G. Larkin, 1682), in Alexander S. Salley, Jr., ed., *Narratives of Early Carolina: 1650-1708* (Charles Scribner's Sons, 1911; reprinted, Barnes & Noble, 1959), 170. Indians selling game to the settlers at *A Relation of Maryland*, in Clayton Colman Hall, ed., *Narratives of Early Maryland: 1633-1684* (Charles Scribner's Sons, 1910; reprinted, Barnes & Noble, 1959), 98.

29. John Winthrop, James Kendall Hosmer, ed., *Winthrop's Journal: "History of New England" 1630-1649* (Charles Scribner's Sons, 1908), 1:191.

30. "Letter of Captain George to Pepys" (1689), in Charles M. Andrews, ed., *Narratives of the Insurrections, 1675-1690* (Charles Scribner's Sons, 1915; reprinted, Barnes & Noble, 1959), 216; "Andros's Report of His Administration," in Andrews, *Narratives of the Insurrections*, 232.

31. Trumbull, Hoadly, *Public Records of the Colony of Connecticut*, 14:419–20.

I. COLONIAL AMERICA

Chapter 1: A Lonely Outpost: Militias in Colonial America

1. William L. Shea, *The Virginia Militia in the Seventeenth Century* (Louisiana State University Press, 1983), 1–3; James Shapiro, *A Year in the Life of William Shakespeare: 1599* (HarperCollins, 2005), 62–64.

2. Leonard Woods Labaree, ed., *Royal Instructions to British Colonial Governors, 1670-1776* (Noble Offset Printers, Inc., 1935; reprinted, Octagon Books, Inc., 1967), 1:392–3.

3. In the 1630s and 1640s, Massachusetts, for example, required every Bostonian to turn out for public works construction and street maintenance. Householders of the town of Boston were required to possess a ladder reaching to the roof, and a "good large swob" on the end of a twelve-foot pole, to extinguish house fires. Refusing to assist a constable in enforcing the law, or refusing to participate in "watches & wardes" (a form of community policing), was punishable by a fine, starting in 1646. Darrett B. Rutman, *Winthrop's Boston: A Portrait of a Puritan Town, 1630-1649* (W. W. Norton & Co., Inc., 1965), 208, 215; Winthrop, *Winthrop's Journal,* 1:113; Shurtleff, *Records of the Governor and Company of the Massachusetts Bay,* 2:150–51.

4. *Code of 1650, Being a Compilation of the Earliest Laws and Orders of the General Court of Connecticut* (Silas Andrus, 1822), 72–73. Other Connecticut statutes to similar effect: in 1636, Trumbull, Hoadly, *Public Records of the Colony of Connecticut,* 1:3–4; in 1637, *Ibid.,* 1:15–16; in 1741, *Ibid.,* 8:379–83.

5. 1630/1: Shurtleff, *Records of the Governor and Company of the Massachusetts Bay in New England,* 1:84; 1631: *Ibid.,* 1:85; 1632/3: *Ibid.,* 1:93; 1634: *Ibid.,* 1:125; 1645: *Ibid.,* 2:122, 3:84; 1647: *Ibid.,* 2:222. See also a 1645 law at *Ibid.,* 2:99 (requiring "all youth" from ten to sixteen to be trained with "small guns, halfe pikes, bowes & arrows . . . ")

6. 1632: William Brigham, ed., *The Compact with the Charter and Laws of the Colony of New Plymouth . . .* (Dutton and Wentworth, 1836), 31; 1636: *Ibid.,* 44–45.

7. 1699: *Laws and Acts of Rhode Island, and Providence Plantations Made from the First Settlement in 1636 to 1705,* in John D. Cushing, ed., *The Earliest Acts and Laws of the Colony of Rhode Island and Providence Plantations, 1647-1719* (M. Glazier, 1977), 57, 106–7; 1718: *Acts and Laws of His Majesties Colony of Rhode-Island, and Providence-Plantations in America* (John Allen, 1179 [1719]), 86–87. (Emphasis added.)

8. 1647: *Proceedings of the First General Assembly of the Incorporation of Providence Plantations and the Code of Laws Adopted by That Assembly, in 1647,* in Cushing, *Earliest Acts and Laws of the Colony of Rhode Island,* 10.

9. 1639: Hoadly, *Records Of The Colony And Plantation Of New Haven,* 25–26; 1643: *Ibid.,* 96–97; 1644: *Ibid.,* 131; 1646: *Ibid.,* 202.

10. 1716: *Acts and Laws, Passed by the General Court or Assembly of the Province of New-Hampshire in New-England . . .* (1716), 91–92, in Clifford K. Shipton, ed., *Early American Imprints, 1639-1800* (American Antiquarian Society, 1967), imprint 1985.

11. *Colonial Laws of New York from the Year 1664 to the Revolution . . .* (James B. Lyon, 1894), 1:52–53.

12. 1668: Aaron Learning and Jacob Spicer, *The Grants, Concessions, and Original Constitutions of the Province of New-Jersey* (W. Bradford, 1752), 78, 86–88; 1679: *Ibid.,* 135–6; 1703: *The Laws and Acts of the General Assembly of Her Majesties Province of Nova Caesarea or New-Jersey* (W. Bradford, 1709), 12–13, in Clifford K. Shipton, ed., *Early American Imprints, 1639-1800* (American Antiquarian Society, 1967), imprint 1412.

13. 1742: *Laws of the Government of New-Castle, Kent and Sussex Upon Delaware* (B. Franklin, 1741), 171–7. While the title page says 1741, this must have been the first of an annual series. See also a 1740 statute, *Ibid.,* 151, imposing similar requirements on the town of Lewes, which was apparently considered especially exposed to naval attack.

14. 1639/40: William Waller Hening, ed., *The Statutes at Large; Being a Collection of all the Laws of Virginia, from the First Session of the Legislature, in the Year 1619* (R. & W. & G. Bartow, 1823), 1:226; 1684: *Ibid.,* 3:13; 1738: *Ibid.,* 5:16–17; 1748: *Ibid.,* 6:116; 1757: *Ibid.,* 7:94–95.

15. 1715: *Laws of North Carolina–1715,* ch. 25, in John D. Cushing, ed., *The Earliest Printed Laws of North Carolina, 1669-1751* (Michael Glazier, Inc., 1977), 2:29–31; 1746: *A Collection of all the Public Acts of Assembly, of the Province of North-Carolina: Now in Force and Use . . .* (James Davis, 1751), 215–16.

16. 1773: Allen D. Candler, comp., *The Colonial Records of the State of Georgia* (Chas. P. Byrd, 1911), 19(part 1):296.

17. Alexander S. Salley, *Journal of the Grand Council of South Carolina* (Historical Commission of South Carolina, 1907), 1:9–12; David J. McCord, *Statutes at Large of South Carolina* (A.S. Johnson, 1840), 7:417–19. See Peter H. Wood, *Black Majority: Negroes in Colonial South Carolina From 1670 Through the Stono Rebellion* (Alfred A. Knopf, 1974), 313–4, for discussion of the 1724 and 1739 statutes, and how the imminent enforcement of the 1739 statute may have encouraged the Stono Rebellion. Salley E. Hadden, *Slave Patrols: Law and Violence in Virginia and the Carolinas* (Harvard University Press, 2001), 16–21, discusses the Barbados origins of South Carolina's militia statutes, and how earlier than most, there was a clear division between the militia (aimed at external threats) and slave patrols.

18. A Springfield, Massachusetts, ordinance is mentioned at Joseph H. Smith, ed., *Colonial Justice in Western Massachusetts (1639–1702): The Pynchon Court Record, An Original Judges' Diary of the Administration of Justice in the Springfield Courts in the Massachusetts Bay Colony* (Harvard University Press, 1961), 124.

19. Portsmouth, Rhode Island, 1639: Bartlett, *Records of the Colony of Rhode Island*, 1:94; 1643, *Ibid.*, 1:79–80.

20. William Hand Browne, ed., *Archives of Maryland* (Maryland Historical Society, 1885), 1:347, 2:557, 3:103, 345, 13:554–6.

21. Browne, *Archives of Maryland*, 75:264; Farley Grubb, "The Statutory Regulation of Colonial Servitude: An Incomplete-Contract Approach," *Explorations in Economic History* 37 [January 2000]:69.

22. James B. Whisker, *The American Colonial Militia* (E. Mellen Press, 1997), vol. 3, ch. 1, http://www.constitution.org/jw/acm_3-m.htm.

23. *Ibid.*, ch. 2. A series of articles in the *Pennsylvania Gazette*, in Accessible Archives online collection, available at http://www.accessible.com, trace this dispute between Quakers and non-Quakers: 10 January 1740; 7 February 1740; 17 June 1742; 2 August 1744; 16 August 1744. For an example of voluntary militia formation, see the *Pennsylvania Gazette*, 22 December 1747.

24. James T. Mitchell and Henry Flanders, ed., *Statutes at Large of Pennsylvania from 1682 to 1801* (William Stanley Ray, 1898), 5:197, 200, 532; Whisker, *American Colonial Militia*, vol. 3, ch. 4.

25. Mitchell and Flanders, *Statutes at Large of Pennsylvania from 1682 to 1801*, 5:609–13.

26. Bartlett, *Records of the Colony of Rhode Island*, 6:78. See *Ibid.*, 6:80, for a statute authorizing purchase of ammunition "sufficient to furnish every soldier"—but not a word about purchasing or providing of guns.

27. *Code of 1650, Being a Compilation of the Earliest Laws and Orders of the General Court of Connecticut*, 72–73. New York had a similar provision: *Colonial Laws of New York*, 1:52–53.

28. Plymouth's 1646 order: Brigham, *Compact with the Charter and Laws of the Colony of New Plymouth*, 84; Virginia: 1757, Hening, *Statutes at Large*, 7:94–95; Rhys Isaac, *The Transformation of Virginia: 1740-1790* (University of North Carolina Press, 1982), 109–110.

29. Edmund S. Morgan, *American Slavery, American Freedom: The Ordeal of Colonial Virginia* (W.W. Norton & Co., 1975), 340–3.

30. Bartlett, *Records of the Colony of Rhode Island*, 1:79–80. Other colonies that required regular inspection to verify compliance: Massachusetts, 1645: Shurtleff, *Records of the Governor and Company of the Massachusetts Bay*, 2:118–19; New Haven, 1644: Hoadly, *Records Of The Colony And Plantation Of New Haven, From 1638 To 1649*, 131.

31. Browne, *Archives of Maryland*, 1:77. The requirement to view arms monthly reiterated in 1654 and 1658 at *Ibid.*, 1:347, 3:345, but the 1658 requirement applied only to members of the trainbands; the 1654 viewing requirement applied to every family. See Russell R. Menard, "The Tobacco Industry in the Chesapeake Colonies, 1617–1730: An Interpretation," *Research in Economic History* 5:111, for conversion of tobacco prices to sterling.

32. Hoadly, *Records Of The Colony And Plantation Of New Haven*, 122–3. Three men fined six pence for "want of flints" and a matchlock owner, "for want of match." Two men fined six pence "for want of worme and skourer" (used for cleaning the channel from flintlock pan to barrel). Eight

men fined three shillings, four pence "for total defect in armes." At *Ibid.*, 486, some years later, a Mathew Camfield fined "for want of some powder last viewing day 12*d.*, and for not bringing his armes to meeting one lecture day, 2*s.* 6*d.*" Henry Pecke and Thomas Marshall fined "for not bringing the[i]r armes to the meeting one day when it was their turne" 2*s.* 6*d.*

33. While married women lacked legal equality with men—and indeed had no separate legal existence or authority from their husband under the doctrine of *femme couverture*—single unmarried women and widows might accumulate substantial assets by inheritance or remarriage. In practice, Colonial law often gave women more control over property than English law.

34. Browne, *Archives of Maryland*, 1:77. See also *Ibid.*, 3:103, for a 1642 law requiring "That all housekeepers provide fixed gunn and Sufficient powder and Shott for each person able to bear arms." A 1658 revision of the law at *Ibid.*, 3:345, however, seems to be specific to men: "every househoulder provide himselfe speedily with Armes & Ammunition . . . ."

35. *A Relation of Maryland*, 94; Matthew Page Andrews, *Tercentenary History of Maryland* (S.J. Clarke Publishing Co., 1925), 1:150.

36. Browne, *Archives of Maryland*, 3:100–1.

37. Learning and Spicer, *Grants, Concessions, and Original Constitutions of the Province of New-Jersey*, 20–21.

38. Winthrop, *Winthrop's Journal*, 2:323–4. A 1652 Massachusetts law at Shurtleff, *Records of the Governor and Company of the Massachusetts Bay*, 3:265, provides that calvarymen were entitled to nominate many higher officers (subject to legislative confirmation), and to choose "all other inferior officers . . . ."

39. John Shy, *A People Numerous and Armed: Reflections on the Military Struggle for American Independence* (Oxford University Press, 1976), 24.

40. *Laws and Acts of the General Assembly of Her Majesties Province of Nova Caesarea or New-Jersey*, 12–13. Other groups exempted from militia duty or the duty to be armed: Virginia: 1624: those settlers who had arrived before 1612, Shea, *Virginia Militia in the Seventeenth Century*, 39–41; 1639/40: free blacks exempted from the obligation to arm themselves, and masters of indentured or enslaved blacks exempted from duty to arm them, Hening, *Statutes at Large*, 1:226; 1757: legislators, Anglican ministers, faculty and students of William and Mary College, the keeper of the public jail, overseers, millers, and "all workers in any mine whatsoever," Hening, *Statutes at Large*, 7:94–95.

41. *Laws of the Government of New-Castle, Kent and Sussex Upon Delaware*, 171–7.

42. Trumbull, Hoadly, *Public Records of the Colony of Connecticut*, 1:95, 96.

43. 1642: Browne, *Archives of Maryland*, 3:103.

44. 1644: Hoadly, *Records Of The Colony And Plantation Of New Haven*, 131–32. See *Ibid.*, 122–3, for men fined for failure to bring their guns to church, and Hoadly, 500, for William Paine's request that he be exempted from this requirement.

45. 2 August 1619, "Proceedings of the Virginia Assembly, 1619," in Lyon Gardiner Tyler, *Narratives of Early Virginia, 1606-1625* (Charles Scribner's Sons, 1907; reprinted, Barnes & Noble, 1959), 273; 1632: Hening, *Statutes at Large*, 1:198; 1738: Hening, *Statutes at Large*, 5:19.

46. 1639: Bartlett, *Records of the Colony of Rhode Island*, 1:94; 1643: *Ibid.*, 1:79.

47. McCord, *Statutes at Large of South Carolina*, 7:417–19.

48. Candler, *The Colonial Records of the State of Georgia*, 19(part 1):137–40.

49. Shurtleff, *Records of the Governor and Company of the Massachusetts Bay*, 1:190.

50. Shurtleff, *Records of the Governor and Company of the Massachusetts Bay*, 1:210.

51. Shurtleff, *Records of the Governor and Company of the Massachusetts Bay*, 2:38.

52. Brigham, *Compact with the Charter and Laws of the Colony of New Plymouth*, 70. By 1658, Plymouth had reduced the requirement so that only one fourth of the militia was obligated to come to church armed on any particular Sunday. In 1675, apparently in response to a current military crisis, all were again required to come to church armed "with att least six charges of powder and shott" during "the time of publicke danger . . . ." *Ibid.*, 115, 176.

53. Hening, *Statutes at Large*, 1:127, 198.

54. Shea, *Virginia Militia in the Seventeenth Century*, 56–57.

55. Shurtleff, *Records of the Governor and Company of the Massachusetts Bay*, 1:85.

56. Shurtleff, *Records of the Governor and Company of the Massachusetts Bay*, 1:190.

57. Bellesiles, *Arming America*, 73; Michael Bellesiles, "Gun Laws in Early America: The Regulation of Firearms Ownership, 1607–1794," *Law & History Review* 16:575 (1998).

58. Trumbull, Hoadly, *Public Records of the Colony of Connecticut*, 1:29.

59. Trumbull, Hoadly, *Public Records of the Colony of Connecticut*, 1:134.

60. J. Franklin Jameson, ed., *Johnson's Wonder-Working Providence: 1628-1651* (Barnes & Noble, Inc., 1959), 231.

61. Shurtleff, *Records of the Governor and Company of the Massachusetts Bay*, 5:48–49.

62. Browne, *Archives of Maryland*, 6 August 1676, 15:123–4.

63. Browne, *Archives of Maryland*, 75:425. See Bartlett, *Records of the Colony of Rhode Island*, 7:268, for a similar marking of public arms, before issuing them to the towns, just before the American Revolution.

64. Browne, *Archives of Maryland*, 52:452.

65. Printed Ephemera Collection; Portfolio 35, Folder 15b, Library of Congress.

66. Massachusetts, Governor (1760–1770: Bernard), "Pay Warrant, 14 June 1763," Miscellaneous Bound Manuscripts, Massachusetts Historical Society.

67. Browne, *Archives of Maryland*, 9:565. Also at *Ibid.*, 31:404, in 1760, and at *Ibid.*, 56:404 in 1761.

68. Walter Clark, ed., *State Records of North Carolina* (Nash Bros., 1907), 21:138.

69. Hening, *Statutes at Large*, 2:294; Philip Alexander Bruce, *Institutional History of Virginia in the Seventeenth Century* (G.P. Putnam's Sons, 1910; reprinted, Peter Smith, 1964), 2:58–59. H.R. McIlwaine, ed., *Journals of the House of Burgesses of Virginia, 1659/60-1693* (The Colonial Press, 1914), 68, suggests that the law may have been passed but not implemented. An order dated 7 March 1675/6 directs "that the late act for providing armes and ammunition be putt into strict and effectuall execution, alsoe that the county courts and militia officers see the smyths accounts for fixing armes, be putt into the collection, and that they be paid according to the act." Morgan, *American Slavery, American Freedom*, 140, discusses the problem of "unfixed" guns in terms of a shortage of skilled craftsmen—not a shortage of guns.

70. Bruce, *Institutional History of Virginia in the Seventeenth Century*, 2:40, 43.

71. Hening, *Statutes at Large*, 2:403.

72. Bartlett, *Records of the Colony of Rhode Island*, 1:226.

73. The very first entry in *Public Records of the Colony of Connecticut* concerns a 1636 complaint that "Henry Stiles or some of the ser[vants] had traded a peece with the Indians for Corne." Trumbull, Hoadly, *Public Records of the Colony of Connecticut*, 1:1, 2. In 1640, George Abbott was ordered to pay a £5 fine for "selling a pystoll & powder to the Indeans . . . ." *Ibid.*, 1:49. Robert Slye fined £10 for "exchanging a gunn with an Indian" with George Hubberd, John West, and Peter Blatchford "for the same" all fined the same amount, *Ibid.*, 1:182.

74. *Pennsylvania Gazette*, 7 June 1764.

75. Charles J. Hoadly, *Records of the Colony or Jurisdiction of New Haven, from May 1653, to the Union* (Case, Lockwood & Co., 1858), 176–77.

76. Shea, *Virginia Militia in the Seventeenth Century*, 92–93.

77. Hening, *Statutes at Large*, 3:13.

78. Browne, *Archives of Maryland*, 1:232–3.

79. George Washington to Robert Dinwiddie, 27 June 1757, George Washington, John C. Fitzpatrick, ed., *The Writings of George Washington, from the Original Manuscript Sources, 1745-1799* (Government Printing Office, 1931–44) (hereinafter *Writings of George Washington*), 2:78–79.

80. Shurtleff, *Records of the Governor and Company of the Massachusetts Bay*, 1:293.

81. Don Higginbotham, *The War of American Independence: Military Attitudes, Policies, and Practice, 1763-1789* (Macmillan Co., 1971), 8–9.

82. Jasper Danckaerts, Barlett Burleigh James and J. Franklin Jameson, ed., *Journal of Jasper Danckaerts: 1679-1680* (Charles Scribner's Sons, 1913; reprinted, Barnes & Noble, 1959), 239, 271.

83. Rutman, *Winthrop's Boston*, 216–17; Winthrop, *Winthrop's Journal*, 1:83, 91–92.

84. Winthrop, *Winthrop's Journal*, 2:42.

85. Danckaerts, *Journal of Jasper Danckaerts*, 239, 271.

86. Morgan, *American Slavery, American Freedom*, 241–2.

87. Weir, *Colonial South Carolina*, 82–85.

88. Shy, *A People Numerous and Armed*, 26; Higginbotham, *War of American Independence*, 8. Morgan, *American Slavery, American Freedom*, 239–40.

89. Browne, *Archives of Maryland*, 6:219, 222, 251, 257, 259, are a few of many examples of his complaints.

90. Browne, *Archives of Maryland*, 9:193, 240.

91. New York (Colony) Legislative Council, *Journal of the Legislative Council of the Colony of New-York: Began the 8th Day of December, 1743; and Ended the 3rd of April, 1775* (Weed, Parson & Co., 1861), 1304.

92. Willard Sterne Randall, *Benedict Arnold: Patriot and Traitor* (Barnes & Noble Books, 1999), 32–33.

93. Clark, *State Records of North Carolina*, 21:122–23.

94. Browne, *Archives of Maryland*, 6:353.

95. Shy, *A People Armed and Numerous*, 27–28; Hadden, *Slave Patrols*, 29.

96. Morgan, *American Slavery, American Freedom*, 112–113.

97. Rutman, *Winthrop's Boston*, 159–61, 244–9.

98. Richard Buel, Jr., "Samson Shorn: The Impact of the Revolutionary War on Estimates of the Republic's Strength," in Ronald Hoffman and Peter J. Albert, ed., *Arms and Independence: The Military Character of the American Revolution* (University Press of Virginia, 1984), 146; Shy, *A People Numerous and Armed*, 29–32; Higginbotham, *War of American Independence*, 9; Richard H. Kohn, *Eagle and Sword: The Beginnings of the Military Establishment in America, 1783-1802* (The Free Press, 1975), 7–8; Shy, *A People Numerous and Armed*, 28–29.

99. Morgan, *American Slavery, American Freedom*, 340.

100. Higginbotham, *War of American Independence*, 22–23.

101. Pauline Maier, *From Resistance to Revolution: Colonial Radicals and the Development of American Opposition to Britain, 1765-1776* (Alfred A. Knopf, Inc., 1972), 16–18. *Ibid.*, 18–22.

102. Higginbotham, *War of American Independence*, 17–18.

103. Maier, *From Resistance to Revolution*, 91–92.

104. Brown, *The South Carolina Regulators*, 29–37, 40, 44–46.

105. Brown, *The South Carolina Regulators*, 53–55, 57, 88–92

106. Nathanael Byfield, *An Account of the Late Revolution in New-England . . . .* (Ric. Chitwell, 1689), in Charles M. Andrews, ed., *Narratives of the Insurrections, 1675-1690* (Charles Scribner's Sons, 1915; reprinted, Barnes & Noble, 1959), 170–3.

107. "Andros's Report of His Administration, 1690," in Andrews, *Narratives of the Insurrections*, 232.

108. Andrews, *Narratives of the Insurrections*, 186–90.

109. Kohn, *Eagle and Sword*, 2–6, 8–9.

Chapter 2: Threatening Shadows: Guns in the Hands of the Other

1. Weir, *Colonial South Carolina*, 26–27.

2. Morgan, *American Slavery, American Freedom*, 127–9, describes the conditions of the first indentured servants of Virginia, and the apparent lack of racial distinction.

3. Shea, *Virginia Militia in the Seventeenth Century,* 10–15, 25–28, 31; Robert Beverley, Louis B. Wright, ed., *The History and Present State of Virginia* (University of North Carolina Press, 1947), 51; Wesley Frank Craven, *White, Red, and Black: the Seventeenth-Century Virginian* (University Press of Virginia, 1971), 51–52; Charles Campbell, *History of the Colony and Ancient Dominion of Virginia* (J.B. Lippincott & Co., 1860; reprinted, The Reprint Co., 1965), 160–65; Morgan, *American Slavery, American Freedom,* 98–99.

4. Shea, *Virginia Militia in the Seventeenth Century,* 39–41. Virginia gave special status to settlers arriving before a certain date in other areas as well. Morgan, *American Slavery, American Freedom,* 94, describes a law giving pre-1616 settlers more land than later arrivals.

5. Shea, *Virginia Militia in the Seventeenth Century,* 47.

6. Bruce, *Institutional History of Virginia in the Seventeenth Century,* 2:4–5. Bruce also reports that Governor Berkeley, when he received his commission in 1641–2, included all men from sixteen to sixty in the colony's militia, with no explicit statement as to whether Berkeley included slaves or not.

7. Hening, *Statutes at Large,* 1:226. It appears that this statute is *not* the same as the one Shea, *Virginia Militia in the Seventeenth Century,* cites at 53–54.

8. Shea, *Virginia Militia in the Seventeenth Century,* 53–54.

9. Shea, *Virginia Militia in the Seventeenth Century,* 73–74.

10. Morgan, *American Slavery, American Freedom,* 246–7.

11. Morgan, *American Slavery, American Freedom,* 238.

12. Leading up to Bacon's Rebellion in 1676, Bacon's supporters in the assembly restored the vote to landless freemen. In the aftermath of the Rebellion, in which poor whites and indentured servants had played a prominent role, this measure expired, again leaving landless freemen without a voice in the government. See Morgan, *American Slavery, American Freedom,* 263, 276.

13. Bruce, *Institutional History of Virginia in the Seventeenth Century,* 2:6–8; Morgan, *American Slavery, American Freedom,* 241–2.

14. Hening, *Statutes at Large,* 2:304.

15. Bruce, *Institutional History of Virginia in the Seventeenth Century,* 2:6–8.

16. Bruce, *Institutional History of Virginia in the Seventeenth Century,* 2:6–8.

17. Morgan, *American Slavery, American Freedom,* 279–81.

18. Morgan, *American Slavery, American Freedom,* 281–3.

19. Morgan, *American Slavery, American Freedom,* 276.

20. Hening, *Statutes at Large,* 3:451; Abbot Emerson Smith, *Colonists in Bondage: White Servitude and Convict Labor in America, 1607-1776* (Peter Smith, 1965), 239.

21. *Laws of the Government of New-Castle, Kent and Sussex Upon Delaware,* 178.

22. Mitchell and Flanders, *Statutes at Large of Pennsylvania from 1682 to 1801,* 5:197, 200.

23. Browne, *Archives of Maryland,* 10:485; Gloria L. Main, *Tobacco Colony: Life in Early Maryland, 1650-1720* (Princeton University Press, 1982), 118.

24. Philip J. Schwarz, *Twice Condemned: Slaves And The Criminal Laws Of Virginia, 1705-1865* (Louisiana State University Press, 1988), 72–73.

25. Browne, *Archives of Maryland,* 75:264; Farley Grubb, "The Statutory Regulation of Colonial Servitude: An Incomplete-Contract Approach," 69. "Freeman" was widely used in New England to distinguish full citizens of the colony, with the right (and sometimes onerous obligation) to hold public office, from inhabitants who were not so obligated. See Rutman, *Winthrop's Boston,* 41, 159–60, for discussion of this distinction and the gradual loss of this distinction. Unless otherwise noted, the term "freeman" throughout this work means a person, regardless of race, who was neither enslaved, nor bound to service.

26. Main, *Tobacco Colony,* 105, demonstrates this decisive change in the period 1684–96.

27. Farley Grubb, "The Statutory Regulation of Colonial Servitude: An Incomplete-Contract Approach," 69; Hadden, *Slave Patrols,* 32–33.

28. Clayton E. Cramer, "The Racist Roots of Gun Control," *Kansas Journal of Law & Public Policy* 4:2 [Winter 1995] 17–25; Robert J. Cottrol and Raymond T. Diamond, "The Second Amendment: Toward an Afro-Americanist Reconsideration," *Georgetown Law Journal* 80:2 [December 1991]:309–361.

29. Morgan, *American Slavery, American Freedom*, 154 n. 69. Hadden, *Slave Patrols*, 8, points out that the lack of English common law to deal with slavery (except externally) caused the American colonies to develop their own legal system from a mixture of invention and borrowing from other nations. Morgan, *Slave Counterpoint*, 8, asserts that the status of the first Africans as servants "is no longer tenable."

30. Hening, *Statutes at Large*, 1:226.

31. Hadden, *Slave Patrols*, 27–28.

32. Hening, *Statutes at Large*, 2:481–2.

33. Morgan, *Slave Counterpoint*, 4.

34. Kathleen M. Brown, *Good Wives, Nasty Wenches, and Anxious Patriarchs: Gender, Race, and Power in Colonial Virginia* (University of North Carolina Press, 1996), 218–19; Schwarz, *Twice Condemned*, 67, 70–71, 85–88.

35. Hening, *Statutes at Large*, 4:131.

36. Schwarz, *Twice Condemned*, 85–88.

37. Hadden, *Slave Patrols*, 31.

38. Hening, *Statutes at Large*, 5:17. Indians and blacks to appear unarmed for muster reiterated in 1757 at Hening, *Statutes at Large*, 7:95.

39. Hadden, *Slave Patrols*, 31.

40. Browne, *Archives of Maryland*, 75:268.

41. Browne, *Archives of Maryland*, 1:533–4, 13:546–9 are 1664 and 1692 examples of the increasingly severe punishments for interracial marriages; *Ibid.*, 33:112 is a 1717 statute enslaving any free black who married a white.

42. Wood, *Black Majority*, 99–100, 23, 25; Weir, *Colonial South Carolina*, 94–96.

43. Wood, *Black Majority*, 125–6.

44. Hadden, *Slave Patrols*, 21.

45. Wood, *Black Majority*, 97, 127.

46. Morgan, *Slave Counterpoint*, 390, 138–9, 152; Wood, *Black Majority*, 117.

47. Hadden, *Slave Patrols*, 22.

48. Wood, *Black Majority*, 196.

49. Morgan, *Slave Counterpoint*, 671.

50. Wood, *Black Majority*, 51, 96, 99–100, 102.

51. Weir, *Colonial South Carolina*, 173–4.

52. Wood, *Black Majority*, 36.

53. Wood, *Black Majority*, 273–6.

54. Wood, *Black Majority*, 299–303. Wax, "'The Great Risque We Run,'" 140–1.

55. Wood, *Black Majority*, 303–7, 309–12, 314; Wax, "'The Great Risque We Run,'" 143; Mark H. Smith, "Remembering Mary, Shaping Revolt: Reconsidering the Stono Rebellion," *Journal of Southern History* 67:3 [August 2001] 513–34, and John K. Thornton, "African Dimensions of the Stono Rebellion," *American Historical Review* 96:4 [October 1991] 1102–1108.

56. *South Carolina Gazette*, March 16, 1734, quoted in Wood, *Black Majority*, 265 n. 94.

57. Wood, *Black Majority*, 314–20.

58. Wood, *Black Majority*, 314.

59. Wood, *Black Majority*, 322–3.

60. Weir, *Colonial South Carolina*, 123–4.

61. Brown, *The South Carolina Regulators*, 17–18, 32. Hadden, *Slave Patrols*, 141–2, and Morgan, *Slave Counterpoint*, 449–51.

62. Hadden, *Slave Patrols*, 140, 288 n. 10.

63. Morgan, *Slave Counterpoint*, 391.

64. *A Collection of all the Public Acts of Assembly, of the Province of North-Carolina: Now in Force and Use . . .* , 215–16.

65. Hadden, *Slave Patrols*, 45, 246 n. 16, 37.

66. John Hope Franklin, *The Free Negro in North Carolina, 1790-1860* (University of North Carolina Press, 1995), 101–2.

67. Hadden, *Slave Patrols*, 32–36.

68. Clark, *The State Records of North Carolina*, 11:45–47.

69. Wood, *Black Majority*, 274.

70. Weir, *Colonial South Carolina*, 111–112, 123–4, 174–6.

71. Shurtleff, *Records of the Governor and Company of the Massachusetts Bay*, 3:268, 397; Rutman, *Winthrop's Boston*, 162.

72. The 1768 Georgia statute's title explained that it was "Establishing and Regulating Patrols" for "Searching and examining any Negroe house for Offensive Weapons Fire Arms and Ammunition." While the statute regulating possession of firearms referred only to slaves, the title of the statute suggests that it applied to any black person, slave or free. The law prohibited slaves possessing or carrying "Fire Arms or any Offensive Weapon whatsoever" except with a permit "from his Master Mistress or Overseer to Hunt and Kill Game Cattle or Mischievous Birds or Birds of Prey." Other provisions allowed a slave to possess a gun while in the company of a white person 16 years or older, or while actually protecting crops from birds. Under no conditions was a slave allowed to carry "any Gun Cutlass Pistol or other Offensive Weapon" from Saturday sunset until sunrise Monday morning. Candler, *The Colonial Records of the State of Georgia*, 19(part 1):76–78.

    A 1722 New Jersey law prohibited slaves from hunting or carrying a gun without permission of his master. *Laws and Acts of the General Assembly Of His Majesties Province of Nova Caesarea or New-Jersey . . .* , 143–5. Delaware's 1742 militia statute clearly prohibited slaves from serving in the militia, or bearing arms. *Laws of the Government of New-Castle, Kent and Sussex Upon Delaware*, 178. It appears that neither the New Jersey or Delaware statutes applied to free blacks.

    Pennsylvania's law was very clear-cut in denying all blacks, free or slave, the right to carry any arms. A provision of the 1700 "Act for the Trial of Negroes" provided that "if any Negro shall presume to carry any guns, swords, pistols, fowling-pieces, clubs or other arms or weapons whatsoever, without his master's special license for the same" he would receive twenty-one lashes on his bare back. The Privy Council repealed this law on 7 February 1705/6. Pennsylvania passed a similar statute, with the same provision, but it did not become law until 1709 remaining on the books until 1780. Mitchell and Flanders, *Statutes at Large of Pennsylvania from 1682 to 1801*, 2:77–79, 233–6.

73. Jameson, *Johnson's Wonder-Working Providence*, 175; Shurtleff, *Records of the Governor and Company of the Massachusetts Bay*, 1:211–12; Winthrop, *Winthrop's Journal*, 1:215; Rutman, *Winthrop's Boston*, 217, mentions that while this quarrel was under way, the Boston men refused "to serve in an Indian expedition to which John Wilson was attached as a chaplain." Winthrop, *Winthrop's Journal*, 1:217, n.1, discusses the refusal of the Boston men to march alongside the chaplain John Wilson, because he was under a "covenant of works." There is no indication that disarming was tied to a failure to perform militia duty. Winthrop, *Winthrop's Journal*, 1:240–1, explains that many were disarmed for petitioning the General Court against banishing Anne Hutchinson, "and would not acknowledge their fault . . . ."

74. Joyce Lee Malcolm, *To Keep and Bear Arms: The Origins of an Anglo-American Right* (Harvard University Press, 1994), 123. Britain and Ireland had different laws disarming Catholics. The Irish law was more restrictive on the possession of arms for self-defense. Compare 1 W. & M., ch. 15 (1689) with the Irish law 7 Will III c.5 (1695).

75. Joyce Lee Malcolm, "The Right of the People to Keep and Bear Arms: The Common Law Tradition," *Hastings Constitutional. Law Quarterly* 10:310 (1983).

76. Browne, *Archives of Maryland*, 25:288–9.

77. Browne, *Archives of Maryland*, 52:454, 474–5.

78. Candler, *The Colonial Records of the State of Georgia*, 18:190–1.

79. Berthold Fernow, ed., *Documents Relating to the Colonial History of the State of New York* (Weed, Parsons & Co., 1887; reprinted, AMS Press, Inc., 1969), 12:96.

80. Brown, *Good Wives, Nasty Wenches, and Anxious Patriarchs*, 177–78.

81. In 1715, Maryland passed a very complex statute that partially fits into this category—and also reminds us that Colonial legislators may have known what they intended, but sometimes failed to define what certain phrases meant. This law prohibited those convicted of certain crimes (involving hunting or stealing of livestock) from hunting or carrying a gun "upon any persons Land whereon there shall be a Seated plantation without the owners Leave . . . ." Along with those convicted of crimes, however, the statute also applied to anyone "of Evill fame or a Vagrant or dissolute Liver . . ." without clearly identifying what identified such a person. Browne, *Archives of Maryland*, 30:305.

Chapter 3: Uneasy Alliances: Guns and Indians

1. Learning and Spicer, *Grants, Concessions, and Original Constitutions of the Province of New-Jersey*, 103. For example, New Jersey prohibited transfer of firearms and ammunition starting in 1675, with a graduated system of fines depending on the value of the goods, and prohibited gunsmiths and blacksmiths from repairing guns belonging to the Indians, but this appears to be the only significant such regulatory measure in that colony.

2. Hening, *Statutes at Large*, 1:525, 2:215, 336–7.

3. "The Beginning, Progress, and Conclusion of Bacon's Rebellion, 1675–1676," in Andrews, *Narratives of the Insurrections*, 17; "A True Narrative of the Late Rebellion in Virginia, by the Royal Commissioners, 1677," in Andrews, *Narratives of the Insurrections*, 124–5.

4. "Bacon's Manifesto," in Robert Middlekauf, ed., *Bacon's Rebellion* (Rand McNally & Co., 1964), 21. See *Calendar of State Papers, Colonial, 1675-1676* (London, 1893), no. 909, quoted in Middlekauf, *Bacon's Rebellion*, 6, for evidence that the Virginians were well-armed.

5. Middlekauf, *Bacon's Rebellion*, 27, 44–45; William Washburn, *The Governor and the Rebel: A History of Bacon's Rebellion in Virginia* (University of North Carolina Press, 1957), 27–28.

6. Adams, *New English Canaan of Thomas Morton*, 21–28; William Bradford, Samuel Eliot Morison, ed., *Of Plymouth Plantation, 1620-1647* (Alfred A. Knopf, 2001), 204, 206–8, 232–3; Shurtleff, *Records of the Governor and Company of the Massachusetts Bay*, 1:196.

7. Sydney V. James, Jr., *Three Visitors to Early Plymouth* (Applewood Books, 1997), 16; Emmanuel Altham at James, *Three Visitors to Early Plymouth*, 32.

8. Winthrop, *Winthrop's Journal*, 1:64, 90.

9. Shurtleff, *Records of the Governor and Company of the Massachusetts Bay*, 2:24; Winthrop, *Winthrop's Journal*, 2:80.

10. Winthrop, *Winthrop's Journal*, 2:74–75, 328.

11. Shurtleff, *Records of the Governor and Company of the Massachusetts Bay*, 4 (part 2):365.

12. Trumbull, Hoadly, *Public Records of the Colony of Connecticut*, 1:1, 2, 79–80, 113–14, 138, 145–6, 197–8.

13. Winthrop, *Winthrop's Journal*, 2:342–3.

14. Trumbull, Hoadly, *Public Records of the Colony of Connecticut*, 1:146–7, 167, 182, 242, 351, 375.

15. Thomas Newe, 17 May 1682, in Salley, *Narratives of Early Carolina*, 182.

16. Weir, *Colonial South Carolina*, 119–20.

17. Carl P. Russell, *Firearms, Traps, & Tools of the Mountain Men* (University of New Mexico Press, 1977), 65–66; S. James Gooding, "The Trade Guns of the Hudson's Bay Company," in T.M. Hamilton, ed., *Indian Trade Guns* (Pioneer Press, 1982), 1–17.

18. Winthrop, *Winthrop's Journal*, 2:161.

19. Joseph B. Mayer, *Flintlocks of the Iroquois: 1620-1687* (Rochester Museum of Arts and Sciences, 1943), 5–6, 18, 32–33.

20. T.M. Hamilton, "Relics from 17th Century Seneca Sites," in Hamilton, *Indian Trade Guns*, 53–55.

21. T.M. Hamilton, "Relics from 17th Century Seneca Sites," in Hamilton, *Indian Trade Guns*, 57; S. James Gooding, "The Trade Guns of the Hudson's Bay Company," in Hamilton, *Indian Trade Guns*, 2.

22. Danckaerts, *Journal of Jasper Danckaerts*, 149, 179–80. (Emphasis added.)

23. Andrews, *Narratives of the Insurrections*, 198.

24. *Pennsylvania Archives* (J. Severns & Co., *et al.*, 1852–1935), 4th series, 1:445, 581, 747, 794. One 1728 delivery contained 100 pounds of gunpowder, 200 pounds of lead, and 500 flints. A 1736 delivery included 100 pounds of gunpowder, 150 pounds of lead, and 200 flints. In 1740, "Three Barrels of Gunpowder. Five Hundredweight of Lead . . . Three Guns. Five Hundred Flints." In 1742, "600 Lead. 600 Powder . . . 1,000 Flints. . . . 24 Guns."

25. Benjamin Franklin, *The Papers of Benjamin Franklin,* Leonard W. Labaree, ed. (Yale University Press, 1961), 4:121.

26. *Pennsylvania Gazette*, March 8, 1748.

27. James B. Whisker, *Arms Makers of Colonial America* (Susquehanna University Press, 1992), 51, 59.

28. T.M. Hamilton, "The Gunsmith's Cache from Malta Bend, Missouri," in Hamilton, *Indian Trade Guns*, 29–52.

29. T.M. Hamilton, *Early Indian Trade Guns: 1625-1775* (Museum of the Great Plains, 1968), 21, 15–32. Two more surviving examples of Type K have also been identified as well as other types of Colonial era English-made guns found in multiple states.

30. Charles Heath to author, 20 March 2001.

31. Russell, *Firearms, Traps, & Tools of the Mountain Men*, 70–73; Henry Family Papers at Hagley Museum and Library (hereinafter, Hagley Henry Papers), accession 1309, Series 2, Folder 9.

32. 12 October 1837, *Journal Of The Executive Proceedings Of The Senate Of The United States Of America*, 1837–1841, 5:45; 11 June 1838, *Journal of the Senate of the United States of America*, 25th Cong,, 2nd sess., 605–606; *Statutes at Large*, 29th Cong., 1st sess., ch. 34; *Statutes at Large*, 30th Cong., 1st sess., ch. 118; *Statutes at Large*, 30th Cong., 2nd sess., ch. 106.

33. T.M. Hamilton, "Relics from 18th Century Osage Sites," in Hamilton, *Indian Trade Guns*, 71–98.

34. Russell, *Firearms, Traps, & Tools of the Mountain Men*, 70–73.

35. Belfiles, *Arming America*, 140.

Chapter 4: Guns in Official Records and Personal Narrative

1. Alice Hanson Jones, *Wealth of a Nation To Be: The American Colonies on the Eve of the Revolution* (Columbia University Press, 1980), 3–6.

2. See Alice Hanson Jones, *American Colonial Wealth: Documents and Methods*, 2nd ed. (Arno Press, 1978). Documentation and methods are available at http://www.icpsr.umich.edu/cgi/archive.prl?study=7329.

3. Main, *Tobacco Colony*, 282; Hanson, *Wealth of a Nation To Be*, 44–45, 349–51.

4. Judith A. McGaw, "'So Much Depends upon a Red Wheelbarrow': Agricultural Tool Ownership in the Eighteenth-Century Mid-Atlantic," in Judith A. McGaw, ed., *Early American Technology: Making and Doing Things from the Colonial Era to 1850* (University of North Carolina, 1994), 332, 342–3.

5. Trumbull, Hoadly, *Public Records of the Colony of Connecticut*, 1:455–6.

6. Because the "armes, and ammunition" are not broken out by value on Porter's estate, I have used the value of £2 specified in the similarly phrased John Elsen inventory.

7. See Patricia Scott Deetz, Christopher Fennell, and J. Eric Deetz, *The Plymouth Colony Archive Project* "Analysis of Selected Probate Inventories," available at http://etext.lib.virginia.edu/users/deetz/Plymouth/probates.html for a list of selected probate inventories. While I make no pretense that these inventories were randomly selected, they were

not selected by me, and there is no reason to assume that they are unrepresentative with respect to the presence of guns.

8. Thomas Willett, *Plymouth Colony Wills* 3:117–128, excerpted in Deetz, Fennell, and Deetz, *The Plymouth Colony Archive Project,* available at http://etext.lib.virginia.edu/users/deetz/Plymouth/P231.htm.

9. Margaret Carpenter, *Plymouth Colony Wills* 3(2):37–38, excerpted in Deetz, Fennell, and Deetz, *The Plymouth Colony Archive Project,* available at http://etext.lib.virginia.edu/users/deetz/Plymouth/P278.htm and Alice Bradford, *Plymouth Colony Wills* 3:3–5, excerpted in Deetz, Fennell, and Deetz, *The Plymouth Colony Archive Project,* available at http://etext.lib.virginia.edu/users/deetz/Plymouth/P178.htm.

10. McGaw, "'So Much Depends upon a Red Wheelbarrow': Agricultural Tool Ownership in the Eighteenth-Century Mid-Atlantic," 332, 342–3.

11. Brown, *Good Wives, Nasty Wenches, and Anxious Patriarchs,* 177, 427 n.106.

12. Main, *Tobacco Colony,* 242.

13. James Lindgren and Justine Lee Heather, "Counting Guns in Early America," *William and Mary Law Review* 43:5 [2002], 1788–89.

14. Lindgren and Heather, "Counting Guns in Early America," 1794.

15. Chris Tami, *New York City Wills* 1–11 (Ancestry, Inc., 1998–99) on http://www.ancestry.com under "New York City Wills."

16. Joyce Hansen and Gary McGowan, *Breaking Ground, Breaking Silence: The Story of New York's African Burial Ground* (Henry Holt and Co., 1998), 51.

17. Roth, "Guns, Gun Culture, and Homicide," 224–7.

18. William P. Palmer, ed., *Calendar of Virginia State Papers and Other Manuscripts, 1652-1781, Preserved in the Capitol at Richmond* (n.p., 1875), 1:81.

19. Kenneth Coleman and Milton Ready, ed., *Colonial Records of the State of Georgia: Trustees' Letter Book 1732-1738* (University of Georgia Press, 1985), 29:311, 319, 332.

20. *Boston Gazette,* 30 May 1720, 24 October 1720; 21 January 1730; 27 January 1730; 2 February 1730; 9 February 1730, 1 March 1730; 9 March 1730; 14 August 1730.

21. *Boston Gazette,* 11 May 1730; 18 May 1730.

22. *Boston Gazette,* 17 November 1741; 1 December 1741; 8 December 1741; 15 December 1741; 19 January 1742; 2 February 1742; [unreadable date], 1742; March [unreadable], 1742; 11 May 1742; 18 May 1742; 25 May 1742; 13 July 1742; 10 August 1742; 24 August 1742; 31 August 1742; [13? September], 1742.

23. *Boston Gazette,* 11 May 1742; 18 May 1742; 25 May 1742; 13 July 1742; 24 August 1742; 31 August 1742.

24. A fairly typical ad was that of a merchant named Peter Turner who, in 1741, liquidated his inventory before returning to London, including "Rifle barrel Guns, . . . with several sorts of fowling Pieces . . . ." A Robert Towers offered, "rifle double barrel and smooth bore guns, pistols, flints, bullet and shot molds . . . ." A Robert Lettis Hooper offered "superfine Rifle Powder by the Quarter Cask or Pound . . . a Parcel of Spanish Muskets, neatly fitted with iron Rods, and small Bayonets, the Locks are large and well made, and the whole Piece very handy and convenient for common Use." Samuel Carruthers offered "a neat Assortment of birding and fowling Pieces, and a valuable Rifle Gun." Francis & Relfe offered "rifle gun barrels and locks, gunpowder." There are many similar ads, as well as ads offering muskets and pistols for sale, parts for making guns, and gunpowder. *Pennsylvania Gazette,* 30 July 1741; 6 September 1764; 22 September 1763; 8 July 1762; 5 March 1761; 4 June 1761; 1 November 1744; 26 September 1745; 3 October 1745; 17 October 1745; 11 February 1746; 17 July 1746; 30 July 1747; 29 March 1748; 5 May 1748; 12 May 1748; 15 September 1748; 25 October 1750; 27 November 1755; 18 January 1759; 2 August 1759; 19 November 1761; 11 February 1762; 19 August 1762; 14 April 1763; 19 May 1763; 16 February 1764; 12 April 1764; 19 April 1764; 14 May 1772; 28 May 1772; 26 August 1772; 17 February 1773; 28 November 1778; 24 December 1783.

25. United Kingdom Public Records Office, Customs 16:85, 109, 171. In 1769: 229,545 pounds; 1770: 410,591 pounds; 1771: 390,558 pounds. These figures are for imports through American ports, and do not include imports through Canadian or West Indian ports.

26. William J. Novak, "*Salus Populi*: The Roots of Regulation in America, 1787–1873," (Ph.D. diss., Brandeis University, 1992), 188.

27. This calculation is based on statutes that assumed four pounds of lead for every pound of gunpowder, and a 0.75 caliber Brown Bess: Browne, *Archives of Maryland*, 1:77; Andrews, *Tercentenary History of Maryland*, 1:150; Hening, *Statutes at Large*, 5:17, 21. Many firearms in Colonial America were smaller caliber, and used less powder, increasing the number of shots that could be fired.

    Edward E. Curtis, *The Organization of the British Army in the American Revolution* (Yale University Press, 1926; reprinted, AMS Press, 1969), 16 n. 38 gives a somewhat lower weight for the bullets than my calculations based on the density of lead would suggest. This would, however, increase the number of shots that could be fired.

28. [William Bradford], "A Relation, or Journal, of the Beginning and Proceedings of the English Plantation settled at Plymouth," in Edward Arber, ed., *The Story of the Pilgrim Fathers, 1606-1623 A.D.; as told by Themselves, their Friends, and their Enemies* (1897), 432. Dwight B. Heath, ed., *Mourt's Relation: A Journal of the Pilgrims at Plymouth* (Applewood Press, 1963), 18–19, relates the same incident, but puts the number of men "well armed" at "fifteen or sixteen."

29. Heath, *Mourt's Relation,* 31.

30. Heath, *Mourt's Relation,* 18 n. 6.

31. Heath, *Mourt's Relation,* 42. Edward Winslow, *Good Newes from New England* (n.p., 1624; reprinted, Applewood Books, n.d.), 10–11, describing preparations for defense in 1622, more ambiguously suggests that all the men were armed with muskets.

32. Heath, *Mourt's Relation,* 85.

33. James, *Three Visitors to Early Plymouth*, 29, 75–77.

34. Bradford, *Of Plymouth Plantation*, 111 n. 7, 342.

35. Bradford, *Of Plymouth Plantation,* 86, 246; William Shakespeare, *The Tragedy of Hamlet, Prince of Denmark*, V. ii., 409–14.

36. Thomas Morton, *A New English Canaan* (Jacob Frederick Stam, 1637), 132, in Charles Francis Adams, Jr., ed., *New English Canaan of Thomas Morton* (The Prince Society, 1883; reprinted, Burt Franklin, 1967), 276–7. Also in Albert Bushnell Hart, ed., *American History Told by Contemporaries* (1898), 1:361–63.

37. The training requirement reduced to eight times annually in 1637: Shurtleff, *Records of the Governor and Company of the Massachusetts Bay,* 1:210. Plymouth's training requirement set at six times annually in 1639: Brigham, *Compact with the Charter and Laws of the Colony of New Plymouth,* 68. Connecticut's training requirement set at six days annually in 1639, reiterated in 1643, Trumbull, Hoadly, *Public Records of the Colony of Connecticut,* 1:30, 97.

38. Winthrop, *Winthrop's Journal,* 1:69.

39. Winthrop, *Winthrop's Journal,* 1:70, 229, 2:194, 1:148. A farthing was worth perhaps six minutes of a daily laborer's wages, assuming an unskilled laborer's daily wages of 2 *s.*, 6 *d.*, and 12 hour days. The equivalent of six minutes of minimum wage labor today would be $0.52. (Lead has become cheaper relative to wages in the intervening three centuries.)

40. Trumbull, Hoadly, *Public Records of the Colony of Connecticut,* 1:33, 50, 115.

41. John E. Soule, Milton E. Terry, and Robert S. Wakefield, comp., *George Soule of the Mayflower and His Descendants for Four Generations*, 3rd ed. (General Society of Mayflower Descendants, 1999), 6.

42. Hoadly, *Records of the Colony and Plantation of New Haven,* 176–7.

43. Hoadly, *Records of the Colony or Jurisdiction of New Haven,* 173–5.

44. Nicholas M. Luccketti, William M. Kelso, and Beverly A. Straube, *APVA Jamestown Rediscovery: Field Report 1994* (Association for the Preservation of Virginia Antiquities, 1994), 28.

45. Beverly A. Straube and Nicholas Luccketti, *APVA Jamestown Rediscovery: 1995 Interim Report* (Association for the Preservation of Virginia Antiquities, 1996), 30–35; William Kelso and Beverly Straube, *1996 Interim Report on the APVA Excavations at Jamestown, Virginia* (Association for the Preservation of Virginia Antiquities, 1997), 15.

46. Kelso and Straube, *1996 Interim Report on the APVA Excavations at Jamestown, Virginia,* 10–11, 28.

47. Beverly Straube and Nicholas Luccketti, *1997 Interim Report on the APVA Excavations at Jamestown, Virginia* (Association for the Preservation of Virginia Antiquities, 1998), 14.

48. Hening, *Statutes at Large,* 1:401–2.

49. Public Record Office, T. 64/88 (Blathwayt's journal), 360, quoted in Morgan, *American Slavery, American Freedom,* 240.

50. Beverley, *The History and Present State of Virginia,* 269.

51. 21 October to 28 October 1737, [Williamsburg,] *Virginia Gazette* (Parks), in Thomas Costa, ed., *Virginia Runaways: Runaway Slave Advertisements from 18th-century Virginia Newspapers* (http://www.wise.virginia.edu/history/runaways/); 13 January to 20 January 1737/8, *Ibid.*; 26 August to 2 September 1737, *Ibid.*; 26 August to 2 September 1737, *Ibid.*; 28 April to 5 May 1738, *Ibid.*, ("Two Fowling-Pieces"); 12 May to 19 May 1738, *Ibid.*; 2 March to 9 March 1738/9, *Ibid.*

52. *Pennsylvania Gazette,* 13 September 1739; 18 August 1743; 18 July 1751; 24 April 1755; 15 September 1763; 11 May 1765; 20 June 1765; 19 September 1771; 12 December 1771; 10 August 1774.

53. 27 June to 3 July 1746, [Williamsburg,] *Virginia Gazette* (Parks), in Costa; 21 April 1775, [Williamsburg,] *Virginia Gazette* (Purdie), in Costa; also in *Pennsylvania Gazette,* 3 May 1775.

54. 15 April to 27 April 1737, [Williamsburg,] *Virginia Gazette* (Parks), in Costa.

55. 24 May 1751, [Williamsburg,] *Virginia Gazette* (Hunter), in Costa; 18 July 1751, 8 August 1751, 24 October 1751, 7 November 1751, 30 January 1752, 10 April 1752, 12 June 1752, 30 July 1752, 17 October 1755, 6 June 1766, [Williamsburg,] *Virginia Gazette* (Purdie & Co.), in Costa; 28 May 1767, [Williamsburg,] *Virginia Gazette* (Purdie & Dixon), in Costa; 23 July 1767, [Williamsburg,] *Virginia Gazette* (Rind), in Costa ("Brass mounted Pistols"); 22 December 1768, 4 May 1769, 14 September 1769, 31 October 1771, 4 February 1773, 24 November 1774, 16 June 1775, [Williamsburg,] *Virginia Gazette* (Purdie), in Costa; 30 June 1775. Supplement, 16 August 1776, Supplement, 5 January 1775, [Norfolk,] *Virginia Gazette or, Norfolk Intelligencer* (Duncan), in Costa. The Georgia *Gazette* for the period 1763 through 1775 found that of 453 runaway slave ads, four reported that the slaves had taken guns; Betty Wood, *Slavery in Colonial Georgia, 1730-1775* (University of Georgia Press, 1984), 170, 185. The low percentage may reflect either Georgia's law severely regulating gun storage, or a reluctance of masters to admit that slaves had obtained a gun anyway.

56. 14 April 1768 [Williamsburg,] *Virginia Gazette* (Rind), in Costa.

57. Wood, *Black Majority,* 255–6.

58. *South Carolina Gazette,* 22 March 1735, quoted in Wood, *Black Majority,* 243.

59. *Pennsylvania Archives,* 4th series, 1:412.

60. Wood, *Black Majority,* 261–2.

61. William Black, "A Practical Joke" in Albert Bushnell Hart and Mabel Hill, *Camps and Firesides of the Revolution* (Macmillan Co., 1937), 43–45.

62. Franklin B. Dexter, *Biographical Sketches of the Graduates of Yale College* (H. Holt & Co, 1896), 2:8.

63. Hart, *American History told by Contemporaries,* 2:267–8.

64. Bradford, *Of Plymouth Plantation,* 276.

65. Franklin, *Papers of Benjamin Franklin,* 4:82–83, 113.

66. William L. Saunders, ed., *The Colonial Records of North Carolina* (Josephus Daniels, 1890; reprinted, AMS Press, Inc., 1968), 8: 30, 114, 130–1, 285, 368, 436, 440.

67. Saunders, *Colonial Records of North Carolina,* 8:200–1.

68. Saunders, *Colonial Records of North Carolina*, 7:722, 8:200–1, 498, 243, 552.

69. Saunders, *Colonial Records of North Carolina*, 8:577, 651, 687–9, 601.

70. 1 August 1771, Saunders, *Colonial Records of North Carolina*, 8:647, 649, 655, 671. See also 8:608–11, 613, 615–16, 637, 642, 647, 693, for other evidence that the Regulators were armed with guns, and this was not regarded as unusual.

71. Saunders, *Colonial Records of North Carolina*, 8:615–6, 655.

Chapter 5: Intent to Kill: Man Against Man and Man Against Nature

1. Winslow, *Good Newes from New England*, 34–35.

2. James, *Three Visitors to Early Plymouth*, 28–29.

3. Heath, *Mourt's Relation*, 82, 84, 86.

4. James, *Three Visitors to Early Plymouth*, 79–80.

5. Francis Higginson, *New England's Plantation Or A Short And True Description Of The Commodities And Discommodities Of That Country: Written By A Reverend Divine Now There Resident* (Michael Sparke, 1630), quoted in http://www.winthropsociety.org/doc_higgin.php, last accessed 2 February 2006.

6. Winthrop, *Winthrop's Journal*, 1:68, 192, 194, 2:348. Winthrop writes in August 1648: "This month, when our first harvest was near had in, the pigeons came again all over the country, but did no harm, (harvest being just in,) but proved a great blessing, it being incredible what multitudes of them were killed daily. It was ordinary for one man to kill eight or ten dozen in half a day, yea five or six dozen at one shoot, and some seven or eight."

7. George Alsop, *A Character of the Province of Mary-land* . . . (Peter Dring, 1666), in Hall, *Narratives of Early Maryland*, 345–8, 357.

8. Hall, *Narratives of Early Maryland*, 338.

9. Aubrey C. Land, *Colonial Maryland: A History* (KTO Press, 1981), 59–60, 74.

10. Browne, *Archives of Maryland*, 1:77, 103, 345.

11. John Hammond, *Leah and Rachel, Or, The Two Fruitfull Sisters Virginia and Mary-land* . . . (T. Mabb, 1656), in Hall, *Narratives of Early Maryland*, 285, 291. Hammond tells us that while there was little hunting when Jamestown was first settled, it was not for lack of interest: "for they durst neither hunt, fowl, nor Fish, for fear of the Indian, which they stood in aw[e] of." But later, the common people felt free "to range the wood for flesh, the rivers for fowle and fish." Referring to his own experiences in Virginia, Hammond writes, "Water-fowle of all sortes are . . . plentifull and easie to be killed. . . . Deare all over the Country, and in many places so many that venison is accounted a tiresome meat; wilde Turkeys are frequent."

12. Hening, *Statutes at Large*, 1:199.

13. Hening, *Statutes at Large*, 2:96–97, 3:328, 3:180.

14. Weir, *Colonial South Carolina*, 17.

15. Morgan, *American Slavery, American Freedom*, 237.

16. Robert Horne, *A Brief Description of the Province of Carolina* . . . (n.p. 1666), in Salley, *Narratives of Early Carolina*, 68–71.

17. Thomas Ashe, *Carolina, or a Description of the Present State of that Country* . . . (Mrs. Grover, 1682), in Salley, *Narratives of Early Carolina*, 150–1.

18. *Ibid.*, 158. See also Thomas Newe, August 23, 1682, in Salley, *Narratives of Early Carolina*, 187, asking his father to send out 200 pounds of pigeon shot.

19. John Archdale, *A New Description of That Fertile and Pleasant Province of Carolina* . . . (John Wyat, 1707), in Salley, *Narratives of Early Carolina*, 289.

20. Danckaerts, *Journal of Jasper Danckaerts*, 60, 70, 92, 108, 123, 126, 206–8, 230.

21. Beverley, *The History and Present State of Virginia*, 153, 309–11.

22. Main, *Tobacco Colony*, 208–209.

23. *Laws and Acts of the General Assembly Of His Majesties Province of Nova Caesarea or New-Jersey* . . . , 143–5.

24. *Laws of North Carolina—1738*, ch. 10, in Cushing, *Earliest Printed Laws of North Carolina, 1669-1751*, 2:128.

25. David Humphreys, "Israel Putnam and the Wolf" in Hart and Hill, *Camps and Firesides of the Revolution*, 9–11.

26. Andrew Burnaby, "In the Woods" in Hart and Hill, *Camps and Firesides of the Revolution*, 51. See also Jameson, *Johnson's Wonder-Working Providence,* 85, for what *may* be a description of Indian fire-hunting of deer in seventeenth century New England. Higginbotham, *War of American Independence*, 127–8, gives a bit more discussion of the Royal Navy's monopoly on white pines, and the resentment that this overbearing policy generated.

27. Hening, *Statutes at Large*, 5:62, 431. Browne, *Archives of Maryland,* 28:348–9 is a 1745 statute that prohibits fire-hunting, although it is not explicit that the "hunters" were using guns. *Ibid.*, 44:21, 36, 39, 173, 180–1, trace the legislative history from the request earlier that year from the backwoods farmers to prohibit fire-hunting and hunting by non-residents to final passage. For reasons not explained, a similar law was debated in 1753 at 50:211 and 251, where it was "referred to the Consideration of next Assembly."

    Connecticut's 1733 statute regulating "Firing the Woods" at Trumbull, Hoadly, *Public Records of the Colony of Connecticut*, 7:456–7, is not explicitly about hunting, nor does it ever mention firearms, but may have been motivated by the same concerns.

    Weir, *Colonial South Carolina*, 17, indicates that the Indians of South Carolina may have regularly burned the woods not directly as part of hunting, but to create an environment better suited to deer. *Ibid.*, 44, mentions whites "seasonally burning the woods" of South Carolina in the mid-eighteenth century, but with no indication that this was hunting related.

28. Hening, *Statutes at Large*, 3:69.

29. J. Thomas Scharf, *History of Western Maryland: Being a History of Frederick, Montgomery, Carroll, Washington, Allegany, and Garrett Counties From the Earliest Period to the Present Day* . . . (L.H. Everts, 1882; reprinted, Regional Publishing Co., 1968), 1:70–71.

30. Alexander Graydon, "A Philadelphia Boy's Sports" in Hart and Hill, *Camps and Firesides of the Revolution*, 184.

31. Saunders, *Colonial Records of North Carolina*, 8:26.

32. Brown, *The South Carolina Regulators*, 42, 47–48.

33. Hening, *Statutes at Large*, 8:592–3.

34. Hening, *Statutes at Large*, 1:401–2.

35. Browne, *Archives of Maryland*, 3:103.

36. Winthrop, *Winthrop's Journal*, 1:60, 62, 63, 2:80–1.

37. *Laws of the Government of New-Castle, Kent and Sussex Upon Delaware*, 175.

38. September 6, 1638, Shurtleff, *Records of the Governor and Company of the Massachusetts Bay*, 1:236.

39. Eugene Aubrey Stratton, *Plymouth Colony: Its History & People, 1620-1691* (Ancestry Publishing, 1986), 188.

40. *Acts and Resolves, Public and Private, of the Province of the Massachusetts Bay* . . . , 3:305–6.

41. Candler, *The State Records of the Colony of Georgia*, 18:294–5. Pennsylvania and Maryland had similar provisions. See Mitchell and Flanders, *Statutes at Large of Pennsylvania from 1682 to 1801*, 2:419–20; and Browne, *Archives of Maryland*, 1:273, respectively.

42. J. Thomas Scharf and Thompson Westcott, *History of Philadelphia, 1609-1884* (L.H. Everts & Co., 1884), 2:998–1029, available at http://www.accessible.com, 5 October 2004.

43. Bellesiles, *Arming America*, 36, 175.

44. Joyce Lee Malcolm, "Concealed Weapons," *Reason,* January 2001, 47–49; Joyce Malcolm, *Guns and Violence: The English Experience* (Harvard University Press, 2002); George MacDonald Fraser, *The Steel Bonnets: The Story of the Anglo-Scottish Border Reivers* (HarperCollins, 1995); Edward L. Ayers, *Vengeance and Justice: Crime and Punishment in the 19th-Century American South* (Oxford University Press, 1984), 21–23; James G. Leyburn, *The Scotch-Irish: A Social History* (University of North Carolina Press, 1962), 3–13, 147–148, 157–168; R.J. Dickson, *Ulster Emigration to Colonial America 1718-1775* (Routledge & Kegan Paul, 1966), 84–85, 96–97; Carlton Jackson, *A Social History of the Scotch-Irish* (Madison Books, 1993), 82–83, 112–113; David Hackett Fischer, *Albion's Seed: Four British Folkways in America* (Oxford University Press, 1989), 621–632.

45. Roth, "Guns, Gun Culture, and Homicide," 234–5.

46. George F. Willison, *Saints and Strangers* (Time-Life Books, 1981), 308. See Stratton, *Plymouth Colony,* 1, for criticism of Willison's work.

47. Bradford, *Of Plymouth Plantation,* 234.

48. Willison, *Saints and Strangers,* 320–21; Bradford, *Of Plymouth Plantation,* 263.

49. Winthrop, *Winthrop's Journal,* 1:96, 111, 123–4, 235–7, 282–3, 2:153, 180, 187–8, 218–19, 317–18, 345, 272–3. See 2:60 for an attempted murder.

50. Augustine Herrman, "Journal of the Dutch Embassy to Maryland," in Hall, *Narratives of Early Maryland,* 314, 316.

51. "A True Narrative of the Late Rebellion in Virginia, by the Royal Commissioners, 1677," in Andrews, *Narratives of the Insurrections,* 111, 130–1.

52. Middlekauf, *Bacon's Rebellion,* 37.

53. Washburn, *Governor and the Rebel,* 88.

54. Brown, *Good Wives, Nasty Wenches, and Anxious Patriarchs,* 162.

55. "Narratives of Thomas Miller, Sir Peter Colleton, and the Carolina Proprietors," in Andrews, *Narratives of the Insurrections,* 152, 156.

56. Bellesiles, *Arming America,* 84.

57. Leonard Strong, *Babylon's Fall in Maryland: a Fair Warning to Lord Baltamore . . .* (Leonard Strong, 1655), in Hall, *Narratives of Early Maryland,* 240–4 (Puritan account); John Langford, *A Just and Cleere Refutation of a False and Scandalous Pamphlet Entitled Babylons Fall in Maryland . . .* (John Langford, 1655), in Hall, *Narratives of Early Maryland,* 260–1. 266 (Cavalier version).

58. *Virginia and Maryland, or The Lord Baltamore's printed CASE . . .* (n.p., 1655), in Hall, *Narratives of Early Maryland,* 204; Strong, in Hall, *Narratives of Early Maryland,* 239–41.

59. *A Letter From a Gentleman of the City of New-York To Another . . .* (William Bradford, 1698), in Andrews, *Narratives of the Insurrections,* 369.

60. *Loyalty Vindicated from the Reflections of a Virulent Pamphlet . . .* (n.p., 1698), in Andrews, *Narratives of the Insurrections,* 391.

61. [Nicholas Bayard], *A Modest and Impartial Narrative of Several Grievances and Great Oppressions . . .* (n.p., 1690), in Andrews, *Narratives of the Insurrections,* 333.

62. Edward Countryman, *A People in Revolution: The American Revolution and Political Society in New York, 1760-1790* (John Hopkins University Press, 1981), 40.

63. Daniel Defoe, *Party-Tyranny, or an Occasional Bill in Miniature . . .* (n.p., 1705), in Salley, *Narratives of Early Carolina,* 244; John Ash, "The Present State of Affairs in Carolina," in Salley, *Narratives of Early Carolina,* 273–4. Weir, *Colonial South Carolina,* 65, 75–80.

64. *Pennsylvania Archives,* 4th series, 1:586–95.

65. Brown, *The South Carolina Regulators,* 14, 19–20, 23–24, 29–37, 40, 54.

66. Roth, "Guns, Gun Culture, and Homicide," 234–5.

67. John Carey, ed., *Eyewitness to History* (Harvard University Press, 1988), 192–3.

68. Hart, *American History told by Contemporaries,* 2:83.

69. Douglas Adair and John A. Schutz, eds., *Peter Oliver's Origin and Progress of the American Rebellion* (1961), 89, quoted in Maier, *For Resistance to Revolution*, 139.

70. Maier, *From Resistance to Revolution*, xv.

71. Plymouth Archaeological Rediscovery Project, "Firearms in Plymouth Colony" (2002), Tables 2 and 4, available at http://plymoutharch.tripod.com/parp/id71.html, last accessed 10 August 2004.

72. Harold L. Peterson, *Arms and Armor in Colonial America: 1526-1783* (Stackpole Co., 1956), 213–14, 202, 205, 209; M.L. Brown, *Firearms in Colonial America: The Impact on History and Technology 1492-1792* (Smithsonian Institution Press, 1980), 312; Frank Klay, *The Samuel E. Dyke Collection of Kentucky Pistols* (The Gun Room Press, 1972), 4–15; Felicia Johnson Deyrup, *Arms Makers of the Connecticut Valley: A Regional Study of the Economic Development of the Small Arms Industry, 1798-1870* (George Banta Publishing Co., 1948), 34.

73. George A. Stickels, "The William Smith Pistols Made by Medad Hills," *The Gun Report*, September 1979, 10–12.

74. *Boston Gazette* issues with one or more ads offering pistols: 30 May 1720, 17 November 1741, 8 December 1741, 2 February 1742, 11 May 1742, 18 May 1742, 25 May 1742, 13 July 1742, 10 August 1742, 24 August 1742, 31 August 1742, [13? September] 1742.

75. *Pennsylvania Gazette*, 31 August 1749.

76. 4 September 1772 and 14 September 1773, *Wochtenlichter Pennsylvanische Staatsbote*, translated and quoted in James Whisker, *The Gunsmith's Trade* (Edwin Mellen Press, 1992), 159–160.

77. *Pennsylvania Gazette*, 1 November 1744; 26 September 1745; 3 October 1745; 17 October 1745; 11 February 1746; 17 July 1746; 30 July 1747; 12 May 1748; 15 September 1748; 25 October 1750; 27 November 1755; 2 August 1759; 11 February 1762; 14 April 1763; 19 May 1763; 12 April 1764; 19 April 1764; 16 August 1770; 28 May 1772; 17 February 1773; 15 September 1773.

78. Winthrop, *Winthrop's Journal*, 2:27, 153, 180, 275.

79. Eliza Lucas Pinckney, Elise Pinckney, ed., *The Letterbook of Eliza Lucas Pinckney* (University of South Carolina Press, 1997), 42, 42 n. 55.

80. *Pennsylvania Gazette*, 7 September 1749.

81. *Pennsylvania Gazette*, 31 October 1745; 20 April 1749.

82. Brown, *The South Carolina Regulators*, 35, 40, 54.

83. *Pennsylvania Gazette*, 15 August 1745.

84. *Pennsylvania Gazette*, 28 December 1774.

85. Winthrop, *Winthrop's Journal*, 1:83, 2:55, 2:72, 317.

86. Winthrop, *Winthrop's Journal*, 1:75, 82, 94, 207, 2:11–12., 220–1.

87. Generally, see Malcolm, *To Keep and Bear Arms*; Shea, *Virginia Militia in the Seventeenth Century*, 1–3.

II. THE SHOT HEARD 'ROUND THE WORLD

1. Ralph Waldo Emerson, "Concord Hymn" (1836).

2. Bellesiles, *Arming America*, 174, 181, 183, 188–91.

Chapter 6: Guns in Revolutionary New England

1. Richard Frothingham, *History of the Siege of Boston, and of the Battles of Lexington, Concord, and Bunker Hill*, 6th ed. (1903), 94–95. The marking of these arms demonstrates that they were privately, not publicly, owned.

2. An 1806 Congressional committee report at United States Congress, *American State Papers: Military Affairs*, 1:198, used the phrase "fire arms and rifles," suggesting that "fire arm" may have been used in a narrower sense than "firearm" is used today, perhaps indicating specifically a military musket. This narrower usage does not appear in standard works on English usage, such as J.A. Simpson & E.S.C. Weiner, ed., *Oxford English Dictionary*, 2nd ed. (Clarendon Press, 1989), 5:948.

3. Frothingham, *History of the Siege of Boston*, 15, 19, 54–55. Frederick Mackenzie, Allen French, ed., *A British Fusilier in Revolutionary Boston* (Harvard University Press, 1926), 31–33, 39–40, describes gun smuggling out of Boston, and soldiers court-martialed and convicted for selling guns and gunlocks "to the Country people."

4. Mackenzie, *British Fusilier in Revolutionary Boston*, 42.

5. Mason L. Lowance, Jr. and Georgia B. Bumgardner, *Massachusetts Broadsides of the American Revolution* (University of Massachusetts Press, 1976), 58.

6. Bellesiles, *Arming America*, 181.

7. Massachusetts Provincial Congress, *The Journals of Each Provincial Congress of Massachusetts in 1774 and 1775* (Dutton and Wentworth, 1838), 98, 99, 109, 756.

8. Massachusetts Provincial Congress, *Journals of Each Provincial Congress of Massachusetts*, 30.

9. *Ibid.*

10. *Essex Gazette*, 17 January 1775.

11. Peter Force, ed., Force, *American Archives: Consisting Of A Collection Of Authentick Records, State Papers, Debates, And Letters And Other Notices Of Publick Affairs* . . . (1837–53; reprinted, Johnson Reprint Co., 1972), 4th ser., 2:580.

12. *Essex Gazette*, 10 January 1775.

13. Massachusetts Provincial Congress, *Journals of Each Provincial Congress of Massachusetts*, 34, 48, 71, 103, 209–10. (Emphasis added.)

14. Library of Congress, Printed Ephemera Collection; Portfolio 38, Folder 32a.

15. Massachusetts Militia, Massachusetts Militia Record of Firearms Distribution [1776], Ms. S–63, Massachusetts Historical Society.

16. Ray Raphael, *The First American Revolution: Before Lexington and Concord* (New Press, 2002), 121–3.

17. "Anne Hulton, a 'Loyalist Lady,' to Mrs. Adam Lightbody," in Andrew Carroll, ed., *Letters of a Nation: A Collection of Extraordinary American Letters* (Kodansha International, 1997), 53.

18. Hart, *American History told by Contemporaries*, 2:459; Ray Raphael, *A People's History of the American Revolution* (The New Press, 2001), 38–41; 132, 136; Countryman, *A People in Revolution*, 45.

19. Peterson, *Arms and Armor in Colonial America*, 179; Whisker, *The Gunsmith's Trade*, 164.

20. Frothingham, *History of the Siege of Boston*, 148.

21. Massachusetts Provincial Congress, *Journals of Each Provincial Congress of Massachusetts*, 41, 50, 97.

22. Massachusetts Provincial Congress, *Journals of Each Provincial Congress of Massachusetts*, 332, 348–49.

23. Bellesiles, *Arming America*, 188–91.

24. Massachusetts Provincial Congress, *Journals of Each Provincial Congress of Massachusetts*, 210, 336–37.

25. Massachusetts Provincial Congress, *Journals of Each Provincial Congress of Massachusetts*, 536–37, 584–93; Force, *American Archives*, 4th ser. 2:1347, 1349, 1353, 1357–62.

26. Massachusetts Provincial Congress, *Journals of Each Provincial Congress of Massachusetts*, 584–585, 591; Force, *American Archives*, 4th ser. 2:1357–8, 1361–3.

27. Massachusetts Provincial Congress, *Journals of Each Provincial Congress of Massachusetts*, 413, 586–7, 692.

28. Frank Warren Coburn, *The Battle of April 19, 1775*, 2nd ed. (n.p. 1922; reprinted, Kennikat Press, 1970), 119–20. Abram English Brown, *Beneath Old Roof Trees* (Lee & Shepard, 1896), 252–4, based almost entirely on oral histories collected from *grandchildren* of the participants, tells roughly the same story.

29. Coburn, *Battle of April 19, 1775*, 139–42; Brown, *Beneath Old Roof Trees*, 262–3.

30. Coburn, *Battle of April 19, 1775*, 151–52.

31. Brown, *Beneath Old Roof Trees*, 306–7.

32. Brown, *Beneath Old Roof Trees*, 315.

33. Massachusetts Provincial Congress, *The Journals of Each Provincial Congress*, 291, 540, 542, 548–9, 551–3.

34. Ezra Ripley, *A History of the Fight at Concord on the 19th of April, 1775* (Allen & Atwill, 1827), 20; Kauffman, *Early American Gunsmiths*, 18.

35. Force, *American Archives*, 4th ser., 4:1336.

36. Trumbull, Hoadly, *Public Records of the Colony of Connecticut*, 14:417–18. See *Ibid.*, 15:188, and Force, *American Archives*, 4th ser., 5:1613, for similar premiums in December 1775, and May 1776 respectively.

37. Trumbull, Hoadly, *Public Records of the Colony of Connecticut*, 15:97; Charles J. Hoadly, ed., *Public Records of the State of Connecticut* (Case, Lockwood & Brainard Co., 1894), 1:242–4.

38. Trumbull, Hoadly, *Public Records of the Colony of Connecticut*, 14:418–19.

39. Hoadly, *Public Records of the State of Connecticut*, 1:242–4.

40. Force, *American Archives*, 4th ser., 5:80.

41. Trumbull, Hoadly, *Public Records of the Colony of Connecticut*, 15:420–1.

42. Hoadly, *Public Records of the State of Connecticut*, 1:71–73, 245. Procedure revised May 1777 at 1:258–9 and August 1777 at 1:377.

43. Hoadly, *Public Records of the State of Connecticut*, 1:91–92, 94.

44. Hoadly, *Public Records of the Colony of Connecticut*, 15:176, 15:127; Washington, *Writings of George Washington*, 20:423–4; 20:423 n.34.

45. Trumbull, Hoadly, *Public Records of the Colony of Connecticut*, 14:419–20; 15:17, 137, 317, 323, 437; Kauffman, *Early American Gunsmiths*, 41,51; Merrill Lindsay, *The New England Gun: The First Two Hundred Years*. (New Haven Colony Historical Society, 1975), 55, 57; Brown, *Firearms in Colonial America*, 325, 350–351; Force, *American Archives*, 4th ser., 5:1621; *Connecticut Archives*, Revolutionary War Series, 5:117–121, quoted in Kauffman, *Early American Gunsmiths*, 75.

46. Hoadly, *Public Records of the State of Connecticut*, 1:246.

47. Bartlett, *Records of the Colony of Rhode Island*, 7:266, 269.

48. *Essex Gazette*, 10 January 1775.

49. Bartlett, *Records of the Colony of Rhode Island*, 6:354–6.

50. Force, *American Archives*, 4th ser., 2:607–8.

51. Gertrude Selwyn Kimball, ed., *The Correspondence of the Colonial Governors of Rhode Island 1723-1775* (Houghton, Mifflin & Co., 1903), 2:439.

52. Force, *American Archives*, 4th ser., 2:1145–6.

53. Stand appears to have referred to the collection of the firearm, bayonet, cartridge box, and all the paraphernalia required to clean and fire the gun in the field.

54. Bartlett, *Records of the Colony of Rhode Island*, 8:191. Another purchase on the same page involving "small arms" does not give a count.

55. Bartlett, *Records of the Colony of Rhode Island*, 7:477–80.

56. Rhode Island. General Assembly, "State of Rhode-Island and Providence Plantations. In General Assembly, May second session, A.D. 1778 . . . ," [Providence : Printed by John Carter, 1778], Early American Imprints 43541.

57. Force, *American Archives*, 4th ser., 2:650–2, 1177–8.

58. Force, *American Archives*, 4th ser., 2:1182.

59. Force, *American Archives*, 4th ser., 5:16–17.

60. Force, *American Archives*, 4th ser., 5:17–18.

61. Force, *American Archives*, 5th ser., 1:52.

62. Force, *American Archives*, 4th ser., 5:7–8.

63. Vermont (an independent nation until 1791) provides little information on this subject, but did impose a requirement in 1779 that every militiaman and "other householder" have "a well fixed firelock, the barrel not less than three feet and a half long, or other good firearms." Allen Soule, ed., *Laws of Vermont* (Howard E. Armstrong, 1964), 1:59.

Chapter 7: Guns in the Revolutionary Middle Colonies

1. *Pennsylvania Archives* 2nd series, 13:271, 292.

2. *Pennsylvania Archives*, 5th ser., 2:4–7.

3. Force, *American Archives*, 4th ser. 2:588.

4. Force, *American Archives*, 5th ser., 1:221l; Steven Rosswurm, "The Philadelphia Militia, 1775–1783: Active Duty and Active Radicalism," in Hoffman and Albert, *Arms and Independence*, 83–84. The Lancaster Committee also reports purchasing rifles from Jacob Dickert, a known gun maker, for a total of £31:7:6, *Ibid.*, 83–4.

5. *Pennsylvania Archives*, 5th ser., 1:4, 2:56.

6. Force, *American Archives*, 4th ser., 5:681.

7. *Pennsylvania Archives*, 5th ser., 2:194.

8. Force, *American Archives*, 5th ser., 2:69.

9. Force, *American Archives*, 4th ser., 3:862, 3:1842; 4:517, 1562, 1568, 1576, 1577; *Ibid.*, 5th ser., 1:1311, 1320, 1326–7, 1329–30, 2:61, 64–65, 69, 76–79, 81, 87; *Colonial Records of Pennsylvania* (J. Severns, 1852), 10:416–8, 471–2, 478, 481, 537, 550–1, 653, 679, 681, 686–7, 696–7, 700.

    Examples of uncertain purchases: "Nathaniel Porter, for Arms bought, £2214*s.*; to be charged to Colonel Hockley." Force, *American Archives*, 5th ser., 1:1319. What arms? How many? Even the amount paid is confusing, although it is probably £22, 14*s.* Other uninformative purchases are at Force, *American Archives*, 4th ser., 6:660, 6:1278, 6:1288, 6:1293, 5th ser., 1:1320, 1323, 1325–6, 1329, 2:64. Hundreds of pounds for arms seized from non-Associators at Force, *American Archives*, 5th ser., 1:1320, 1323–5.

10. Pennsylvania Provincial Council, *Minutes of the Provincial Council of Pennsylvania*, 10:696, £107:2:6; Force, *American Archives*, 5th ser., 2:62, "for Arms taken from Non-Associators" £402:0:1; *Ibid.*, 5th ser., 2:65, £89; *Ibid.*, 5th ser., 2:75, £20:18:9; Pennsylvania Supreme Executive Council, *Minutes of the Supreme Executive Council*, 11:140, £10:19:6, "for the amo't of arms taken from Non-Associators in New Hanover Township, Philadelphia County."

11. Force, *American Archives*, 5th ser., 2:65–6, 76.

12. *Colonial Records of Pennsylvania*, 10:288.

13 Force, *American Archives*, 4th ser., 6:1289.

14. *Colonial Records of Pennsylvania*, 10:480; Pennsylvania Provincial Council, *Minutes of the Provincial Council of Pennsylvania*, 10:289–90, 356, 358, 471, 473, 483–5, 503, 514, 525, 537, 550, 648, 650, 652, 687, 697; Force, *American Archives*, 4th ser., 4:517, 1576, 6:1290, 5th ser., 1:1319, 1326. *Pennsylvania Archives*, 3rd ser., 6:376. This is doubtless a very incomplete list of gunsmiths, for a short period of time.

15. *Colonial Records of Pennsylvania*, 10:230, 233; Force, *American Archives*, 4th ser., 4:517; Henry Family Papers at Historical Society of Pennsylvania, 1:21, 37, 39, 41, 43, 2:20, 2:29–30; *Ibid.*, "Account of Expenditures for Arms & Military Accoutrements" in vol. 2.

16. Fernow, *Documents Relating to the Colonial History of the State of New York*, 15:57, 5, 83.

17. Force, *American Archives*, 4th ser., 2:665–6.

18. Fernow, *Documents Relating to the Colonial History of the State of New York*, 15:42–43, 47–49.

19. Fernow, *Documents Relating to the Colonial History of the State of New York*, 15:31–32, 54, 67.

20. Fernow, *Documents Relating to the Colonial History of the State of New York*, 15:89, 95.

21. Force, *American Archives*, 4th ser., 6:628. A 30 May 1776 report concerning a Minuteman regiment of Suffolk County lists eight companies, six of which reported that their "State of Ammunition

and Arms" was either "Complete in arms, &c." or "Complete except bayonets." The seventh company reported, "Want fifteen guns and a number of bayonets "while the eighth reported "Complete except one man."

22. Fernow, *Documents Relating to the Colonial History of the State of New York,* 15:12–13, 38–39.

23. Force, *American Archives,* 5th ser., 1:1467–8.

24. Fernow, *Documents Relating to the Colonial History of the State of New York,* 15:72, 82; Force, *American Archives,* 4th ser., 5:147–148.

25. Pennsylvania Provincial Council, *Minutes of the Provincial Council of Pennsylvania,* 10:508.

26. Force, *American Archives,* 4th ser., 5:1455–6. The Committee of Safety responded that they knew that these were good muskets, and indicated that they would be quite happy to use them elsewhere. They also knew "that several more very good arms may be purchased in your Precinct."

27. Shy, *A People Numerous and Armed,* 185–6; Higginbotham, *War of American Independence,* 150.

28. Force, *American Archives,* 4th ser., 3:912.

29. Force, *American Archives,* 4th ser., 5:1451.

30. Fernow, *Documents Relating to the Colonial History of the State of New York,* 15:99, 103, 113, 127–128.

31. Fernow, *Documents Relating to the Colonial History of the State of New York,* 13:103; McCusker, *Money and Exchange in Europe and America,* 165.

32. Does "arms" here mean guns? Apparently so, because the order specifies that "each man who shall not have arms bring with a Shovel, Spade or Pick axe or a Scythe straightened and fixed on a Pole." The first three items would be useful for building fortifications. The straightened scythe is clearly a weapon—and yet not considered as "arms" by this order.

33. Fernow, *Documents Relating to the Colonial History of the State of New York,* 15:8–10, 13–14, 111, 123.

34. Whisker, *The Gunsmith's Trade,* 178–179.

35. Force, *American Archives,* 4th ser., 4:1100, 5:1401, 1396.

36. Fernow, *Documents Relating to the Colonial History of the State of New York,* 15:92.

37. Force, *American Archives,* 4th ser., 5:390–92.

38. Browne, *Archives of Maryland,* 11:89–91.

39. Browne, *Archives of Maryland,* 11:126, 127, 464, 438–39, 12:192, 12:3, 16:190–1.

40. Force, *American Archives,* 5th ser., 1:1331, 1340, 1349, 1350, 1352, 1356, 1357; Browne, *Archives of Maryland,* 12:9, 47, 134, 174, 179, 192, 242, 246, 252, 256, 257, 263, 267, 269, 293.

41. Force, *American Archives,* 4th ser., 5:1509, 1514–15. Orders to disarm Tories in parts of Baltimore County at Force, *American Archives,* 4th ser., 5:1510, 1513–15, 1518.

42. See Force, *American Archives,* 5th ser., 1:1337, or Browne, *Archives of Maryland,* 12:54.

43. Browne, *Archives of Maryland,* 16:121, 131, 138, 163, 167, 179, 235, 249, 326, 367, 375, 379, 471, 557, 21:13, 70, 138, 201. I used the 1774 conversion factor from Jones, 1706, for 1776 purchases. Later in the war, the Maryland government paid higher prices for guns. In 1777, Maryland purchased at least twenty firearms averaging £4:16:9. The following year, the records show six firearms averaging £4:6:8. It is unclear how much of this price increase was caused by scarcity, and how much was wartime inflation of Maryland's money supply.

44. Browne, *Archives of Maryland,* 12:297.

45. 19 August 1776, Force, *American Archives,* 5th ser., 1:1355–6. See also 24 August 1776, *Ibid.,* 1:1358 involving military accoutrements for 100 long guns—but no long guns, and 28 September 1776, Browne, *Archives of Maryland,* 12:308, for orders to get cartridge boxes, kettles, canteen, and flints—but no guns. A September 1776 order directed the forming of "a company of militia of not less than fifty men . . . the said company finding their own arms and blankets." Maryland State Archives, Microfilm MSA SC M3145, 277.

46. Force, *American Archives,* 4th ser., 5:1543; 5th ser., 1:1338, 1354; Browne, *Archives of Maryland,* 11:214, 353, 524, 12:47, 54, 248, 255.

47. Force, *American Archives,* 4th ser., 3:130–1, 448–9, 5:1526, 1544, 1546, 5th ser., 1:363, 892, 1331, 1337–8, 1352, 3:1025; Browne, *Archives of Maryland,* 11:75–77, 81–82, 99–100, 108, 155, 180–1, 314, 326, 333, 356, 402, 406–8, 440, 444, 455, 472, 499, 525–6, 535, 549–50, 553, 12:10, 54, 59, 93, 128, 134, 141, 238, 269, 412, 16:167, 219, 21:69, 71:215; Brown, *Firearms in Colonial America,* 350–1, 407.

48. Force, *American Archives,* 5th ser., 1:892.

49. Force, *American Archives,* 5th ser., 1:365, 667, 1354; Browne, *Archives of Maryland,* 12:142; Maryland State Archives, Microfilm MSA SC M3145, 284.

50. Force, *American Archives,* 5th ser., 1:365.

51. Force, *American Archives,* 5th ser., 1:366.

52. A. Van Doren Honeyman, ed., *Documents Relating to the Colonial History of the State of New Jersey,* 1st ser. (Unionist-Gazette Association, 1923), 31:162.

53. Force, *American Archives,* 4th ser., 3:1236–9.

54. Force, *American Archives,* 4th ser., 5:134–36.

55. David A. Bernstein, ed., *Minutes of the Governor's Privy Council, 1777-1789* (New Jersey State Library, 1974).

56. Force, *American Archives,* 4th ser., 6:1666–8.

57. E.M. Woodward & John F. Hageman, *History Of Burlington And Mercer Counties, New Jersey, With Biographical Sketches Of Many Of Their Pioneers And Prominent Men* (Everts & Peck, 1883), 664–748, available at http://www.accessible.org, October 2, 2004.

58. Force, *American Archives,* 4th ser., 5:89. See Bellesiles, *Arming America,* 192, and Brown, *Firearms in Colonial America,* 315. (Empahsis added.)

59. Claudia L. Bushman, Harold B. Hancock, and Elizabeth Moyne Homsey, ed., *Proceedings of the Assembly of the Lower Counties on Delaware 1770-1776, of the Constitutional Convention of 1776, and of the House of Assembly of the Delaware State 1776-1781* (University of Delaware Press, 1986), 208, 228–9.

60. Marie Windell, "News Notes and Book Reports," *Delaware History* 5[March 1953]:3, 218–19; Ruthanna Hindes, "Delaware Silversmiths, 1700–1850," *Delaware History* 12[October 1967]:4, 256–7; Whisker, *Arms Makers of Colonial America,* 39.

Chapter 8: Guns in the Revolutionary South

1. Force, *American Archives,* 4th ser., 2:167–70.

2. Force, *American Archives,* 4th ser., 2:612–13.

3. Frothingham, *History of the Siege of Boston,* 227–8; Randall, *Benedict Arnold,* 150–1.

4. John Harrower, "Diary . . . .1773–1776," *American Historical Review* [October 1900]:100.

5. Frederick W. Ricord and William Nelson, ed., *Documents Relating to the Colonial History of the State of New Jersey* (Daily Advertiser Printing House, 1886), 10:644.

6. Honeyman, *Documents Relating to the Colonial History of the State of New Jersey,* 1st ser., 31:181.

7. Hening, *Statutes at Large,* 9:12, 20, 28–29.

8. Higginbotham, *War of American Independence,* 308–9.

9. Hening, *Statutes at Large,* 9:28–29.

10. H.R. McIlwaine, ed., *Journals of the Council of the State of Virginia* (Virginia State Library, 1931), 1:30.

11. Morgan, *Slave Counterpoint,* 390.

12. Palmer, *Calendar of Virginia State Papers,* 1:267–9.

13. Palmer, *Calendar of Virginia State Papers,* 1:266–98.

14. McIlwaine, *Journals of the Council of the State of Virginia,* 1:2, 38.

15. McIlwaine, *Journals of the Council of the State of Virginia,* 1:2–3, 7, 10–13, 15–17, 19–23, 25–27. Excluded from the average price and count are four guns, whose price was combined with "provisions . . . furnished the Militia of Gloucester County" for a total of £30:19:6 at 1:28.

16. *Ibid.,* 1:6, 7, 8, 10, 12, 13, 14, 15, 23. Not included in this total is a transaction of £1368:18:0, "the balance of his account for arms Linen, Leather breeches, and military accoutrements" on 1:23; £38:17:1 on 1:44, "the balance of his account for arms"; £18:11:11 "for Arms, hunting Shirts, Leggins, and other articles" on 1:47.; and £114:10:0 "for hunting shirts, Blanketts, arms &c" on 1:51.

17. *Ibid.,* 1:6 ("large Rifle Gun purchased of Mr. John Pryor"), 12, 16, 17, 26, 30, 45, 48–50.

18. *Ibid.,* 1:15.

19. Daniel D. Hartzler, *Arms Makers of Maryland* (George Shumway, 1977), 275.

20. Force, *American Archives,* 5th ser., 1:892.

21. Bellesiles, *Arming America,* 192.

22. Nathan Swayze, *The Rappahannock Forge* (American Society of Arms Collectors, 1976), 1–31; Peterson, *Arms and Armor in Colonial America,* 207.

23. Force, *American Archives,* 4th ser., 3:209–10; Saunders, *Colonial Records of North Carolina,* 10:215–20, 993–4, 22–23.

24. Saunders, *Colonial Records of North Carolina,* 10:197–8.

25. Saunders, *Colonial Records of North Carolina,* 10:328.

26. Saunders, *Colonial Records of North Carolina,* 10:560–2.

27. Saunders, *Colonial Records of North Carolina,* 10:680 overleaf.

28. Saunders, *Colonial Records of North Carolina,* lead and gunpowder: 10:10, 29, 135–37, 163–64, 186, 230, 247, 253–4, 312, 316, 321, 337–8, 346–7, 350–1, 356–8, 394, 524, 565–6; shortages of guns: 10:13, 113, 314, 447, 719.

29. Saunders, *Colonial Records of North Carolina,* 10:437–9, 29, 163, 433; Maier, *From Resistance to Revolution,* 244.

30. Saunders, *Colonial Records of North Carolina,* 10:593. The earliest reference of foreign imports is March 1776, Clark, *State Records of North Carolina,* 11:287, describing arrival of 8,000–9,000 pounds of gunpowder from the French West Indies.

31. Saunders, *Colonial Records of North Carolina,* 10:643–4, 683, 719–20, 727–8, 755; Clark, *State Records of North Carolina,* 11:271–2, 274, 310, 3:333; 338.

32. Saunders, *Colonial Records of North Carolina,* 10:566, 615, 662, 671; Clark, *State Records of North Carolina,* 11:319. These records also show that Hugh Montgomery and Matthew Lock were authorized by the North Carolina Provincial Congress on 6 May 1776, to purchase "any quantity of lead, not exceeding 20 tons . . . ." On 26 July 1776, President Page of Virginia acknowledged having sent at least two tons of lead at the request of the North Carolina Council of Safety, and promised to send five tons more.

33. Force, *American Archives,* 4th ser., 5:1329–30; Saunders, *Colonial Records of North Carolina,* 10:524–6.

34. Saunders, *Colonial Records of North Carolina,* 10:291–2.

35. Saunders, *Colonial Records of North Carolina,* 10:418.

36. Saunders, *Colonial Records of North Carolina,* 10:358, 422, 556, 571, 611, 635, 687, 724–5, 952; McCusker, *Money and Exchange in Europe and America,* 219.

37. Saunders, *Colonial Records of North Carolina,* 10:627. On 12 June 1776, the Provincial Congress directed Colonel Ebenezer Folesome, "one of the Commissioners for purchasing Guns in Cumberland County, deliver to Captain Arthur Council as many of the said Arms as shall be sufficient to Arm his said Company." Folesome had apparently purchased more than enough to arm Captain Council's company.

38. Saunders, *Colonial Records of North Carolina,* 10:358, 571, 635; McCusker, *Money and Exchange in Europe and America,* 219.

39. Clark, *State Records of North Carolina,* 11:262–3.

40. Clark, *State Records of North Carolina,* 11:299.

41. Saunders, *Colonial Records of North Carolina,* 10:158. See also 25 November 1776 Provincial Congress hearings concerning an August 1776 armed robbery in Chatham County involving a rifle, pistol, and dirk, and how the two victims then went out and *bought* two guns with which to protect themselves in the future.

42. Saunders, *Colonial Records of North Carolina*, 10:467, 472, 555–6, 593; Clark, *State Records of North Carolina*, 11:282–3, 286–7.

43. Saunders, *Colonial Records of North Carolina*, 10:406.

44. Governor Martin to Lord George Germain, Saunders, *Colonial Records of North Carolina*, 10:489. See also 10:491 for Martin's discussion of the failure of many of the Highlanders and Regulators to show up.

45. Saunders, *Colonial Records of North Carolina*, 10:485–6.

46. Charles Stedman, *The History of the Origin, Progress, and Termination of the American War* (J. Murray, 1794), 2:216.

47. Stedman, *History of the Origin, Progress, and Termination of the American War*, 2:222. See John Bivins, Jr., *Longrifles of North Carolina*, 2nd ed. (George Shumway, 1988), for surviving examples of American-made rifles of the colonial and Revolutionary era of the sort that would have been carried by these backwoodsmen—there are dozens of them still in existence.

48. Saunders, *Colonial Records of North Carolina*, 10:680, 881–2, 729, 846. See also Clark, *State Records of North Carolina*, 11:349.

49. Saunders, *Colonial Records of North Carolina*, 10:629, 716–7, 723–4, 754–5, 811–13, 840, 869–70, 963, 985–8, 999–1000; Clark, *State Records of North Carolina*, 11:300, 331–3, 345, 350–1, 496.

50. Connecticut: Hoadly, *Public Records of the State of Connecticut*, 1:243. Pennsylvania: Force, *American Archives*, 4th ser., 5:1609, 6:1290; 5th ser., 1:1326; 2:83–85. Maryland: *Ibid.*, 5th ser., 1:1353, 3:1025; Browne, *Archives of Maryland*, 11:472, 489; 12:449. Delaware: Bushman, Hancock, and Homsey, *Proceedings of the Assembly of the Lower Counties on Delaware 1770-1776*, 247–9. Virginia: McIlwaine, *Journals of the Council of the State of Virginia*, 1:18, 31, 35, 43. Kentucky: James Rood Robertson, *Petitions of the Early Inhabitants of Kentucky to the General Assembly of Virginia 1769 to 1792* (John P. Morton & Co., 1914; reprinted, Arno Press, 1971), 43–44. New York: Force, *American Archives*, 5th ser., 1:1466, 1468. South Carolina: Salley, *Journal of the General Assembly of South Carolina*, 58, 72–74, 78.

51. Saunders, *Colonial Records of North Carolina*, 10:629, 719; Thomas Jefferson, Julian P. Boyd, ed., *The Papers of Thomas Jefferson* 8:407 (Princeton University Press, 1950), 4:206.

52. Saunders, *Colonial Records of North Carolina*, 10:354–5.

53. Force, *American Archives*, 4th ser., 5:1330.

54. Saunders, *Colonial Records of North Carolina*, 10:952.

55. Force, *American Archives*, 4th ser., 5:1410.

56. Saunders, *Colonial Records of North Carolina*, 10:358, 439, 631, 1002.

57. Saunders, *Colonial Records of North Carolina*, 10:539.

58. Saunders, *Colonial Records of North Carolina*, 10:929, 958, 1001; Clark, *State Records of North Carolina*, 21:168–9; Brown, *Firearms in Colonial America*, 315; Saunders, *Colonial Records of North Carolina*, 10:630. Saunders, *Colonial Records of North Carolina*, 10:981. Bivins, *Longrifles of North Carolina*, 16–18.

59. William Edwin Hemphill and Wylma Anne Wates, ed., *Extracts from the Journals of the Provincial Congresses of South Carolina, 1775-1776* (South Carolina Archives Department, 1960), 55.

60. Clark, *State Records of North Carolina*, 11:267.

61. William Edwin Hemphill, Wylma Anne Wates, and R. Nicholas Olsberg, ed., *Journals of the General Assembly and House of Representatives 1776-1780* (University of South Carolina Press, 1970), 129–30, 171.

62. Salley, *Journal of the General Assembly of South Carolina*, 89–95.

63. Stedman, *History of the Origin, Progress, and Termination of the American War*, 2:72.

64. Force, *American Archives*, 4th ser., 5:580–1.

65. Candler, *Colonial Records of the State of Georgia*, 19(part 2):103–108.

Chapter 9: Guns in the Continental Army & Revolutionary Militias

1. Brown, *Firearms in Colonial America*, 306.
2. Worthington C. Ford, *et al.*, ed., *Journals of the Continental Congress, 1774-1789* (Government Printing Office, 2:188. [Emphasis added.])
3. Washington, *Writings of George Washington*, 7:209, 215–16.
4. Washington, *Writings of George Washington*, 9:140–41; see also 7:123. Frothingham, *History of the Siege of Boston*, 285, thus described Washington's army in early 1776: "A large number had brought into the field their own fire-arms."
5. Washington, *Writings of George Washington*, 11:322–3.
6. Washington, *Writings of George Washington*, 6:386–7, 18:86.
7. Force, *American Archives*, 4th ser., 6:1121–22.
8. Washington, *Writings of George Washington*, 4:337–38.
9. Ford, *Journals of the Continental Congress*, 7:345, 362, 370–1, 8:429.
10. Washington, *Writings of George Washington*, 18:9. (Emphasis added.)
11. Ford, *Journals of the Continental Congress*, 4:276, 292–3; 5:432, 663, 6:867–8, 977, 7:303, 351, 8:680.
12. Ford, *Journals of the Continental Congress*, 4:205. (Emphasis added.)
13. Force, *American Archives*, 4th ser., 5:693–4, 713–14.
14. Higginbotham, *War of American Independence*, 270.
15. Mitchell and Flanders, *Statutes at Large of Pennsylvania From 1682 to 1801*, 9:110–14.
16. 18 USC 922(g)(7).
17. Ford, *Journals of the Continental Congress*, 4:220–21. (Emphasis added.)
18. Washington, *Writings of George Washington*, 10:190.
19. Curtis, *The Organization of the British Army in the American Revolution*, 21.
20. *Colonial Records of Pennsylvania*, 10:322.
21. Whisker, *The Gunsmith's Trade*, 169.
22. Whisker, *Arms Makers of Colonial America*, 68.
23. Ford, *Journals of the Continental Congress*, 11:611–12, 577.
24. Washington, *Writings of George Washington*, 22:258, 427.
25. Saunders, *Colonial Records of North Carolina*, 10:773, 782.
26. Peterson, *Arms and Armor in Colonial America*, 200–3.
27. Browne, *Archives of Maryland*, 12:404–5.
28. Clark, *State Records of North Carolina*, 11:331, 367; Palmer, *Calendar of Virginia State Papers*, 1:266–98; Hoadly, *Public Records of the State of Connecticut*, 1:71; Higginbotham, *War of American Independence*, 303–6.
29. 10 USC § 311.
30. Bellesiles, *Arming America*, 174, 178–9.
31. David Ramsay, Lester H. Cohen, ed., *The History of the American Revolution* (Liberty Fund, 1990), 1:178, 181–2, 207.
32. Frothingham, *History of the Siege of Boston*, 102–3, 141–42, 197.
33. Ford, *Journals of the Continental Congress*, 2:169.
34. Richard Henry Lee, James Curtis Ballagh, ed., *The Letters of Richard Henry Lee* (Macmillan Co., 1911; reprinted, Da Capo Press, 1970), 1:130–31; Maier, *From Resistance to Revolution*, 168–9, 222–3, 242, 256.
35. James Madison, William T. Hutchinson and William M.E. Rachal, ed., *The Papers of James Madison* (University of Chicago Press, 1962), 1:153.
36. Higginbotham, *War of American Independence*, 120 n.9.

37. Scharf, *History of Western Maryland,* 1:130.

38. "From The Virginia Gazette (1775)" in Hart and Hill, *Camps and Firesides of the Revolution,* 230.

39. Randall, *Benedict Arnold,* 150, 211.

40. Scharf, *History of Western Maryland,* 1:131; Frothingham, *History of the Siege of Boston,* 227–8.

41. John Harrower, "Diary . . . 1773–1776," 100.

42. Ford, *Journals of the Continental Congress,* 4:156.

43. Peterson, *Arms and Armor in Colonial America,* 197–98.

44. Peterson, *Arms and Armor in Colonial America,* 160.

45. Robert K. Wright, Jr., "'Nor Is Their Standing Army to Be Despised': The Emergence of the Continental Army as a Military Institution," in Hoffman and Albert, *Arms and Independence,* 53–54, 58, 70.

46. Washington, *Writings of George Washington,* 7:198, 22:257.

47. Stedman, *History of the Origin, Progress, and Termination of the American War,* 1:120.

48. Mackenzie, *British Fusilier in Revolutionary Boston,* 55–58, 67.

49. John Keegan, *The Face of Battle* (Penguin Books, 1978), 70.

50. Saunders, *Colonial Records of North Carolina,* 10:618b.

51. Higginbotham, *War of American Independence,* 45–48, 160.

52. Massachusetts Provincial Congress, *Journals of Each Provincial Congress of Massachusetts,* 681.

53. Higginbotham, *War of American Independence,* 61–64.

54. Gage to Barrington, "Private," 26 June 1775, *Gage Correspondence,* II, 686–87, quoted in Shy, *A People Numerous and Armed,* 104.

55. Stedman, *History of the Origin, Progress, and Termination of the American War,* 1:147–48, 178–82, 280–81.

56. Higginbotham, *War of American Independence,* 74–76, 192–5.

57. Shy, *A People Numerous and Armed,* 150–1, 161, 200–201; Higginbotham, *War of American Independence,* 361–3, 372–3.

58. Shy, *A People Numerous and Armed,* 175–7, 199, 209–11; Maier, *From Resistance to Revolution,* 92–93; Randall, *Benedict Arnold,* 58–59, 77–78.

59. Higginbotham, *War of American Independence,* 164–5.

60. Ramsay, *History of the American Revolution,* 1:307, 2:340–1, 375, 441.

61. Higginbotham, *War of American Independence,* 7, 155–8, 161, 166–168, 186–187, 364, 366–7, 369–70.

62. George Washington Papers at the Library of Congress, 1741–1799, Series 3a Varick Transcripts, Letterbook 2, image 116.

63. Higginbotham, *War of American Independence,* 192–5.

64. George Washington Papers at the Library of Congress, 1741–1799: Series 2 Letterbooks, Letterbook 7, Image 152, Series 3b Varick Transcripts, Letterbook 3, Image 279.

65. Randall, *Benedict Arnold,* 94–104, 137–237.

66. Buel, "Samson Shorn," in Hoffman and Albert, *Arms and Independence,* 145–9; James Kirby Martin, "A 'Most Undisciplined, Profligate Crew': Protest and Defiance in the Continental Ranks, 1776–1783," in Hoffman and Albert, *Arms and Independence,* 123–5; Higginbotham, *War of American Independence,* 393–7; "In Congress, 14 April 1777 : Resolved, that it be recommended to the executive powers of each of the United States, to enquire into the conduct of all officers on the recruiting service . . . ," Evans 15564; Higginbotham, *War of American Independence,* 104.

67. Wright, "'Nor Is Their Standing Army to Be Despised,'" 273–5.

68. Higginbotham, *War of American Independence,* 10–11, 104–105, 159, 164–5.

69. Shy, *A People Numerous and Armed,* 216–17.

70. Ramsay, *History of the American Revolution,* 1:181–2, 207.

71. Higginbotham, *War of American Independence,* 101–103; Randall, *Benedict Arnold,* 136.

72. Randall, *Benedict Arnold,* 90.

73. Rosswurm, "The Philadelphia Militia," 91–100. Pennsylvania (State) Council of Safety, In Council of Safety, Lancaster, 25 October 1777, "An ordinance for the more effectual levying the monies advanced for substitutes, in the militia, and fines due to the public, for disobedience to the militia laws ...," Library of Congress, Printed Ephemera Collection; Portfolio 144, Folder 37; Mitchell and Flanders, *Statutes at Large of Pennsylvania from 1682 to 1801,* 9:75–94, 131–6, 167–9, 185–9, 10:144–73.

74. Higginbotham, *War of American Independence,* 101–103.

75. Randall, *Benedict Arnold,* 150–1.

76. Wright, "'Nor Is Their Standing Army to Be Despised,'" in Hoffman and Albert, *Arms and Independence,* 52–53; Buel, "Samson Shorn," in Hoffman and Albert, *Arms and Independence,* 142–3; Maier, *From Resistance to Revolution,* 172–3, 187–8; Higginbotham, *War of American Independence,* 111, 205–208, 210–11, 12–14, 434–5.

77. Thomas Auburey, *Travels Through the Interior Parts of America* (1791), 2:329–30, quoted in Morgan, *American Slavery, American Freedom,* 378–9.

78. Burgoyne to Lord George Germain, 20 August 1775, Germain Papers, Clements Library, quoted in Shy, *A People Numerous and Armed,* 103.

III. The Early Republic

Chapter 10: Militias in the Early Republic

1. Candler, *Colonial Records of the State of Georgia,* 19(part 2):348–56.

2. *Annals of Congress,* 1st Cong., 2nd sess., 2141–2150. This is the militia proposal that appears starting at *American State Papers: Military Affairs,* 1:6.

3. Kohn, *Eagle and Sword,* 130–3.

4. *Statutes at Large,* 2nd Cong., sess. 1, Ch. 33 (1792), 1:271–74.

5. 10 December 1794, *Annals of Congress,* 3rd Cong., 2nd sess., 1396–99.

6. Kohn, *Eagle and Sword,* 225.

7. 16 May 1798, *Annals of Congress,* 5th Cong., 2nd sess., 1734.

8. *Statutes at Large,* 7th Cong., sess. 2, Ch. 15 (1803), 2:207

9. *American State Papers: Military Affairs* 1:198.

10. *Commonwealth* v. *Stephen Annis,* 9 Mass. 31 (1812).

11. Bellesiles, *Arming America,* 241.

12. United States Congress, *American State Papers: Military Affairs,* 1:159–62, 258–62, 297–301, 303–4. At 1:165, 168–72, there are somewhat larger numbers of firearms in a "Return of the Militia" compiled less than two months later, after New Hampshire, Massachusetts, Connecticut, New York, North Carolina, Georgia, and Kentucky sent in their returns. This increases the number of firearms a bit, but does nothing to support the claim that these are comprehensive censuses of firearms in the United States, or that they list all privately owned firearms.

13. *American State Papers: Military Affairs,* 1:168, 171–2.

14. Bellesiles, *Arming America,* 241, 241 n. 123.

15. *American State Papers: Military Affairs,* 1:198. Pennsylvania militiamen receiving payment "for the use of my gun" while on militia duty in 1794 at *Pennsylvania Archives,* 6th ser., 5:70–71.

16. *Annals of Congress,* 10th Cong, 1st sess., 1022–4.

17. *Annals of Congress,* 10th Cong, 1st sess., 1022–4, 1026–7.

18. Bellesiles, *Arming America,* 249.

19. Mark Pitcavage, "An Equitable Burden: The Decline of State Militias, 1783–1858," (Ph.D. diss., Ohio State University, 1995), 1:132–3. Compare Karl Bernhard, Duke of Saxe-Weimar-Eisenach, *Travels Through North America, During the Years 1825 and 1826* (Carey, Lea & Carey, 1828), 1:74, with its description of a Buffalo, New York, militia "not all provided with muskets" and *Ibid.*, 2:41, of a New Orleans volunteer company, "pretty well equipped."

20. Pitcavage, "An Equitable Burden," 1:101–106.

21. Bellesiles, *Arming America*, 249; William C. Claiborne, Dunbar Rowland, ed., *Official Letter Books of W.C.C. Claiborne* (Mississippi Department of Archives and History, 1917), 1:39, 152, 155, 182–83, 237. (Emphasis in original.)

22. Kohn, *Eagle and Sword*, 42–43, 51.

23. *Annals of Congress*, 6th Cong., 1st sess., starting at 286, present both arguments at excessive length.

24. Hadden, *Slave Patrols*, 144–7, gives several examples of how slave patrols provided the first line of defense while the militia organized.

25. *Annals of Congress*, 6th Cong., 1st sess., 284.

26. Maier, *From Resistance to Revolution*, 137–8.

27. Kohn, *Eagle and Sword*, 87–88, 134–5, 132–3, 102–103, 107–110, 113–120.

28. *Annals of Congress*, 6th Cong., 1st sess., 297; Kohn, *Eagle and Sword*, 52–53, 164, 172, 259–62.

29. George Washington, 1 May 1783, Peace Settlement, George Washington Papers at the Library of Congress, 1741–1799: Series 3a Varick Transcripts, Letterbook 7, Image 55.

30. Kohn, *Eagle and Sword*, 49–50.

31. *American State Papers: Military Affairs*, 1:7.

32. Higginbotham, *War of American Independence*, 447–8.

33. Kohn, *Eagle and Sword*, 74–75, 162–70.

34. Clayton E. Cramer, *For the Defense of Themselves and the State: The Original Intent and Judicial Interpretation of the Right to Keep and Bear Arms* (Praeger Press, 1994), 9–15.

35. Kohn, *Eagle and Sword*, 81–83.

36. James Madison, "Federalist 46," in Jacob E. Cooke, ed., *The Federalist* (Wesleyan University Press, 1961), 320–1.

37. *Annals of Congress*, 2nd Cong., 1st sess., 337–9.

38. Kohn, *Eagle and Sword*, 222, 225–7, 229–31, 250–2.

39. *Annals of Congress*, 5th Cong., 2nd sess., 1736, 1744–5, 1760.

40. *Annals of Congress*, 6th Cong., 1st sess., 305.

41. *Journal Of The Executive Proceedings Of The Senate Of The United States Of America, 1789-1805*, 1:304.

42. Hadden, *Slave Patrols*, 46–47, 75.

Chapter 11: Ammunition in the Early Republic

1. Arlan K. Gilbert, "Gunpowder Production In Post-Revolutionary Maryland," *Maryland Historical Magazine*, 52:3 [September 1957], 187–8, 198–9. An incomplete list of Revolutionary advances and guarantees encouraging industrial production of gunpowder and saltpeter (one of gunpowder's essential ingredients): Pennsylvania Provincial Council, *Minutes of the Provincial Council of Pennsylvania*, 10:471–2, 479, 482, 501; Force, *American Archives*, 4th ser., 5:390–92; Palmer, *Calendar of Virginia State Papers*, 1:268–9; Force, *American Archives*, 4th ser., 3:209–10; Saunders, *Colonial Records of North Carolina*, 10:215–20.

2. Victor Du Pont, "Riflemen, Attention!: Gunpowder of the First Quality— Manufactured by E.I. Dupont de Nemours & Co.—to be Had—by Applying to the Subscriber." (James Wilson, 1806). Courtesy of the Hagley Museum and Library.

3. Gilbert, "Gunpowder Production In Post-Revolutionary Maryland," 188 n. 7.

4. Gilbert, "Gunpowder Production In Post-Revolutionary Maryland," 189 n. 8.

5. New Brunswick (N.J.) Common Council, "Gun-powder: an Ordinance, to Prevent the Storage, or Otherwise Keeping, within Half a Mile of the Line of Buildings of This City, Certain Quantities of Gunpowder," (A. Blauvelt, 1813). Hagley Museum and Library.

6. Boston Board of Fireworks, "An Act, Further Regulating the Storage, Safe Keeping, and Transportation of Gunpowder, in the Town of Boston, Together With the Rules and Regulations of the Firewards, Relative to the Same" (n.p., 1821). Hagley Museum and Library.

7. Boston (Mass.), "Blank License to Keep and Sell Gunpowder in the City of Boston," (s.n., 1833?), Massachusetts Historical Society.

8. Center to Prevent Handgun Violence, *Second Amendment Symposium: After the Emerson Decision, Setting the Record Straight on the Second Amendment*, 64, http://www.gunlawsuits.org/pdf/defend/second/symposium.pdf, last accessed 25 September 2004.

9. "An Act in Addition to the Several Acts Already Made For The Prudent Storage of Gun-Powder Within the Town of Boston" (1786). Professor Cornell provided me a copy of the ordinance, 22 September 2004.

10. Fortescue Cuming, *Sketches of a Tour to the Western Country Through the States of Ohio and Kentucky; A Voyage Down the Ohio and Mississippi Rivers . . .* (Cramer & Bierbaum, 1810), 163.

11. Henry Bradshaw Fearon, *Sketches of America: A Narrative of a Journey of Five Thousand Miles Through the Eastern and Western States* (Longman, Hurst, Rees, Orne, and Brown, 1818; reprint, Benjamin Blom, 1969), 245, 383.

12. Tench Coxe, *A Statement of the Arts and Manufactures of the United States of America, for the Year 1810* (A. Cornman, 1814), 33.

13. "Sales of Gunpowder and Remanufactured Gunpowder Period 1810 to 1815 Inclusive," Du Pont Company Legal Dept. files, box 32, Hagley Museum and Library; Coxe, *Statement of the Arts and Manufactures of the United States of America, for the Year 1810*, 33. Other gunpowder manufacturers appear in early Republic business directories, such as "A. & A. Watson, Powder Manufacturers, near Pittsburgh," in Lyford, William G., *The Western Address Directory: Containing the Cards of Merchants, Manufacturers, and Other Business Men . . . .* (Joseph Robinson, 1837), 144.

14. Novak, "*Salus Populi*," 187–8.

15. Berkeley R. Lewis, *Small Arms and Ammunition in the United States Service, 1776–1865* (Smithsonian Institution Press, 1956), 20–22.

16. Lewis, *Small Arms and Ammunition*, 24.

17. Du Pont Company, "Sales of Gunpowder and Remanufactured Gunpowder Period 1810 to 1815 Inclusive," Du Pont Company Legal Dept. files, box 32, Hagley Museum and Library.

18. "Gun Factory," October 30, 1821, *Cleaveland* [Ohio] *Herald*, 3; "New Goods," *Ibid.*, 4.

19. John West, *The Boston Directory: Containing the Names of the Inhabitants* . . . (John Russell, 1800), 55; John West, *The Boston Directory: Containing the Names of the Inhabitants* . . . (E. Lincoln, 1803), 63. Edward Cotton, *The Boston Directory: Containing The Names Of The Inhabitants, Their Occupations, Places Of Business, And Dwelling-Houses* . . . (David Carlisle, 1805), 63.

20. James M. Riddle, *The Pittsburgh Directory, for 1815* . . . (n.p., 1815), 61.

21. E. Copeland, Jr., "Dupont's Superior Gunpowder: A Constant Supply of Dupont's Gunpowder, Warranted of the First Quality, and Assorted Sizes . . . " (Davies, ca. 1819), Courtesy Hagley Museum and Library.

22. Coxe, *Statement of the Arts and Manufactures of the United States of America, for the Year 1810*, 17.

23. James Lakin, *Baltimore Directory and Register, for 1814–15* (J.C. O'Reilly, 1814), 200.

24. Bernhard, *Travels Through North America*, 2:100.

25. Baird, Robert. *View of the Valley of the Mississippi . . . .* (H.S. Tanner, 1832), 207, 223; Bernhard, *Travels Through North America*, 2.

Chapter 12: Pistols in the Early Republic

1. Bellesiles, *Arming America*, 306, 322–25, 378, 450.

2. Bellesiles, *Arming America,* 378. It important to note that while "handgun" and "pistol" are technically interchangeable terms, common usage today distinguishes pistols from revolvers, both of which are handguns.

3. *Pennsylvania Gazette,* 2 May 1781.

4. *Pennsylvania Journal,* 24 November 1781, quoted in Kauffman, *Early American Gunsmiths,* 71.

5. Edward Pole, *Military Laboratory, at No. 34 . . .* (R. Aitken, [1789]), in Library of Congress Printed Ephemera Collection, Portfolio 147, Folder 9a.

6. 13 October 1785, *South Carolina Gazette & Public Advertiser,* quoted in Henry J. Kauffman, *Early American Gunsmiths: 1650-1850* (Bramhall House, 1952), 23.

7. 21 September 1791, *Federal Gazette,* quoted in Kauffman, *Early American Gunsmiths,* 14.

8. 26 April 1798, *Pennsylvania Packet (Claypoole's American Daily Advertiser),* quoted in Kauffman, *Early American Gunsmiths,* 66.

9. 18 December 1812, *Pittsburgh Gazette,* quoted in Kauffman, *Early American Gunsmiths,* 45.

10. 8 January 1818, *Somerset* [Pennsylvania] *Whig,* quoted in Whisker, *The Gunsmith's Trade,* 155.

11. James E. Hicks, *Notes on United States Ordnance* (James E. Hicks, 1940), 1:28.

12. 30 June 1790, 4 July 1798, *Pennsylvania Gazette.*

13. Klay, *Samuel E. Dyke Collection of Kentucky Pistols,* 18–27.

14. Lindsay, *New England Gun,* 85–91.

15. Hartzler, *Arms Makers of Maryland,* 61, 65–68.

16. Kauffman, *Early American Gunsmiths,* 76.

17. Whisker, *The Gunsmith's Trade,* 200.

18. S.E. Dyke, *Thoughts on the American Flintlock Pistol* (George Shumway, 1974), 13–60.

19. 21 September 1816 and 4 October 1816, *Richmond Commercial Compiler,* quoted in Whisker, *The Gunsmith's Trade,* 163; Whisker, *The Gunsmith's Trade,* 203–204.

20. Kauffman, *Early American Gunsmiths,* 6.

21. 8 May 1823, *Cleveland* [Ohio] *Herald,* quoted in Kauffman, *Early American Gunsmiths,* 4.

22. Kauffman, *Early American Gunsmiths,* 5.

23. Courtesy Pennsylvania Longrifle Heritage Museum.

24. Lyford, *The Western Address Directory,* 385, 418.

25. "Guns, Pistols, Bowie Knives," *Nashville Daily Republican Banner,* 2 October 1837, through 25 November 1837, 1.

26. *New York* [City] *Morning Herald,* January 1, 3, 4, 5, 6, 9, 10, 11, 12, 13, 15, 16, 17, 1838.

27. "Gun and Locksmith," Huntsville, Alabama *Free Democrat,* 23 May 1837, 1.

28. Isaac Weld, *Travels Through the States of North America, and the Provinces of Upper and Lower Canada, During the Years 1795, 1796, and 1797* (John Stockdale, 1807), 1:117–19, 234, 2:150.

29. Elias Pim Fordham, Frederic Austin Ogg, ed., *Personal Narrative of Travels in Virginia, Maryland, Pennsylvania, Ohio, Indiana, Kentucky; and of a Residence in the Illinois Territory: 1817-1818* (Arthur H. Clark Co., 1906; reprinted, Library Resources, Inc., 1970), 137, 155, 219–20, 195–6. (Emphasis added.)

30. "A Proclamation. Mayor's office, Washington Dec. 23, 1828," Printed Ephemera Collection; Portfolio 193, Folder 10, Library of Congress.

Chapter 13: Guns and Sport in the Early Republic

1. George Frederick Ruxton, Leroy R. Hafen, ed., *Life in the Far West* (University of Oklahoma Press, 1951); John Palliser, *Solitary Rambles and Adventures of a Hunter in the Prairies* (John Murray, 1853; reprinted, Charles E. Tuttle Co., 1969).

2. Weld, *Travels Through the States of North America,* 1:117–19, 234, 2:150.

3. Francis Baily, Jack D.L. Holmes, ed., *Journal of a Tour in Unsettled Parts of North America in 1796 & 1797* (Southern Illinois University Press, 1969), 26, 35, 39–41, 43, 62, 70, 91, 93, 97–98, 115, 139.

4. Cuming, *Sketches of a Tour to the Western Country,* 30, 42, 114, 118, 135, 156.

5. Cuming, *Sketches of a Tour to the Western Country,* 42, 30.

6. David Robertson, *Reports of the Trials of Colonel Aaron Burr . . .* (Hopkins and Earle, 1808; reprinted, Da Capo Press, 1969), 1:582.

7. William C. Smith, *Indiana Miscellany* (Poe & Hitchcock, 1867; reprinted, Library Resources, 1970), 18–22, 39, 77–78.

8. Robert Carleton [Baynard Rush Hall], *The New Purchase, or Seven and a Half Years in the Far West* (D. Appleton & Co., 1843), 1:125.

9. [Hall], *The New Purchase,* 1:50, 61, 80, 101, 150–1, 171–7, 195–8, 218–223, 2:253–63, 1:84–85, 99.

10. [Hall], *The New Purchase,* 1:122–36.

11. [Hall], *The New Purchase,* 1:126–36, 2:29–30.

12. [Hall], *The New Purchase,* 1:41, 287–9.

13. [Hall], *The New Purchase,* 2:30–31, 255, 262–3.

14. [Hall], *The New Purchase,* 2:253–63, 290–1, 314.

15. Abraham Lincoln, Roy P. Basler, ed., *The Collected Works of Abraham Lincoln* (Rutgers University Press, 1953–55), 1:386–8, 4:62.

16. Fordham, *Personal Narrative of Travels,* 95–96.

17. Fordham, *Personal Narrative of Travels,* 125–6.

18. Fordham, *Personal Narrative of Travels,* 109, 205.

19. Fordham, *Personal Narrative of Travels,* 143, 147.

20. Fordham, *Personal Narrative of Travels,* 181, 200, 213, 223–225, 237.

21. Anne Newport Royall, *Letters from Alabama, 1817-1822* (University of Alabama Press, 1969), 181–9, 203.

22. Henry Rowe Schoolcraft, intro. by Milton D. Rafferty, *Rude Pursuits and Rugged Peaks: Schoolcraft's Ozark Journal 1818-1819* (University of Arkansas Press, 1996), 63.

23. Schoolcraft, *Rude Pursuits and Rugged Peaks,* 54–56, 60–62, 72–74.

24. Schoolcraft, *Rude Pursuits and Rugged Peaks,* 54–55.

25. Schoolcraft, *Rude Pursuits and Rugged Peaks,* 23.

26. John Stillman Wright, *Letters from the West; or a Caution to Emigrants* (n.p., 1819; reprinted, University Microfilms, 1966), 21.

27. Richard Flower, *Letters from the Illinois, 1820-1821: Containing An Account of the English Settlement at Albion and Its Vicinity . . .* (J. Ridgway, 1822), 14.

28. E.I. du Pont de Nemours & Company, "Hagley Mills: IIF Gunpowder," Courtesy Hagley Museum and Library.

29. E. Copeland, Jr., "Dupont's Superior Gunpowder: A Constant Supply of Dupont's Gunpowder, Warranted of the First Quality, and Assorted Sizes . . . " (Davies, ca. 1819), Hagley Museum and Library.

30. William N. Blane, *An Excursion through the United States and Canada, during the Years 1822-3* (Baldwin, Cradock, and Joy, 1824; reprinted, Negro Universities Press, 1969), 88, 95–96, 145, 173–5, 302–4.

31. Bernhard, *Travels Through North America,* 1:70–71, 116, 128–9, 138, 173–4, 183, 186–8, 176, 2:35, 118–9, 146–7.

32. Sandford C. Cox, *Recollections of the Early Settlement of the Wabash Valley* (n.p., 1860; reprinted, Books for Libraries Press, 1970).

33. Philip Gosse, *Letters from Alabama* (Morgan & Chase, 1859), 130–1.

34. Gosse, *Letters from Alabama,* 130–1.

35. Gosse, *Letters from Alabama,* 132–3, 226–34, 256–72.

36. Alexis de Tocqueville, *Journey to America,* trans. George Lawrence, ed. J.P. Mayer (Greenwood Press, 1981), 95.

37. Tocqueville, *Journey to America*, 281.

38. Baird, *A View of the Valley of the Mississippi* . . . (H.S. Tanner, 1832), 229, 325–7.

39. Baird, *A View of the Valley of the Mississippi* . . . , 171, 206, 224, 238, 222, 323.

40. Harriet Martineau, *Retrospect of Western Travel* (n.p., 1838, reprinted, Haskell House, 1969), 2:20.

41. Gert Göbel, *Länger als ein Menschenleben in Missouri* (1877), 80–81, quoted in Walter L. Robbins, "Christmas Shooting Rounds in America and Their Background," *Journal of American Folklore,* 86:339 (1973) 48–52.

42. Robbins, "Christmas Shooting Rounds in America and Their Background," 49–51.

43. Rebecca Burlend, *A True Picture of Emigration: Or Fourteen Years in the Interior of North America* . . . (G. Berger, 1848), 29–30.

44. Frances Wright, ed. Paul R. Baker, *Views of Society and Manners in America* (Belknap Press, 1963), 150.

45. Thomas Cather, Thomas Yoseloff, ed., *Voyage to America: The Journals of Thomas Cather* (Thomas Yoseloff, 1961; reprinted, Greenwood Press, 1973), 132.

46. Frederick Marryat, ed. Jules Zanger, *Diary in America* (Longman, Orme, Brown, Green & Longmans, 1839; reprinted, Indiana University Press, 1960), 288–9, 237–42.

47. Caroline Matilda Kirkland, *A New Home—Who'll Follow? Or, Glimpses of Western Life* (C.S. Francis, 1839), available at http://etext.lib.virginia.edu/toc/modeng/public/Eaf240.html, 13, 45, 108–9, 123, 126, 130, 201, 215–16, 253.

48. Shirley S. McCord, ed., *Travel Accounts of Indiana, 1679-1961* (Indiana Historical Bureau, 1970), 183.

49. John James Audubon, *Delineations of American Scenery and Character* (G.A. Baker & Co., 1926), 3, 6–9, 11–12.

50. Audubon, *Delineations of American Scenery and Character*, 26, 33.

51. Audubon, *Delineations of American Scenery and Character*, 41–47, 82, 122.

52. Audubon, *Delineations of American Scenery and Character*, 206.

53. Audubon, *Delineations of American Scenery and Character*, 57, 59–63.

54. Heath, *Mourt's Relation*, 88.

55. Audubon, *Delineations of American Scenery and Character*, 88, 93.

56. Audubon, *Delineations of American Scenery and Character*, 68–75, 177, 210–16, 281–6.

57. Ole Rynning, ed. and trans. Theodore C. Blegen, *Ole Rynning's True Account of America* (Minnesota Historical Society, 1926).

58. Charles Augustus Murray, *Travels in North America* (R. Bentley, 1839; reprinted, Da Capo Press, 1974), 118–19.

59. "Gun Factory," 30 October 1821, *Cleaveland* [Ohio] *Herald*, 3; "New Goods," *Ibid.*, 4.

60. Charles H. Haswell, *Reminiscences of New York by an Octogenarian* (Harper & Bros., 1896), 261.

61. Bellesiles, *Arming America*, 322–25.

Chapter 14: Guns and Violence in the Early Republic

1. See Clayton E. Cramer, *Concealed Weapon Laws of the Early Republic: Dueling, Southern Violence, and Moral Reform* (Praeger Press, 1999) for a detailed examination of the intersection of honor culture, dueling, and early Republic weapons regulation.

2. New York (State) Court of Oyer and Terminer (Dutchess County), *An Account Of The Trial Of Jesse Wood For Shooting His Son Joseph Wood* . . . (n.p. 1806).

3. *Pennsylvania Gazette*, 30 May 1787; 1 August 1787; 21 November 1787; 1 October 1788; 31 December 1788; 22 June 1791; 13 June 1792; 15 May 1793; 10 June 1795; 20 January 1796; 11 May 1796; 7 December 1796; 30 August 1797; 20 September 1797; 6 December 1797; 6 December 1797; 27 February 1799; 13 November 1799; 27 November 1799; 12 March 1800; 24 December 1800. There were many more examples covered in just this one newspaper.

4. *Pennsylvania Gazette*, 30 May 1787; 1 August 1787; 21 November 1787; 1 October 1788; 31 December 1788; 15 May 1793; 11 May 1796; 7 December 1796; 30 August 1797; 6 December 1797; 27 February 1799. There were many dozens more articles that showed up in the search. I found dozens of examples from 1837–38 in which pistols appear in accounts of crimes, and are never treated as remarkable. A few typical incidents can be found at the Huntsville, Alabama *Democrat*, 4 April 1837, 2; 25 April 1837, 4; 23 May 1837, 1, 3; Tuscumbia *North Alabamian*, 23 June 1837, 2; 12 January 1838, 1; 26 January 1838, 2.

5. Cuming, *Sketches of a Tour to the Western Country,* 54, 209.

6. [Hall], *The New Purchase,* 1:23, 29–30, 32–33, 232–5.

7. [Hall], *The New Purchase,* 1:231–5.

8. [Hall], *The New Purchase,* 1:23, 29–30, 32–33, 232–5.

9. Peter Cartwright, *Autobiography of Peter Cartwright, the Backwoods Preacher* (Jennings & Graham, 1856), 200–1, 206, 223–5, 238.

10. "Communicated," *Brookville Enquirer & Indiana Telegraph,* 14 January 1820, 3.

11. William Oliver Stevens, *Pistols at Ten Paces: The Story of the Code of Honor in America* (Riverside Press, 1940), 39–40.

12. *The Upland Union,* 27 December 1825, from http://www.accessible.com.

13. Blane, *An Excursion through the United States and Canada,* 161, 305–6, 352.

14. Blane, *An Excursion through the United States and Canada,* 378, 385.

15. Karl Bernhard, Duke of Saxe-Weimar-Eisenach, *Travels Through North America,* 1:74, 117, 182, 191, 2:70, 96, 118, 170.

16. Bernhard, *Travels Through North America,* 1:70–71, 116, 128–9, 138, 173–4, 183, 186–8, 176, 2:35, 118–9, 146–7.

17. Quadroon balls: A New Orleans event at which women who were one-quarter black would meet white men, often becoming their mistresses.

18. Bernhard, *Travels Through North America,* 2:61, 70, 130.

19. Audubon, *Delineations of American Scenery and Character,* 3, 6–9, 11–12.

20. Audubon, *Delineations of American Scenery and Character,* 16–22.

21. Bellesiles, *Arming America,* 306.

22. Haswell, *Reminiscences of New York,* 312–3.

23. Haswell, *Reminiscences of New York,* 244.

24. *Enumeration of the Inhabitants of the United States, 1830* (Duff Green, 1832).

25. Charles Dickens, *American Notes for General Circulation* (1842), 185–186, 215, 275–282, at http://etext.lib.virginia.edu/toc/modeng/public/DicAmer.html.

26. Tocqueville, *Journey to America,* 103.

27. 19 April 1832, US Congress, *Journal of the House of Representatives of the United States,* 25:611.

28. "Our Town," (Tuscumbia) *North Alabamian,* 24 February 1837, 2.

29. "More of the Effects of Carrying Concealed Weapons," (Milledgeville, Ga.) *Southern Recorder,* 16 January 1838, 3.

30. "Fatal Rencontre at Columbus, Geo.," (Tuscumbia) *North Alabamian,* 17 February 1837, 2.

31. "A Young Man by the Name of Alexander H. Dixon . . . ," *Nashville Daily Republican Banner,* 13 October 1837, 2.

32. "Horrid Rencontre," *Nashville Daily Republican Banner,* 7 October 1837, 2.

33. Cather, *Voyage to America,* 143–144.

34. Marryat, *Diary in America,* 195–6.

35. William F. Pope, *Early Days in Arkansas* (Frederick W. Allsopp, 1895), 103. (Emphasis in original.)

36. Edward Beecher, *Narrative of Riots at Alton* (1838; reprinted, E.P. Dutton & Co., 1965), 14, 64, 75, 84.

37. Cassius Marcellus Clay, *The Writings of Cassius Marcellus Clay*, edited by Horace Greeley (Harper & Brothers, 1848; reprinted, Negro Universities Press, 1969), 257. (Emphasis in original.)
38. Murray, *Travels in North America*, 142–3, 214–15.
39. *Delaware County Republican*, 15 February 1839, from http://www.accessible.com.
40. US Congress, *House Journal*, 39:848.
41. *Report of the Debates and Proceedings of the Convention for the Revision of the Constitution of the State of Kentucky 1849* (A.G. Hodges & Co., 1849), 822.
42. Frederick Law Olmsted, Charles E. Beveridge and Charles Capen McLaughlin, ed., *The Papers of Frederick Law Olmsted* (Johns Hopkins University Press, 1981), 2:232–3. (Emphasis in original.)
43. Cramer, *Concealed Weapon Laws of the Early Republic*.
44. Bellesiles, *Arming America*, 378.

Appendix: Firearms Glossary

1. Photograph courtesy C.W. Slagle of Scottsdale, Arizona. There were *dozens* of similar early pepperboxes at the gun show where I photographed this one.

Index

gunsmiths, 83, 100, 102, 103, 105, 110, 116, 118, 120, 126, 136, 137, 146, 195, 197–199, 201, 228

Hagerstown, Maryland, 206
Hagley Mills (see Du Pont gunpowder manufacturing), 123
Halbach & Sons, 198
Hall, Baynard Rush, 208, 225
Hanger, George, 154
Hart, Aaron, 195
Haslett, James, 197
Hastings, Samuel, 191
Haswell, Charles H., 223, 229
Hawk, Nicholas, 197
Henry Family, 49, 199
Higginson, Francis, 69
Houston, Samuel, 230
Hudson Bay Company, 45
Hutchinson, Anne, 38
hunting
    accidents, 85, 209
    for alligators, 222
    for bears, 35, 70, 73, 203, 206, 207, 210, 211, 217, 220
    for birds (fowling), 67–70, 72, 73, 75, 142, 206, 207, 210, 211, 217, 220
    for deer, xix, 67, 68, 70, 72, 73, 75, 76, 206, 215, 220, 222
    for squirrel, xix, 73, 75, 116, 207, 208
    for sport and sustenance, x, xiii, xvii, xviii, xix, 33, 34, 40, 46, 47, 49, 50, 55, 64, 68–73, 75, 76, 94, 97, 127, 130, 134, 140, 147, 148, 171, 173, 179, 193, 194, 204–206, 208, 210–217, 219, 220, 233, 235, 237
    for wild pigs, 40, 70, 71, 73, 216
    guns and artillery, 94, 127, 134, 140, 142, 147, 148, 173, 179, 192, 207, 217, 228
    statutes and regulations, 70, 71, 73, 75, 76
    with fire (fire-hunting), 74

Illinois, 192, 201, 210, 211, 213, 217, 232
indentured servants, 5, 18, 21, 24-30, 31, 33, 38, 39, 40, 62, 69, 70, 164, 171
    freedom dues for, 30-1

Indiana, 174, 201, 207–210, 213, 215, 217, 219, 225, 226, 234
Indiana Miscellany (Rev. William C. Smith), 207
Indian
    ambassadors, 147
    attacks (or threat of attack), 3, 4, 6, 20, 25, 28, 29, 33, 34, 59, 178, 180, 184
    gun ownership and use, 23, 24, 32, 41-50, 57, 59, 60, 63, 134-5, 147, 207
    hunting practices, xix, 68, 69, 71
    laws and regulations, xvii, 11, 14, 15, 32, 33, 37, 41, 43
    rights, 28, 29, 79
    slaves, 32, 33, 41
    statutes, 41, 42
    war
        French & Indian, 14, 16, 19, 21, 23, 39, 74, 148, 158, 165, 166
        Pequot, 11, 18
        prisoners of, 24
        Yamasee, 18, 33
Irish, 28, 37, 62
Iroquois Indians, 46

Jamestown, Virginia, 1, 61
Jefferson, Thomas, 174, 177, 185
Jews, 40
Journal of American History, x–xii
Journey to America, (Alex de Toqueville), 216, 230

Kentucky, 134, 135, 189, 199, 206, 210, 216, 217, 221, 222, 225, 228, 232–234
King Charles II, 11, 29
King, Isaac, 197
King Philip's War, 18
King's Mountain, 161
Kirkland, Caroline, 219
Knox, Henry, 141, 172, 181, 182

Lancaster County, Pennsylvania, 45, 47, 50, 108, 109, 125
Lee, Arthur, 150, 151
Lee, General Charles, 160
Lee, Richard Henry, 151
Leisler, Jacob, 80
Leman, H.E., 50
Letters from the Illinois (Richard Flowers), 213

Letters from the West (John Stillman Wright), 213
Lexington,
    and Concord, 21, 91, 149, 156, 159, 166
    Battle of, 91–93, 97, 98, 130, 156, 158, 166
    Kentucky, 189
liberalism, 179, 180
Lincoln, Abraham, 210
Lindgren, James, xv
Long Island, Battle of, 162, 164
Louisbourg, Cape Breton Island, 17
Lovejoy, Elijah P., 232
Loyalists, 114, 130, 133, 138, 147, 160, 165
loyalty oaths, 144
    Test Act (1777), 144

Mackenzie, Lieutenant Frederick, 92, 156
Madison, James, 94, 151, 183
Malcom, Joyce Lee, 39
Malta Bend, Missouri, 47
marksmanship (of colonists), 103, 141, 149, 150, 152, 155, 157, 159, 164, 204, 207, 212, 214, 215, 219
"maroon" community, 36
Martineau, Harriet, 217
Marryat, Frederick, 219, 231
Maryland, 4, 7–9, 12, 14, 15, 19, 20, 30, 31, 33, 34, 39, 54, 63, 69, 70, 72, 74, 78, 80, 81, 116–118, 121, 126, 135, 139, 147, 152, 165, 174, 187, 198, 205
Maryland "Act for Military Discipline: (1638), 7
Maryland militia, 81
Maryland militia statutes, 4, 5, 12, 33, 38, 70, 74, 76
Massachusetts, 23, 38, 43, 69, 76, 77, 85, 94–101, 104, 106, 107, 110, 137, 173, 183
Massachusetts Bay Colony, 10, 11, 38, 43, 59, 78, 86, 91
Massachusetts Bay Company, xiii
Massachusetts militia, 11, 17, 100, 142
Massachusetts Provincial Congress, 94-8
Massachusetts statutes, 43, 77, 95, 101
McDowell, Joseph, 185